the ADULTEROUS MUSE

For Martin Carney and Laura Caffrey

the ADULTEROUS MUSE

MAUD GONNE,
LUCIEN MILLEVOYE
and W.B. YEATS

Adrian Frazier

THE LILLIPUT PRESS
DUBLIN

First published 2016 by
THE LILLIPUT PRESS
62–63 Sitric Road, Arbour Hill
Dublin 7, Ireland
www.lilliputpress.ie

ISBN 9781 8435 1 6781

1 3 5 7 9 10 8 6 4 2

A CIP record for this title is available
from The British Library.

Set in 10.5 pt on 14 pt Minion with
Trajan display titling by Marsha Swan
Printed in Navarre, Spain, by Castuera

CONTENTS

Acknowledgments   VII

Introduction   3

I   The Origins of Maud Gonne's Hatred of the English   11

II   The Secret Alliance   35

III Foreign Affairs   51

IV   From Millevoye to Yeats to Millevoye   63

V   A Single Mother in the Nineteenth Century   79

VI   The Millevoye Affair and the Norton Affair   93

VII An Ibsenite Heroine   123

VIII Millenarian Exaltations   149

IX   Sexual Love, Spiritual Hatred   179

X   The Crack-Up   217

XI   Fallen Majesty and the Rising   237

Notes   265
Bibliography   291
Index   299

ACKNOWLEDGMENTS

This book is dedicated to Martin Carney, my wife Cliodhna's father, and Laura Caffrey. In 2014 Laura, a poet, was working part-time for us as a childminder while completing her post-graduate qualification to be a teacher. The two of them, Martin and Laura, obliged me by reading the chapters of *The Adulterous Muse* as soon as I had finished them. One or the other would ask, 'But why did this happen?' or simply remark, 'That's so strange but clearly it's true,' or best of all, 'Hurry up, I want to see what happens next.' Their responsiveness was crucial to my ability to keep the chapters coming, or to repair one I had just completed. If I could read in the faces of these readers a degree of confusion, or, alas, boredom, I knew another try was required on my part. They really helped write this book.

Also, certain scholarly friends and writers agreed to give me their opinions of a just completed manuscript: Professors Lucy McDiarmid, Nicholas Grene, Jordan Smith, and Kevin Barry. Frank Miata rescued the author with a particularly helpful report on the chapters involving nineteenth-century French politics. Norman Berke gave the manuscript a review on behalf of the intelligent general reader, uncompromised by academic affiliations. Galway friends John Behan and Daniel Rosen took the time to read a late draft and give me their thoughts. Any author will realize how important it is to have friends whom you trust, and who will tell you quickly, honestly, and clearly just what they think of a manuscript, page by page, and as a whole. There is no point in asking for such opinions if you are not going to heed them, and I incorporated responses to each of these readers' suggestions within the text.

As this book is so much about Maud Gonne in France, and I am a scholar of neither French nor the history of France, I found the help I needed in Pierre Ranger and Pierre Joannon. I discovered Dr Ranger through his thesis in history and political science, *La France vue d'Irlande. L'histoire du mythe français de Parnell à l'État Libre* (2011), which partly focuses on the influence of French right-wing republicanism on Irish nationalism. That is a theme that *The Adulterous Muse* approaches by means of biography. Dr Ranger assisted me personally with on-the-spot archival research and research in official records in the Bibliothèque nationale de France.

After Pierre Joannon and I met at a 2013 George Moore conference in Paris, he was kind enough to loan me his copy of the doctoral thesis by Anne Magny, *Maud Gonne: Réalité et Mythe, Analyse d'une présence historique et littéraire* (1992). The value of Dr Magny's work was not, I hope, lost on me. Pierre Joannon also made me a gift of original copies of French periodicals from the 1890s in which Maud Gonne had published, real treasures. Finally, a historian himself, with many books on Ireland and its relationship with France, he read the final draft of *The Adulterous Muse*, and enabled me to present it with confidence to the public.

Another generous forerunner was Conrad Balliet, the author of nine ground-breaking articles on Maud Gonne. He answered questions in a lengthy series of emails, and sent copies of his work, both published and unpublished.

Deirdre Toomey, scholar and editor of *Yeats and Women* (1992), provided a tip in the course of email correspondence about the uncollected poem 'The Glove and Cloak'. Her information forced a reconsideration of what Yeats knew about Gonne's Paris love life, and when he knew it. Integrating that insight into the narrative of Yeats's relationship to his muse, and into the poetry, is a driving force of *The Adulterous Muse*.

John Kelly, general editor of the Oxford University Press edition of Yeats's letters, drew from his dragon's hoard of anecdotal jewels one about Yeats's visit with Maud Gonne to the studio of Rodin, a proper treat.

Parts of this book were periodically aired in lectures, and I thank the colleagues who organized those events, so important for work-in-progress: Dan Carey for the Moore Institute; Adrian Paterson for 'Yeats and the West' in the Model Gallery, Sligo; Susan O'Keefe for 'Yeats Day,' Sligo; Stoddard Martin and Conor Montague for City Lit, London; Jordan Smith for Union College, New York; and Michel Brunet, Fabienne Dabrigeon and Mary Pierse for 'George Moore in Paris', Centre Culturel Irlandais, Paris. Drafts of some parts of the book were also published earlier in *The Sewanee Review* (April 2013), *W.B. Yeats in Context* (Oxford UP, 2010), and *George Moore's Paris and his Ongoing French Connections* (2015).

I am grateful to Nicholas Allen and Sean Ryder, directors of the Moore Institute at the National University of Ireland for support, and to the NUI Galway Triennial Grant for covering part of the cost of travel in France, particularly to Royat, Laval, Saint-Raphaël and Paris. The Grant-in-Aid-of-Publication committees of the National University of Ireland, Merrion Square, and the National University of Ireland, Galway, have enabled this book to be published to a high standard. For their courtesy and promptness in providing photographs and permissions, I wish to thank the staffs of the National Library of Ireland, the New York Public Library, Getty Images, the National Portrait Gallery (London), the Bibliothèque nationale de France, the Agence photo de la Réunion des Musées nationaux et du Grand Palais, and the Library of Congress (Washington, DC).

My agent Jonathan Williams was part of this project from early in its conception. What would the final product be without his readings of drafts and proofs? Antony Farrell and Djinn von Noorden of Lilliput Press worked with their customary care and élan in preparing the manuscript for publication. I was delighted that Marsha Swan, the designer of *Hollywood Irish*, took on *The Adulterous Muse*; there is no one better.

Finally, I want to thank the members of my immediate family. The author of this book becomes, while writing, self-absorbed and driven to a degree that, if not immoral, is uncivil, and Delia, Lesy, Clea, and, most of all, Cliodhna, have had much to forgive.

the ADULTEROUS MUSE

INTRODUCTION

There are a number of assumptions in most accounts of Maud Gonne (1865–1953) and her love affair with W.B. Yeats (1865–1939). This book probes those suppositions by means of the discovery and narration of previously untold stories. She was a glamorous 'Irish' rebel who roused great crowds in Ireland against the injustice of the British dominion; but both her mother and father's families were English, going back at least several generations. So why was Maud Gonne either anti-British or pro-Irish?

It is taken as known that Maud Gonne had an affair with a Frenchman and bore him a child. That too is true, but why has no one found out all that can be known of this man, Lucien Millevoye, the Boulangiste? And what exactly is a Boulangiste? Did Millevoye, or Boulangism, have any influence on Maud Gonne? Why did she prefer Lucien Millevoye to William Butler Yeats, who loved her for so long, so eloquently, so publicly?

Throughout the time that Maud Gonne was having an affair in Paris (1887–1898), and giving birth to children, how is it that Yeats never found out? He saw her very frequently in Dublin and London, and kept up a correspondence with her. His friends were often in Paris; sometimes Yeats was too. Or did he know of the liaison with Millevoye? It is a given that he was utterly fooled, but maybe he was not, not utterly.

It is taken as true, because it came from Maud Gonne herself, and was reported by Yeats, that the great beloved had a 'horror and a terror of physical

3

love'. But then she bore not one but two children of Millevoye's before she made this statement in 1898, and a son by John MacBride followed in 1904. Were those the outcomes of forced, or dreaded, or unpleasant intercourse? Is it even possible to ascertain the answer to such a private question?

Yeats is inclined to depict Maud Gonne as divinely beautiful and apocalyptically charismatic, but imprudent and even dangerous in her politics. Thankfully, he often reflects, she was never more than a woman who wasted her life screaming to ignorant crowds. What were the results of her oratory, fund-raising, political journalism, conspiracies, newspaper ownership, agitation and continuous subversive activities?

Information that can shed light on some of these presuppositions is now easier to find, thanks to the digitalization of books and newspapers. What has been missing from accounts of Maud Gonne is a close investigation of her years in France, which was, after all, her primary residence from the age of twenty to her early fifties. It is as if her biographers have been standing on Dawson Street in Dublin, or in Bloomsbury in London, and we see Maud Gonne coming to one or the other only from the shadows of another life in another country, romantic and unknowable.

But, in fact, not unknown then, or very difficult to know now. The Bibliothèque Nationale has an electronic portal, Gallica, and the search terms 'Gonne' and 'Millevoye' are not common words or names in France. They turn up hundreds and hundreds of hits. Neither Gonne nor Millevoye were publicity-shy. They sought out newspaper reporters and photographers and became celebrities, whose comings and goings were regularly reported, if they boarded a ship, or arrived at a spa, for example. One can follow their movements almost day by day. Furthermore, their friends and associates in France tended to be activists in politics, literature, or society; they too left footprints in the digital record. Maud Gonne's secret life in Paris was never really secret at all, but now one can return to it along a broad documentary road. It is as if someone has put on the lights in one of history's dark rooms. For one so long regarded as an Irish personality, it is amazing to see Maud Gonne lit up in her full Parisian flower.

Readers who come to this book out of an interest in Yeats, or in Maud Gonne as *la sublime vierge de la libération irlandaise*, may at first regard the turn of the narrative into the history of General Boulanger and the right republicans in France as a digression. How can such out-of-the-way matters be important? The point of this book is that Maud Gonne did not simply have an affair with Lucien Millevoye; she was part of a political team with him. The

'Secret Alliance' with Millevoye may have begun partly as a euphemism for an adulterous affair, but it became an ongoing mutual political commitment to bring about nationalist revolutions in France and Ireland, sometimes by secret means. In the course of their life together, Millevoye influenced Maud Gonne, and Maud Gonne influenced the Irish national movement. How much a single individual can do to bring about change in a country is debatable, but a reader should be prepared to find that Maud Gonne, although a woman, and an English woman too, achieved a great deal more than one might expect. She mattered not just to W.B. Yeats but to modern Ireland.

Knowing the truth about Maud Gonne in Paris forces one to read Yeats's poetry differently. Yeats himself said that a poet's 'life is an experiment in living and those that come after have a right to know it' because poetry is not 'a rootless flower but the speech of a man'. We cannot really know his life without knowing hers, the primary inspiration, subject, and audience of so much that is great in the poetry of Yeats. Was the relationship of poet to muse founded on fantasies, lies, ignorance? That would be a flower without a root.

2

There is a key difference between the muse of a male poet and any intriguing, elusive woman with whom a man happens to fall in love. I accept the view that what Yeats as a writer sought in Maud Gonne was not so much gratification of bodily desire as 'some knowledge or power [to] come into his mind from beyond his mind'.[1] For the sake of his poetry he was willing to be possessed of what he could not possess, and to permit his experience of an alien, inconquerable spirit to erupt in his poetry. That Maud Gonne was beautiful, fabulously rich, literally larger than life (six feet two inches), conversational and maddeningly inaccessible were all functions of her role as his muse. Had she agreed to his first offer of marriage, she would not have served him, as poet, nearly so well. In *W.B. Yeats and the Muses* Joseph Hassett aptly quotes Denis de Rougemont: the muse is 'the woman-from-whom-one-is-parted: to possess her is to lose her'.[2]

The role of muse has fallen into desuetude with the rise of women's equality. One of the last great muses, Laura Riding, denounced the work of Robert Graves, the poet she inspired, as simply exploitative: 'I never meant anything to Graves but as a means of his elevating himself to a level of public success as a literary figure that his given native endowments could not be made to effect by the mere force of ambition.'[3] Riding called Graves's entire theory of poetic inspiration, *The White Goddess*, 'a literary machine designed for seizure of the essence of my reality, out of the literary plunder remaining from the destruction of the personal fact of me.'[4] This is not a jilted lover's speech of recrimination but the clear voice of modern feminism.

The literary practice and interpersonal relationships of 'courtly love' came to be execrated in light of dawning equality between men and women. Love in the late twentieth century was not to be the same as courtly love in twelfth-century France. As a literary code, medieval and renaissance courtly love involved the poet speaking of himself as the vassal of the lady, customarily a woman of wealth, beauty and position, married to another (a knight who might be off on a crusade). Love at first sight was succeeded by elegant declarations of desire, refused by the lady, but ardently repeated in a kind of siege by the lover, who pleaded for pity (a euphemism for sexual submission). The lover proved himself worthy by means of heroic deeds, stipulated by the lady, on the mythological template of Hera requesting labours of Heracles. Tales of Tristan and Isolde, and Lancelot and Guinevere, served as patterns of conduct for courtly lovers. Dante and Beatrice, Petrarch and Laura, Ronsard and Cassandre Salviati, Sir Philip Sidney and Penelope Rich became models for subsequent poets and muses, in an increasingly self-conscious and etiquette-governed relationship. Coming to manhood during the nineteenth-century revival of Arthurianism through the poetry of Tennyson and Swinburne and the philosophy of Ruskin and William Morris, Yeats saw himself in the lineage of these courtly love poets – he adopted their code of noble lovemaking.

Of course, every literary lover in the nineteenth century was not a Lancelot or a Galahad. In his 'Don Juan trilogy', George Moore outlined various paths for the privileged male of the late nineteenth century. He could be a homosexual as in *A Mere Accident* (1887), a husband as in *Spring Days* (1888), or a Don Juan as in *Mike Fletcher* (1889). To be a *poète maudit* and prey to the demonic power of a prostitute was yet another convention in life and literature, illustrated by Moore's *Flowers of Passion* (1877). Moore did not even touch upon the courtly love option. The nihilistic role of the Don Juan was the antithesis of the idealistic Lancelot.[5]

With the male population of Britain reduced by imperialist wars of the nineteenth century, and professions barred to women, the times were favourable for Don Juans, as giddily celebrated by Moore in *Confessions of a Young Man* (1889):

The position of a young man in the nineteenth century is the most enviable that has ever fallen to the lot of any human creature. He is the rare bird, and is feted, flattered, adored. The sweetest words are addressed to him, the most loving looks are poured upon him. The young man can do no wrong. Every house is open to him, and the best of everything is laid before him; girls dispute the right to serve him; they come to him with cake and wine, they sit circle-wise and listen to him, and when one is fortunate to get him alone she will hang round his neck, she will propose to him, and will take his refusal kindly and without resentment ... To represent in a novel a girl proposing marriage to a man would be deemed unnatural, but nothing is more common; there are few young men who have not received at least a dozen offers ...

While there is no reason to doubt that the Victorian male often took a crudely cavalier rather than a courtly love approach to the woman he desired, Yeats was a Lancelot.

Maud Gonne was herself a proto-feminist or 'New Woman'. Yet, unlike Laura Riding, she embraced the role of muse. She worked it for all it was worth. As both an orphan and an heiress, she had no curbs and vast potential. When she met W.B. Yeats in January 1889 she knew how to play the part of lady in the courtly love tradition, and Yeats's poems to her gave her further instruction. Yet this was not the only part she played. She was already the doom-stricken object of a Don Juan in the shape of Lucien Millevoye. For both men, the one in politics, the other in literature, she was not a prize but an inspiration.

As a muse, Maud Gonne was not limited to two men. She constructed an effigy of herself as a contemporary Joan of Arc, but with a difference – she would be Ireland's Joan of Arc. Like the maid of Orleans, she meant to lead and inspire the troops to fight a war against the English. She fashioned an image, militantly virginal, to spur Irish people to give their lives in a war against England. 'Irishmen are no cowards,' she wrote, 'and they will strike for their motherland. Over Ireland the cloud-cloak of the *Mor Riga* [or Morrígan] will wave once more from her war chariot, and through the smoke, and the fire, and the darkness, life, light, and regeneration will come.'[6] The Morrígan is the Irish goddess of battle and (what goes with battle) death. Maud Gonne played that part too. In his last play, *The Death of Cuchulain*, Yeats represents her as a goddess furnishing the severed heads of warriors with which Cuchulain's wife Emer can dance.

In relationship to W.B. Yeats, Maud Gonne was remarkably self-conscious about the psychodynamics of the literary role of muse. One time when Yeats begged her to marry him and 'give up this tragic struggle' for Irish independence, she says that she replied:[7]

'Willie, are you not tired of asking that question? How often have I told you to thank the gods that I will not marry you. You would not be happy with me.'

'I am not happy without you.'

'Oh yes, you are, because you make beautiful poetry out of what you call your unhappiness and you are happy in that. Marriage would be such a dull affair. Poets should never marry. The world should thank me for not marrying you.'

Years later, in September 1911, Maud Gonne declared that, while never his wife, she had actually been 'the Father' of his poems, 'sowing the unrest and storm which made them possible'.[8] She was proud to have taken charge of his imagination.

3

In a letter to Yeats of October 1899, Maud Gonne makes a bizarre reference to Octave Mirbeau's recent *Jardins des Supplices* (translated as *The Torture Garden*). She first expresses delight with recent Boer victories over British forces in South Africa. The ordinary Tommies killed in action can be pitied, but[9]

> ... as for [Joseph] Chamberlain [Colonial Secretary during the Boer War] & the English Cabinet & financiers responsible for this war, all the Chinese tortures invented by Mirbeau's diseased brain in his *Jardin des Supplices* would not be bad enough for them.

It is startling that Maud Gonne has been reading a book regarded by English contemporaries as pornography. Mirbeau's novel is actually in a particularly French line of politico-philosophical libertine fiction that stretches from the Marquis de Sade's *Justine* to Georges Bataille's *L'histoire de l'oeil* (*Story of the Eye*). With respect to Chamberlain, Maud Gonne surprisingly assumes the role of the character Clara in the novel, who leads the unnamed narrator/protagonist into a world of sexual tortures. Why she takes that point of view is a puzzle.

When Clara first encounters him, the protagonist is an amoral, hapless, venal French politician, on a voyage to discover the biological origins of life in the South Indian seas, a scientific endeavour for which he is completely unqualified, but the mission serves the purpose of a high French minister to remove a potentially embarrassing person from the political scene in Paris. Once she discovers the moral weakness of the protagonist, Clara, hitherto standoffish, reveals herself as the muse of *eros-thanatos*:[10]

A light flashed in her green pupils, and in a low, almost raucous voice, she said: 'I'll teach you terrible things ... divine things ... you'll know at last what love really is! I promise you'll descend with me to the very depths of the mystery of love ... and death!' And smiling an evil smile which made a shiver run through my bones, she said again: 'Poor baby! You thought yourself a great debauchee ... a great rebel! Ah! your little remorse ... do you remember! And now your soul is as timid as a little child's!'

Clara leads the protagonist, as Maud Gonne hoped to lead Joseph Chamberlain, to a China right out of the French imaginary, in which sex and death are united in hideous rituals. It is revealed to the protagonist that love and hate, life and death, aggression and affection all grow from a single root:[11]

On high stalks, flecked with black and scaly like snake-skins, there were enormous spathes, sort of bell-shaped trumpets ... like the split thoraxes of dead beasts. From the bottom of these trumpets there issued long sanguinolent spadices, assuming the form of monstrous phalluses. Attracted by the cadaverous odor these horrible plants gave off, flies hovered about in compact swarms ... And along the stalks, fingerlike leaves contracted and twisted like the hands of tortured men. 'You see, my darling,' instructed Clara, 'these flowers are not the creation of any sickly soul, nor of a raving genius ... they are natural.'

Individuals must abandon social lies, Clara concludes, and live 'in the dazzling and divine immorality of things'. Maud Gonne's letter shows that she was acquainted with the *fin-de-siècle* confrontation between civility and barbarism, repression and disinhibition, idealism and immoralism.

There is a particular reason why Maud Gonne may have been reading *Jardins des Supplices*, which may explain why she found it possible to assume the standpoint of Clara. During the Dreyfus affair, Octave Mirbeau, a left-wing anarchist, had been an opponent of the proto-Nazi Lucien Millevoye. In September 1898 Millevoye challenged Mirbeau to a duel (the offer was declined).[12] Maud Gonne could hardly read Mirbeau's novel a year later and not think that its protagonist was reminiscent of Millevoye, perhaps vindictively so.

Mirbeau's text triggered no particular reference to her. Clara is simply a literary personification of the life/death principle as female, supplied with a delicious figure and a cynical philosophy. Maud Gonne was the specific subject or inspiration of many other literary works, mostly but not all by Yeats, yet she remains herself, unconquerable by literary parasitism, a distinct biographical subject, politically if inexplicably committed to a single cause, significantly but not completely knowable as a character.

The father of Maud Gonne rose by merit through the ranks to become the head of British forces in Ireland; with a like courage, and similar capacity for command, his daughter achieved a supremacy over a leading right-wing French politician, a great Irish poet, the first generation of Irish female activists and a broad-based nationalist movement dedicated to violent insurrection against the country of her birth and the country of residence for her extended family. She industriously constructed a public Maud Gonne, 'the Irish Joan of Arc', through costuming, posing for professional portraits, hosting a salon, speech-making, managing press relations, packaging her image, editing a newspaper, writing articles, picking lovers, acting in plays, founding organizations, coordinating demonstrations, starting riots and inspiring the literary efforts of a number of writers, most triumphantly, W.B. Yeats. As a muse, she was not primarily woman-as-object-of-desire, but, in this at least like Clara, a woman in command.

I

THE ORIGINS OF
MAUD GONNE'S HATRED
OF THE ENGLISH

Previous page: *Maud Gonne, c. 1900. (Library of Congress)*

I n 1945 Richard Ellmann, demobilized from the US Navy, was in Dublin
writing his Yale doctoral dissertation, Yeats: The Man and the Masks (1948).
He established a rapport with the poet's widow, George Yeats (in the winter
of 1947 he sent her a ton of coal),[1] but the young American, a Jew, had his
reservations about Maud Gonne. In the 1979 revised edition, Ellmann makes
those reservations explicit:[2]

> She claimed Irishness for reasons which, though creditable, remain puzzling …
> Her passion for her adopted country was in many ways admirable, but it was
> adulterated by a fanatical quality which led her from the time of the Dreyfus case
> to anti-semitism, and from the time of Hitler to pro-Nazi sympathy. Hitler was to
> carry out the attack on Britain for which she had always longed.

The puzzle of Maud Gonne's claim to be Irish remains. The origins of her trea-
sonous hatred of the country of her birth are even more difficult to specify.

There was an obvious play-acting aspect to her chosen role as the female
embodiment of Ireland. In the Birmingham Post on 26 May 1893, a gossip
columnist, considering her accent and clothes, snidely saw it as some sort of joke:

> The liberty and prosperity of England is being attacked in France by the truest
> type extant of the real Irish colleen. Her name is Maud Gonne. She is young, fair,
> and rich; therefore made to be listened to, be courted and admired, particularly

by Frenchmen … Whence comes the heroine? 'From Ireland, shure.'– the brogue betrays this one fact clearly enough – but from what part of the Green Isle? Here there is rivalry amongst her admirers, who cannot agree as to the identical locality of her birth. Some say Limerick, some say Tralee; others again vote for Mullingar, because of the presence of many dialects in the many varieties of brogue which adorn her speech …

She wears a bright-green poplin with flounces *tourmentes de blanc*, and a Connemara cloak of bright scarlet.

'The national costume tempered by French taste,' whisper the ladies as she enters.

'A true Celtic heroine, the Bragella of Ossian's poem!' murmur the men.

The article's sarcasm is underlined by the fact that James MacPherson's 'Ossian', with its 'true Celtic heroine', is the most notorious literary fraud in English literature.

Six years later in October 1899, a Kildare man, reading news of Maud Gonne's successes as an agitator for Irish independence, lost his temper and wrote a letter to the London *Daily Mail*. It was high time Miss Gonne was charged with treason. 'I knew her as a girl,'[3] the correspondent explained:

She is the daughter of Colonel Gonne, who commanded the 17th Lancers, and who was at one time DAAG [Divisional Army, Adjutant General] in Dublin. This is the only connection she ever had with Ireland. Not a drop of Irish blood in her veins, and not a sod of land in the country does her family possess.

Ramsay Colles, unionist editor of *Irish Figaro*, was similarly outraged by Gonne's attacks on the March 1900 visit of Queen Victoria to Dublin. He published a contemptuous article on 'the woman Gonne'. The lady, 'if a liar can be a lady', was not as she so often claimed, an Irish citizen. Arthur Griffith, editor of *The United Irishman*, the weekly financed by Gonne, then went around to the Grafton Street office of *Le Figaro*. The editor was at an upstairs window watching the royal procession in the street below.

'Are you Colles?' Griffith asked.

'Yes.'

'Then take that!' Griffith said, knocking Colles's silk hat off with a Boer *sjambok*. Colles removed his coat, placed his hat atop it, handed Griffith a sword, and drew another sword himself.

'Defend yourself, or you will not leave this place alive!'[4] The two men evidently ended up in a harmless struggle on the carpet. Griffith subsequently got two weeks in jail for the attack. He had made his point: the authenticity of Maud Gonne's Irishness was not to be questioned.

But it was questioned again, this time by Maud Gonne's husband John MacBride. In the course of the couple's 1905 Paris divorce trial, MacBride's lawyer, Fernand Labori, put into the record that Maud Gonne was unable to produce a document proving she was Irish. Maître Cruppi, on behalf of Gonne, vehemently protested, and read out a birth certificate. It indicated that she was born in Ireland in 1866. 'Her ancestors', Cruppi claimed, 'had always lived in Ireland.'

Within a few months Maud Gonne was able to obtain from Henry Gonne, her nephew, a family tree showing that Gonnes first came to Ireland in 1560 from Caithness in Scotland.[5] These proofs, however, failed to satisfy P.T. Daly, secretary of Cumann na nGaedheal. When Gonne was nominated vice-president of that party, he ruled that she was ineligible for election to an organization she had helped found. According to its rules, official positions were restricted to those born in Ireland, and, he added, Maud Gonne's 'grandfather and uncles are Portuguese, her father English ... and her son French.'[6]

2

Maud Gonne was, in fact, born on 20 December 1865 at Tongham Manor, Surrey. Her father, Lieutenant Thomas Gonne, was stationed at Aldershot, the big army camp nearby. One day earlier, at the last socially possible moment, Captain Gonne, thirty years old, had married Edith Cook, a 21-year-old heiress, in East Peckham, Kent, near her grandfather's Tudor manor.[7] The circumstances that led to Maud Gonne being born within just twenty-four hours of illegitimacy are unknown.

Those circumstances did not include lack of eligibility on the part of either her mother or father. Edith Cook brought into the marriage a dowry of £25,344. At the time it produced an annual income of £760 (an amount with an income value of approximately £600,000 in 2013). Lieutenant Gonne was himself not a poor man. In 1855 he was able to purchase a commission of the rank of coronet in the 2nd Dragoons. By means of a further payment he increased his rank to captain in 1862.[8] When his father Charles Gonne died in 1877, Thomas inherited a quarter of an estate valued at approximately £90,000. This would be about £62 million in today's money. They were a rich couple any way you calculate it.

Edith Cook's paternal grandfather William, still alive at the time of her marriage, had been born on a Norfolk sheep farm in 1784. He went from selling linen in a shop in Norfolk to becoming one of the biggest manufacturers, wholesalers, warehousers and insurers in Britain, with business premises at St Paul's churchyard, London, and a Tudor manor house, Roydon Hall, in Kent.[9] He was one of the richest men in a country that was then the richest in the world. At his death in 1869 William Cook left an estate of £2 million to his son Francis, Edith (William II's heir and Maud Gonne's mother), and his three daughters Augusta, Caroline Louisa and Mary Anne Cook.

The linen-manufacturer's children adapted themselves to the privileges of the very rich. Mary Anne Cook became the second wife of Comte de Monier de la Sizeranne (1797–1878), playwright, former deputy under the July Monarchy, and senator during the Empire of Louis Napoleon.[10] 'Aunt Mary', the comtesse, remained in France after the death of her husband, where she would one day play a key role in the life of the young Maud Gonne.

Francis Cook (1817–1901), Maud Gonne's uncle, left the wholesale business to his employees and became a collector of Old Masters. On the walls of his private gallery built onto Doughty House, Richmond, he had fine examples of work by Holbein, Dürer, Rembrandt, Botticelli, Tintoretto, Van Dyck, Velásquez, Rubens and El Greco.[11] In reports of loan exhibitions of paintings, his name is sometimes listed among the donors, alongside that of Baron Lionel de Rothschild; he was a magnate of that order.[12]

Francis Cook did not stop with Old Masters; he also collected silver, antique furniture, Italian majolica and racehorses. A long-term project was the enlargement and improvement of his pleasure garden at Sintra, northwest of Lisbon. He had the Sintra mountainside planted with bougainvillea and eucalyptus.[13] In recognition of his investments in the country, Francis Gonne was 'raised' to the title Viscount de Montserrat by the King of Portugal.

On her father's side, Maud Gonne's family, like anyone's, could be traced back to not just one progenitor, but to many collateral ones. Family trees are a species of fiction. A line of descent can be made to originate at a chosen point between anyone and Adam. A further difficulty is that Irish genealogical records before the nineteenth century are incomplete. The surname Gonne does appear, with the family forenames of William, Henry, and Thomas, in surviving Church of Ireland records for the parish of St Mary's in Dublin from the early eighteenth century. The earliest record concerns a Thomas Gonne being buried in St Mary's churchyard in 1729.[14]

Many settlers from Britain came to Ireland in the Elizabethan and Cromwellian plantations of the sixteenth and seventeenth centuries. In what fashion Maud Gonne's ancestors arrived in Ireland, how long they stayed, where they lived and how they left, are uncertain questions. In later years Maud Gonne told the story, and perhaps believed it, that the Gonnes had been settled for many years in counties Kerry and Mayo before disinheritance forced one of them to emigrate.[15] Her great-grandfather William Gonne, she said, left Ireland in the eighteenth century for Portugal, where he went into business as a wine trader.

Indeed, William Gonne supplied Britain with a product for one of its most British customs: the drinking of port. His son Charles, Maud Gonne's grandfather, having been born in Oporto, Portugal's second city, made his residence near Portman Square, London. In 1824 he married Susanna Beale of Fitzroy Square, and the couple settled at 19 Gloucester Place.[16] It was in this 'substantial, spacious, and elegant Family House, with coach-house and stables at the back' (as described in an 1846 auctioneer's advertisement) that Maud Gonne's father Thomas was born in 1835.[17]

Charles Gonne originally intended his son Thomas to work in the family wine-trading business, and sent him abroad for an education.[18] Thomas learned French, Italian, German and Portuguese. But the boy discovered that he had no taste for the business and turned instead to a military career. Thomas Gonne grew up to be no ordinary officer in the army of the Empire. He served in one British colony after another, starting with Ireland in 1856. In India he was the Hindustani interpreter on the regimental staff (he had a gift for languages). With the 17th Lancers, he participated in the suppression of the Indian Mutiny of 1857.[19] In time, he was singled out for intelligence work and diplomatic assignments. In May 1866 when Maud was just five months old, Thomas Gonne wrote a letter to *The Times* from the Hotel des Capucins in Amalfi, Italy, diplomatically giving tourists the all-clear to return, now that Garibaldi's army had been dispersed, and a firm Italian government put in place.[20]

The following year he was posted as brigade major to the Curragh camp, near the racecourse in County Kildare. For 1868 he took the lease on a racing lodge, Athgarven, for his family, which now included his wife, his three-year-old daughter Maud, and her newborn sister Kathleen.[21] The following year, he moved the family into the suburbs of Dublin, to a house called Floraville in Donnybrook.

In 1871 Edith Gonne was with child for a third time. She was worrisomely weak. Doctors suspected tuberculosis, so she came back to England for the 'lying in'. After giving birth to a third daughter, Margaretta Rose, Maud Gonne's mother died on 15 June 1871. There was no coroner's report, but had there been, Edith Gonne would possibly have been treated as a casualty of childbirth in the nineteenth century. However, the family tradition was to mourn her as a victim of consumption (tuberculosis). The infant without its mother failed to thrive, and died two months later at Rocklands, Tunbridge Wells, not far from the Cooks in Sussex and the Gonnes in Kent.

What was Captain Gonne to do now? He had two surviving daughters, aged five and three, and no wife. His orders were to return to the Curragh camp. He employed a nurse, Mary Ann Meredith (nicknamed 'Bowie' and 'Biddy Bounce-Bounce'), and returned to duty in the autumn of 1871, eventually housing his daughters near the Curragh.[22] In the summer of 1872 he found a place for the girls and their nanny in Howth, a fishing village and headland at the end of a long arm of land encircling Dublin Bay to the northeast. The village itself lies around the harbour on the leafy north side of the peninsula, while above the village rises a treeless promontory covered in heather and gorse, and twined with footpaths. The headland falls away in steep cliffs on the eastern side. The Baily Lighthouse is on the southeast side. Great colonies of seabirds – not just seagulls, but kittiwakes, fulmars, and guillemots – nest along the cliffs of the peninsula, and soar in the winds that rise from the sea.

In Howth Maud Gonne passed the childhood days that she remembered all her life. This was her Irish idyll. In addition to Mary Ann Meredith, the girls had an Irish nurse, who lived in a cottage by the Baily Lighthouse. The time spent at Howth, Gonne remembered, was broken up by stays with the Cook relatives in London. She and her sister 'hated these visits after our free Irish life where we were allowed to play with the children of the many mud-cabins which existed then everywhere'.[23] To have no mother and a father in the colonial army is a sore deprivation for a child, but it can also mean – especially if one's family is well off, and servants are employed – a remarkable experience of liberty. The children of Howth and the two lonely English girls were a wonder to one another. Maud Gonne remembered a time during a rain shower when she and her sister ran into the mud cabin of their playmates. The *bean an tí* (woman of the house) took off the girls' shoes and socks and laid them out to dry. Her own children were barefoot, but she kept her pity for Kathleen and Maud: 'The creatures, God help them, they have lost their mother.' This maternal kindness went right to the young orphan's heart, and made an impression that lasted to Maud Gonne's eightieth year.

The Howth idyll did not last long, maybe just a year, perhaps as little as a summer or two. In February 1874 Captain Gonne was appointed to the position of garrison instructor at Aldershot.[24] Maud and Kathleen were then transferred to the care of Edith Cook's aunt, Augusta Tarlton. She was married to the Reverend Thomas Tarlton and lived in a large white residence at 24 Hyde Park Gardens, London.

It is unknown what caused Aunt Augusta to give up the children. Their next stop was Doughty House, the grand mansion (with the famous art gallery) of Edith Cook's Uncle Francis.

Perhaps these periods of being fostered out are what the elderly Maud Gonne recalled as the hated 'visits' to her Cook relatives in London, in which there was not enough love and too much propriety. They were really more than visits. They continued a good deal longer than Maud Gonne's sojourn in Howth. She spent six years in London between the various big homes of her aunts and uncles while her father moved from post to post in his military career.

Maud Gonne's girlhood was like that of Eloise in Kay Thompson's series of children's books: left by her distant mother, Eloise lives in the Plaza Hotel with her English nanny and pets, or in Paris, or Moscow. Like Eloise, Maud Gonne had her own precocious views on the stuffy lives of adults, and cherished a poignantly romantic regard for her beloved millionaire papa, who wrote her delightful letters, and occasionally arrived bearing gifts, but could never be persuaded to give her much of his time.

In February 1876 Thomas Gonne was appointed military attaché to Austria. He remained in Vienna until October 1878. His service won him a promotion on merit to Lieutenant Colonel of the 17th Lancers. In February 1879 the Lancers were ordered to embark on a troopship for Natal, South Africa, to put down Zulu resistance to British occupation. While training officers ahead of departure, Gonne was accidentally shot in the thigh.[25] The troops left for South Africa, but he stayed behind to recuperate. So in the winter of 1879 thirteen-year-old Maud was able to spend some months with her father.

In her 1938 autobiography, *A Servant of the Queen,* Maud Gonne wrote that her father worried about her health and about tuberculosis in particular; all his tender regard, we are to understand, had passed from her dead mother to herself (her ever-present sister Kathleen rarely comes into the frame of the picture she shows the reader). The following July, when orders were published that Colonel Thomas Gonne was to assume command of the Lancers, now in India,[26] he made arrangements for the girls to stay on the French Riviera. Its climate was thought to be salubrious for those with weak chests. Maud and Kathleen were still being minded by Mary Ann Meredith. In Provence she was assisted by a governess from Cannes named Miss Austen. In later years, Gonne remembered this governess as instilling in her charges a reverence for a republican form of government. Maud and Kathleen remained in the South of

France until 1881. In April of that year, Colonel Gonne took a post as military attaché to Russia.[27] Before leaving for St Petersburg, he arranged for his daughters (along with Mary Ann Meredith) to attend Rosemont School in Torquay.[28]

In *A Servant of the Queen*, Maud Gonne never mentions Rosemont School. She tells, instead, of being left on her own in Italy:

> I was sixteen and Tommy [it was Maud's normal practice to address her father by his first name] left us in Rome with an old Friend of Mama's while he returned to Ireland to take up an appointment of Assistant Adjutant General in Dublin. He had kept his promise to Mama; he had never sent us to school and he had saved us from the clutches of the aunts. He intended that we should stay abroad another year. But one night, visiting the Coliseum by moonlight, a young Italian had proposed to me – it was the first proposal I had received.

She says that she accepted this first of her many proposals in spite of the fact that she would have preferred if it had come from another man; for instance, the young American who was painting her portrait.

This charming tale of her beauty, naiveté and scampishness is variously inaccurate. In fact, 'Tommy' Gonne did not keep his daughters from their aunts and uncles, though evidently Maud Gonne wishes he had done so. And he did indeed send the girls to school. Rosemont was either so unpleasant or so unromantic that it was never afterwards mentioned. Finally, Tommy did not become Assistant Adjutant General in Dublin until four years after Maud Gonne's sixteenth year. Maybe the undocumented Coliseum-by-moonlight episode happened at another time.

Before going to Dublin in 1885, Thomas Gonne spent a year and a half as military attaché in the court at St Petersburg.[29] Afterwards, he considered giving up the exciting but vagabond life of an intelligence officer. *The Times* of 31 October 1884 reports that 'Col. T. Gonne, 17th Lancers, yesterday was unanimously selected by the Liberal Party in Bridport [Dorset] as their candidate.' Maud Gonne wrote that her father discussed with her his desire to resign his commission and run for Parliament:[30]

> He told me that the Land War had made him realise that as an Irishman he felt he must resign from the English Army and that he intended standing as a Home Rule candidate at the next election; that the only thing that was troubling him was the change this would make in our social position and how it would affect me. He said he had accepted the post as Adjutant General in Dublin because he wanted me to have a good time on 'coming out'. We were both so happy when we found our thoughts were as one, for I worshipped my father. He died of typhoid fever before he could put his resolve into effect.

If this story is dated according to the *Times'* announcement of Colonel Gonne's nomination as a parliamentary candidate, it raises the question of whether his eldest daughter could have had fully formulated 'thoughts' about the Land War in 1884; she had not been in Ireland since she was a child. Nor is there any evidence that Colonel Gonne ever governed his life according to what he thought to be his duties as an Irishman. Ireland was just one of many stopping places in the remarkably international pilgrimage of Thomas Gonne. The Colonel had been a dutiful servant of the Queen on missions of high importance in Russia, Turkey, Armenia, Ireland and India. Was he a spy? Or just a non-clandestine military intelligence officer? Whichever, he was a servant of the Empire.

In 1884 Thomas Gonne may have talked to Maud, then just nineteen, about whether the time had come for him to resign his very high rank in the army to run for parliament. He would then be able to spend more time with his family. In parliament he would find another field in which to exercise his expertise in international relations. Then again, the offer of command over the whole British army presence in Ireland was tempting. In that position, he could launch his daughters into society with every advantage.

3

Colonel Gonne arrived in Dublin to take up his new post in January 1885. Maud Gonne may have visited him in Dublin for a number of weeks, because a 'Miss Gonne' is reported on 27 February 1885 among the departures from Dublin by Royal Mail steamer.[31] She may have been on her way back for further forgettable months of finishing school at Rosemont. It was not until the following year that the Gonne sisters made their formal debut in Dublin. The *Irish Times* reported that 'Miss Gonne and Kathleen Gonne' came to the 'First Drawing Room' of the Dublin Castle Season on 27 January 1886 to be kissed by the Lord Lieutenant.

That was just the beginning of the heady whirl of the Dublin Castle Season, during which British military officers and administrators danced, dined and intermarried with Anglo-Irish families of place or property. George Moore's *A Drama in Muslin* (1886) is a rich record of this festival of high-society matchmaking against the background of the Land War. Moore took notes on the Castle Season of 1885, and he even dared to return in 1886 for

'St Patrick's Ball'[32] while his controversial novel was being serialized in *The Court and Society Review*.[33] In that novel, Big House daughters arrive from Galway and other counties beyond the Pale to join the chase for husbands. The women are said to hunt in packs, and an unmarried lord is the equivalent of a 'ten-antler stag'.[34] Dublin is described as a colonial parade with floats on imperial themes, a parody of the reality:[35]

> We are in a land of echoes and shadows. Smirking, pretending, grimacing, the poor shades go by, waving a mock-English banner over a waxwork show: policemen and bailiffs in front, landlords and agents behind, time-servers, Castle hirelings, panderers and worse on the box ; nodding the while their dollish cardboard heads, and distributing to an angry populace, on either side, much bran and brogue.

As Moore's heroine, Alice Barton, her sisters and mother, travel by closed carriage from the Shelbourne Hotel to Dublin Castle, they pass through streets

> ... lined with vagrants, patriots, waifs, idlers of all sorts and kinds. Plenty of girls of sixteen and eighteen come out to see the 'finery'. Poor little things in battered bonnets and draggled skirts, who would dream upon ten shillings a week; a drunken mother striving to hush a child that dies beneath a dripping shawl; a harlot embittered by feelings of commercial resentment; troops of labourers battered and bruised with toil: you see their hang-dog faces, their thin coats, their shirts torn ... and when the block brought the carriages to a standstill, sometimes no more than a foot of space separated their occupants from the crowd on the pavement's edge. Never were poverty and wealth brought into plainer proximity.[36]

Maud Gonne was not one of the unmarried Anglo-Irish girls from an over-mortgaged estate beyond the Pale. No, she was on a higher plane altogether. Yet Moore accurately depicted the sights to be seen by Maud Gonne, and the society in which she made her brilliant debut.

In public Colonel Gonne treated Maud not like his child but as his companion. She was delighted when people drew the conclusion that they were romantically involved, not just married but 'a honeymoon couple'.[37] This is decidedly strange, either as behaviour by the father, or as a fantasy by the daughter. 'I was not seventeen [she was in fact just twenty-one] and, everybody said, too young to be at the head of Tommy's house without chaperone, and I was terribly anxious to show I was efficient.'[38] She carried off the role so well that the *Irish Times* reported 'Colonel and Mrs Gonne' being present at the Viceregal Court when the new Lord Lieutenant and his wife, Lord and Lady

Aberdeen, were received.[39] Having been deprived of her father's company so often over the years, Maud Gonne was understandably overjoyed to be beside him day after day and to see that he was proud of her.

Naturally she also wished to be the belle of the many balls. At St Patrick's Ball, she says with half-ironic vanity, she caught the eye of the Prince of Wales. That must be a mistake, because the future King Edward VII was not there. Perhaps she meant Prince Edward of Saxe Weimar (1823–1902), who was the guest of honour at that ball. Since Prince Edward's wife was in bed with an 'indisposition', the 63-year-old Prince was free to dance with all those young ladies he thought fairest. 'No one enjoyed the country dance more than Prince Edward', according to the *Freeman's Journal*.[40] Or perhaps Maud Gonne was recalling the Castle Ball on 10 April 1886, when she danced with Prince Albert Victor, son of the Prince of Wales. There were princes enough to confuse a person's memory. She threw herself into the Castle Season with flair. In the amateur theatricals staged at the Royal Hospital Kilmainham, she took the part of the Marquise de St Maure in Tom Robertson's *Caste*.[41]

Even a sceptical reading of her memoir, however, suggests that Maud Gonne did, early in her first year in society, notice the ugly side of colonial Ireland. She tells a story of going to a fox hunt at a Big House outside Dublin. M. Hollmann, solo violinist to the King of Holland, was to provide the entertainment, and she wished to hear him. The host turned out to be a hard drinker. He was late to dinner, holding up everyone, and then banged on about the Land League, and how it was the ruin of the country. His wife tried to change the subject, but the master of the house could not be diverted. The tenants, he complained, were getting in the way of the hunters riding through their fields. He had told the cottiers on his estate not to join the Land League. One did anyway, so he had to turn him out. Now he had seen the man's ailing wife out on the road: "'And you did nothing about it,' I exclaimed. "Let her die," he answered. "These people must be taught a lesson."' A shocked Maud Gonne left first thing the next morning.

This story may be true. Advertisements for string concerts by M. Hollmann appear in the Dublin papers in February 1886. The detail goes some way to confirming that Maud Gonne, an open-hearted and idealistic young woman, received a nasty shock to her sense of right and wrong early in her first Castle season.

In 1893 Maud Gonne gave an account of this episode to interviewer Adolphe Brisson for a newspaper profile. For the sake of verisimilitude and colour, she added many details, but it is clearly a story about the same events:

It was winter, it was freezing cold. I travelled in a carriage, when I saw a woman who had fainted at the door of a cottage in ruins.

I run, I pick up the poor thing, I give her a drink of cordial, I question her. She told me that, having failed to pay her meagre rent, she was just put out by the landlord, who gave orders that her cottage should be demolished; she added that she has not eaten for two days, and her husband, by the name of Duncan, had gone to pick up some potatoes, at the risk of being arrested by the manager of the estate.

I put a piece of gold in her hand, and I arrived, my heart full of pity, at the house of my host, with my mind made up to speak of these sorrows, and to beg him to help the woman in her misery. Then, on entering the salon, do you know what words I heard? The lord spoke in a loud haughty voice, and he said, 'I won my bet. Last year I warned Duncan, a bad tenant, that in six months his wife would be lying in a ditch. Well, there she is. And she stays there, and there she will die. That will be an example to others and teach them to pay their rent fully.' I did not say anything; I could not find the words; but that evening, I buckled up my trunk and walked away from the home of this monster. I vowed to devote myself to the enfranchisement of the Irish slaves; I would devote my life to this sacred mission. I try always to live up to this oath.

Another variant of this story was given by Gonne to the *New York Herald* in 1896. Her conversion to the Irish cause was due to a dramatic incident, which she witnessed the night after her return from a long sojourn as a schoolgirl in England. Near to the Gonne homestead was the home of a Land Leaguer named M'Grath, who had won worldwide fame through his long and heroic struggle against being evicted from his farm. M'Grath was a sort of Land League hero, and in the middle of his fight took sick of a fever and died. Along with his homeless wife and children, Maud Gonne saw him waked. From that time on, the Land League had no heartier supporter, and a little later no more lavish contributor, than this Orange girl:[42]

George Moore explained to readers of *A Drama in Muslin* that he had set the main action in Dublin Castle because in that place 'are endured the bitterest griefs that a young girl's heart may know'.[43] He was thinking of those soon-to-be spinsters who fail in their pursuit of a prize husband. The sentiment may also apply to the dawning recognition by a young woman of privilege that she was the beneficiary of a system of outrageous injustice.

4

For the summer of 1886, Maud Gonne was sent by her father to Paris to stay with her great aunt, Mary *née* Cook, Comtesse de Sizeranne. While Maud Gonne was away from Dublin, the Colonel secretly became a father once again. Whatever his daughter thought about him treating her as his companion, unbeknownst to her he had a regular bedmate. He had begun an affair after his arrival in Dublin with a woman known as Margaret Wilson, although Wilson may not have been her original surname. On 18 July Margaret gave birth to a daughter, Eileen Constance. The baby was baptized in St Matthias', a Church of Ireland building, on 10 November 1886. The father was registered as Thomas George Wilson, the clerk on duty.[44]

5

Aunt Mary's husband, the Comte de Sizeranne, had been a trusted member of the court society of Napoleon III. He had a particular appreciation for the womanly arts of the Empress Eugénie. She had a wit, he observed, just sufficient to enforce her will. *Littérateurs*, in particular, were fascinated by her beauty and rank, and gave her greater credit for intelligence than he himself believed was her due, their own understandings having been confused by her laughter, poses and talent for listening.[45] His widow, the 75-year-old Comtesse, herself took a keen interest in these gifts that conquer men. In her view, male companions were permitted to be ugly, but women must be beautiful, and this required cultivation. 'She loved to discover and present to the world a beautiful girl,' according to *A Servant of the Queen*. In fact, 'her chief hobby was launching professional beauties'.[46] Once she had Maud Gonne in her care, Aunt Mary had the young woman perfumed, powdered, hatted and dressed, then brought her out into the Bois de Boulogne, where *demi-mondes* put themselves on show. Aunt Mary was delighted with her niece: Maud Gonne was the Comtesse's latest 'artistic production'.[47]

Aunt Mary, as described by Gonne, was anything but conventional. She kept what would now be called a toy boy, a 'young English secretary whom she addressed as Figlio ... and his secretarial duties were fictional.'[48] From Paris Aunt Mary brought her niece away to Hamburg, where she had rooms in a fashionable hotel. Maud Gonne was shown off at the Casino, and put on display in the balcony boxes of theatres. Within a short time, the project was show-ing signs of success. Photographers were asking for permission to photograph the new 'professional beauty'. Her photograph was printed in newspapers. Strangers asked for her autograph.

Maud Gonne (Undated studio photograph;
Print Collection, NYPL)

In time, the Prince of Wales arrived in Hamburg. He was obese, but reputedly the greatest roué of his era.[49] Aunt Mary promised Gonne they would soon be invited to dine with the Prince. It was inevitable. Would Aunt Mary be so bold as to leave her niece alone with Bertie at the end of the evening?

The Prince did indeed approach Maud and Aunt Augusta on the promenade. The young lady, unforgettably tall, had been presented to him only the previous May at Buckingham Palace. Before things could proceed further, according to *A Servant of the Queen*, Colonel Gonne arrived in Hamburg. He announced that he was taking his daughter to Bayreuth (Wagner's *Tristan and Isolde* was being performed that summer). Aunt Mary protested. He was spoiling everything; an invitation to a private supper with the Prince was surely about to arrive. That was just the problem, the Colonel answered: 'If I refuse to let her go, my military career would suffer, and I don't choose she should be talked about.'[50]

It is strange, given Maud Gonne's political views at the time of writing, that she depicts herself as having been content to play out to the last act a sex comedy with the Prince of Wales, although the script was written by others. Her vanity seems caught up in the notion that, when young, she was so beautiful that she was picked out to be a mistress of the future King of England, who had had much practice in the selection of mistresses. Aunt Mary may not have got her way in the summer of 1886, but she had planted a seed: Maud Gonne could expect to attract the attention of someone very important in the world, and for no conventional end.

6

In the *Servant of the Queen* version of Colonel Gonne's conversion to Home Rule, the scene is laid when he was lodged in the official residence in the Royal Barracks, Dublin.

Father and daughter have just been watching a Land League procession led by a marching band towards the Phoenix Park, where Michael Davitt and others would be speaking. Tommy remarks to his daughter, 'They are quite right … The people have a right to the land.' Then he brings her inside his residential quarters and shows her a draft of an election address he has composed. She is delighted. 'I would love it. I would help you. It would be wonderful.'

Royal, now Collins Barracks, Dublin, where Colonel Gonne died in 1886.
(Photograph by Robert French; Lawrence Collection, NLI)

There is no doubt that Maud Gonne MacBride truly would have had such sentiments at the time of writing, in the late 1930s. She would have loved her father to have been a Home Rule Liberal MP, but he never was; he was always a loyal 'servant of the Queen'. The author had acquired her chronic enmity of England long before the time of writing, and thus an animadversion to what had been an honoured title for her father. In using the epithet as the title of her memoir, she somewhat laboriously reinterprets its meaning. Her own life, she explains, was spent in service to 'Cathleen ni Houlihan', the allegorical queen of Ireland. Actually, on stage and off, Maud Gonne was never inclined to servitude; however, she would often give queenly magnificence to impersonations of Cathleen herself.

After recounting Thomas Gonne's political volte-face, *A Servant of the Queen* takes up the story with the Gonne family planning to spend a weekend at Captain Claude Cane's country house, St Woolstan's, in Celbridge, Co. Kildare. At the last moment, however, the Colonel sends his two daughters on alone, because he feels unwell. These events, if they occurred, might well have coincided with the baptism of Colonel Gonne's last daughter, on 10 November 1886. It is unknown whether Thomas Gonne attended the ceremony as an observer. Certainly, he was not registered as the infant's father.

When the Gonne girls returned from Celbridge, according to *A Servant of the Queen*, they found their father in bed with a high temperature. Week by week his condition worsened. He became delirious. On 1 December 1886, Thomas Gonne died of typhoid fever. The old barracks drained into the River Liffey, and at high tide sewage was driven back up whence it came. The whole edifice was unhealthy. Even the unionist *Irish Times* said it was high time the barracks were demolished.[51]

7

The doubly orphaned Maud Gonne now had nowhere to go except back to London and into the care of aunts and uncles. She and Kathleen spent time with Aunt Augusta Tarlton, the reverend's wife; Sir Francis Cook, the art collector; and Thomas Gonne's brother Charles, an official with the Bombay Civil Service, before the orphans finally settled with William Gonne, the oldest of Thomas's brothers, and their legal guardian. He lived at 11 St Helen's Place, a Georgian street off Bishopsgate. To judge from *A Servant of the Queen*, the

Gonne girls would have preferred to remain at the home of Charles Gonne in Ascot because he had two daughters, Catherine ('Chotie'), born in 1861, and May, born in 1864.[52] The four girls had taken it upon themselves to plan their own futures. May wanted to be a nurse, and Kathleen and Chotie wanted to go to art school. What would become of Maud?

William, trustee of Thomas Gonne's estate, had ideas of his own about what was becoming for a young woman. His niece did not like his ideas. She thought William Gonne 'rich, old, and crusty'.[53] He expected his nieces to be up early and to say prayers at breakfast, but they appeared to him not to understand the great importance of punctuality. One cold Sunday morning he waited for Maud Gonne in order for the family to depart for church. She was very tired. She had, she said, coughed all night long. William indicated that it was necessary to come along to prayer services anyway. This was a rude shock. Her father had always shown great respect for her cough, and he never made much fuss about religion. Tommy had loved her style. Maud Gonne writes that she subsequently came down with pneumonia. She leaves the reader to understand that her illness was the clear result of being dragged to church by Uncle William on a cold winter morning.

Maud and Kathleen were put on an allowance, and it was a tiny one: two shillings and sixpence a week. Uncle William requested a written account of how the money had been spent. If the girls could show him that there was reason for an increase in the allowance, he would be good enough to enlarge it. Perhaps William Gonne was attempting to prepare his nieces for being women of independent means; they would soon require an ability to keep track of their money. Yet this was evidently the first time either girl had encountered any limits being placed upon their power of purse. Maud Gonne spiritedly began to draw up fraudulent accounts for Uncle William's inspection. In her eyes, a state of war prevailed. In such circumstances, she decided, honesty was not required.

Uncle William hated it when his niece said the Gonnes were really an Irish family. That he hated her saying it did not stop her from doing so, often. He did not think of the family that way at all. It was absurd. The Gonnes were identified with the importation of port wine, and with all the associations of that brand: Britishness, middle-class domesticity and polite conviviality around the family dinner table. So what if the family name derived from the French language, and a branch of the family had once been planters in Ireland? Now they were more British than the British. Obviously his late brother's daughter had turned out to be (as far as he was concerned) a truly difficult child.

She remembers Uncle William saying 'I fear my poor brother brought you up very badly.' In her bereavement, and having lost not only a father, but her self-determination, Maud Gonne could not interpret such a statement as other than hateful.

8

There are many factors that caused Maud Gonne to come to possess, or be possessed by, an outright hatred of the country of her birth: the lost idyll in Howth; the cold welcome from aunts and uncles in London, and maybe even resentment on their part of children who were always being left on their hands, sometimes for years at a time; the 'family romance' in the Royal Barracks in Dublin. But the perfect storm occurred in 1887: a debutante with a classic Electra complex, reeling from the sudden death of her 'good father' in Ireland, being forced into a 'bad father' dependency upon a possibly bewildered but certainly insensitive English guardian.

Perfidious Albion had imposed 'tyranny' on a free Irish girl, at a time of momentous trauma in the life of Maud Gonne. That winter of woe in 1887 saw the birth of her lasting and ultimately abstract hatred of England. She had been famished of paternal attention for years, then intensely spoiled for a season. She was traumatized by her father's sudden and unpredictable death. Her adolescence was in its raging late bloom. These are conditions in which a person's character can take its final shape. Maud Gonne did not underestimate the importance of William Gonne's role in her life. A whole chapter of *A Servant of the Queen* is entitled 'Uncle William', yet he was not sufficient cause for the change in her life; the other factors are necessary too.

Maud Gonne was not accustomed to looking at herself diagnostically. She understood her feelings to arise out of pure sources of ethical inspiration. Her love of Ireland and her hatred of England were to her mind warrants for action; they were never interrogated.

Things went from bad to worse with Uncle William. One of his hobby horses was that socialism was going to be the ruin of Britain. He announced one morning that the girls were forbidden to go out that day; it would be too dangerous. A big demonstration was to be held in Trafalgar Square, organized by Tom Mann, the trade unionist and renowned orator. As soon as William left the house, Maud Gonne caught a bus into London. Where to? Trafalgar Square, of course. She claims that, once she arrived, some in the crowds, out of respect, lifted her up from the crush of people onto the speakers' platform, right beside the stone lions at the centre of Trafalgar Square. The setting is truly operatic. Tom Mann then asked what cause she had come there to represent. 'None at all' would have been the plain truth, but 'Ireland' was her answer. He invited her to address the crowd on behalf of her people. She did so, and thus began Maud Gonne's brilliant career as an Irish nationalist grandstand speaker. That career, by her telling, had its origin in angry defiance of Uncle William.

One event etched into Maud Gonne's memory was a time when she came into Uncle William's drawing room to find him standing stiffly with his back to the fireplace. Opposite him, sitting, was a woman in widow's weeds. She was crying. William was in the course of saying, 'That letter is no proof the child was his ... Please go at once. Can't you see how improper your presence is here?'[54] The woman, 'pale and rather beautiful', turned to the tall girl: 'Miss Gonne, won't you help me?' 'If I can,' she said quietly. She went over to the woman. 'Are you Mrs Robbins?'

She remembered the name because Colonel Gonne, being too weak to write in his last weeks, had asked his daughter to address an envelope to a woman of this name. The document enclosed was later returned because it was illegible. It had been a cheque. Mrs Robbins explained, according to *A Servant of the Queen*, that her baby girl was just six weeks old, and Colonel Gonne had died before mother and daughter left the period of bed rest that traditionally followed birth. Now she found herself alone and impoverished.

Some of the details in Gonne's dramatization of this episode are false, such as the child's age (not six weeks but eleven months in May 1887). The fairy-tale elements in it are reminiscent of an episode in the crowning achievement of literary romances, Edmund Spenser's *The Faerie Queene*, involving the 'False Florimel'. The real Florimel is a beautiful maiden devotedly in love with Marinell, and an inspiration of all that is innocent and good, but she was initially rejected by her beloved. The 'False Florimel' looks exactly the same. She, however, is crafty, lustful and dangerous. The False Florimel must be got rid of, before the real Florimel's wedding to Marinell can occur. The 'pale and rather beautiful' Margaret Wilson may have been seen by Maud Gonne as her double, a sort of False Florimel, but the story of her visit to Thomas Gonne's house in Portman Square is not all fairy tale. In part, it is factually supported by its outcome. Six years later, Maud Gonne arranged for Margaret Wilson to go into service as a governess with Count Ignaty Platonovich Zakrevsky, a Russian lawyer in St Petersburg.[55] The Count discovered Mrs Wilson to be a 'tall, very good-looking woman, with a great deal of poise,'[56] and was pleased to employ her as part of his household. The sorry side of this charitable act by Maud Gonne was that Margaret was forced to leave behind her daughter Eileen, to be raised as the adopted child of Mary Ann Meredith, the Gonne girls' old nanny, now settled in Hampshire. Maud Gonne evidently took in her stride the possibly shocking news that her father had a lover and an illegitimate child. Her *savoir faire* set her still further apart from William Gonne and English hypocrisy.

9

The next plot point in Maud Gonne's story of her turbulent times in England is another scene with Uncle William. He calls his obstinate niece in for a word, and then informs her that her father had been unwise with his money. Her expectations of an inheritance were going to be sadly disappointed. Now she would have to do as William wished, or go to work – and what work could she do? Maud reflected on the question. Nursing – one of the few professions open to women – was out because of her tricky lungs, so she secretly decided to go on stage. This would be, in the eyes of William Gonne, about the most *déclassé* thing a young woman could do, apart from selling her body.

According to *A Servant of the Queen*, Herman Vezin (the best-known acting coach of the day) had spotted her talent during the amateur theatricals of the 1886 Dublin Castle Season. He now helped her find a part – the leading part, naturally – in an English touring production of *Heartsease*, Charles Klein's adaptation of *Adrienne Lecouvreur*.

This turn in the story may appear to be just one more instance of Maud Gonne seeing herself, with childlike vanity, as the princess in a fairy tale. If there is a prince at a ball, he must dance with her all evening; if there is a fox hunt, she must be in at the kill and 'win the brush'; if there is a gigantic crowd, she is thrilling it with a heartfelt speech; and if there is a play, she must be its star. The reader is expected to exclaim again and again, not in doubt but in admiration, 'It is unbelievable!' Maud Gonne's life, however, was in fact amazing, with her knee-weakening beauty, great height and magical wealth. Sometimes, what she says happened did happen, and more or less as she says it did. For instance, in relation to her going on tour in a play, a classified advertisement appeared in the London papers on 2 May 1887 for a production of *Heartsease*. The timing is right, and so is the bill of fare. However, on 11 May the *Times* reports that 'Miss Gonne and Miss May Gonne' were presented at the Drawing Room, Buckingham Palace. It would be difficult for a young woman, even one with Maud Gonne's determination, to manage both rehearsals for the lead role in a play and, no doubt chaperoned by her uncle, making her curtsies at Buckingham Palace before the Prince and Princess of Wales.

At any rate, she never appeared in the play, but she is recorded as being present in Buckingham Palace. According to *A Servant of the Queen*, the pressure of rehearsals caused her to become ill – that weak chest again – and she was forced to withdraw. In this way, she explains, the stage lost a star, but Ireland gained a champion.

A family council was convened to discuss what was to be done with Maud Gonne. It was agreed that poor Uncle William, although he meant well, had been unwise to tell the girls that they had no money and thus no choice. He had simply wished to insist that either they must behave or go to work. He never expected Maud Gonne to choose the latter course of action, much less to enter such a disgraceful profession as acting. Yet everyone knew that Maud and Kathleen were going to inherit a fortune when they came of age, so in fact they had neither to work nor to behave. Maud Gonne, being already twenty-one, was in fact due her money as soon as her father's will cleared probate.

According to *A Servant of the Queen*, inheritance left Kathleen and Maud 'not rich but with enough to live on'.[57] That depends on what one means by rich. To be precise, Thomas Gonne left £28,828 to his daughters, which would have an income value of £21 million in 2013. Maud Gonne got half of that. That counts as rich by any standard, and the total does not include additional money coming to her from her mother's estate, and by way of the slow cascade of inheritances through her maternal grandfather's family.

With that matter settled by family conference, Maud Gonne left England in the summer of 1887 to join Aunt Mary, Comtesse de Sizeranne, in France. Release of his niece into the hands of the Comtesse by the very moral William Gonne was surely equivalent to her father's family giving Maud Gonne up for lost. From his point of view, it was a relief that whatever she was going to do with herself would at least now be done out of the country. One of the strangest departures from fact in *A Servant of the Queen* is that Maud Gonne makes her 'Aunt Mary' into a Gonne, when she was really a Cook. The book places Aunt Mary at the family council concerning Maud Gonne's attempt to go on stage. She speaks up for her niece's rights as a woman of independent fortune. Surely Maud Gonne knew that her aunt was a Cook and not a Gonne. Embarrassment about ostracism may have had something to do with the mis-characterization. It served as a token of fealty to one who had been willing to take her in.

II

THE SECRET ALLIANCE

Previous page: *The ancient road to the Romanesque church in Royat; the Hôtel des Marronniers is along this road. (Library of Congress Prints and Photographs Division Washington, D.C.)*

Those readers who bought copies of *A Servant of the Queen* in 1938 because of their interest in W.B. Yeats were in for a surprise. There is very little about him in the book. When the poet does get mentioned, it is sometimes with condescending humour. Maud Gonne regularly takes the liberty of referring to him in print as 'Willie'. Before publication, Yeats had given her permission to quote from his poems and to publish whatever she liked about him, but, after reading the book on 26 October 1938, he admitted to his wife George that he was 'sufficiently upset by it to have a not very good night'.[1]

Maud Gonne conceived her life as one great love story, yet Yeats plays a very small part in that story, on a par with a number of other males in supporting roles. Nor does the hero turn out to be the former husband of Maud Gonne, Major John MacBride; he is nearly left out of the book entirely. The romantic lead is instead taken by a French politician whom she met shortly after leaving England in 1887.

Maud Gonne recalls that upon falling ill during rehearsals for *Heartsease*, her doctor ordered her to go south to a spa, and to take a 'cure' there. And so, chaperoned by Aunt Mary, she arrived in Royat in the Auvergne for a therapeutic holiday in the midst of a 'sultry' French summer. Since Roman times, resorts had been constructed in Europe around mineral springs. In the nineteenth century, with the rise of both a leisure class and of tuberculosis, new spa towns were developed, seventy in France alone. A proper spa town would have a theatre, a casino, a formal garden with a band pavilion, confectioners' shops and patisseries, exquisite restaurants, hot and cold bathhouses for hydrotherapy and the consumption of minerals, groomed footpaths through wooded hills and a number of first-class hotels.[2] Local mythology about the ancient, miraculous powers of the waters was also a customary part of the package. In the course of her life, Maud Gonne would frequent many of them.

Eugen Weber explains the anthropology behind the explosive development of health resorts in nineteenth-century France:[3]

> A normal town, however small, had specific functions … trade, exchange, administration, justice. Resorts, on the other hand, were centres where people came together in pursuit of interests that had little or nothing to do with business, but with leisure and pleasure: concerts and shows, promenades, excursions, dancing, gambling, meeting each other and, especially, the opposite sex. Once they abandoned their walls (and remember that, more than a figure of speech, city walls were a stifling nuisance into the last third of the century!) townsfolk also abandoned many restrictions and constraints that the walls represented. What was exceptional in everyday life became the rule on holiday. The ease with which people once removed from the rigidities of life at home struck up new friendships, flirted, courted, was a special attraction of resorts. So too were the gargantuan meals and the gambling – above all, the gaming in casinos one could not find elsewhere and whence a large part of the resort's revenue was drawn.

The spa town of Royat is built high in a valley leading from Clermont-Ferrand to the Puy-de-Dôme (a former volcano, nearly 5000 feet high). It sits 1480 feet above a flat plain that is often roasting in July and August. Royat was put on the holiday map in 1862 when it was visited by Napoleon III and Empress Josephine. The emperor particularly enjoyed the trout fried in butter served at the Hôtel des Marronniers (now called Hôtel Belle Meunière), an event that made the fortune of both the dish and the restaurant.

The new thermal bathhouse at Royat was eighty metres long. *Curistes* entered, bought a ticket for the services prescribed by their physician, then went to the left of the vestibule if they were men, to the right if women, into large galleries, each with twenty-six baths, made of marble, volvic stone and enamelled iron. At the end of the gallery a pulverizer sprayed thermal mists. Patients could take baths in carbonic acid, sit in an amphitheatre encircling an umbrella-like spout of steam, retire to private rooms for massages, and swim in the *piscine*. Depending on whether a patient aspirated the spray, drank the waters, bathed, soaked or swam in them, the Royat bathhouse offered to cure many otherwise incurable ailments: gout, arthritis, asthma, herpes, tuberculosis and anaemia. Testimonials from doctors with practices in Paris and London swore to the efficacy of the waters. According to an English medical specialist in 1881:[4]

> Pale emaciated, stooping girls evidently brought up in convents or schools, without proper food, fresh air, and out-of-door exercise, crowded at night into dormitories, without ventilation, are seen by dozens at Royat; the change which takes place under the influence of the Ferro-arsenical water, combined with the exercise they take on the verdant hills surrounding the Valley, is very remarkable.

Another factor that might bring colour to these young girls' cheeks was the presence in Royat of officers from the huge military camp in Clermont-Ferrand, two miles down the mountain.

Postcards of Royat

When, after the nine-hour train journey from Paris, Maud Gonne and the Comtesse de Sizeranne arrived in Royat at the height of the fashionable season (15 July to 25 August), they found the town well populated with military men. General Georges Boulanger, the popular ex-Minister of War, had been reassigned away from Paris and confined to base in Clermont-Ferrand. Boulanger spent his idle time in Royat, followed by military aides and a sizeable party of his nationalist co-conspirators. Masses of Frenchmen had been thrilled by the General's rapid rise to prominence, and not just Frenchmen – Frenchwomen were mad for the red-bearded general on his black horse. A young woman employed in a Royat hotel remembered her excitement the night before his arrival in Clermont-Ferrand:[5]

> Sunday, July 10. Am I too suffering from what our old friend and doctor jokingly called the 'Boulangite'? It seems that this evil is rampant among women. I believe instead it's just a variation on what all good men and women of France feel. But I hardly slept that night because of my mad desire to go see the General. I got up out of bed, I was on tenterhooks, counting the minutes and seconds.

Second only to the visit of Napoleon III, the General's presence in Royat was a heyday in the history of the town; there is a diorama illustrating the event in the town museum.

In *A Servant of the Queen*, Maud Gonne recalled one particular scene with slow-motion, hyper-real particularity. She and the Comtesse were seated along the promenade listening to the band. A black cloud hung over the Puy-de-Dôme; a thunderstorm was imminent:[6]

> The wife of a French general, Madame Feline, a friend of Aunt Mary and her daughter Berthe … came and sat with us. People were slowly walking up and down. A couple of Frenchmen came up; there were introductions. One of these men I was certain I had met before. He was a tall man of between thirty and forty and looked ill; he was also at Royat for his health. I kept wondering where I had met him before. At last I asked him. 'But no, Mademoiselle, it is impossible; I would never have forgotten if I had met you.'

The man was 37-year-old Lucien Millevoye, a confederate of General Boulanger. Comtesse de Sizeranne may have already become acquainted with him through royalist or Bonapartist circles. Just then the storm began to break. Aunt Mary invited Monsieur Millevoye to accompany the ladies to their hotel. In the parlour, Aunt Mary's young male companion, Figlio, began to play the piano; outside, it thundered. Maud Gonne arose and left the salon. She recalls a sudden urge to walk right out into the rain, where 'petals of roses were being dashed to pieces by the deluge' – a blatantly symbolic touch. Who was this behind her? What a surprise! Monsieur Millevoye. Aunt Mary had dispatched him, to make sure that Maud was all right. It was in the nature of Aunt Mary's matchmaking skills to infallibly catch a murmured word, the squeeze of a hand, a small start of surprise. By her standards, Maud Gonne's exit was a shockingly bold signal.

Out on the veranda, Millevoye asks if the young lady is not afraid of lightning. 'One must never be afraid of anything, even death,' Maud Gonne has herself replying, reciting a piece of advice often heard from Tommy. Have they really not met before? she asks. He understands this line as bearing its customary flirtatious import. He puts his arm around her and kisses her 'dripping wet arm'.[7] A feverish passage of Marcel Prévost's Les Demi-Vierges spells out in further detail these stereotyped conventions of French seduction:[8]

> She tore off the left glove of a sudden; her arm suddenly appeared naked. [He] put his lips first on the fingertips, then slowly and greedily, he applied kisses to the wrist, forearm, winning his way past the elbow … [H]er eyes half closed, mouth open, [she] did not move her outstretched arm, till she suddenly withdrew it when his moustache tickled a vein – enough for today, she said.

In the days that followed, Lucien Millevoye and Maud Gonne went to the baths together, took walks in the hills – they were never apart. He told her of his beliefs, which were political in nature. He came from a family of Bonapartists. He did not believe in royal dynasties, but in the idea that a nation incarnates itself in a man of outstanding genius, who enjoys during his lifetime 'the right to rule despotically'. General Boulanger was now the man of the moment. If only Maud Gonne were French, he said, they could work together for revenge on Prussia and the return to France of Alsace-Lorraine. 'With a woman like you, a man could accomplish anything.'

'I shook my head. "I am Irish, and the whole of my country is enslaved."'

Later, Millevoye made a proposal, but it was not a marriage proposal. That would be impossible. He was already married, and the father of a son, Henri, facts Maud Gonne fails to mention in A Servant of the Queen.[9] What Lucien Millevoye offered was another sort of alliance, a secret one, in which as a pair they would do all they could to harm England, she for the sake of Ireland, and he for Alsace-Lorraine. What England had to do with continued German possession of these two French provinces is unclear. Maybe Millevoye just hated England because that is what many French people did, or because

Wellington defeated his hero Napoleon, or because now England stood in the way of an alliance between France and Russia against Germany, a long-range strategy for which Millevoye was scheming. Maybe he just wanted to enjoy sexual intercourse with Maud Gonne, and so he told her what she wished to hear; i.e., that this was undercover politics, top secret and very deep, and not just sex. Sex was only the way to put a fatal seal on the *alliance*.

In Maud Gonne's telling, this is the fundamental moment in her life story. She binds herself by oath to Millevoye, and – it is to be tacitly understood – subsequently seals that oath by sexual intercourse. The binding took the place of both a marriage ceremony and an initiation into a revolutionary secret society. The one thing the Secret Alliance is never said to be is an adulterous affair: Madame Adrienne Millevoye does not get a mention in *A Servant of the Queen*.

2

Some days later (according to *A Servant of the Queen*), Lucien Millevoye presented the young Englishwoman with a new self-conception. Instead of becoming a famous actress on the English stage – that would be beneath her – why not play the part of Joan of Arc in real life? Just as St Joan freed France from the English, Maud Gonne might free Ireland. His words, she said, brought to mind another saying of Thomas Gonne: if one's will is strong enough, one can do anything. Associations with her military father crowded around the 2-metre-tall Millevoye. With these fair omens, she accepted the heroic role he offered.

Joan of Arc, in addition to being a historical figure, is an archetype of changing significance in France. She is *la pucelle*, the virgin maid of whom it was said at her trial that she had never had a period. She is the defender of the King of France, and thus a royalist; the leader of a populist rebellion, and so a democrat. She embodies noble hatred of the perfidious English. She is a female knight, a child of nature, a Catholic saint and a patriot.[10] A large statue of Joan of Arc was commissioned for Paris after the Franco-Prussian War, erected in 1874 on the Place des Pyramides, where it immediately served as a focus for the restoration of national pride. For those in the Third Republic longing for a return to dynastic rule, Joan of Arc became a symbol of their own cause.[11] Against the grain of a period of growing scepticism, St Joan has an unquestioning, visionary heroism; she hears voices calling her to be a martyr for *la patrie*. Sarah Bernhardt was Joan of Arc on stage;[12] Maud Gonne would play her in real life.

3

The story of her life that Maud Gonne has to tell is painfully reminiscent of Henry James's *The Portrait of a Lady*. Isabel Archer, the young heroine from Albany, New York, is given a vast fortune by her uncle in England in order to 'put a little wind in her sails'. Money, it is hoped, will enable her 'to meet the requirements of her imagination'.[13] But no sooner is Miss Archer made free by this inheritance than she chooses to surrender much of that freedom by marrying Gilbert Osmond, a middle-aged widower with a daughter in need of womanly care.

What is strange and tragic about both stories is the eerie passivity with which a fresh and independent spirit surrenders her freedom. Maud Gonne permits Millevoye to take her body, permits him to veto her plan to be an actress, and accepts from him a new destiny. The behaviour seems out of character for such a publicly independent, proto-feminist woman. But that is the secret her book reveals: Maud Gonne's amazing public life hid a private, exciting dependency. It is wrong to expect of either a fictional character like Isabel Archer, or a real one like Maud Gonne, even if both are laden with wealth and freed from parentage, to act like models of triumphant modern feminism. Many of the conditions required for the equality of the sexes, or even steady progress towards it, were not in place in the 1880s. All the odds were against a woman on her own.

The parallel with Isabel Archer does not, of course, work in many respects: Maud Gonne does not and cannot marry Millevoye. As a Catholic, Millevoye cannot divorce his wife to marry Maud Gonne. And Maud Gonne was not cleverly manipulated by her worldly Aunt Mary so much as unwisely led. Unlike Isabel Archer, Maud Gonne never learned to repent her choice: owing to her continuous absence of reflection, she became impenetrable to herself. What Anna Magny calls her 'auto-mythification' was complete.[14]

4

Lucien Millevoye was born in Grenoble in 1850, the son of a Lyon magistrate. He came of age just after the Franco-Prussian war. He experienced the loss of imperial glory as personally traumatic. He turned to the study of classics at Rouen, then law in Grenoble. From 1872 to 1875 he was called to the bar in Lyon. In 1877 he became a substitute magistrate in that city. From these facts alone one could conclude that, after terms for peace were agreed with Prussia, Millevoye, in line with family tradition, began taking measured steps toward a privileged position in conservative Lyon.

But after 1870 nothing was quite what it had been in France. In the wake of Napoleon III's humiliating defeat in the war with Prussia, social fragments still surviving after the explosion of the French Revolution vied for supremacy. On the right, some royalists wished to re-establish the line of the Bourbons, the dynasty that had reassumed power in France after the fall of Napoleon in 1814. Henri, Comte de Chambord, was now the Bourbon claimant of the crown. Other royalists supported the descendant of Louis-Philippe, Duc d'Orléans, who ruled France in the 'July Monarchy' from 1830 to 1848. The Orleanists' hopes currently rested on the Comte de Paris. Other deputies in the French Assembly schemed on behalf of the Napoleonic line, of which there was more than one possible representative. A number of French notables wanted no supreme head at all: they aimed for a constitutional rule by a senatorial body composed of men of title and property.[15]

On the left were the followers of Léon Gambetta, one of the only heroes France had to show for the 1870 war. They placed their hopes in a constitutional republic based on universal suffrage.[16] A number of Communards who had briefly taken power in the Commune of 1871 had been exiled from France, but after amnesty in 1880 socialists gathered growing support from the organized wage-earning classes in the 1880s and nineties.

The 1875 constitution, on which the Third Republic was ultimately founded, was a compromise document: it did not clearly settle which of these social segments was to dominate. On its terms, a return to monarchy was possible, and so was progress towards democracy. There were many parties in play: all claimed to represent the true France, and all promised ultimately to vindicate the glory of the nation against Germany.

In 1877 a government led by Jules Ferry wrested power from the reactionary Marshal MacMahon, who in his four years as president had shown himself hostile to democratic, secular republicanism and inclined toward an ultimate return to monarchy. Catholicism since the French Revolution had been a bulwark of the royalists. Once in power, Ferry passed laws in 1879 and 1880 banning clergy from teaching in state or private schools. All religious orders not authorized by the state were outlawed. Over 250 religious houses were closed. Five thousand monks were designated for expulsion. Rather than carry out this law, many Catholic jurists resigned. The Church had the names of 200 of these Catholic jurists inscribed in a 'Golden Book' of martyrs to their faith. Lucien Millevoye was one of them. He sacrificed his career as a magistrate nearly as soon as it had begun.[17]

After his resignation, thirty-year-old Millevoye began to write for *Revue de la Société Littéraire, et archéologique de Yerle,* a monarchist journal. The Ferry government soon suppressed it.[18] Millevoye then found other right-wing, anti-government journals to publish his articles. He also employed himself as an advocate for men of property who aspired to recognition by the heraldry council.[19] An alliance of reactionaries had been formed between the royalists of every stamp and the Bonapartists, so Millevoye's work with the heraldry council is not out of place. However, in May 1886 Millevoye joined a Bonapartist group in Périgueux that repudiated this pact. Their rally concluded with the cry, *Vive Napoleon!*[20] A few months later, Millevoye was charged with writing an article with the intention of stirring up civil war. His offence was his proposal that the soldiers in the French army had the solution to the problems of France on the points of their swords.[21] At his trial, Millevoye protested his astonishment at the construction placed on his words; he had no such thought at all; he had just brought a bit of rhetorical colour to legitimate opinions.

His actual plans at this time emerge from an 18 August 1886 letter to a comrade. The right-wing's policy of abuse, obstruction and noise in the Chamber of Deputies, Millevoye had concluded, was not serving its cause any longer. The right must lead the country, not just harass its current leaders. He admitted that it might be difficult for the right to retain the allegiance of its current anarchist supporters, but patriotic men of vision now needed to establish a stable rule in France. The initial headway could be made by publicity. 'By fame the public is to be administered, to be governed.'[22] Suffrage was the means; a plebiscitary dictatorship was the end.

5

All Millevoye's hopes for overthrowing the current regime and establishing a right-wing government in France had come to rest on General Boulanger. Millevoye had been one of the first to start a press campaign on the General's behalf in March 1885. Boulanger was then the leader of the occupation forces in Tunisia, France's protectorate since 1881. The representative of France's civil power in the colony was Paul Cambon. He did not have a high opinion of the newly arrived young general, or of his family:[23]

> The General has more energy than intelligence. He needed it to reach the position he holds at his age, but he lacks a cultivated mind. He has no conversation either. You feel that here is a man who has read little, who has thought little about higher things, and who has no wide-ranging ideas. His whole mind is directed towards advancement and personal politics … Madame Boulanger talks a lot, about everything, without rhyme or reason, in a loud voice, and a tone that admits no reply. The two girls are plain …

The General soon found a means in Tunis to advance his popularity in France. After a fight broke out at a theatre and an Italian beat up a French soldier, Boulanger issued an order that his men could draw the sword on anyone who insulted them, whether native Tunisian or colonial Italian. Disrespect for a man in uniform was to be treated as an attack on France itself. Cambon revoked the order as one likely to cause trouble. This left a stalemate between the civil and military authorities in Tunisia, with Boulanger blustering that Cambon had brought shame upon the tricolour. The press took up the conflict, and Millevoye rowed in on behalf of General Boulanger and the honour of France. When General Boulanger returned to Paris in April 1885 he received a celebratory welcome, and not just from right-wing Catholic Bonapartists like Millevoye. Boulanger had also been supported in his struggle with Cambon by Georges Clémenceau, a radical deputy and the editor of *La Justice*. Growing up together in Nantes, Boulanger and Clémenceau had once been schoolmates, and according to some sources they were cousins. Now Clémenceau had in mind – using his great parliamentary influence – to promote General Boulanger as minister of war in the next government, whenever the current ministry should collapse. Clémenceau had a particular talent for bringing about the collapse of ministries.

Yet General Boulanger was not obviously a radical like Clémenceau. He had supporters of all types. Senator Alfred Naquet, a Jew and author of divorce legislation, allied himself with Boulanger. The former communard and vitriolic editor Henri Rochefort ('arguably the most accomplished blasphemer of the nineteenth century') and Georges Laguerre, once the personal secretary of Louis Blanc, a socialist, took his side.[24] Thomas Dillon, a businessman with experience of the methods of American electioneering, offered his services. Paul Déroulède, soldier, poet, orator and leader of a civilian army of 182,000 members (La Ligue des Patriotes), volunteered his forces.[25] Ambitious men from all sides gathered around this unknown quantity in a uniform. Female novelists like 'Gyp' 'endowed the General with the qualities of conquerors, which, in the event, he lacked: audacity, steadfastness, bravery, intelligence, and guts.'[26]

On 8 January 1886 Boulanger, aged fifty, became minister of war under Prime Minister Charles de Freycinet ('the white mouse').[27] A number of Boulanger's initial policies carried out the ideas of Georges Clémenceau.[28] Military service was made obligatory for all, even for the clergy. Buy-out clauses for the rich were no longer permitted; all young men had to serve their time in the army. Boulanger downgraded officers who, at a weekend party in a château, had reportedly slighted the republic. He withdrew his second daughter from the convent so as not to offend his radical supporters.[29] He purged the princes of the Orléans dynasty from the officer ranks of the army. These actions were all very satisfactory to the left wing. He pleased his nationalist followers in the Ligue des Patriotes by sabre-rattling. Great hopes were raised in the lost provinces:[30]

> The Lorrainers at first believed in him ... there were pasted up pictures of a yellow-bearded general, covered with [ribbons] and crosses, in lonely cottages, where solitude and hard toil prepared the simple husbandmen for belief in legends and miracles ... It was in Lorraine that a beginning was made for the future military dictatorship in France.

France, however, was far from being prepared to fight and win a war with Germany. In April 1887 M. Schnaebele, a French customs official who ran a string of spies in the lost provinces, was tricked by a German commissioner into a meeting at a border crossing in Metz.[31] Finding no one there on his arrival, Schnaebele wandered a few metres into German territory. A soldier then leapt up from a ditch and arrested Schnaebele as a spy. Out of such incidents wars can be made, but France was in no position to start one. And, in fact, General Boulanger had been infiltrating spies into the captured provinces, even if Schnaebele was not himself one of them so much as he was their supervisor (a fact not admitted by France at the time). When it became clear that France could do nothing but bluster, Schnaebele was released. The affair wound up being an embarrassment to France, but it also served as an opportunity for the next government (formed on 30 May 1887) to dismiss General Boulanger from his post for having proved himself a blunderer.

A better reason for the government's dismissal of the General is that, urged on by his supporters, early in May Boulanger had allowed his name to go forward for election in a large number of departments. While as an officer he was disqualified from holding office or even taking an active part in politics, he came top of the poll in more than one constituency. The results were a clear threat to the government in office; the people had indicated they would rather have been led by the General.

During May 1887 Boulanger dined at the Café Anglais with Alfred Naquet and Clémenceau. Naquet saw the General as carrying the standard for the left. That had been Clémenceau's expectation as well. Naquet now proposed that the time was ripe for a *coup d'état*. The General considered the proposal, but concluded that the right moment had not yet arrived. If the attempt were successful, Germany might invade, and France was still not ready for war. Clémenceau was horrified that Boulanger had no other than a pragmatic reason for refusing to lead a coup. To him, the republic was sacred, and he had previously thought Boulanger shared these sentiments.[32] Along with others, he too began to fear Caesarism and a general who had become too popular.[33]

General Boulanger's departure from Paris for Clermont-Ferrand was announced for 8 July 1887. Whether it was a spontaneous expression of popularity, or the result of operations undertaken by Boulanger's experts in mass mobilization, huge crowds appeared on the day at the Gare de Lyon, singing the 'Marseillaise'.[34] Some of those present thought a march on the Elysée Palace and a quick coup were about to occur before their eyes, but it did not. The train simply pulled out of the station. Socialists like Paul Lafargue then mocked 'the general, pale and undone by his triumph, [who] leaves by locomotive without saying a word to the crowd that acclaims him'.[35] Boulanger's departure from Paris, however, was anything but a retreat. He had in his hands the wherewithal for a coup, but had deferred the day of its occurrence.

6

When the tourists left Royat at the end of its high season, 25 August 1887, Maud Gonne remained behind with Lucien Millevoye. The nature of the plans discussed at that moment by General Boulanger and his confederates was the object of speculation in the capitals of Europe. In the *Fortnightly Review*, an expert on foreign affairs surmised that what actuated the General was no particular principle, but just a desire for power:[36]

> Ambition is his hope, his life, his mistress, his present and his future; his very being is bound up by his insatiable craving for some intangible 'beyond' … Each in turn, from Radical Left to royalist right … has received from time to time some particular, though by no means binding, mark of favour from the astute General … He is in reality neither Conservative nor Radical, Opportunist nor Socialist, Monarchist nor Republican; he is simply *Boulangiste*.

If ambition was his mistress, it was not his only one. The previous January in Paris General Boulanger had won the favours of Marguerite Brouzet, the Vicomtesse de Bonnemains. She was separated from her husband and held a salon in the Rue de Berri. It was the wealth of Madame Bonnemains, many believed, which enabled the General to mount lavishly advertised campaigns in the May 1887 elections.[37]

On 22 October 1887 Marie Quinton, concierge in the Hôtel des Marronniers in Royat, received two visitors, one very tall. They behaved quite mysteriously. The two men wanted to inspect whatever rooms the concierge had available. Their inspection complete, they booked her best suite for two guests whose identities, they insisted, must be kept secret. The booking was for five days. Two days later Madame Bonnemains arrived to take possession of the suite. That night, two men showed up at the hotel's door, both wearing false beards. One handed over a suitcase, and in Marie Quinton's hearing, said, 'Tomorrow, then, at nine.'[38] The other man, who proved to be General Boulanger himself, then went up to his mistress.

According to *A Servant of the Queen*, Lucien Millevoye explained to Maud Gonne that he had a surprise in store for her: a private dinner had been arranged. In fact, it was a top-secret engagement. Maud Gonne would be introduced not just to the brave general, but to the famous Madame Bonnemains, 'a woman of great beauty and charm and very influential.'[39] Millevoye offered his companion the treat of an awesome proximity to power, wealth and beauty, the best of the best in France. The young Englishwoman was not, in the event, overawed. In *A Servant of the Queen*, she allows that the General was very good-looking, and his manners were never less than charming, but she says that she was able to see right away that he did not have the ruthlessness required for the part he aimed to play (Maud Gonne is writing with the benefit of hindsight). When she told Millevoye of her assessment, he replied: 'It depends on Madame de Bonnemains. If she is strong enough for the role, all will be well; he is crazy about her.'[40]

Apart from the chivalry of this praise for the importance of a woman to a man's success, Lucien Millevoye was grooming Maud Gonne for the role he intended for her to play. She would be his Madame Bonnemains. She too was a woman of fortune. She could, with his aid, become influential, not just in Ireland, but in France. A salon would be required. Some celebrity could be organized. Most essential would be the man through whom, if she were strong, she would fulfil herself.

III

FOREIGN AFFAIRS

I n November 1887 Maud Gonne decided to take up the invitation of a fellow
English debutante, Lila White, to visit Constantinople. Gonne would not
be an ordinary tourist in an ordinary Turkish hotel. Miss White's father,
Sir William, was the British Ambassador to Turkey. Such private access to the
person in charge of British foreign policy in the region cannot but have been
interesting to Lucien Millevoye. Turkey was currently a centre of strategic
diplomacy. Bulgaria and Armenia were in an unsettled condition. They were
pulled on one side by the 'Triple Alliance' – Germany, Austria-Hungary, and
Italy – and on the other side by France and Russia. Maud Gonne could keep her
ears open at the dinner table, couldn't she?

Before she embarked for Constantinople, Maud Gonne enjoyed a clandestine rendezvous with Millevoye in Marseilles. She called into a pet shop and
bought a little monkey, to which she wittily gave the name 'Chaperone'. From
now on, she would have no other; Aunt Mary, the Comtesse, was no longer
accompanying the young heiress. In Marseilles Millevoye visited a gunsmith
and bought his mistress a small revolver. When she expressed surprise at this
ominous love token, he said it was 'to protect our Alliance'.[1] In *A Servant of
the Queen*, Maud Gonne makes her excitement plain. She was being given not
just a gun but a dangerous mission in 'the great game' of international state-
craft. That was the world in which her father had spent the best years of his life.
Wouldn't he be proud of her! In her memoir, it does not occur to Maud Gonne
that perhaps the Colonel would have been horrified.

2

After Maud Gonne had left for Turkey, the murky stratagems of the Boulangistes became truly bewildering. Even the General's nearest allies could not follow what he was up to. On 19 November 1887 Georges Clémenceau managed to bring down yet another government by means of an 'interpellation' in the Chamber of Deputies – that is, a demand for an explanation from an officer of the government. Clémenceau's challenge concerned the sale of state honours by President Grevy's son-in-law, Daniel Wilson. After the successful passage of a resolution by the opposition in the Chamber, negotiations began on the formation of a new government.

On the nights of 28 and 29 November radical deputies tried to find a formula for a new government that would be led by Charles Floquet or Charles de Freycinet, both thought to be weak leaders, and which would include Boulanger and Clémenceau in the cabinet, understood to be men with the strength to impose their will. One night at the home of Marguerite Durand (Georges Laguerre's mistress) Clémenceau came to realize that a rump of Boulanger's followers, including Millevoye, Laguerre, Henri Rochefort and Alfred Naquet were not going to wait for a favourable coalition in the Chamber; they had begun to plot a coup. Clémenceau, shocked, asked General Boulanger where he stood on this matter. Boulanger said that his army would not stand in the way of such a move. 'Just think,' Clémenceau said to Madame Durand, 'a French General is giving ear to such proposals!'[2] From then on, Clémenceau ceased to be an ally and became an enemy of the Boulangistes, in fact, their bitterest enemy.

The disgraceful doings of that night were far from complete. The same evening Boulanger directly reached out to the royalists. On 1 November, three weeks earlier, he had already done so indirectly, by sending his election agent, Count Dillon, to meet the Comte de Paris in London. Boulanger's message to the prince was that he now regretted the expulsion of the royalist princes; as a matter of fact, he had never really been comfortable with the radicals. He was now ready to serve the royalist cause in France; all the Comte de Paris needed to do was give the order.[3]

After the departure of Clémenceau on the night of 29 November, Boulanger went to a meeting with Baron de Mackau, a chief royalist. The General presented a plan for a coup on behalf of the Comte de Paris.[4] Boulanger seemed to have forgotten that he was in the French army. He conspired with enemies of the regime that he was supposed to serve.[5]

A month later, on 26 December 1887, Boulanger had a second meeting with Baron de Mackau. He repeated his willingness to back a coup on behalf of the Comte de Paris, but first he needed money to run for election. These electoral tactics would soon demonstrate his popularity, and thus force the government to reappoint him to the cabinet. Once he was Minister of War, all would be well for the Orleanists. A week later, Boulanger went to Switzerland to meet the man who carried the hopes of the Bonapartists, Prince Jérome Napoleon, the direct rival of the Comte de Paris. Boulanger wanted money and political support from him as well, but the prince made no promises.[6]

Although Boulanger travelled to these secret meetings he was actually under orders not to leave his base in Clermont-Ferrand. The current minister of war made arrangements to keep him under watch; however, Boulanger employed disguises when he travelled, and aliases and secret codes when he wrote messages. His actions were usually undertaken not in his own person but by his agents, men such as Dillon, Déroulède and Millevoye.[7]

In the periodic by-elections that followed the formation of a new government, General Boulanger once again was on the ballot in multiple jurisdictions. Officially, these polls were not campaigns for office by the General. They were just, it was to be assumed, an expression of the general will (*volonté générale*), spontaneously manifesting itself. When Boulanger was questioned directly by the minister of war if he had been party to the nominations, he said he knew nothing about them. After making this denial, the General wrote privately to Millevoye:

> Did you see that the Minister put the question to me if it was with my consent that my nomination for office was publicized? I responded as laconically as possible and I could not do otherwise, although knowing full well that such behaviour would take away votes.[8]

The only problem Boulanger sees with lying to his superior is that in this case the lie might reduce his vote count. Obviously, his letter assumes a moral community with Millevoye on such political necessities.

Early in 1888 Boulanger consolidated his alliance with the Ligue des Patriotes. It had formerly been an organization open to all parties. Now its leader, Paul Déroulède, declared that henceforth the Ligue des Patriotes would concern itself

> ...with internal and external policies, that is to say with the reorganization of the Republic ... General Boulanger ... is the symbol of the Parti national ... We protest the usurpative constitution of 1875 and ministerial parliamentarianism.[9]

The Ligue advocated a plebiscite and one-man rule.

Each time there was a by-election to fill a seat in the Chamber of Deputies, Boulanger's name was listed among the candidates. Picture posters of the General on his horse went up all over the area in which the vote was to be held. Illustrated song sheets with ditties about the brave general were distributed. Newspapers were paid to write favourable articles about him. Mass meetings were organized. Orators were deputized to speak on his behalf, and against the government. Elections were won north and south. Who was doing all this?

It was obvious that General Boulanger was not minding his military business in Clermont-Ferrand. Orleanist riches flooded into these political campaigns, ultimately on behalf of the Comte de Paris, and a return to monarchy. One of the principal sources was the vastly wealthy Duchesse d'Uzès. When asked by an English journalist if she had given three million francs to Boulanger for his election campaigns, she did not deny it. Sitting on her bed in the state bedroom of her château, she told the journalist that she was ready to give General Boulanger anything he needed, slapping her riding crop on the counterpane to emphasize her words – anything at all.[10]

On 14 March 1888 General Logerot, Minister of War, had had enough of Boulanger's clandestine operations. Boulanger had been explicitly reminded in February that he did not have permission to leave his base, but he nonetheless repeatedly snuck away to Paris, disguised behind dark blue glasses and a black beard, and faking a limp. On three occasions, these ruses failed to deceive the police detectives assigned to his case.[11] Put on notice by General Logerot, Boulanger suddenly began to fear the punishment in store for him. He liked being General Boulanger. What would it be like to be just plain Georges? Why, he might be exiled! He poured out his heart to Lucien Millevoye. If barred from the army, 'I expect that one would wither in France and abroad to an unheard of extent that just hit me.'[12] Boulanger made one last plea to the minister of war. He had been compelled to make these unapproved journeys because his mistress Madame Bonnemains was 'sick' in Paris, and had called for his help. To be frank, she was having a miscarriage.[13] In such circumstances, a Frenchman had to do his duty.

In spite of his ingenious appeal, Boulanger was suspended from military service on 15 March 1888.

3

If this suspension, with a 40 per cent cut in pay, was intended to clip the General's wings, it failed in its purpose. Out of the army it was harder for Boulanger to lead a coup, but easier for him to make France ungovernable by others. The following day, 16 March, Boulanger joined the list of inactive military officers and simultaneously entered politics as the figurehead of a 'Republican Committee of National Protest'.[14] The committee's name is a classic combination of politically emotive but ambiguous terms, of a kind to attract followers who cherished contradictory hopes.

Voters from all sides rallied to the General. Royalists saw him as a king or a king's champion; to republicans, he was the embodiment of true liberty; to imperialists, a Caesar; to patriots, he would fight for the return of Alsace-Lorraine; to peaceable people, he would guarantee the benefits of simple law and order; and those who longed for something unknown found in Boulangism an adventure that would enable them to escape their problems.[15] Even young intellectuals saw in him the potential for their multifarious desires to be fulfilled.

Édouard Vaillant ran for office as a socialist and Boulangiste. In his election speech, he put to supporters the question: What is Boulangism? It was not only a movement of reactionaries, he said. The people as a whole was making its will known through this one man:[16]

> Le Boulanger is the expression of the people's discontent; the people are excitable, always ready to respond to a new current ... All these malcontents are the nation's unconscious; they do not know where they are going, but wander in obedience to the mysticism of our race, and their belief in the individual.

The writer Maurice Barrès became a passionate Boulangiste too. Barrès was the author of a novel, *Sous l'oeil des Barbares*, the first volume of his trilogy *Le Culte du moi* (*The Cult of the Self*). It expressed the yearning of a generation of post-Imperial, post-Catholic sceptics for a principle of order in a chaotic world. Their prayer began, 'O master, if you exist somewhere, in axiom, religion, or prince of men ...'[17]

Barrès proclaimed in *La Revue Indépendant* (the organ of the Symbolistes) that Boulanger 'was that Master and that prince of men. Boulanger has the merit that he is outside existing political parties. Politicians are farceurs, they poison existence. France needs a man from every party and no party.'[18] Barrès was the bellwether of his generation, with many followers. They were all sick of 'the Republic of atheism and demagoguery',[19] or, in other words, ordinary democratic polity.

4

On 19 April 1888 Georges Boulanger, a general no longer, entered the Chamber having been elected as a deputy for the Nord. A banquet was held at Café Riche in his honour. One of those seated close to Boulanger was Lucien Millevoye. He was described in the press report of the banquet as 'currently the chief of the Bonapartist party in Corrèze [a department in the northwest Massif Central]': 'He sends, many times a week, ultra Bonapartist articles to the *Journal de Lot-et-Garonne*, the *Echo de la Dordogne*, the *Corrèzien*, the *Conciliateur de la Corrèze*, etc., in short, all the imperialist newspapers in the region.'[20] Millevoye, the paper archly observed, is 'the sort of republican Boulanger represents' [i.e., not one at all].

On 30 April Millevoye addressed a heated article on an issue raised by a column in the newspaper *Le Nord*. It had claimed that Russia was unhappy about the success of the Boulangistes. A government under the former general could be the source of serious complications in Europe, such as a war with Germany. The Czar did not want this outcome. Millevoye spoke for Boulanger in saying there were no grounds for such a fear:[21] 'I cannot with too much energy protest against this sentiment. The sincerity of our feelings is absolute … We slander democratic France by suggesting that we have a plan for aggression, to which for my part I have been and remain resolutely opposed.'

That the Czar might harbour doubts about the ultimate intentions of Boulanger would have been reasonable; no one really knew what they were. It was necessary for the Boulangistes to remove these doubts. The alliance between Russia and France was essential to their master plan (vague as to detail) for the ultimate recovery from Germany of the lost provinces. Personal diplomacy and documents of the highest authority would both be necessary to reassure Russia. For that diplomatic assignment, Lucien Millevoye relied on no other than Maud Gonne.

5

During this period of hectic, devious, and seditious manoeuvres by the Boulangistes, there is no evidence that Maud Gonne was in France. It is known that she went over to Dublin for the Castle Season of 1888, and saw her sister Kathleen presented to the Lord Lieutenant. A meeting could have occurred between Millevoye and Gonne in London on 26 April 1888, when Deputy Boulanger was on a publicity tour to Britain; Millevoye was normally a part of his retinue.[22] Or perhaps the couple met upon Boulanger's return to Paris for the Café Riche banquet.

In *A Servant of the Queen*, Maud Gonne remembers being summoned by telegram to meet Millevoye in Paris.[23] She was brought to the salon of Juliette Adam, the famous mistress of Léon Gambetta. Money, beauty, intelligence and a flair for popular fiction made the wife of Edmond Adam into a force in her own right. The particular aspect of Gambetta's programme that Juliette Adam embraced was the idea that universal education should be established so that each French child could be taught a single lesson: 'A cause exists to which it must give everything, its life, its future, its family, and that this cause is France.'[24] Maud Gonne would one day pursue with equal passion the nationalist indoctrination of Irish children. The part of Gambetta's republicanism Madame Adam did not accept was his populism. She was a French nationalist, but she wanted the masses led by an elite, while Gambetta believed the people could be educated to govern themselves.[25]

In 1881 Madame Adam started a new journal to advance her principles, especially *revanche* ('revenge' – a war against Germany to recover lost territories). The literary lights of her salon and of *La Nouvelle Revue* included Millevoye's friend Paul Déroulède, as well as Paul Bourget, and later on, the anti-semite writer Léon Daudet (son of novelist Alphonse Daudet).[26]

Madame Adam had long been a Russophile. She was party to the mission of Déroulède in 1886 to meet pan-Slavic leaders on behalf of Boulanger. Déroulède had then conveyed Boulanger's message that he would support Slavic rebellions in the Balkans against both Turkish and Austro-Hungarian rulers. In late April or early May 1888 Madame Adam helped to prepare Maud Gonne for a secret errand to St Petersburg. The Boulangistes wished to communicate with the Czar or one of his top advisors as soon as possible; however, they could not trust the regular post. Would Maud Gonne carry these secret documents? It would be necessary to leave straight away. She also must take care not to be followed. What decided her to accept the mission, according to *A Servant of the Queen*, was the warning that her mission would not only be undertaken without the approval of the French government, but it would also be utterly contrary to British policy.[27] Not for the last time, she applied the amoral logic that the enemy of my enemy is my friend. If a course of action would be harmful to Britain, it was a good action. No further information was required.

Madame Juliette Adam (photograph from Atelier Nadar, pub. 1910;
Bibliothèque Nationale)

The documents were sewn into her dress and Maud boarded a train for St
Petersburg via Berlin. While *A Servant of the Queen* leaves the impression that
she went to Russia alone, Millevoye came along too. The value of Maud Gonne
to the enterprise was that no one would dare to search this elegant English lady.
Princess Catherine Radziwill recalled meeting the pair upon their arrival in St
Petersburg and wrote that she had tried to help Millevoye obtain a conference
with the Czar, but he 'did not display the tact he might have done'. Meanwhile,
the Russian authorities requested from Boulanger confirmation that Millevoye
was truly empowered to speak on his behalf. Boulanger, embarrassed by public
exposure of the scheme, denied that he had anything to do with Millevoye's
mission. In the end, the whole intrigue collapsed.[28] As the French historian
Bertrand Joly brutally put it, you can find Millevoye on every page of the
history of the radical right in France 'whenever there is a disaster to organize'.[29]

It happened that W.T. Stead, editor of the *Pall Mall Gazette*, was in St Petersburg in May 1888. Unlike Millevoye, he was afforded generous access to the Czar. His bombshell interview – by English standards, sympathetic – would later be published in London.

Stead, although a puritanical finger-pointer when it came to the peccadilloes of others, had a long-lasting attachment to a woman not his wife, Madame Olga Novikoff. (Some believed this old charmer was managing Stead on behalf of the Russian secret service.) It was acceptable, he reasoned, for a married man like himself to have a second love, so long as the 'secondary female' did not 'step over [the threshold of] the monogamous household'.[30] What was to be done when, far from the monogamous household, you found yourself with a 'secondary' lady in a grand hotel?

Or a third and a fourth lady. Madame Novikoff, Princess Radziwill and Maud Gonne were all staying in the Grand Hotel de l'Europe in St Petersburg. This hotel became the setting for scenes that, as dramatized in *A Servant of the Queen*, seem right out of a French farce. Princess Radziwill urges Maud Gonne to find out what Stead's real purpose is in Russia. Was he or was he not laying the groundwork for an alliance between Russia and England? Maud Gonne seeks out the editor's company. She asks him question after question, then listens to his lengthy answers with apparent admiration. Maud Gonne's eyes are dewy. They are huge. A man could get lost in them.

Somehow, Stead got around to the subject of sex, no matter what topic she raised. Her untiring interest in him was interpretable as a sign that she wished him to start something. Her failure to match his bid in a game of two-handed flirtation was puzzling. So he bid higher. She interpreted his interpretation as evidence of a congenital 'sex obsession'. When she called him on it, he was left in confusion. That night, by way of apology, Stead wrote Maud Gonne a long and amorous letter. How could a man not be obsessed with sex when he was with a young woman as beautiful and daring as Maud Gonne was?

The next day, returning from a drive with a Russian who had befriended her father at the time he was military attaché in St Petersburg, Maud Gonne found Madame Novikoff waiting at her apartment. She had always wanted to meet the Russian *grande dame*. As soon as Maud Gonne entered, however, Madame Novikoff excused herself and hurried away. The following morning Stead burst into Gonne's suite, weeping. How could Maud Gonne have been so heartless as to show his letter to Madame Novikoff? But she had not done so. Then it dawned on Gonne that the Russian lady, like any good spy, had in Gonne's absence taken the liberty of reading her private correspondence.

The giddy skit that Madame MacBride makes of all this in *A Servant of the Queen* may accurately capture the spirit in which a young Maud Gonne played Mata Hari. Her 1888 trip to Russia winds up in 1938 as a tale of hilarious risks taken, wild thrills enjoyed. Its literary development, like Gonne's neglect to mention Millevoye having been in St Petersburg, may function as a cover for a humiliating failure in the life of her lover.

At the end of that section of the autobiography dealing with her trip to Russia, Madame MacBride attempts to conclude on a serious note. What she had carried sewn into her skirts, she can now reveal, was a draft treaty that would in a few years change the face of European diplomacy.[31] International relations were then altered, she notes, in a direction the very opposite of that sought by Britain. In addition, she had exposed Madame Novikoff as a double agent who was really working for Britain. In the contest of Gonne with Novikoff, the 'Irish' lady is shown to have triumphed. She had even unintentionally stolen the affections of a besotted London editor. In the wisdom of her old age Madame MacBride is delighted by the treasonable high jinks of her youth, set in the city where her father had once been the British military attaché. Sometimes a reader may still exclaim 'Unbelievable!' but, exaggeration aside, the adventures of Maud Gonne were wonderful enough, and she was only getting started.

IV

FROM MILLEVOYE TO YEATS
TO MILLEVOYE

ONTO THE IRISH STAGE, THEN
A MYSTERIOUS DISAPPEARANCE

Previous page: *Cover from* L'Univers illustré, *10 October 1891.*
The suicide of General Boulanger. (BNF)

The time had come for Maud Gonne to make a beginning as the 'Irish Joan of Arc'. The September 1888 'Parnell Fund' campaign gave her an opportunity to show on what side she stood. Parnell had sued *The Times* for libel after it published letters seeming to prove that the leader of the Irish Parliamentary Party had conspired with terrorists in the 1882 Phoenix Park murders. In 1889 those letters would be proven to be forgeries by Irish journalist Richard Pigott. Gonne's September 1888 donation of £2 6s. to the fund to cover Parnell's legal costs put her near the top of the published list of contributors, just below the names of Irish bishops of the Catholic Church.[1] An accompanying letter to the press urged

> ... all Irishmen and women to show their sympathy and admiration of those who so nobly maintain the struggle against wrong and oppression.
>
> Faithfully yours,
> Maud Gonne

One imagines Uncle William Gonne spitting out his tea when he read that item in the morning newspaper. 'Wrong and oppression' indeed! What will she do next?

What Maud Gonne did next was to move her base of operations to Airfield House, Dublin, home of the Jameson family. Owners of a big distillery, and unionists, Mr and Mrs Jameson were unlikely on the whole to sympathize with Gonne's projects, but Ida Jameson was another story. Maud Gonne's friend from the Castle Season of 1886, Ida was persuaded to join Maud in becoming very Irish very publicly. After all, Lady Aberdeen herself, the Lord Lieutenant's wife, was in favour of demonstrations of personal sympathy with the people. Who could object? The two young heiresses bought gold rings and had them inscribed 'Eire'.[2] This gesture was not revolutionary, but Maud Gonne had tried to get advice from Michael Davitt about the best way to contribute to the national cause, and he would not grant her a meeting. Given her background as the elder daughter of the former chief of British forces in Ireland, Maud Gonne encountered reasonable resistance before being allowed to play a part in the nationalist movement. Furthermore, many Irish national organizations had by-laws that ruled out full membership by women, even when attendance by female guests was permitted on social occasions. Yet Maud Gonne was unstoppable.

At five o'clock on the afternoon of Thursday, 11 October 1888 she presented herself at the weekly meeting of the Society for the Preservation of the Irish Language. Count Plunkett presided. Gonne applied for membership, paid her fee and was admitted, giving as her address 'Airfield, Donnybrook'. The event was reported in *The Nation*.[3] It was newsworthy that someone at the Jamesons' home supported the Irish language revival. Maud Gonne's visibility was beginning to be established.

She showed up at meetings on College Green of the Contemporary Club, a discussion group set up by Charles Oldham, a Protestant Home Ruler and mathematics lecturer at Trinity College Dublin. He was also vice-president of the Dublin Young Ireland Society. Rules against female membership of this society did not keep Maud Gonne from fully participating when present. It was probably through the Young Ireland Society that she first met John O'Leary – like Oldham, a Protestant nationalist – and one of the original Young Irelanders.

John O'Leary became a Fenian and took part in several failed uprisings in his twenties. In 1859 he was arrested for treason-felony and sentenced to twenty years, of which he did five years' hard labour in Portland Prison in England. Fifty-eight years old in 1888, O'Leary looked like the ancient of ancients, with a lofty forehead and a long white beard. He made a practice of giving fatherly encouragement to young Irish patriots, lending out books from his personal library of Irish literature and history. O'Leary was instrumental in leading W.B. Yeats to see his destiny in Irish terms. In some ways, his persona of scholarly gentleman in retirement was a mask. He also had another identity as the undercover president of the Irish Republican Brotherhood, a secret society devoted to revolution (but under O'Leary's guidance, in no hurry to start one). Young visitors to his library would be vetted before being invited to join the IRB. Maud Gonne was not asked to join – yet. It seemed to some that the impetuous young English woman who was crashing the meetings of all the nationalist societies in Dublin might turn out to be a particularly maladroit spy.

According to Samuel Levenson, Gonne visited the City of Dublin Hospital at first with a view to taking up the study of nursing, but after a discussion with the matron, she decided instead to raise money for the hospital.[4] Ida Jameson and Charles Oldham were drawn into her plan for a series of benefit performances by herself and others (Ida performed too), announced by the *Freeman's Journal* on 30 October 1888. At the first concert on 3 November the works recited by Maud Gonne may be the result of browsing in John O'Leary's library: 'The Banshee' by John Todhunter, 'Emmet's Death' and 'The High-born Ladye' by Thomas Moore, with its premonitory advice that Irish bachelors ignored at their own risk:[5]

> In vain all the Knights of the Underwald wooed her,
> Tho' brightest of maidens, the proudest was she;
> Brave chieftains they sought, and young minstrels they sued her,
> But worthy were none of the high-born Ladye.

Gonne was back on stage less than two weeks later for another benefit concert, this time doing the death scene from *Romeo and Juliet*.[6] In a second appearance on that evening, Gonne recited 'Nationality' by Thomas Davis. The following month, on 18 December, she was one of the elocutionists at the 'Grand Public Recital' in Molesworth Hall, where she reprised her performance as Juliet taking the poison.[7] In these months, Gonne's activities were covered by the Dublin daily papers over and over: three charity concerts, big advertisements ahead of those concerts, news reports following them and appearances at patriotic clubs that were noted in the press. She was taking the city by storm.

Maud Gonne made a woman friend in Dublin too, the painter Sarah Purser. Around Christmas 1888 Purser wrote to her classmate from the Académie Julian, Louise-Catherine Breslau, about the young woman who was making such a stir.[8] For a relative stranger to the city, Maud Gonne had located key figures in cultural nationalism with impressive speed. On 16 December she attended Dr George Sigerson's Sunday 'At Home'. Sigerson, a tall, bearded fellow, looked like one of his Viking ancestors. Formerly a student of Dr Charcot in France, he translated and wrote Irish poetry, in addition to his medical practice. Thereafter, whenever Maud Gonne needed medical attention in Ireland, it was to Dr Sigerson she turned. Douglas Hyde, not yet the founder of the Gaelic League, noted in his diary Maud Gonne's presence that night:[9] 'To Sigersons in the evening where I saw the most dazzling woman I have ever seen: Miss Gonne, who drew every male in the room around her ... We stayed talking until 1.30 AM. My head was spinning with her beauty!'

Charles Oldham was another drawn into that circle of men under the spell of Maud Gonne, moths around a very tall candle. While John O'Leary could see that she was enchanting, and he liked her obvious enthusiasm for the cause, he was wary. O'Leary would warn the sculptor John Hughes: 'She looks at yeh as tho' she was dying in love with yeh – but she isn't.'[10] Still, when Maud Gonne left Dublin to visit her relatives in London, O'Leary told her to look up W.B. Yeats in Bedford Park: O'Leary, who had done so much for Yeats with his reading lists, was sending him something else a poet may require – a dominant, mercurial muse.

2

On 30 January 1889 Maud Gonne arrived at the Bedford Park address of John Butler Yeats. She told her taxi to wait, though her visit would not, in fact, turn out to be a short one. She carried a letter of introduction to John Butler Yeats from his old friend and Trinity College classmate John O'Leary. Inside the house she found, in addition to the father, his daughters Lily and Lolly and his son Willie. Lolly made an acidulous note of the event in her diary:[11]

> Miss Gonne, the Dublin beauty (who is marching on to glory over the hearts of Dublin youths), called to-day on Willie, of course, but also apparently on Papa. She is immensely tall and very stylish and well dressed in a careless way. She came in a hansom all the way from Belgravia and kept the hansom waiting while she was here. Lily noticed that she was in her slippers.

W.B. Yeats recorded the event decades later in his memoirs. The passage is worth quoting at length:[12]

> I was twenty-three years old when the troubling of my life began. I had heard from time to time in letters from Miss O'Leary, John O'Leary's old sister, of a beautiful girl who had left the society of the Viceregal Court for Dublin nationalism. In after years I persuaded myself that I felt premonitory excitement at the first reading of her name. Presently she drove up to our house in Bedford Park

with an introduction from John O'Leary to my father. I had never thought to see in a living woman so great beauty. It belonged to famous pictures, to poetry, to some legendary past. A complexion like the blossom of apples, and yet face and body had the beauty of lineaments which Blake calls the highest beauty because it changes least from youth to age, and a stature so great that she seemed of a divine race. Her movements were worthy of her form, and I understood at last why the poet of antiquity, where we would but speak of face and form, sings, loving some lady, that she paces like a goddess. I remember nothing of her speech that day except that she vexed my father by praise of war, for she too was of the Romantic movement and found those incontrovertible Victorian reasons, that seemed to announce so prosperous a future, a little grey. As I look backward, it seems to me that she brought into my life in those days – for as yet I saw only what lay upon the surface – the middle of the tint, a sound as of a Burmese gong, an overpowering tumult that had yet many pleasant secondary notes.

She asked [me] to dine with her that evening in her rooms in Ebury Street, and I think that I dined with her all but every day during her stay in London of perhaps nine days, and there was something so exuberant in her ways that it seemed natural that she should give her hours in overflowing abundance.

Mixed with those 'many pleasant secondary notes' left by Maud Gonne's calamitous arrival into Yeats's life were sounds of a more menacing kind. In the days that followed in the privacy of her Ebury Street rooms, surrounded by the cages of singing birds and the little monkey with which 'she always travelled … even upon short journeys', Maud Gonne talked to the young poet of her 'desire for power, apparently for its own sake'. When the two spoke of politics, all she appeared to care about, he recalled, was 'mere effectiveness'. According to *Memoirs*, 'Her two and twenty years had taken some colour, I thought, from French Boulangiste adventurers and journalist *arrivistes* of whom she had seen too much.' This apparent reference to Lucien Millevoye (journalist *arriviste*), undisguisedly snide, was surely added with the benefit of hindsight. Only subsequently would Yeats learn to resent the fact that when he first met Maud Gonne, the lady had already been taken, and that he was not told of the fact.

Before leaving for Paris, Maud Gonne talked of her desire to act on a Dublin stage – not in *Romeo and Juliet* again, but in a truly Irish play. This seemed a deliberate commission. Yeats told her a story he had collected in *Fairy and Folk Tales of the Irish Peasantry* about 'Countess Kathleen O'Shea' who, in a time of Famine, sold her soul for gold, and then used that gold to buy grain to feed her starving Irish tenants. He would be pleased to write a play on this theme for her to act in Dublin. On her table, he had noticed a copy of *Tristram of Lyonesse*. He aimed, he said, to become a poet who would write works of that kind. How could he know that she might have given to Swinburne's story of an Irish princess with a forbidden French lover a personal application, and one that had nothing at all to do with him?

At the end of the nine-day wonder of Maud Gonne's passage through London, Yeats felt that he had met a woman who in her womanhood was as great as any man could become in his manhood. He made a sacrifice of his 23-year-old heart to her, as if swearing by the Arthurian oath of courtly love:[13]

> To speak no slander, no, nor listen to it,
> To honour his own word as if his God's,
> To lead sweet lives in purest chastity,
> To love one maiden only, cleave to her,
> And worship her by years of noble deeds,
> Until they won her; for indeed I knew
> Of no more subtle master under heaven
> Than is the maiden passion for a maid,
> Not only to keep down the base in man,
> But teach high thought, and amiable words
> And courtliness, and the desire of fame,
> And love of truth, and all that makes a man.

In the wake of the departure of his muse, there was nothing much Yeats could do but get to work on that play.

3

During the same week that Yeats was experiencing something deceptively like intimacy with Maud Gonne, in Paris Georges Boulanger stumbled into, at, and over the climactic opportunity of his political insurgency. After the debacle of Millevoye's discountenanced overture to Russia, Georges Boulanger took his place in the Chamber of Deputies, and in June 1888 put forward a proposal for the revision of the constitution. He wanted the Senate abolished and a government established that was composed of just one Chamber, led by a president elected by popular vote, as in the United States. Laws passed by the Chamber were to be ratified by plebiscite. It was not expected by Boulanger, or intended, that this proposal would pass; the newly elected Chamber of Deputies was not going to vote itself out of existence. But the proposal was a political threat because it was so conceived as to appear to be a vehicle for the expression of a Rousseau-like general will. Prime minister Charles Floquet took the podium and wondered aloud why former General Boulanger considered himself to be the incarnation of a purer Republic, when his personal predilections led him to haunt sacristies and the antechambers of various princes.[14] Boulanger called Floquet a liar and resigned his seat (possibly setting a record in France for brevity of service by a deputy).

The duel was held the next day, 13 July. Charles Floquet was sixty years old, fat, and unathletic. No one thought he would survive the encounter. As soon as the words '*Allez, monsieurs*' signalled the start of the conflict, Boulanger charged forward with his rapier extended. Floquet retreated, stumbled backwards, and fell sitting into a bush, with his sword clutched in both hands, and the pummel in his stomach. But Boulanger in his hell-bent rush slipped too, and fell forward, spitting himself on Floquet's sword; it ran right through his neck.[15] The wound nearly killed him. This ridiculous defeat did not in fact damage the former general's public standing. His political agents managed to spin the story into a demonstration of Boulanger's willingness once again to shed his blood in the cause of *La Patrie*.

After recuperating in Spain with Madame Bonnemains, Boulanger returned to the campaign trail. Parliamentary elections were to be held at the end of January 1889. On 2 December 1888 the Boulangistes gathered for a large rally in Nevers. The opening speaker explained that the new Boulangiste constitution for France would be 'a powerful weapon placed in the hands of the people'. They would gain control over the opportunist politicians now in office. 'Down with the thieves!' came the cry from the crowd. Then Lucien Millevoye took his turn at the podium:[16]

> They call us warmongers! That is a slander. Here, we take an oath to do away with national enemies. These men now in the Chamber of Deputies are there neither for your benefit, nor for glory. Some do not even have the right to an honest name, but they dare proclaim, dare publish, that the party of national hope is a party of provocation and of war.

The campaign was succeeding in whipping up the passions of the voters. On New Year's Day 1889 Georges Boulanger was able to raise an optimistic toast to his followers: 'If 1889 is as prosperous for us all as 1888 has been, by 1890 we will have completed our work, and we can just live.'[17]

Election night was set for 27 January 1889. In the run-up to the vote, the speeches of the Boulangistes made it ever more clear that they intended, if elected, to take over the state and reconfigure it to their purposes. At one rally, Millevoye said he spoke in place of a leader who, like the flag of France, floated above the fray:[18]

> This is not an oration; it is a simple statement ... My voice is the echo of thousands and thousands of voices from the depths of the public consciousness, from points the most opposite in the country, combined in a large patriotic concert, all the voices alarmed, outraged, with wounded pride, and with a cry to the one glorious soldier that still remains standing, intact: 'Sir, my General, let not the Republic and the Fatherland be tarnished! You have heard our hope ... Raise our Honour!'
>
> I belong to the legions of patriots, the democrats whose number every day increases, an expression of the dedication, the zeal of Republicans of the National Republic. I say to them, 'Infants, children of our immortal Revolution, heirs of our common glories and sorrows, brothers in a threatened Patrie, open your ranks, make a place for those who offer to defend a Republic of good people, honest people of the Republic, with clean hands, a Republic enlarged, and purified by General Boulanger.' The edifice of Parliament is day by day threatened in its corridors and clans by the shadow of intrigue with a sudden collapse ...
>
> We are asked, who is our master? The people, or our Prince? Our obedience is to the wishes of the people. Alone they have the right to elect their leader. They alone ... After twenty years, our democracy is still seeking its way, indecisive, confused, unhappy about the weak instruments that have now been tested and broken. We need a permanent reorganization of public powers – such is the urgent requirement that dominates today all calculations. What will become the work of the future? Is it this Parliament? Is it the nation? We say that only the people, strong workers, have hands strong enough to build Right and Liberty.
>
> With the current Constitution, the disorder, the anarchy, are everywhere; responsibility nowhere. We have an anonymous system, where faults are committed by anonymous representatives; their liquidations of public money are anonymous. It is time to stop. The delegation of power must be direct. Parliament must be replaced by the country.

This appeal by Millevoye may be floridly rhetorical and it is certainly demagogic, but its drift is plain enough: it is a request for a popular vote for one-man rule by Georges Boulanger.

On election night, 27 January, Boulanger's supporters gathered at Café Durand to celebrate a decisive victory. Frank Harris, editor of *The Fortnightly Review*, claimed to have been present with his friend Henri Rochefort. Rochefort introduced the leader to Harris, and wittily chatted away, talking over Boulanger without a break. Afterwards, Harris said, 'The General seems strangely quiet.' 'The flag does not need to be articulate,' Rochefort replied, evidently implying that the imminent new government would really be a sort of junta, not a dictatorship.[19] But would the General now act? Would he lead a march to the Elysée? The paramilitary army of the Ligue des Patriotes and Blanquistes waited outside in the Place de la Madeleine. The cries went up in waves, '*Vive Boulanger!*' In his dramatization of the incident, Frank Harris characteristically gives himself both an eyewitness vantage-point and a speaking part:[20]

> 'Surely, General, it is time. The hour has struck!'
> 'What do you mean?' he asked with perfect composure.
> 'The Elysée Palace is just over there,' I pointed, 'hardly a quarter of a kilometre to go.'
> He shook his head. 'We have no forces. We have made no preparations. We are not ready.'

At midnight Paul Déroulède again pressed for an immediate coup. Boulanger still demurred. 'Why do you expect me to seize power by illegal means when I can be sure of getting it in six months by the unanimous vote of all France?'[21] By half past twelve, it was clear to everyone that nothing was going to happen. 'Nothing has changed, Paris has only one more deputy.'[22] Two days later *La Presse* reported the General as saying, 'By 24 February I will be President of the Council, and on the first of May I will be appointed President of the Republic. I will open the Exhibition, and the calm inside and outside will be perfect.'[23]

Things did not go according to this plan. While Georges Boulanger was elected in Paris with 100,000 votes more than his opponent, and a handful of his followers were elected to the Chamber, the parliamentary majority remained with the constitutional republicans.[24] In the first week of February a new Minister of the Interior was appointed, Ernest Constans. After his appointment, Constans ran into Georges Laguerre, vice-president of the Ligue des Patriotes. He extended his hand, but Laguerre hesitated. 'Go ahead and shake it,' Constans said, 'because I promise that it will shake you.'[25] On 14 February Constans outlawed the Ligue des Patriotes. He ordered the suppression of street demonstrations, one of the main tools of Boulangiste opposition. A hundred police were assigned to shadow Boulanger's confederates.[26] Constans briefed reporters on the prospect of Boulanger facing a Senate trial for treason.

Madame Adrienne Millevoye sent out invitations for a 27 February ball at the Grand Hotel to celebrate the General's electoral victory, but when the day came around, the mood among the Boulangistes was no longer celebratory. Madame Millevoye felt unwell, but insisted on being present. She lay on a couch, surrounded by ladies, so Lucien Millevoye redoubled his efforts to welcome the guests at the door. Alfred Naquet, Thomas Dillon, Henri Rochefort and George Laguerre were among the first to gather, around eight o'clock. Later, while Louis Andrieux was giving a speech, word arrived that the office of the Ligue des Patriotes in Place de la Bourse was being searched by the Attorney General and a force of gendarmes. Laguerre and Déroulède, respectively vice-president and president of the Ligue, rushed by cab from the banquet to the office, but, though enraged, they could do nothing to prevent the search from being completed and papers being carried away. Déroulède said to his aides, 'Do not complain about the mess they are making; the police are correct to do as they are told. In a year, with the same conscientiousness, they will do what we tell them to do.'[27]

This *sang-froid* was more than General Boulanger could manage. Constans had succeeded in causing him to believe that his arrest for treason was imminent. On 1 April Boulanger with Madame Bonnemains boarded a Brussels-bound train at Gare du Nord. Constans's agents watched him go. When the train arrived at the Belgian border, the agents let the couple pass unhindered through customs. Flight in such circumstances could only humiliate Boulanger and destroy his cause. *Le brav' General*, it was then said, had 'skipped off like a pimp', 'slipped out like an enema'.[28]

On 2 April an emergency meeting of the Committee of the Parti Nationale was called. Millevoye and Déroulède were there, shocked to the core. After a stormy debate, Déroulède proposed a motion that they should all agree to lie about why the General had left. He cannot be thought by the public to have been afraid. A press release from the Parti Nationale would declare that the General did not wish to go, but his party had ordered him to leave the country. It was to be said that his life and freedom were in danger because of the irresponsibility and corruption of the present government of France. In order to maintain the strength of the reform movement he represented, the General finally accepted the necessity of a temporary departure. A motion to adopt these 'talking points' was passed.[29] Members of the committee, including Millevoye, then set off for Belgium in an attempt to save the situation.[30]

To keep their cause alive, the Boulangiste cadre organized a 'Banquet de Versailles' on 20 April. The theme for the evening was that democracy and Boulangiste one-man rule were really one and the same. The first speaker declared that it was impossible to allow 'national degradation by parliamentary dictatorship' to go any longer. The speaker himself – and he was sure many would agree with him – would be glad to 'bow to the orders of a personal power, the authority of an honest and loyal man, like my friend General Boulanger, in place of this bunch of epileptics or freaks we call a Parliament!' He proposed a toast to the 'Boulangiste revolution, the newest phase of the democratic solution'. It was Lucien Millevoye's turn next. The movement was not in decline, he declared:[31] 'Real force is the people, the people of France. It is not spent; it is not ephemeral; it is not made of wind.' But really this was hot air, and the ovation he received was just noise.

A few days later Millevoye joined the party boarding the special train that would carry General Boulanger and Madame Bonnemains onward to London.[32] He was no longer welcome in Belgium, and was being forced farther into exile, accepting sanctuary in the home of the historic enemy of France, perfidious Britain. Neither the General nor his mistress would ever return to France. They ultimately bought a seaside villa in Jersey. Periodically, Boulanger sent messages to the Parisian press suggesting that he would return in triumph, but those were widely understood to be laughable fantasies. Two years after they settled in Jersey, Madame Bonnemains died of cancer. Just two months later, on 30 September 1891, Boulanger shot himself in the head on the grave of his mistress. Madame Séverine, once a follower, immortalized the General in an epitaph: he 'began as Caesar, continued as Catiline, and died as Romeo'.

4

Sometime during those weeks of the dizzy descent of General Boulanger, Maud Gonne came to Lucien Millevoye's side, and, in a passionate moment, a child was conceived. But when? And where?

After Maud Gonne left W.B. Yeats for Dublin, Yeats wrote to John O'Leary's sister Ellen: 'Did I tell you how much I admire Miss Gonne? She will make many converts to her political belief. If she said the world was flat or the moon an old caubeen tossed up into the sky I would be proud to be of her party.'[33] Yet there was competition. Douglas Hyde had offered Maud Gonne free private lessons in how to speak Irish, and she came to him on 11 and 13 February. He brought her to the Dublin Theosophical Society; she let him take her home in a cab at the end of the evening. On 18 February Hyde called on her, supposedly to continue language lessons. He stayed for a couple of hours, but 'we did not do much Irish'. [34] His hopes that his love would be requited were possibly as high as those of Yeats.

The Irish poet Katharine Tynan – not herself a beauty – was getting annoyed that 'the heads of all my male friends, young and old' were 'flustered' by Maud Gonne.[35] 'So I hear you have taken up with Maud Gonne,' Tynan wrote to Yeats. 'Who told you?' Yeats asked by return on 21 February. It had been thought at one time that Yeats might marry Katharine Tynan. He was understandably defensive:[36]

> I think she is 'very good looking' and that is all I think about her. What you say of her fondness for sensation is probably true. I sympathize with her love of the national idea rather than any secondary land movement but care not much for the kind of red Indian feathers in which she has trapped out that idea. We had some talk as to the possibility of getting my 'Countess O'Shea' acted by amateurs in Dublin and she felt inclined to help, indeed suggested the attempt herself if I remember rightly. I hardly expect it will ever get outside the world of plans.

Maud Gonne's triumphal car rolled on. At the Kildare Hunt Ball at Palmerstown House, she and her sister were on the dance floor for the polka, waltz, lancers, gallop and quadrille, as reported in the *Freeman's Journal* on 30 March. No one could have suspected that her heart was engaged elsewhere.

It is possible that, on 8 April 1889, Maud Gonne left Dublin for a rendezvous with a desperately needy Millevoye. A 'Miss R Gonne' is reported as among those who departed by boat; maybe that 'R' is a misprint. Or it could be that the pair reunited in London two weeks later, after Millevoye arrived on the special train carrying General Boulanger into exile. What is not just possible but likely is that Maud Gonne came to her lover when his hopes for the future lay in pieces at his feet. His speeches indicate that he was in a state of exaltation – frantic, despairing, pretending defiance. And what is not just likely but certain is that, after seeking comfort in her arms, he left her with child.

5

Maud Gonne reappeared in Paris in May, after tending to her sister Kathleen in London, where she was recuperating from a liver ailment.[37] Sarah Purser met Maud Gonne at the Paris Exhibition and introduced her to the painter Louise-Catherine Breslau. Purser's biographer John O'Grady believes that it was at this time that Gonne consented to sit for Purser, and work began on a 6-foot-tall portrait, to be put up for sale at public exhibitions. Gonne is posed with her pet monkey Chaperone in a fashion that Yeats acutely detected was meant as a witty allusion to Marie Bashkirtseff, a painting student at the Académie Julian, who died at just age twenty-five. The frontispiece of Bashkirtseff's posthumous (and wildly popular) confessions is similar to Purser's picture. Both Maud Gonne and Marie Bashkirtseff were brilliant, beautiful and ambitious for fame, yet terrified that a cough that never entirely went away signalled tuberculosis and an early grave. That would be tragically true for Bashkirtseff, but not for Maud Gonne, who, in spite of her reasonable fears, appears to have had the lungs of a healthy horse.

Gonne may not have known she was pregnant while posing for Purser, but soon there can have remained no doubt. She vanishes from the public eye in the summer of 1889. She kept her name in print with a July contribution to the 'Summer Sketch Book' of the *Freeman's Journal.*[38] It seems likely that she found discreet quarters in Samois-sur-Seine, near Fontainebleau, and with easy rail access to Paris, to go along with her apartment on Avenue Wagram in Paris.

Samois-sur-Seine; Le Pont de Bois et la villa Rose.
(Ed. Thibault, Fontainebleau-Melun)

In October Maud Gonne returned to her sister's bedside in London when Kathleen came down with a further episode of her liver ailment.[39] Surprisingly, when eight months pregnant, Maud came to London again for Kathleen's 13 December wedding to Captain Thomas Pilcher. On neither visit to London did she tell W.B. Yeats that she was in town. Even clothed in the voluminous dresses and winter wraps available from Paris shops, she would have found it difficult to conceal her condition.

Maud Gonne so often says that she lived by her father's advice to be afraid of nothing, that one suspects she repeats the saying as an apotropaic charm to put down her many fears, especially that of tuberculosis. Of her courage, however, there can be no doubt: it is hard to fathom how she worked up the nerve to brave detection of her condition by William Gonne, Aunt Mary and all the others gathered at St Mary's Church, Graham Street, for the wedding of her sister.

V

A SINGLE MOTHER IN THE NINETEENTH CENTURY

Previous page: *Police travelling to an eviction.* (Illustrated London News, *1 May 1886)*

On 11 January 1890 Georges Silvère Gonne was born in Samois-sur-Seine. The die had been cast. Maud Gonne's future life would be a double life. She would have one existence in France, and another in Britain and Ireland.

In France, the fact that the father of her child was a prominent man who happened to be married and Catholic meant that the relationship had to obey certain proprieties. One had to mind the distinction between what is 'not done' and 'the way things are done'. The child would have to be raised at a discreet distance from one's formal residence in the city. If the child were to appear, it would have to be called one's nephew or ward. It would have to be taught from the start not to address one as 'Mama'. Alternative nicknames would serve as terms of affection. A devoted nanny was essential, such as 'Biddy Bounce-Bounce' had been for Maud Gonne and her sister.

Still, a highly esteemed position remained open to Maud Gonne. The great women of the French salons of the *fin de siècle* – like Gambetta's Madame Adam; Geneviève Bizet, Proust's muse; or Anna de Noailles, the target of Maurice Barrès' literary desires – were all women of richly complex private lives. The hint of sexual mystery did not damage their public image – on the contrary – but they did have the advantage over Maud Gonne of having at least first passed through a stage of wedlock.

In Ireland, none of the effects of an active sexual relationship by an unmarried woman could be allowed to become visible: not the tacit relationship with Lucien Millevoye, not the establishment in Samois, not the existence of a ward. These would all be signs that she was a 'fallen woman'. As such, she would not be free to carry out her plans for anti-British, Irish nationalist agitation, which, to be successful, required a popular following and thus the respect of the common people. A magnificent virginity was, if not essential, advantageous.

Pregnancy and motherhood certainly imperiled Maud Gonne. What is amazing is how little in the event they impeded her. Her wealth cancelled out some of the disabilities of her condition. She could afford the multiple establishments required and the staff for each of them: a Paris apartment at 61 Avenue Wagram, a little house and garden in Samois, and eventually rooms on Nassau Street in Dublin. But the fact that Millevoye was Roman Catholic and married also meant that not only could she not become his wife, but she did not have to do so, as would likely have been the case had he been single, or capable of divorce and remarriage. In the eyes of outsiders, she was free. She thereafter affected to despise the institution of marriage.

It seems most unlikely that Maud Gonne had planned to become the unwed mother of a child by Lucien Millevoye, or that her first thought upon the realization of her condition was delight. Between September 1888 and March 1889 when she was turning the heads of all the men in Dublin, and spending nine long flirtatious days with W.B. Yeats in London, she may not have yet considered herself as monogamously bound by a 'Secret Treaty' with Millevoye; maybe at the time, there were moments when she hoped for an Irish companion in life. Once she had gone to Millevoye during the collapse of the Boulangiste putsch, and pregnancy occurred, the possibility of a full companionate love in Ireland became remote. She might again wish for that, but how could it become a reality?

2

During the month when Georges Silvère Gonne was born, his father was a busy man. In the new session of the French Chamber, three Boulangistes who had been elected as deputies – Déroulède, Laguerre and Millevoye – tried to prevent Jules Joffrin, appointed to take Boulanger's seat, from assuming his duties. 'Let him first be elected!' Déroulède shouted. 'I insist this man must not be heard.'[1] Others on the radical right banged on the lids of their desks. Déroulède was censured. The session was suspended; everyone left the Chamber; army officers then removed Déroulède. After the session reopened, Millevoye practised the same disruptive tricks. The session was suspended, and he was removed. The whole process was repeated a third time with Laguerre. These histrionics made the Parnellite tactics of obstruction of British parliamentary business seem courteous.

On 18 January 1890 Millevoye attended a big meeting of the radical right in Neuilly. Francis Laur was the Boulangiste candidate for a parliamentary post there, running against a communist journalist, Prosper-Olivier Lissagaray, the first lover of Eleanor Marx.[2] Here for the first time, the Boulangistes made common cause with anti-Semites. There were 1500 present in the workers' hall, including a number of prominent princes, dukes and *marquises*. Edouard Drumont, author of the best-selling *La France juive* (1886) was the principal speaker. When he mounted the rostrum, the cry 'War with the Jews!' went up. Drumont's election speech was one long diatribe: 'Do you know what Rothschild's millions are? His three millions mean the salary of three million French workers working throughout one year, without a day of rest, at three francs a day.'[3] The next speaker, Marquis de Mores, having returned to France from ranching in the American Wild West, said the deputies now in the Chamber were under the thumbs of the Jews: 'In America, they would in good order have a lynching. In the name of God! I do not want the pigs of German Jews to prevent me from serving my country.' The meeting passed a resolution that acclaimed Francis Laur, the Boulangiste deputy, as 'the enemy of Rothschilds, republicans and communists.'[4]

Boulanger seems himself to have had no personal feeling against Jews (Naquet, one of his closest lieutenants, was a Jew.) But when Naquet asked the General to denounce the new direction being taken by his followers, Boulanger was characteristically indecisive. In a 24 February reply to Naquet, he said he aimed to keep 'an even balance between the partisans and adversaries of an alliance with Drumont.'[5] 'An even balance' was not Drumont's own style. On 4 March he published a savage attack on Boulanger. He provided a reading of Boulanger's palm: it showed, Drumont explained, an absence of lines of superiority; expert study proved it to be the hand of a liar. Worst of all, Boulanger's career had been launched by a Jew, Cornelius Herz; he was advised by a Jew, Alfred Naquet, and he was invisibly controlled by a Jew, Rothschild.

Alarmed by this frontal attack, Boulanger called a meeting of his deputies on 5 April. He demanded that they cut ties with Drumont and the Marquis de Mores. Some of the deputies took their time in choosing between the

General and the Jew-haters, but after lunch, Francis Laur said he had made his choice: he would remain loyal to Boulanger. Everyone applauded. Then Laur went home and gave a newspaper interview in support of Drumont. The Boulangistes were coming to pieces.

In August a series of articles began to be published in *Le Figaro*: 'Les Coulisses du Boulangisme'.[6] These were the work of 'Mermeix', pen-name of Gabriel Terrail, himself a Boulangiste deputy for the 7th arrondissement. Repentant after his realization that the head of the movement to which he belonged was a traitor who had plotted the overthrow of the Republic, Mermeix spared no one. He revealed in irrefutable detail the alliances forged by the Boulangistes with the royalists, with the Bonapartists and with the Catholics, and the huge funding released by these duplicitous alliances. He published the facts about the plot for a *coup d'état*. Conversations and letters of the Boulangistes were printed verbatim.

What Mermeix wrote was embarrassing, but difficult to contradict. His former confederates therefore challenged him to duels. Millevoye issued an initial announcement to the press that he had sent his seconds to Mermeix. After reflection, he retreated to a conditional offer to meet Mermeix on 'the field of honour':[7]

> If M. Castelin, my colleague in the Chamber, fights with M. Mermeix, then I will not refuse a meeting with the latter. However, I reserve the right to present my seconds to the author of *Les Coulisses du Boulangisme*. Yet regarding [what Mermeix wrote about] the meeting at Café Riche, I do not owe him any reparation in return. However, if Mr Mermeix thinks that a duel with him could exonerate him from the charge of dishonour, I would be far from approval.

Two 'if's, two 'however's, two 'not's and one 'yet' – Mermeix cannot have been certain just what was expected of him. First, at any rate, he fought a duel with the Boulangiste deputy Léon Dumonteil on 17 September, in the course of which he received a slight but painful wound.[8] Mermeix then requested a 'meeting' with Millevoye outside Paris on the morning of 22 September.

The men fought with swords. On the sixth encounter, Millevoye received a deep wound in his hand. The fight was stopped by the doctors. Millevoye, shamed by the wild justice of single combat, later demanded a 'jury of arbitration'. This was held on 24 September. Millevoye's representatives alleged that Millevoye was wounded after he had lowered his rapier upon the order of the umpire of the contest. As a result, Mermeix, by taking unfair advantage of his opponent, was the one who had been dishonoured.

Later, Millevoye withdrew a second challenge he had issued to the publisher of Mermeix's articles, due to the fact that he had already obtained full satisfaction from Mermeix. *The Times* reported these matters in scornful detail. In the bloodied and defeated Millevoye, 'we have a man who has a fancy for a very curious satisfaction'.[9]

3

Maud Gonne was not in Samois, or in Paris, during the publication of Mermeix's controversial *Les Coulisses du Boulangisme*.[10] By the summer of 1890 she had left her infant son in the care of another and resumed her quest to be the Irish Joan of Arc. It was not the custom even for married women of her class to be the primary caregivers of their children: sometimes, birth was followed by a sea voyage by mother and father to recover, while the infant remained at home with a wet nurse. Her own childhood accustomed Maud Gonne to the notion that children need not be closely minded by their parents; others could be paid to do that. That Maud Gonne did not deem the existence of her illegitimate child to mark the end of her freedom as a woman, or the ruin of plans she had made before her pregnancy, does not mean she loved that child any the less than her father had loved her.

In June 1890 Maud Gonne went to Barrow-in-Furness in the northwest of England to give campaign speeches on behalf of a Liberal Home Rule candidate, J.A. Duncan. In August she joined a delegation of liberal English visitors who came to Ireland to review the evictions on the Clongorey Estate in County Kildare. She attended a meeting at the farm of Mrs Kelly presided over by the parish priest and surrounded by police. The priest told the people that they 'should be extremely grateful to Miss Gonne [*cheers*], who had worked for the Home Rule candidate in Barrow.' Then it was Maud Gonne's turn to speak, and she spoke as an Irishwoman:[11]

> She said she was too proud of her country and her countrymen not to tell them, first of all, that she was an Irishwoman [*cheers*]. She had been, however, a long time in England, and she felt that she must, to a certain extent, speak on behalf of the people of England; for when she was over in Barrow recently the people there asked her to say to the Irish that they, at least, would no longer be responsible for the wrongs that were being done in this country [*cheers*]. They had been kept in ignorance over there for a long time, but when they learned the true state of

affairs they did not rest satisfied until they had ousted the Liberal Unionist and returned a good Home Ruler in his stead.

Two weeks later, she was on the Clanricarde Estate in County Galway, one of the most famous estates in Ireland for its extent, the poverty of its tenants and the evictions perpetrated by its landlord. At a meeting opposite the chapel outside Woodford, Maud Gonne spoke to a crowd of 500, with eighty police constables present. She said she heard in the shouts of the evicted tenants 'an echo of the indignation in the hearts of women' (a remarkable and unusual identification of the Irish struggle for freedom with women's struggle for equality). They were fighting a great battle and they were sure to win it. They could take comfort in the words and deeds of Irish heroes in the past. Irish nationality was indestructible.

Police Inspector Ready summarized the character of Maud Gonne and her activities that summer. She had great dramatic talent, he thought. She was observed taking lessons in shooting a gun. She organized dinners without the least regard to their expense, and associated with William Murphy, John O'Connor, and C.H. Oldham. Ready concluded that she was a 'fanatic'.[12]

4

In September and October, following a speaking tour with the Liberal MPs, Maud Gonne's name disappears from the Irish press. It is possible that she was called back to France on account of the duel of Lucien Millevoye, or perhaps to visit her child, now eight months old.

She next shows up in Gweedore, Co. Donegal, in early November. Famine conditions were reappearing, with a local failure of the potato crop. There had been evictions on the Olphert Estate for the refusal by those tenants allied with the Plan of Campaign to pay any rent at all. J.G. Swift MacNeill, an Irish Protestant nationalist MP, had come with Gonne to witness the work of the battering ram and the suffering of those turned out on the roads. The scenes of desperation activated her large capacity for pity and radicalized her rhetoric:[13]

> I am proud to be among you, with the right, as an Irishwoman, to call myself your sister, and stand side by side with you in this struggle. A terrible calamity, the potato blight, shadows the country. It is in the face of this distress that Mr Olphert chooses to carry out that work of destruction and desolation already

so terribly begun on his estate. When I think of what those evictions mean to you – turned out from the houses you have built with your own hands – driven off the ground which you have reclaimed, whose whole value you yourselves have created, and on which the landlord has never expended a farthing – when I think of the suffering of your wives and children and what the sight of their tears, as they are torn from the homes which, in spite of poverty, they love so dearly, must be to you, I wonder at the marvellous and the admirable patience you have shown. You have made a brave fight here in Gweedore, and you have been winners. Have not Hill, Nixon and Massey, and other landlords, had to give in before you? ... Olphert is backed by his class and by his fellow landlords, by the landlord syndicate ... So much the more reason for you tenants to stand firmly together, and by your united efforts to defeat their combination and conspiracy ... I am willing to go to jail for you if that is necessary.

In the following days Maud Gonne was eyewitness to an eviction in Falcarragh, Co. Donegal, along with a party of observers, which included her cousin, May Gonne, Norma Borthwick (an English artist, later a Gaelic League scholar), Mrs Sheldon Amos and her daughter, four Irish MPs and five priests. The forces of the state backing the landlord included one hundred men with police batons, fifty more with rifles, and a half-dozen police cars. They marched an hour and a half over a mountain to the house of Neal Ferry and his wife and their five children. The Ferrys owed six years' back rent, two pounds in total. The armed force put up ladders, ripped off the thatch, blocked the chimney, stuffed the windows with furze bushes and boarded up the doorway.

They then moved on to the cottage of the next family to be evicted. Here lived the widow Hegarty, with her son, his wife, and their eight children. The son came out from the door shouting wildly in Irish for the priest, who rushed forward, thinking someone inside lay in need of the Last Rites. It was the son's wife. She was in bed after giving birth. The surgeon entered and deemed her sufficiently healthy to be evicted. She was brought out holding her baby and laid down on some sacks by a gable, weeping. Maud Gonne and the other English women in the party came forward to give her comfort.

This event was crucial for Maud Gonne. Time and again in her future orations she drew upon details of the incident. One need not invoke her own recent experience of childbirth, or her memory of being an orphan herself, to explain its lasting impact. The profound inhumanity of the scene would be an indictment of the British government of Ireland for anyone who witnessed it. The evictions continued the next day. Two hundred and fifty families had already been turned out; one hundred more remained with writs hanging over them.

270   UNE HEURE CHEZ MISS MAUD GONNE

Après l'éviction. — La famille du tenancier est jetée dehors; la porte est barrée. — Défense d'entrer sous peine d'emprisonnement.

reçois des centaines de lettres où l'on me dénonce des abus, où l'on me demande des secours. Je suis en communication avec nos comités de bienfaisance, qui se chargent de distribuer les sommes que je recueille. Tout ce que je gagne, le produit de mes confé-rences et de mes quêtes, s'en va là-bas. Et, lorsque j'y vais moi-même, le peuple me remercie, m'acclame et me récompense de mes peines. Il incarne en moi ses espérances, s'abusant, hélas! sur mes moyens d'action et sur mon autorité...

Miss Maud étend la main vers un guéridon et y prend une brochure :

— Voici le Bulletin officiel des pénitenciers de la Grande-Bretagne. J'ai eu mille peines à me procurer ce document, réservé aux seuls ministres d'État. On y trouve des détails navrants sur le sort des Irlandais, accusés d'avoir conspiré contre la reine, et détenus dans le bagne de Portsmouth. Ils sont là, depuis bientôt dix ans, assimilés aux criminels de droit commun, astreints à des travaux rebutants, et traités avec une bar-barie digne, tout au plus, du moyen âge. Songez que les geôliers, le directeur, les sur-veillants, les gardes-chiourmes sont Anglais, c'est-à-dire ennemis-nés de nos captifs, ennemis de religion et de race. Aussi s'ingénient-ils, chaque jour, pour inventer des tortures. Je puis vous en donner un exemple : L'un des prisonniers contracte derniè-rement, grâce à l'humidité malsaine de son cachot, une inflammation d'oreille qui dégénère en abcès. Le médecin y introduit la sonde. Le patient pousse un cri de douleur et laisse échapper ces mots : « Prenez garde, mon ami, vous me faites mal. » — « Votre ami, dit le docteur furieux, votre ami... Je ne suis pas l'ami d'un traître! Apprenez à mieux parler! » Et, d'un mouvement brusque, il lui casse dans l'oreille sa sonde de

'After the Eviction' (La Revue Illustrée, 1892)

Gonne established herself in rooms above Morrow's Bookshop and Library on Nassau Street, Dublin. From there, she made her trips back and forth to the northwest.[14] She was in Donegal seeking to organize the construction of new shelters for evicted tenants when she found herself pestered by marriage proposals from a 'Sir John' (can she mean to suggest John Morley, Liberal Chief Secretary of Ireland?).

Then word arrived from Millevoye. He was in Donegal, laid up sick in Dunfanaghy. He had wanted to see why she had been away so long from Paris, and what she was doing up in this wild country. In *A Servant of the Queen,*

Maud Gonne says she was mightily annoyed that he had come after her. He demanded that she leave Ireland. She could, he argued, combat Britain better from France. What did it matter if she succeeded in winning some concessions from Mr Olphert for his tenants? The two quarrelled. She refused to travel with Millevoye back to France (perhaps out of consideration for her reputation in Ireland). Through her influence with a priest, Maud Gonne arranged a covered carriage for Millevoye, and made her own way back to Dublin alone.[15]

When she arrived at Nassau Street, Dr Sigerson noticed her cough. Her condition worsened over the coming days. Sigerson stayed up all night applying poultices. He warned her of consumption, and recommended a course of injections such as he was giving to the poet Rose Kavanagh. Gonne refused, while Rose Kavanagh died a few months later on 26 February 1891.

5

In the New Year 1891 Maud Gonne spent a period of time in Provence, quite possibly in Saint-Raphaël on the Côte d'Azur, as suggested in her autobiography. She wrote from the South of France to Sarah Purser, asking if anyone had purchased her large portrait. Ten shillings were sent from Saint-Raphaël to a Mr Boyd, an evicted tenant in Donegal, along with Maud Gonne's letter for publication, expressing her sympathy. She composed another letter to the editor of *La France Nouvelle* concerning Balfour's Distress Fund for Evicted Tenants: 'England sends us alms – we expect justice.'[16]

Her major preoccupation while in Provence was the composition of her first major piece of political journalism, an article for *La Nouvelle Revue Internationale* entitled 'Le Peuple Opprime'. Millevoye helped her 'a great deal' with this article. He was also in a position to place it for her. The editor of the *Revue*, Madame Ratazzi, was, by a father from Waterford, the daughter of Laetitia Bonaparte and thus in Millevoye's Bonapartist political circle.

Anna Magny argues that in the course of writing this article Maud Gonne acquired a journalistic style that she never significantly altered. It is energetic and passionate, elaborately courteous to France ('Ah, France! Always ready to extend a generous hand to poor Ireland, her sister in blood, by religion, and by history') and unqualifiedly aggressive towards England. Every example of Irish suffering is extreme. Details are melodramatized in pursuit of a heart-rending effect: the peasant turned out of his cottage is 'nearly dead'; he is opposed by 'the entire force of the army', which seizes him with 'rude hands'. Yet the author insists on the truthfulness of her highly coloured account because she saw it with her own eyes.[17] As in the work of Millevoye, anaphora is a common trope – repetitive sentence structures that vary their concluding phrases in a rising declamatory beat of indignation. But unlike the work of Millevoye, Gonne's writing allied itself with the female tradition of sensibility. Yeats pointed this out in a review of one of her subsequent lectures:[18]

> From first to last it is emotional and even poignant, and has that curious power of unconsciously seizing salient incidents which is the distinguishing mark of the novel written by women … A man or woman trained on the political platforms of the day would have given figures and arguments and have been forgotten ten minutes after.

'Le Peuple Opprimé' is a powerful piece of Boulangiste polemic, and a sensational beginning to Maud Gonne's career as a propagandist in France.

In recounting the time in Saint-Raphaël, *A Servant of the Queen* includes one chilling episode regarding W.B. Yeats. Maud Gonne was just beginning to recover her full strength – going for hikes in the hills where Millevoye hunted game with his brother, and shooting a bird herself – when a letter arrived from the Irish poet with this poem:[19]

A Dream of Death

I dreamed that one had died in a strange place
Near no accustomed hand;
And they nailed the boards above her face,
The peasants of that land,
And wondering, planted by her solitude
A cypress and a yew.
I came and wrote upon a cross of wood –
Man had no more to do –
'She was more beautiful than thy first love,
This lady by the trees';
And gazed upon the mournful stars above,
And heard the mournful breeze.

Gonne was 'greatly amused' by this epitaph 'written with much feeling'. Millevoye, who was staying with her, was presented with a good opportunity for a laugh over Yeats's lines, 'Near no accustomed hand' and 'solitude'!

6

Yeats waited eagerly in Dublin during July 1891 and extended his stay, hoping to meet Maud Gonne. She finally appeared on 22 July; he had not seen her since before the previous Christmas. Yeats called to Nassau Street and found her 'exhausted, depressed, vulnerable', and therefore to him utterly lovable. She might have seemed depressed because Madame Bonnemains had died of cancer on 16 July, and she had just come from her Brussels funeral attended by an assembly of dismal Boulangistes. Or maybe she wished she were out of all that.

After seeing her, Yeats had to leave Dublin for a prearranged stay with a friend in County Down. Gonne headed off to make herself prominently present at the 30 July release of John Dillon and William O'Brien from Galway Gaol.[20] On 3 August, back in Dublin, she wrote to Yeats to ask if he would not return. She told him in the letter of a dream she had had. In it they were brother and sister, and had been sold into slavery in Arabia. That seemed to suggest intimacy, if not exactly of the right kind. Yeats hastened to Maud Gonne's side and asked her to be his wife:[21]

> I remember a curious thing. I had come into the room with that purpose in mind, and hardly looked at her or thought of her beauty. I sat there holding her hand speaking vehemently. She did not take her hand away for a while. I ceased to speak, and presently as I sat in silence I felt her nearness to me and her beauty. At once I knew that my confidence had gone, and an instant later she drew her hand away. No, she could not marry – there were reasons – she would never marry; but in words that had no conventional ring she asked for my friendship.

If Yeats had not suffered from lack of confidence, ignorance or down-right terror upon sensing the nearness of this beautiful woman, if he had not believed a 'man had no more to do' than hold his beloved's hand and ask her to be his wife, would his relationship with Maud Gonne have developed differently? It seems unlikely. There was just then no clear path forward for Maud Gonne with Yeats, or for Yeats with Maud Gonne, even had both of them wished to find one.

They went together to Howth, a place where they had each spent years of their childhoods, and walked together along the cliffs. Yeats read to her from his draft of *The Countess Cathleen*, and he thought he noticed signs of emotion when she heard the line 'the joy of losing joy, of ceasing all resistance'.[22] These all seemed favourable omens to a man in pursuit of a woman, but Yeats still did not see what steps could lead directly to a reversal of her mysterious but firm statement that marriage to him, or to anyone else, was for her impossible. He sent Maud Gonne a poem arising from their cliff walk in Howth. In it he dreams of an impossible metamorphosis:[23]

The White Birds

I would that we were, my beloved, white birds on the foam of the sea!
For we tire of the meteor before it can pass by and flee;
And the flame of the blue star of twilight hung low on the rim of the sky,
Has awaked in our hearts, my beloved, a sadness that never may die.

A weariness comes from those dreamers, dew-dabbled, the lily and rose;
Ah, dream not of them, my beloved, the flame of the meteor that goes,
Or the flame of the blue star that lingers hung low in the fall of the dew:
For I would we were changed to white birds on the wandering foam: I
    and you!

I am haunted by numberless islands, and many a Danaan shore,
Where Time would surely forget us, and Sorrow come near us no more;
Soon far from the rose and the lily and fret of the flames would we be,
Were we only white birds, my beloved, buoyed out on the foam of the
    sea!

Maud Gonne no sooner received this poem, which mingles wish fulfilment with defeatism, than she also received a telegram summoning her back to France. She confided to Yeats that the message had to do with a secret political society in which she was involved. She had lost, she said, all respect for its members' characters, but this one last time she had to answer its summons. The *Freeman's Journal* records her departure from Kingstown on 8 August 1891. Maud Gonne lied to Yeats about why she had to go back to Paris. Her little boy, now nineteen months old, had fallen sick. Twenty days after she returned to her apartment at 66 Avenue de la Grande Armée, Georges died.

There really was no reason for Maud Gonne to blame herself. The cause of death was meningitis, untreatable at the time. Maternal neglect had nothing to do with it. It was merely an accident that when her child fell ill she was listening to proposals from the greatest Irish poet of his time. But Maud Gonne was nonetheless left with 'a sadness that never may die'. She ordered the construction of a temple-like crypt in Samois for her son's burial vault. It still stands large and mysterious at the back of the country cemetery. The child's parents were listed as unknown on the death certificate.

VI

THE MILLEVOYE AFFAIR AND
THE NORTON AFFAIR

HOW MUCH DID YEATS KNOW?

Previous page: 'Le Martyre de L'Irlande', with cover portrait of Maud Gonne (Journal des Voyages, June 1892). The other scenes show (bottom right) a man defending his cottage with a scythe against men in top hats handing him a notice of eviction; (bottom left) a man led away in chains between files of policemen bearing arms; and (top left) a woman prostrate outside the cabin from which she has been evicted, her few sticks of furniture scattered on the ground.

It is incorrect to say that Yeats, even in 1891, was completely in the dark about Maud Gonne's double life. He was not, although for form's sake he allowed himself to appear to be so. He followed a gentlemanly code 'To speak no slander, no, nor listen to it'[1] and 'To love one maiden only, cleave to her, / And worship her by years of noble deeds.' Until the woman by such devotion was won, he pledged himself. 'Not only to keep down the base in man, / But teach high thought, and amiable words / And courtliness, and the desire of fame, / And love of truth' … He knew no other way to love than in the 'old high way of love' derived from 'Precedents out of beautiful old books.'[2] But the antique code that governed his public behaviour did not prevent him from becoming aware of more than he would allow himself to say.

His apprehensions could, however, be insinuated into lyrics intended for Maud Gonne herself. In the summer of 1891 during which he first asked for her hand and was refused – there were reasons why she could not marry, not anyone, not ever – Yeats began to write out poems for her in a vellum book he entitled *The Flame of the Spirit*. One of those poems is dated 1 September 1891, three weeks after her departure for Paris:[3]

> We poets labour all our days
> To make a little beauty be
> But vanquished by a woman's gaze

> And the unlabouring stars are we;
> So I, most lovely child of Ir,
> Rising from labour bow the knee
> With equal reverence to the fire
> Of the unlabouring stars and thee.

It is a poem of defeat. What has conquered him is both the way she gazes into his eyes (this makes him love her), and the 'stars', his destiny and hers too, as written in the zodiac (these make her not free to return his love). They might have been husband and wife, but an infinitely remote, blameless and unchange-able system of chance deemed otherwise. He does not hold her responsible; she is just a child, in fact the 'most lovely child of Ir' [Ireland; a flattering fiction]. The poem has a graceful syntactical motion of winding up and then unwinding its phrases, in a movement from desire to frustration to submission, closing with a Sir Galahad-like gesture of courteous fealty.

Yet if this poem seems wholly reluctant to pursue on a human level the question of why exactly his beloved can never be his, even though he must always be hers, then a poem Yeats entered into his vellum book in October is less reticent:

> He who bade the white plains of the pole
> From the brooding warm years be apart;
> He has made me the friend of your soul, –
> Ah he keeps for another your heart.

The last line records his understanding that she is committed elsewhere, although the door is left open to the interpretation that she is not committed elsewhere now but it is the will of God that one day she will be. It is not her fault they are poles apart; God made things this way. The image in the second line – 'brooding warm years' – may be applied to a woman's fertile time of life, and thus hint at Maud Gonne as a mother. That would leave Yeats with nothing but a wintry sterility ('the white plains of the pole'). Even if that sense were present, it is sufficiently vague not to require acknowledgment by the one to whom the poem was addressed.

These tentative, ceremonious probings for a tender spot in the beloved are contemporary with the changing course of Maud Gonne's own private life. However, in 1916 when Yeats wrote the first draft of that part of his autobiog-raphy, he knew pretty much the whole story. He had come through a hellish month of painful enlightenment by Maud Gonne (December 1898); years of suppressed rage and weary-hearted devotion; the period of her separation and divorce from Major MacBride (1904–06), when Yeats provided loyal support and had the grim satisfaction of knowing that she bitterly regretted her choice of husband; then a short, disappointing spell of sexual consummation (December 1908), which released a wave of rage that surprised both Gonne and Yeats. He had come through that too.

In the chapters of *Memoirs* written in 1916, the motivation of the narrative is to show that even in the early stages of his infatuation with Maud Gonne, Yeats held pieces of the puzzle of her life in his hands. He conceives of himself as one who was never blindly in love and not really the victim of a deception. Sometimes this is unconvincing. For instance, when narrating the first week of his acquaintanceship with her in February 1889, 51-year-old Yeats says that at twenty-three he had observed that (as mentioned earlier) Maud Gonne's thinking had taken 'some colour' 'from French Boulangiste adventurers and journalist *arrivistes* of whom she had seen too much'.[4] He only knew that to be so later. How much later is a question that cannot be answered except by careful inference and by making allowance for many possible degrees of awareness, the tendency of humans to hide the truth from themselves, and their unwillingness to make public the secret life of the one they love.

2

After the death of her child, Maud Gonne did not long remain in France. She returned to Dublin by way of England on 11 October 1891, travelling on the same boat that carried the body of Charles Stewart Parnell back to Ireland. The crowds at the pier drew the conclusion that her mourning clothes and grief-stricken countenance were for Parnell's sake. She explained to Yeats that a child she had adopted had died. He recounts:[5]

> I met her on the pier and went with her to her hotel, where we breakfasted. She was dressed in extravagantly deep mourning, for Parnell, people thought, thinking her very theatrical. We spoke of the child's death. She had built a memorial chapel, using some of her capital. 'What did money matter to her now?' From another I learned later on that she had the body embalmed. That day and on later days she went over the details of the death – speech was a relief to her. She was plainly very ill. She had for the first days of her grief lost the power of speaking French, which she knew almost as well as English, and she had acquired the

> habit, unlearned afterwards with great difficulty, of taking chloroform in order to sleep. We were continually together; my spiritual philosophy was evidently a great comfort to her. We spoke often of the state of death, and it was plain that she was thinking of the soul of her 'Georgette' [It is unclear how Yeats got the idea the child was a girl.]

Loss of the ability to speak French, sleeplessness, reliance on sedatives, the shocking details recited again and again: these are symptoms of trauma. Yeats, as her closest Irish confidant, was in a position to draw the conclusion that such intense grief signified the loss of someone closer than an adopted child being raised by others in a foreign country.

While she was in this fragile state, Yeats offered her the comforts of his spiritual philosophy. Death, he believed, was a human invention; individuals continued to exist as individuals on the other side of the veil, both conscious and articulate, and could be reached through invocation or by means of a gifted medium. The lost child was not necessarily lost. There was a possibility it would be reborn. Maud Gonne was already open to the idea of reincarnation, and that individuals could recall former avatars through dreams. The previous July she had told Yeats her Arabian dream of having been his sister in a former life. On 20 October Yeats gave her a poem on this theme, 'Cycles Ago'.[6]

Yeats's friend George Russell ('Æ') offered his own notions of comfort. Russell, a full-bearded young man with flaming eyes, came from an Ulster Protestant family, but he had moved on from Calvinism through Buddhism to his own Celtic take on Madame Blavatsky's syncretic, multicultural belief system. He told the bereaved woman that a child who died could not only be reincarnated, but could be born again to the same parents by means of a renewal of their relationship. This was hardly the advice that Yeats can have liked Maud Gonne to be given, yet he could see that she was 'deeply impressed' by it.[7] 'Mourn, and then Onward', the title of his newspaper poem on the death of Parnell, was counsel more suitable to his own purpose.

Yeats did not wish Gonne to be converted to Æ's Celtic Buddhism, but to something stranger still, his own Celtic Rosicrucianism. One of his first lyric retorts to her rejection of his marriage proposal – later entitled 'To a Sister of the Cross & the Rose' – was a vision of a bright apocalyptic future beyond all such 'good common hopes' as matrimony:[8]

> No daughter of the Iron Times,
> The Holy Future summons you;
> Its voice is in the falling dew,

In quiet star light, in these rhymes,
In this sad heart consuming slow:
Cast all good common hopes away
For I have seen the enchanted day
And heard the morning bugles blow.

Dublin

August 1891

Where was this enchanted world? When would it dawn? The first step towards it was to be taken in London. On 2 November Yeats brought the bereaved Gonne to be initiated as a 'Sister' of the Order of the Golden Dawn, the magical society to which the poet gave a large part of his energies.[9]

At some time during October in Dublin, Æ had told Gonne that he had had a vision in which she was haunted by a 'grey woman'. This figure, he said, was a lost part of a past personality when she had been a priestess in an Egyptian temple. The soul of this priestess was divided from itself as a result of having fallen 'under the influence of a certain priest who was her lover [and who] gave false oracles for money'. A deliberate allegory of Millevoye?[10] That divided soul was now seeking reunion with her living avatar. Behind this mystagoguery there may lie the work of an amateur therapist in possession of a fragment of Gonne's personal background and a portion of genuine insight.

In November at the temple of the Order of the Golden Dawn, Gonne told MacGregor Mathers, the chief warlock, about a 'beautiful dark woman ... whom as a child, I had seen bending over my cot'.[11] That is your 'Ka', she was told, one of the three parts of which the Egyptians believed the soul to be composed. The 'Ka' was the spark of life given to a person at birth. Yeats and Mathers speculated that it had survived from a former incarnation.[12] In a later seance, Moina Mathers (Mathers's wife and a sister of Henri Bergson) invoked Maud Gonne's 'grey lady'. During that seance, Yeats himself could see nothing, but Mrs Mathers heard a wraith confess to having killed a child, and watched as it wrung its hands in remorse.

These seances meddled dangerously with the feelings of a disturbed woman. The whole otherworldly drama of passion, grief and infanticide seems to have been spun by Yeats and his friends out of two hints. The first is Maud Gonne's dream of a past life with Yeats as brother and sister, which appears to have been her way of intimating that she was open only to a platonic friendship. The second hint she provided was her childhood memory of a woman (possibly her mother) bending over her cot.

Maud Gonne was already beset with guilt. Any newly bereaved parent feels that way. The news of the child's mortal illness had come just at the time Gonne was listening to Yeats's proposal of marriage. It would not be unreasonable to have momentarily entertained the wish to be free to consider different lives than the one to which her illegitimate child had destined her. Tales of mothers eternally suffering remorse in the next world are unlikely to have been therapeutic.

2

In December Maud Gonne was back in Paris to host a banquet of the Union Mediterranean, held two days after Christmas 1891. She gave the first of a series of lectures in France on two themes: England as oppressor, and Ireland for the Irish. W.B. Yeats was not best pleased with this new stage in the life of his sweetheart:[13] 'I was jealous too of all those unknown helpers who arranged her lectures – had she not told me too a French friend, seeing her unhappy, had suggested her first lecture?' His fears were justified. Lucien Millevoye re-established himself in Maud Gonne's life as her impresario. After the death of their child, she was persuaded to resume her career as the Irish Joan of Arc in Paris.

Among the hundred who attended the banquet to hear her speak, the most prominent were Millevoye's Boulangiste friends, such as Clovis Hugues, Maurice Barrès and several deputies. The *Journal des Voyages et des Aventures de Terre et de Mer* subsequently acclaimed the 'young girl … suddenly revealed to France through a speech marked by an ardent and convinced patriotism'. 'The evening before, she was unknown; today, she is a celebrity.' The *Journal des Voyages* commissioned an essay from Gonne on 'The Martyrs of Ireland'. Gonne accepted the offer in a public note:[14]

> I have seen from up close the misery of my poor country. The terrible scenes which took place in front of me moved me more than I knew how to say. Ireland is my country and Ireland bleeds. My whole soul revolted from what I saw. I resolved to shout above the suffering. I swear to spread these miseries in the eyes of civilized nations.

The editor of the *Journal des Voyages* was Emile Driant, the husband of one of General Boulanger's daughters and a confederate of Lucien Millevoye.[15]

Yeats leant a hand with Maud Gonne's French campaign by writing an article entitled 'The New "Speranza"' (the 'old' one was Lady Wilde) published in *United Ireland*, but Millevoye had a nationwide political network in France to employ on her behalf.

In January Jeanne Royannez Hugues, a sculptor and the wife of Boulangiste Clovis Hugues, was doing a bust of Maud Gonne. Lucien Puech stopped by the studio to interview 'the Irish girl' for *Gil Blas*. The article vividly captures the setting, Maud Gonne's 'presence', and the newsworthy, testifying quality of her conversation:[16]

'Can you tell us, Miss, how you started this campaign for the Irish?'

'It was because I was revolted by scenes I saw of the expulsion of tenants from their homes. You cannot imagine, you Parisians, the suffering of the Irish people. All the large factories in Ireland that managed to become profitable, since they came into competition with English factories, were subjected to taxes of all kinds; it did not take long to bring about their ruin.'

'What remains for the Irish people to live on? The soil?'

'But the land is all in the hands of the millionaires who sub-let it to farmers at exorbitant prices. Taxes, taxes, always increasing every year, with ruin soon to come, then bankruptcy, then expulsion from the home. Oh! These evictions! I have seen hundreds of them. Each is more distressing than the last. I could give example after example. One day, I saw a large crowd gathering. This must be an eviction, I thought. I was not mistaken. Two hundred policemen are gathered to shut up a poor dwelling. Two hundred policemen to evict a family consisting of three persons. Distraught, the husband had in his arms a baby. As soon as he saw me, he approached to say: "Please go into the house, my wife is about to have a baby." They let me go inside because the police knew I was a correspondent of English newspapers. So I could see the poor woman who lay on the floor; the police took away her bed in spite of our supplications, despite our prayers. And these horrible scenes recur every day in Ireland.' ...

'The English must be furious with you?'

'They are, indeed. They therefore search for ways to discredit me. Unfortunately, they have found nothing in my life to my discredit. They suggested I was theatrical, and that once I'd played my comedy show, I'd be done; my trip to Paris had only one goal: fame. This is very little, is it not, to have been able to invent about me? I understand what they meant by this word: advertising. They tried to convince the French government I came here for the purpose of trouble-making and agitation. This is false. I am simply telling what I saw in the bogs of Ireland, without comment. The facts speak for themselves.

Minor untruths aside, this is brilliant propaganda, to which Maud Gonne adds a courageous – albeit implicit – challenge to the French press not to betray her by revealing her relationship with Millevoye. It was bad enough that the

English were already 'search[ing] for ways to discredit' her patriotic efforts.

Ten days later, *Le Voleur illustré: cabinet de lecture universel* published a cover story on *l'agitatrice Irlandaise*. Maud Gonne provided the interviewer with a partly fanciful life history, according to which she was born in Dublin and raised on one of her family's many properties in Kerry. As a young woman, she had been presented to the King in Ireland. Her beauty had made her the queen of the Dublin balls. After the death of her father, she became the preferred pupil of the Fenian chief, John O'Leary, who sent the 'patricienne' forth to preach the doctrine of republican independence. One day, ordered to be silent by a soldier of the Queen's regiments, she refused, so the soldiers fired into the crowd: several were killed and others wounded. For her part in the affray, Maud Gonne was sentenced to six months in prison. In England, however, they never put high-born ladies in prison, so the sentence was not carried out.[17] Miss Gonne, the interviewer concluded, was *grande, très grande*, with classic looks; she could easily be a 'professional beauty' if she wished.

Before her 20 February lecture to the *Cercle catholique des étudiants de Paris* in the Rue de Luxembourg, Maud Gonne prepared lantern slides of evictions and took lessons in enunciation from an actress in the Comédie-Française. The lecture went down a storm. According to a newspaper report, 'Deep in the soul of the good students assembled in the hall, there was heard the painful complaint of the girl. They gave a great roar of applause every time that the speaker, in a slow chant, cursed the English people.'[18] One of her thrilling passages of invective against the British prime minister began with these phrases, 'I am only a weak woman, but I say to Lord Salisbury ...' The Sarah Bernhardt-like chanting of this line inspired Lucien Gillain, one of the young men in the audience, to write a poem that compared Maud Gonne to Antigone, since both young women led struggles *contre un envahisseur infame* ('against the infamous invader').[19]

The lecture to the circle of Catholic students was the first of many given by Gonne around France over the next two months. Her 'brave peregrinations' came to an end with a final fundraising lecture (tickets sold for ten francs) on 25 April at the Grand Hotel, Paris, introduced by Clovis Hugues.[20]

A clippings agency kept track of the lecturer's publicity. She reported to Yeats that over two thousand articles about her had appeared in the French press.[21] Thanks to Lucien Millevoye and her own great gifts, she had become a top-flight Parisian celebrity.

3

W.B. Yeats drew Maud Gonne back out of the limelight in France in order to help set up the National Literary Society branch in Dublin. In May 1892 he had organized a reading from the stage of *The Countess Cathleen* for copyright purposes, and it remained his aim to liberate Gonne from her self-destructive commitment to the sufferings of the Irish poor, and to join him in more refined forms of cultural nationalism.[22] The immediate aim of the National Literary Society was to change a situation in which the Irish people, though 'proud to consider themselves a more imaginative people than the English', in fact 'read nothing but a few song books and second-rate books of stories'.[23] Maud Gonne was in the Rotunda in Dublin on 9 June to support Yeats's resolution to promote rural libraries in Ireland. He urged Irish people[24]

> ... to recognize the individual responsibility, which lay upon them to make some practical effort to help their race take its proper place amongst the nations of the earth ... Ireland remained captive at the feet of a country, which was morally and intellectually its inferior [*applause*]. Irishmen succeeded everywhere but in Ireland [*applause*].

Maud Gonne praised the spirit of self-sacrifice in Ireland. John O'Leary replied ironically to her idealization of the people. He wished he could believe that what she said were true; if he could believe that, he could believe anything; in fact, the Irish people showed 'rather an inclination to sacrifice others', a line that earned laughter from the crowd.[25]

An English Liberal, E.J.C. Morton, had begged Maud Gonne to marry him, and, in lieu of that, at least to support his June 1892 campaign for a seat in parliament with a week of speech-making in Devonport. If she did not help him and he lost, he would, he said, never speak to her again.[26] She failed to gratify his wishes, but she did go to England for the birth of her sister Kathleen's child, Thora Pilcher, on 24 July.[27] The day before the birth Maud Gonne attended an event at Oak Tree House, Hampstead, to mark the inauguration of the Irish Literary Society in London.[28] Among the 200 people present were many established Irish literary figures: Charles Gavan Duffy, John O'Leary, T.W. Rolleston, Edmund Downey, Lady Wilde, Standish O'Grady and John Todhunter.

Gonne returned to Ireland, as did Yeats, O'Leary and Duffy, in order to attend a second Dublin meeting of the National Literary Society on 16 August regarding its rural library scheme. At this meeting Yeats again spoke in a somewhat lordly manner of his desire 'to elevate, at any rate, some section of the people'.[29]

The poet's plan to draw Maud Gonne into his own cultural enterprises, and away from her anti-landlord campaign in the west, her propaganda campaign on the French lecture circuit and E.J.C. Morton's campaign for a seat in parliament and the obscure operations of Millevoye, enjoyed a measure of success in the summer of 1892. She had been on the platform for two of the meetings of the National Literary Society. However, in mid September Maud Gonne returned to France. She was taking temporary leave of all campaigning.

4

When passing through Paris, the 'beauty queen Maud Gonne' told reporters for *Le Gaulois* and *Le Matin* that she now needed to look after her health. She would return to her work in November. A series of autumn lectures was being organized for her by prominent political figures.[30] On 25 September 1892 *La Presse* (a right-wing paper) printed on page two the news item that Monsieur Millevoye had gone to Clermont-Ferrand because he was suffering from a lung problem; the following paragraph reports that 'Miss Maud Gonne also just arrived.' The successive mentions, and that little word 'also', are a wink and a nod. The deputy for the Somme and the celebrated Irish patriot were by now, for French readers, a well-known couple.

After a month together with Millevoye in Royat, Maud Gonne undertook a lecture tour in order to publicize the cases of 'political prisoners' (Irish dynamitards) in British prisons. She gave a long interview to *La Presse* while passing through Paris on 26 October. While she explained the purpose of her trip, the reporter admired 'the proud figure of the young heroine, her face at once energetic and soft, bright-eyed and caressing. When talking about the woes of her beloved Ireland, a shining but furtive and sincere tear forms in her eye'. In demanding amnesty for the Irish prisoners, it was not, Maud Gonne explained, her intention to make things difficult for Gladstone at the start of his new government. The prime minister had promised Home Rule, and she wished to see that promise fulfilled. By exposing the historic injustices of British administration in Ireland, she aimed to strengthen Gladstone's case. Since Gladstone's election, Irish landlords had served 30,000 notices of eviction. It was plain that the landlords had conspired to provoke the tenants to acts of illegality, and thus to demonstrate that Gladstone was unable to keep the peace.[31]

At Bordeaux, Perigueux, La Rochelle and Arras, Gonne lectured on the history of Ireland and the present plight of its people. She now was able to attract large audiences – 2000 at La Rochelle. Her lecture began with the Elizabethan plantations and ended with a tearful account of cottiers ordered out of their hut, which, when they resisted, was knocked to pieces by a battering ram. 'Then out of the doors, along with their furniture, were thrown the old and infirm, the woman in labour, the baby.'[32] The baby was the keynote of her tale of heartbreaking national misery.[33]

One of the main forms of distress Gonne aimed to relieve by raising money through these lectures was that of dynamitards in British jails. Gladstone had promised a 'peace treaty' should his Second Home Rule Bill pass (it was brought forward on 13 February 1893). Then amnesty would be declared for those men who had been imprisoned in the fight against British rule in Ireland, such as John Daly and Thomas Clarke. Gonne had plunged herself into the cause of these prisoners. In an interview published by *Gil Blas* on New Year's Eve 1892, she made their situation appear to be as pitiful as that of the evicted tenants. Readers had no doubt heard of the Russian prisoners of the Czar:

> But it is worse here. There are at the moment nineteen prisoners in Portland [Dorset], one has been imprisoned there twice; two have been poisoned; three have gone mad. Another, with enteritis, was led to the bathroom, a room without windows, with screens on the floor, and was forced to take a cold bath, and to wash his own clothes! The unfortunate man died.

Newspapers at the time were full of articles on the bomb exploded outside Dublin Castle on Christmas Eve 1892, an event that cast a shadow over the previously fair prospects of release for the Irish dynamitards. Evidently intended for John Morley, the bomb blew to pieces a police detective on night duty. Gonne told the *Gil Blas* reporter that she was sure that 'The Conservative Party was the author of that attack.'[34] It was a trick meant to bring Irish nationalists into disrepute. *Le Figaro* published a leading article on the dynamite attempt on Morley's life that developed the same conspiracy theory, and quoted 'the words of that admirable Maud Gonne'.[35] She was becoming a woman of influence in affairs of state.

On 11 January 1893 the *Freeman's Journal* published Maud Gonne's letter congratulating the Gweedore prisoners on their release (four men originally jailed for beating to death a police inspector). Her letter accompanied a donation to be shared among the four by the Lord Mayor of Dublin, 400 francs (£16) in all. The list of subscribers to this fund include Maud Gonne with 100 francs, and Millevoye and 'Séverine' (the Boulangiste journalist) with 50 francs each.

Gonne appeared in public with Millevoye on 16 January when he hosted a banquet for the 'Defenders of Paris'. When unseemly rancour broke out in the restaurant between veterans of the Paris Commune and members of the right-wing Parti National, Millevoye diplomatically called on Gonne, who silenced the room with a speech, ending with a toast to 'France and the freedom of Ireland'.[36]

A winter 1893 letter that Gonne wrote 'very sincerely' to her 'friend', 'dear Mr Yeats', informed him that she remained weak from illness and had not left the house. She had amused herself in her confinement, she said, by painting her visions, one in particular of 'the grey woman in the dancing glory of life'.[37] This, her first extant letter to Yeats, must have been written at least a week or two after Millevoye's banquet.

On 8 and 9 February *Le Matin, La Lanterne, Le Gaulois, Le Journal*, and *La Presse* all reported that Maud Gonne was in bed with a 'fluxion of the chest', or possibly pneumonia, and thus had been forced to put off a series of lectures in Ireland on behalf of the New Irish Library. A woman may be grey with a chest cold, but still be said to be in the glory of life when that fact is published as news of interest to all Parisians.

Gonne was back at the podium on 11 March speaking of the sufferings of Irish men in British prisons, followed by a composition by Augusta Holmes, 'L'Opprime', and a passionate recitation by celebrity actor Edouard de Max of Clovis Hugues' poem 'Toast to Ireland', dedicated to Maud Gonne:

> The masters, crowned with a despicable laurel,
> Sit in a circle, presided over by Death,
> Their monstrous banquet stands in its glory:
> Now the offspring of their crimes gather around, ready to drink
> The tears, the blood, the wine from the overladen table.
> As for me, I am shaking in fear of their swords ...
> They insult the defeated, they mock their mourning.
> In the name of the stream and of the grave,
> I drink to an Ireland that still can dream,
> Shaken by the wind of the sea.

And so on for nine stanzas, each concluding with the poet drinking a toast to an Ireland that can, successively, dream, kiss, burn, weep, struggle, believe and finally conquer.

Clovis Hugues, 1900. (Atelier Nadar, BNF)

Clovis Hugues is a character with a wide assortment of attributes: a miller's son from Provence, then a student for the priesthood, supporter of the Paris Commune, prisoner in Marseilles, deputy for the French Workers' Party in 1881, next a Boulangiste deputy, husband of a murderess, and from birth a hunchback; he is also the author of a book-length *Ode to the Vagina*. His hatred of the British oppressor was evidently acquired out of sympathy with Maud Gonne. It went along with his hatred of Jews, expressed in scores of despicable verses, published side by side with his 'Toast to Ireland' in *Les Libres Paroles*.[38]

Clovis Hugues was a regular at Maud Gonne's 'At Homes' at 66 Avenue de la Grande Armée. Another figure of note in attendance at her salon was Maurice Barrès, novelist, newspaper editor and Boulangiste deputy. On New Year's Day 1893, Millevoye sent Barrès a telegram urging him to come for a meeting the following Tuesday at Maud Gonne's to exchange an 'important and urgent communication'.[39]

This was the period in which the Panama Affair reached crisis proportions.[40] In 1880 Ferdinand de Lesseps, the French entrepreneur responsible for the construction of the Suez Canal, formed a company to build a sea-level canal across Panama joining the Atlantic and Pacific oceans. He employed two financiers, Jacques Reinach and Cornelius Herz; they both happened to be Jewish. These two succeeded in raising over a billion francs in private loans. In 1888 a law was passed authorizing another seven hundred million in government bonds, good money thrown in after bad, as the project was hardly going anywhere. Workers were dying of tropical diseases at a terrible rate. Reinach and Herz paid newspapers to publish favourable articles about the canal and not to publish unfavourable ones.[41] To retain the backing of parliament, the two financiers put a number of deputies on retainer. The whole thing was a stew of corruption, in which many famous editors and statesmen were immersed – de Lesseps, Gustave Eiffel, two former prime ministers, and Georges Clémenceau.

When the Panama Company did go bankrupt, the French public was left with its debt. Late in 1891 the Chamber committed itself to an inquiry into the Panama Affair. In September 1892 an alarmed Jacques Reinach very unwisely leaked the names of deputies he had bribed. Idiotically, it was to Edouard Drumont, anti-semitic editor of *La Libre Parole*. Reinach may have wished in this way to save his own skin, but Drumont was incapable of mercy. He described the entire Panama Affair as a Jewish plot. With the legal net tightening around him, Baron Reinach was found dead, apparently poisoned, on 19 November 1892.

On 20 December Paul Déroulède seized an opportunity to take revenge on Georges Clémenceau, the erstwhile friend of General Boulanger. Déroulède asked why one of the two financiers, Cornelius Herz – 'a German born in France' – should have been made an officer of the *Légion d'honneur*. Who was his patron? Everyone knew that among the newspapers that Herz had funded in the mid 1880s, one was *La Justice*, edited by Georges Clémenceau.

291 _ *PARIS* _ L'avenue de la Grande-Armée._   A05£

Avenue de la Grande Armée; Gonne lived at number 66 in 1893.

Georges Clémenceau, 1893. (BNF)

Déroulède continued:

This complacent, this dedicated, this tireless intermediary, so active and dangerous, his name is on everyone's lips, but not one of you will say it, because you fear three things: his sword, his gun, and his tongue. Well! I brave the three. It is Clémenceau.

Clémenceau turned to face Déroulède: 'I did not deserve that; you know it is an abominable falsehood, yet, knowing this, you have uttered it.' The only reason he was being charged by Déroulède, Clémenceau declared, was that he had turned against General Boulanger, whom, he added, had no greater friend or supporter at the start of his political career than Cornelius Herz. His final words were a formal challenge: 'There is but one reply to make: you have lied.'[42] The two faced one another in a duel on 9 December, and exchanged six shots. Clémenceau was a dead-eyed marksman, but murder by duel was not the custom in 1890s' France.[43] Both men walked away unharmed.

At 2.30 pm in the afternoon on the day that Déroulède brought his accusation against Clémenceau in the Chamber, the Attorney General announced that the names of those to be prosecuted in the Panama Affair would soon be announced. The deputies divided into 'the suspects, with their allies, personally honest, but brought together by a scandal which strengthened their opponents, and the attackers quivering while feeling for an opening to attack'.[44]

At 3 pm the president announced that there would be five deputies prosecuted. The names, when announced, did not include that of Clémenceau. The silence that followed the reading of the names was broken by Lucien Millevoye: 'On evidence so slight, and coming from Reinach, a suicide, you ask the House to dishonour five great parliamentarians? You cannot ask us to abandon colleagues without seeing all the evidence.' Maurice Barrès admired 'the fake sweetness' of Millevoye's voice as his 'eyes were measuring the weight of the enormous brief-case clutched under the arm of the Attorney General.'[45] Millevoye wanted all the Attorney General's documents made public in the hope of bringing about the ruin of even more enemies of the radical right, and in particular the ruin of Georges Clémenceau.

After the duel between Déroulède and Clémenceau had been organ-ized, Lucien Millevoye issued his own challenge to 'The Tiger'. The offence for which he sought satisfaction from Clémenceau was not to himself, but to the late General Boulanger, whose honour had been tainted, according to Millevoye, by association with the name of Cornelius Herz. This was a characteristically over-the-top gesture by Millevoye, who tended to ape the behaviour of Paul Déroulède, the chief of the Parti National, even in how he wore his hair (long) and the clothes in which he dressed (a frock-coat).[46] The seconds of Millevoye and Clémenceau fell to haggling over the choice of weapon (which according to protocol should have been the prerogative of the challenged party), so the two men never met.[47] Had that duel gone ahead, and with pistols, so great was Clémenceau's dislike of Millevoye that he might well have ignored the current custom of mercy on the field of honour, and put a bullet in the Boulangiste's heart.

At Maud Gonne's salon, Millevoye was free to meet with his confeder-ates and plot the best way to bring down the government, or at least to destroy Georges Clémenceau. Those accused of corruption in the Panama Affair were scheduled for trial in March, so it was out of order to bring up the subject in parliament. Nonetheless, Millevoye and Déroulède did so, seven times. Each interpellation failed to come close to winning a majority of votes. But the pair did not give up hope. Bertrand Joly gives a brutal description of Millevoye's stature as a political leader during the last stage of the Panama Affair: 'Everything revolved around this slow, mediocre and obtuse mind; he was going to grow, swell, and produce the overwhelming *escroquerie* [swindle] of which he became the victim.'[48]

At the salon held on Sunday, 26 March 1893, Millevoye gathered a number of journalists from the right-wing press, along with poet René Ghil and his wife, and some of Gonne's Irish friends in Paris. The Irish Joan of Arc was, according to a newspaper paragraph on this *soirée*, about to go to Britain and Ireland on behalf of political prisoners.[49] The article failed to mention that Millevoye travelled with her to Britain and Ireland. The couple paid a courtesy call on James Stephens in Sutton, near Howth; the old Fenian chief had lived in exile in France for many years before returning to Ireland in 1891.[50] While in Britain, Maud Gonne applied for permission to visit the Irish prisoners in Portland Gaol.

On her return to Paris, Gonne held a salon and spoke to a reporter for *Le Gaulois*:

> After dinner, Miss Maud Gonne lit a cigarette and expressed herself in the following terms. (Do you know Miss Maud Gonne? She is this Irish young person of whom you have heard us speak, who roams the world, writing, speechifying, preaching in favour of her brothers persecuted by perfidious Albion. She is pretty, she is blonde, she has eyes as changeable as the sea, turning from turquoise to steel-grey. Her smile is delightful, but some disquiet, unknown to me, causes her eyes to close, and become impenetrable to strangers.)
>
> Certainly, she says to me, we must recognise Mr Gladstone for his efforts ... But we are not entirely satisfied with the steps he has so far taken. We wish that as an act of justice, Mr Gladstone would out of pity grant clemency, and release fourteen poor persons, fourteen innocents who have been dying for eleven years on the treadmill at Portland Gaol.
>
> The voice of Miss Gonne trembles, and her beautiful eyes plead.
>
> See, she resumed, I cannot speak about this terrible thing without being moved by it. For this reason, I am leaving soon to go to Portland Gaol to try to communicate with these marytrs. Will I be permitted to approach them? I am afraid that my petition will be rejected. While robbers and murderers get free passes out of prison on certain days, and their parents and their friends get to see them, our poor people of Ireland, who have committed no other crime than to have spoken for the freedom of their fatherland, are *séquestrés*, isolated from the world, weaned from all commerce with their familiars ...
>
> They are fed like the most base of animals, and driven by the lash of the whip. They wear their lives out dragging wagons full of stones, their backs bleeding under the weight of heavy stones, their feet torn by brambles and bruised by rocks. And when, after fifteen hours of this superhuman job, they return to their shelter, it is to be locked up to sleep in damp underground vaults, deprived of air and light. And don't think that I go too far or that I invent. I have a document in my office, it is unique, never published. It is the story by one of these captives, the tortures he was subjected to.

> As soon as any journalist hears of an unpublished document, he would damn his soul to get it. I plead, Miss Maud Gonne, please, let me have a look at this precious manuscript. She granted, gracefully, my request.
>
> First, she says, it is necessary that I explain the background to you. This prisoner is called John Daly …

At the end of May Gonne was allowed to visit prisoners in Portland Gaol. Her account of the atrocious conditions in which they were kept led to the release of one prisoner, Gilbert, who suffered from a serious illness.[51]

5

In early June a Mauritian named Norton, after offering his wares to the editors of many other newspapers, came to Edouard Ducret at the right-wing *La Cocarde*. He introduced himself as an interpreter employed by the British Embassy in Paris. He had documents in his possession that would show that a number of French deputies were in the pay of the British crown. Ducret could have copies of these documents for 30,000 francs; the originals would cost him 100,000.

For an exposé to have its fullest effect, Ducret suggested, highly placed supporters were required. It would best for Norton to win over Lucien Millevoye. The surest way to 'capture the imagination of Millevoye', he explained, was to secure the support of Miss Maud Gonne.[52] Ducret would bring Norton to Gonne's salon and introduce him as a political leader from Mauritius. Norton could talk about the oppression of small countries by big ones, and then lead on to the matter of French deputies whom he knew for a certainty to be lackeys of the British Empire. To perfect the evidence required to destroy Clémenceau and his followers, Ducret provided his own documents for Norton to translate into English and write out onto British Embassy notepaper.

On 15 June the Mauritian showed Millevoye a list of names of those in the pay of the British Embassy, and the amount that each suborned deputy was paid. One of the names on this list was Georges Clémenceau. Thirty thousand francs seemed a small price to pay for such evidence. Millevoye obtained that money and more from M. Marinoni, proprietor of *Le Petit Journal*.[53]

Paul Déroulède, leader of the radical right faction, had not decided how best to 'weaponize' the stolen documents by the time the Chamber next met in session on 19 June. He charged Millevoye to keep the matter under wraps for the time being. Yet the burning enmity of both men for Clémenceau had clearly been blown up into a white heat. When Clémenceau rose to speak from the rostrum, Déroulède barracked him mercilessly: 'Herz! Talk about Cornelius Herz! Speak English!'[54] Clémenceau paused, then turned to Déroulède: 'I am ready to have an explanation with you when you like, and to remind you of the night when you proposed to me that we should march against the Chamber of Deputies,'[55] referring to the evening at Madame Durand's in November 1887 when Clémenceau, still a Boulangiste, was invited to join a conspiracy to carry out a coup.

Déroulède defended himself by saying that he at least was untainted by the Panama Affair, and so would be forgiven by most deputies for the vehemence of his attack on Georges Clémenceau. When Déroulède returned to his seat, Millevoye began to rise.

'Millevoye, sit down. You are not in a strong position,' Déroulède said.

'No, I have something to say.'

Taking the tribune, Millevoye made a brief statement. 'M. Déroulède has a reason for his wrath, and I will give it to you Thursday: we have evidence that M. Clémenceau is a traitor to France.'[56] Déroulède was shocked by Millevoye's indiscipline.

Everything would now depend upon the so-far unproven validity of Norton's documents. Millevoye and his allies brought the papers to the President, Charles Dupuy, and the Minister of Foreign Affairs, Jules Develle. Some of the documents were letters from Thomas Villiers Lister of the Foreign Office to Austin Lee at the British Embassy in Paris. Yet Lister's initials were given on the letters as 'T.W.' instead of 'T.V.' And his signature did not match that of a sample in the hands of the French deputies. This was not necessarily a difficulty; Norton had admitted that the documents were his own copies, claiming that it would have been unsafe to remove the originals from the embassy. Develle exacted a promise from the deputies that they would not make public the contents of letters that concerned foreign affairs. President Dupuy said nothing, apart from expressing his shock that such a man as Clémenceau should be involved, and declaring that a deputy who did a thing like that should be made to disappear.

On Thursday Millevoye arrived at the Chamber of Deputies after a sleepless night. He was suffering from influenza and visibly nervous. Because the letters had not been fully verified, he had promised his cohorts that he would read only a few passages. A government inquiry could then investigate the details. To avoid any blunders, he had written his speech. The President of the

Chamber opened the session and gave the floor to Deputy Millevoye. As he arose, Déroulède tried to restrain him one final time, saying, 'Swear to me you will leave out the list!' Millevoye agreed. As soon as he reached the tribune, unsympathetic deputies called out, 'You said you had evidence of high treason. Out with the proof.'

'O, you say you have stolen documents. Why have you not given them to the police?'

'I say I have proof of the treason of M. Clémenceau. I guarantee the validity of the documents,' Millevoye replied, going off script.

'Liar! Liar! Liar!' shouted Clémenceau.

In his confusion, Millevoye forgot his promises about what to read and what not to read. Since the subject matter of those letters from which he read included passages concerning foreign affairs, the Minister of Foreign Affairs was asked if he approved of their publication in this manner. No, he did not; he could not in any way endorse Millevoye's conduct. But other deputies were shouting, 'Read on! Read on!' Millevoye retraced his steps, and read over again what he had falteringly read earlier. He read on and on through a 'carnival of jeers and insults'. Maurice Barrès described Millevoye at this moment as 'an honest man bewitched to brainlessness by a frenetic cast of rogues'.

Foreign Minister Develle broke in and said to Millevoye, 'Because you read out parts of the documents dealing with foreign affairs, which you had promised not to read, you force me to say that in the Council of Ministers this morning, I told my colleagues that while you may be acting in good faith, you are the victim of a horrible hoax.'

Déroulède rose and shouted at his colleagues, 'You all disgust me! Politics is the worst profession; politicians are the worst men. I have had enough. I resign.' He stormed out of the Chamber. Clémenceau, no longer able to contain himself, laughed and laughed, patting himself with his hands: yes, he was not dreaming, and he was safe. He climbed up on his desk and did a dance.

Millevoye stood at the lectern, stunned. Deputies shouted at him, 'You said you had a list. Read it. Read your list!' Millevoye began to read, and with each name, its owner, livid, stood and denounced the speaker. At the end, Millevoye moved from the lectern to the door; he too was departing. Really, he had no other choice.

6

One of those on Millevoye's ill-fated list was, to everyone's surprise, Henri Rochefort, a confederate of the Boulangistes, now resident in London. He directed his scorn at Millevoye, who had suddenly vanished from the public eye. Where was he? Probably with Maud Gonne, Rochefort sneered.[57] In Millevoye's disgrace, the veil of privacy was being torn from his relationship with Gonne.

The *Echo de Paris*, a daily newspaper, aired the rumour that the letters, or the embassy stationery on which the letters were forged, may have been provided by Gonne. Her interest in the conspiracy would have been to harm Britain. She replied in a letter to the editor:[58]

> I read in the *Echo de Paris*, consecrated to corridor gossip, that in order to create a current of antipathy against England, of which my country is the victim, I would deliver or am delivering the letters published by *La Cocarde*.
>
> May I count on your impartiality to deny this ridiculous report.

> Believe me, sir, Maud Gonne

Journalists camped out at the door of her apartment, but not for the purpose of writing adulatory cover stories. Gonne said she could not come to the door; she was ill. She did not seem sick to the journalist from *Le Figaro*, for she declared 'in a very clear strong voice that she would not see us'. She was in France only as a visitor, she explained, on behalf of her poor countrymen in Ireland. She knew nothing of this scandal. Her only topic of discussion with M. Millevoye was Ireland.

But she had been travelling abroad with Deputy Millevoye in April, was it not so?

He had come to meet her parents at their home in Dublin. He was an old friend of the family. She had been introduced to him on her first visit to Paris over ten years earlier, when she was still a child.

Yet she did have a terrible hatred of Britain, didn't she?

Maud Gonne 'repeated with great vehemence that she had nothing against England'. She was simply against the high taxes on Ireland and the terrible treatment of Irish prisoners in English gaols.[59] In her panic, she made many excuses that could easily be shown to be lies: that she had a mother and father to meet, that she had a home in Ireland, that Millevoye was an old friend of her parents and nothing more, that she knew nothing of French politics, that she did not hate England. The journalists were not hoodwinked; they all already knew about her affair with Millevoye. What was new was that they were writing about it and doing so from a standpoint of hostility.

W.T. Stead published an insinuating article at the time that combined the names of Gonne and Millevoye. Stead remarked that he had met Millevoye in Paris, and found him to be 'a kind of French Maud Gonne'. He expressed his disgust with the charges Millevoye was bringing against Clémenceau in the French Chamber of Deputies. No one believed, and there was no evidence to show, that Clémenceau had been bribed to support British interests against the French Republic, as Millevoye claimed: 'Pigott in England, Ahlwardt in Germany, and Millevoye in France constitute a remarkable trio, whose fate will, it is to be hoped, discourage for some time to come the employment of bogus revelations as a weapon in political warfare.'[60]

Maud Gonne left Paris and scandal behind in early July, but she did return in time for the trial of Ducret and Norton, to which Millevoye was summoned as an unindicted co-conspirator. Clémenceau enjoyed a seat on the prosecution bench.[61]

Norton, after being arrested, rapidly confessed that he had never worked at the British Embassy and had never had in his possession any authentic diplomatic correspondence. His role was simply to translate into English documents prepared by Ducret, editor of *La Cocarde*.[62] Norton's particular qualification for this work was that he was willing to do it and had already been convicted three times for fraud.

Ducret wildly denied everything Norton had said. For his part, Millevoye represented himself as the innocent dupe of Ducret and Norton, acting in concert. He testified that once he had started down the road of belief, he could not stop himself because he 'was accustomed to seeing the hand of England in so many of the sorrows of his country. Finally he had the proof in his hand'.[63] When it was Clémenceau's turn to put Millevoye on the witness stand, Millevoye screamed abuse and refused to answer questions. Clémenceau closed his question time with the remark that on the day of Millevoye's interpellation he had received a private message from the ministers that all the documents that Millevoye was about to read were apocryphal, and Clémenceau had nothing to worry about. In other words, the government had knowingly allowed Millevoye to be caught in his own trap. At least, at the end of the trial Millevoye did not have to go to prison with Ducret and Norton, since he enjoyed immunity for things said in the Chamber of Deputies.

In his summation, Clémenceau made a speech that was immediately celebrated for its dignity. He began by explaining that he was only present in court because he was instructed by barristers that his absence could be understood to mean he did not wish to contest the accusations of treason made against him. The court, unfortunately, could not prosecute the person who was truly guilty of these libels – that was Lucien Millevoye. He was the true culprit.

The judge intervened, and requested that Clémenceau show moderation towards the witnesses who had deposed against him:

> Mr Chairman, I thank you for your criticism this early of what I have not said. But you will allow me, without responding to the prodigious insults heaped upon me, to make a legal rebuttal. I am not here to speak against the two men on trial. It does not matter to me whether it was M. Norton or M. Ducret or whomever that forged the documents. What matters to me is that it be seen in Court that the papers were fakes. Who made the fakes? Maybe we shall never know. But we can come to understand the feeling that gave rise to this behaviour. M. Millevoye said that I had taken the pretty part in this play. If I am not to lose this pretty part, I must impeach the charges brought against my name.
>
> M. Millevoye is a witness, not an accused. But does he make excuses? Yes. His first excuse is that he was driven by the rage of his friends … This is part of a manhunt, and those two men you have arrested are only its agents, its hounds. M. Millevoye had evidence that the documents that were brought to him were false, but he concluded that the copies were genuine. He should resign from the Chamber of Deputies.
>
> Mr Déroulède insulted me. He is not here to face me; he is at the other end of France.
>
> I who am a victim of these fakes am not here to point the moral of the affair. Why I'm here, men of the jury, I do not know. The law asks you to judge without passion. You have to do something here. It is wrong to dismiss the charges. That would smear people who do not wear Déroulède's frock-coat with the charge of not being patriots.
>
> You can stop it. There is an important thing for France to avoid: false accusations that may affect our freedom. There is no greater crime than having sold one's country, especially when that country is defeated and dismembered. The homeland is not just the crowd of people in it; it is the community of hopes and passions for *revanche*.
>
> Gentlemen of the jury, let us not say there was in France a French deputy who sold himself abroad. I ask for a vote of guilty.

7

Given the shower of nasty articles about Lucien Millevoye – and about Maud Gonne too – printed throughout the summer of 1893 in newspapers in France, Britain and Ireland, it would be surprising if W.B. Yeats knew nothing at all about the Norton Affair. At the end of June, when Millevoye was committing his transcendent gaffe and Maud Gonne was pretending to be too sick to talk reporters at 66 Avenue de la Grand Armée, Yeats was in Sligo with his uncle, George Pollexfen. On 30 June he completed a draft of 'Into the Twilight':[64]

> Out-worn heart, in a time out-worn,
> Come clear of the nets of wrong and right;
> Laugh, heart, again in the grey twilight,
> Sigh, heart, again in the dew of the morn.
>
> Your mother Eire is always young,
> Dew ever shining and twilight grey;
> Though hope fall from you and love decay,
> Burning in fires of a slanderous tongue.
>
> Come, heart, where hill is heaped on hill,
> For there live the mystic brotherhood
> Of the flood and flame, of the height and wood,
> And laugh out their whimsey and work out their will.
>
> And Time and the Word are ever in flight,
> And God stands winding His lonely horn,
> And love is less kind than the grey twilight,
> And hope is less dear than the dew of the morn.

The poem could be a poem of discouragement, addressed by the poet to his own weary heart, and bidding it to find consolation in the hills of the west. Why would the heart of a healthy young man be worn out? Perhaps because in April, when Maud Gonne had come to Britain and Ireland with Millevoye and visited James Stephens, she had also seen Yeats. She behaved coldly to the poet, and he felt a 'great breach' had been opened up between them; he could not say why.

But in June 1893 Yeats may have come to know more than he did in April. The 'fires of a slanderous tongue' could be a reference to the ways in which Maud Gonne was being torched in the Parisian press, or to word-of-mouth gossip about her compromised life in France. Her *ménage* with Millevoye was hardly secret. In that case, the 'you' in this poem would be Maud Gonne, not Yeats. She is the one burning in those fires; she is the one caught in the nets of wrong and right. What she must do, Yeats tells her, is come to Ireland to recover her spirits and find her soul.

If the poem is addressed to Maud Gonne, then it is a love poem ('Come, heart'), but a very gentle one. The poet invites her to join in a 'mystic brother-hood'; he does not insist on his own passion. It is conceded that she had loved another, and had cherished great ambitions for what she could do with her life, but now love had shown itself to be cruel and hope had proved costly. The poem's apparent sympathy with her plight would carry the insinuation that the poet understands her circumstances in unspecified detail.

The poem is a Celtic Twilight lyric; in other words, it is written according to an aesthetic of deliberate vagueness and an escapist response to conflict. These qualities make it difficult to read the poem in a biographical manner; however, when Maud Gonne received the lyric, she heard Yeats speaking to her about matters near her heart.

After the August trial of those implicated in the Norton Affair, Gonne left France. Her ultimate destination was Limerick, where a huge rally was being organized by the Amnesty Association for 17 September 1893 on behalf of John Daly, a prisoner in Portland Gaol, who had been placed on the ballot for a Home Rule seat in parliament. Travelling from France to Ireland, Gonne evidently met Yeats in London, and gave him a cover for a manuscript book. Yeats had hand-made paper cut to fit the book cover. On 5 September 1893, he wrote into this book 'On a Child's Death':[65]

> You shadowy armies of the dead
> Why did you take the starlike head
> The faltering feet, the little hand?
> For purple Kings are in your band
> And there the hearts of poets beat;
> Why did you take the faltering feet.
> She had much need of some fair thing
> To make Love spread his quiet wing
> Above the tumult of her days
> And shut out foolish blame & praise.
> She has her squirrel & her birds
> But these have no sweet human words

> And cannot call her by her name
> Their love is but a woodland flame.
> You wealthy armies of the dead
> Why did you take the star-like head.

If not the greatest Yeats ever wrote, these lines are constructed to be heart-rending for Maud Gonne, and a lesson to her as well. He perceives that two years after the death of Georges, her life is still built on top of a void, so that no matter how many pets she keeps, or how many lectures she gives, or how many newspaper spreads are published about her ('the tumult of her days'), hers remains a hollow life. What she needs is love.

Shortly thereafter Yeats wrote into this manuscript book another lyric entitled 'The Glove and the Cloak'. This is an important lyric for the understanding of Yeats's relationship with Maud Gonne and her double life. First of all, it shows he knew that she lived a life of concealment; second, that he let her know that he knew; third, that she was not required to tell him any more than she had. Finally, the poem promises that he will continue to love her, no matter how much she keeps from him:[66]

> I saw her glitter and gleam,
> And stood in my sorrow apart,
> And said, 'She has fooled me enough,'
> And thought that she had no heart.
>
> I stood with her cloak on my arm,
> And said: 'I will see her no more,'
> When something folded and small
> Fell at my feet on the floor, –
>
> The little old glove of a child:
> I felt a sudden tear start,
> And murmured: 'O long grey cloak,
> Keep hidden and covered her heart!'

Maud Gonne acknowledged receiving this poem on 13 October when she had returned from Limerick to Paris: 'Thank you for the poem but I must ask you most earnestly not to publish it.'[67] He did not include the poem in any of his collections, but he did publish it in 1897 in *Roma*, an Italian periodical unlikely to be seen by Gonne's friends, or by Yeats scholars either, who have rarely mentioned the poem.

It is obvious why Maud Gonne could admit to understanding 'The Glove and the Cloak', yet insist that no one else should be allowed to see it. It records an accidental revelation of her personal life. After the death of Georges Silvère Gonne, his mother had kept one of his little sock booties (not a glove, as in the poem). She carried it with her everywhere. Indeed, she left instructions that she was to be buried with the memento. While giving orations, she clutched this little sock in her hand. It is unknown whether the purpose was to calm her emotions, or raise them to a pitiful pitch.[68]

'The Glove and the Cloak' enables one to picture a scene in which the poet and his muse are on a platform. He is bitterly thinking thoughts such as those articulated in his autobiography, that his 'devotion might as well have been given to an image in a milliner's shop, or to a statue in a museum, but romantic doctrine had reached its full development'. [69] She gives him her cloak to hold, when out of its pocket falls this little sock. Suddenly, he realizes everything: that she has a double life, that she is a fallen woman, that she has lost her child, that she is tragically broken-hearted, and ultimately that she is a tremendous woman for putting on a brave face and carrying on her public life. In short, Yeats saw through Maud Gonne's statement that the child was adopted. It was common practice in the period for unmarried mothers to say that their illegitimate children were 'wards' or 'adopted'. Gonne's claim that she was in mourning for the death of an adopted child came with the social understanding: Don't ask me about this – the answer involves something unmentionable – the death of an illegitimate yet beloved child, my own, or that of a kinswoman.

Before this moment of insight, 'The Glove and the Cloak' also quite plainly records Yeats's frustration at the one-sidedness of his relationship with Maud Gonne. It vents his dismay at her insincerity, her superficiality. She is all surface; there is nothing inside, no heart. But then, seeing the glove, he understands that yes, she has been lying to him, but while he had thought it was just about another man in her life, the deception was deeper than that: it was about a pregnancy, and ultimately about the death of a child.

Maud Gonne behaved after the birth of her first child (and would again after the birth of her second) as if she were a 'lawless woman without home or child'.[70] She left Georges while he was still a small infant for a long period in the care of another while she went to Ireland. Was she not worried that this might increase the probability of his death? The story could appear to be like a chapter out of George Moore's *Esther Waters* (1894) about 'baby farmers': middle-class women giving their illegitimate children to industrial-sized 'baby farms', so that they would die and leave the women free to pursue their lives. Yet Yeats sees through this outward appearance of heartlessness into the poignancy of the inner life of his beloved. He sees, yet he does not ask her to drop her mask. No, keep the cloak on, the poem says; keep that troubled heart snugly covered. He comprehends why she must wear a mask, but he also signals to her that he knows what it is about which she cannot speak, and, knowing it, he loves her even more.

VII

AN IBSENITE HEROINE

In October 1893 while W.B. Yeats was laying siege to the heart of Maud Gonne, she was actually free to listen to proposals for a life of another kind. She was no longer an unmarried mother. Disgrace still hung over the head of Lucien Millevoye, and her own reputation in France was clouded by the Norton Affair. Yet she remained wildly popular across Ireland. She could have decided at this point to change her place of residence, but Maud Gonne did not decamp from Paris.

In his *Memoirs* Yeats says he put his own despair into the composition of his one-act play *The Land of Heart's Desire*: 'I could not tell why Maud Gonne had turned from me unless she had done so from some vague desire for some impossible life, for some unvarying excitement like that of the heroine of my play.'[1] He was wrong. It was not some vague desire for a renewed tumult in her days that animated Maud Gonne; she wanted to have another child with Lucien Millevoye. As Roy Foster puts it, 'Gonne's life was spectacularly different from the fantasy WBY had incarnated in *The Countess Cathleen*, if no less surreal.'[2]

The story is often repeated that after hearing from Æ that a dead child could be reincarnated in the same family, Maud Gonne brought Millevoye to the memorial chapel at Samois, and there conceived a second child, Iseult Gonne. It is not incredible that a person so theatrical, and a mother so guilt-stricken, would place her hopes in sex magic. Yet it is unlikely that Maud Gonne and Millevoye had intercourse just once after the death of Georges, that once was enough to guarantee conception, or that they had sex only in the memorial chapel. Iseult was conceived more than two years after Gonne's conversation with Æ about reincarnation, probably in early November 1893. During that two years, Maud Gonne and Millevoye had become a well-known couple in Paris. She hosted a salon on his behalf; he put his press contacts and political affiliates at the service of her Irish propaganda and her personal celebrity. She stood by him through the hideous trials of the Norton Affair. There is every sign that, in fact, she loved him.

She loved him most when he was down and out, and she was the only one still to love him. Both times that Gonne conceived a child by Lucien Millevoye follow great crises in his life. Georges was conceived just after the cowardly flight of General Boulanger from Paris to Brussels: a crushing blow for Millevoye's fantasy that he had found a second Bonaparte. Iseult was conceived in the wake of the humiliations of the Norton Affair, when Millevoye had become a laughing stock, publicly dishonoured. The date and place of Iseult's conception cannot be pinpointed, but the most likely period for this event is the second week of November, when Maud Gonne was lecturing in the Low Countries – at Ghent, Groningen, Arnheim and other towns.[3] If she were organizing a magical reincarnation, perhaps the couple returned to the place in or near Brussels where Georges was conceived. On the other hand, pregnancy may have occurred as an unintended outcome of Gonne's long-running and publicly established intimacy with Lucien Millevoye.

There is no sign in Adolphe Brisson's October 1893 interview, a month before becoming pregnant, that Gonne had in mind anything but a renewal of her campaign against the British position in Ireland. Brisson's *Portraits intimes* of famous people, bound into volumes, were widely admired in France. While he maintained an edge of light comedy and sceptical distance from Maud Gonne, the interview ultimately served to restore her name in the wake of the Norton Affair.

He dubs her the 'Velleda of Ireland', after the Germano-Celtic prophetess who foresaw victories by her northern tribe against the Romans:

> Velleda is huge, she measures at least 1.85 metres, which is equivalent to size of a fine policeman. Beautiful? Not precisely. But curious. The head is surrounded by a blonde halo, very thick, tousled, which evokes the idea of *Eau des Fées*, the 'Cherry Blossom' and other elixirs for the maintenance of women's hair. The chin is resolved, the mouth energetic, nose slightly coquelinesque, i.e. *à la* 'Roxelane'.
>
> Finally the eye could not be more interesting. Not bright, nor petulant, at times dreamy and passionate. It is an indeterminate expression; I cannot comprehend

it; the expression is vague and enclosed. Some foreign people (Saxon or Slavic) are puzzles to us and their souls remain incomprehensible.

Miss Maud Gonne receives me warmly, like a woman accustomed to rub shoulders with men of letters and journalists. Vigorous handshake.

The interview was conducted in the wake of the 2 September 1893 passage of Gladstone's Home Rule bill on its third reading. Was Maud Gonne not at last satisfied, Brisson asked, as the 'British government finally decided to fulfil your dearest wishes?' This slight sarcasm was not appreciated:

A pout is drawn on the lips of Miss Gonne.

– Home Rule is only an initial concession. If it is of some benefit to the dignity of Ireland, the misery, alas! suffered by that unfortunate country will still not be relieved.

– Is the misery truly as atrocious as you pretend? Is there not a certain exaggeration in the descriptions of travellers?

Velleda took on a grave air.

– Those lectures are pictures of the truth. Few people know Ireland. For to know it truly, you would have to do as I have done and travel by horse (as cars are not able to move on the rutted roads) to its isolated hamlets, far from the city … It's there that the worst landlords commit their abominations. They are very quiet … Like the gentry of the twelfth century, they cut back, they starve, they squeeze the peasants who are in reality their slaves, they tear the bread from their mouths and reduce them to starvation.

Some … come to eat grass, like beasts, and even the grass, which they harvest by the sea, they are obliged to pay for or steal, they cannot pick and feed on it because they are under the supervision of the police. And what police! A police hateful, vindictive, composed of sectarians, all the more cruel because they know they are protected by the highest authority.

I will paint you a picture of these horrors. I saw with my own eyes expelled from his house a man 103 years old. I had to pay the last term of his tenancy.

I saw, in winter, the policemen seize a pregnant woman and deposit her in the snow outside her house, threaten the neighbours who gathered to defend her with prison, and put out the fire that charitable neighbours had lit to warm her frozen limbs, so the unfortunate woman, suddenly taken with labour, gave birth to a stillborn child.

Every day such scenes occur. Everyone knows in England, and no one says anything.

This 'out Hecubas Hecuba', but Gonne's sense of purpose caused Brisson to conclude that she was not going to be stopped by scandals like the Norton Affair:

I felt what this woman possesses. She shall not commit indiscretions, she will continue her work for months, for years, without compromising its influence by useless provocations. And I admired this tenacity, this courage.

Full of admiration, I remained quiet. It was not normal for a woman to abandon her position in the world, renounce the joys of marriage, the prerogatives of her blood, break with the prejudices of her caste, and throw herself into a life of adventures.

Gonne admitted that her dedication to the cause of the Irish people was not entirely selfless; she enjoyed fame, admiration and power. 'For myself, I am repaid with fame and gratitude for my pains. I embody their hopes. Alas, on my means and on my authority they depend.' Toward the end of the interview Gonne told a story about British spies that implied that any defamation touching her was the result of malicious political opposition:[4]

[I]f the police leave me at large, they are still watching me closely. Of this, I recently had proof. I had a servant here in Paris, who had served me with good grace and dedication, and inspired in me complete confidence. Then one day I found her opening my letters, my documents, my dispatches. She had been bought by the English. I experienced real shame, but not surprise.

While Brisson begins the interview with sarcastic, sceptical questions, Maud Gonne is more than equal to the challenge of turning him to her favour before its conclusion. This *portrait intime* was just the beginning of the relaunch of Gonne's career as a celebrated *harangueuse* in the wake of the Norton Affair. The continuation of her campaign for rehabilitation would have to wait, however, until after the birth of her second child.

2

On 9 February 1894 W.B. Yeats, having completed *The Land of Heart's Desire*, travelled to Paris to stay with MacGregor and Moina Mathers. This couple had established an offshoot of the Order of the Golden Dawn in Paris, the 'Isis Temple'. Paris was even more mad for the occult than London or Dublin. Stanislas de Guaita and Sar Péladan had started the Cabalistic Order of the Rosy Cross in 1888. Maurice Barrès, Paul Adam, and the magician Papus were original members; poet Catulle Mendès was an early associate.[5] The writer Joris-Karl Huysmans, disgusted with Zola's naturalism and his progressive politics, turned to the occult possibilities of the Cabalistic Order, and in particular to Satanism. There was a large overlap in membership of the Order of the Rosy Cross, the Symboliste writers, and right-wing political figures; Barrès, for instance, was all three.

Edouard Drumont, though deeply Catholic, believed in the occult, as did Millevoye, although these two harboured suspicions that some Rosicrucian cells were covert branches of the Masonic order. To their way of thinking, Masons were part of a Protestant and Jewish conspiracy against Catholic social power. Maud Gonne herself had been dismayed by the middle-class Protestant clergy-men among the membership of the Order of the Golden Dawn – 'an awful set'.[6] She was also repelled by the Hebrew letters so prominent in the rituals.

In June 1890, Sar Péladan – Symboliste poet, novelist, and magician – started a new cabalistic order purged of all non-Catholic elements, because 'I could not take occultism in its entirety with me to Mass, and I refuse to rub shoulders with spiritualism, masonry, or Buddhism.' His new 'Order of the Catholic Rose Cross, the Temple, and the Grail' was exclusively for 'Roman Catholics, Artists, and Women'.[7]

Sar Péladan achieved a major success with his 1892 'Salon de la Rose Croix', which attracted 30,000 visitors to view paintings by Gustave Moreau, Puvis de Chavannes, and others. 'Our aim is to tear love out of the western soul and replace it with the love of Beauty, the love of the Idea, the love of Mystery … If you create a perfect form, a soul will come and inhabit it.'[8]

Péladan started a civil war among the occultists by accusing his former confederate, Stanislas de Guaita, of murdering another warlock, Abbé Boullan, by means of spells operating from afar. Abbé Boullan's occult take on Christianity was that since Adam and Eve brought about the fall of humanity through an act of culpable love, it was by means of acts of love accomplished in a religious spirit that the redemption of all humanity could be achieved. Intercourse with 'celestial entities' was a road to redemption for certain supe-rior individuals. When they in turn had intercourse with inferior beings, it would help those unfortunates to ascend the ladder of life.[9] Huysmans attended a black mass organized by Boullan in the course of his research for *Là-Bas* (1891).[10] The devil, he learned, had a bifurcated member that could penetrate the female in two orifices at once. Huysmans' friend Félicien Rops did an illustration of the feat.

While Mathers guided Yeats into the penetralia of the French occult, the poet awaited word from Maud Gonne that he might visit her.[11] Several weeks after his arrival in Paris, she agreed to go along with him to a performance of

Axel by Villiers de l'Isle-Adam, the quintessential example of French symbolist occult drama.

As they went to their seats, Yeats noted that Gonne had difficulty climbing the stairs; she was over three months' pregnant. Yeats had little French, but Maud Gonne cannot have translated the play as a whole for him; it was five hours long:[12]

> All the favours of other women are not worth my cruelties. I am the most inhuman virgin ... I know the secret of infinite pleasures and delectating cries, the secret of voluptuous sensations where every hope expires ... Let me veil you in my hair so you may inhale the attar of roses of all time! ... Yield. I shall make you pale beneath stinging joy; I shall be merciful when you are under this torture! My kiss for you will be like nectar from Heaven.

Axel admits he that he wants to 'crush and penetrate' Sara: 'My desires swell and die in you ... only to revive in your beauty.' This tumescence is permitted only to be verbal. Axel will not allow either Sara or himself to succumb to what they both want, so sure is he that physical consummation would prove a disappointment. It is better to die and leave no trace behind.

The play's Wagnerian *Liebestod* provided Yeats with formulae that worked for him both in his relationship with Gonne and in his poetry. The plot of *Axel* handily reversed the situation of Yeats and Gonne: the hero-magician-poet turns down the beautiful witch. The 'hair tent' image from Sara's speech – 'Let me veil you in my hair so you may inhale the attar of roses of all time!' – is multiplied throughout the poems of *The Wind Among the Reeds* (1899).[13] Sometimes the hair tent serves as a picture of erotic shelter, sometimes of entrapment. Axel's odd preference for verbal over physical consummation also appealed to Yeats as a stance in relation to Gonne. Yeats had desires, but he also feared consummation.

He knew Maud Gonne was sexually experienced; she had that frightening advantage over him. He had had a dream-vision one night of a thimble (female symbol) and a lump of meerschaum not yet made into a pipe (male symbol, but not in working order): 'She was complete; I was not,' he concluded.[14] Ultimately, for Yeats, as for Axel, the best condition, or the safest way out, was never to beget. By means of magic, natural failure became a symbolist victory.

On this visit to Paris, Maud Gonne herself gave Yeats no reason to hope for any other kind of triumph. In the poem he wrote on his return to London, his references to 'the breath of slander' and 'the thread of my folly', suggest that while in Paris others tried to apprise Yeats of Maud Gonne's real situation – that she was the acknowledged mistress of Lucien Millevoye. Nonetheless, the poet reaffirms his commitment to her:

I will not in the grey hours revoke
The gift I gave in hours of light
Before the breath of slander broke
The thread my folly had drawn tight

The little thread weak hope had made
To bind two lonely hearts in one
But loves of light must fade & fade
Till all the dooms of men are spun.

The gift I gave once more I give
For you may come to winter time
But still your [white] flower of beauty live
In a poor foolish book of rhyme.

10 March 1894

One cannot say that Yeats unconsciously made a fool of himself. He knew there was little hope that his love would be requited. He knew the stories about Gonne must be true.

The poem splits the beloved into one who will live in his book (white as a virgin) and one who will not. That one will grow old – winter will come – and then she may be grateful for his foolish devotion, and take comfort in the virginal eidolon that on its pages never ages. The fact that his beloved will not by him be loved in a physical way is not necessarily a problem. She can still be a very good muse.

3

On 15 April W.B. Yeats attended the writers' dinner in London to launch *The Yellow Book*. He was seated opposite the novelist Pearl Craigie, George Moore, and the wife of Hope Shakespear, Olivia:

> At a literary dinner I noticed opposite to me between two celebrated novelists a woman of great beauty. Her face had a perfectly Greek regularity though her skin was a little darker than a Greek would have been, and her hair was very dark. She was quietly dressed with what seemed to me very old lace over her breast and had the same sensitive look of destruction I had admired in Eva Gore Booth. She was it seemed alone of our age to suggest to me an incomparable distinction.

Olivia Shakespear took the initiative: she contacted Yeats through her cousin the poet Lionel Johnson. When they met, at first all that Yeats could do was talk to Olivia about how broken-hearted he was over Maud Gonne, and his futile struggle with an invisible rival. Over the next year, however, he began to write Olivia Shakespear 'unconscious love letters' from Sligo. They took the form of commentary on her novel-in-progress. The hero of her tale, he wrote, was one of those men who think themselves in love with a woman with pink cheeks, but[15] 'whose character they have never understood, whose soul they have never perceived, & whom they would have forgotten in a couple of months' (6 August 1894). 'I wonder how you would fare were you to pick out some eccentric man, either from among those you know, or from literary history, from the Villiers De Lisle Adams & Verlainnes [*sic*], & set him to make love to your next heroine?' (28 November 1894). 'I have never come upon any new work so full of a kind of tremulous delicasy [*sic*], so full of a kind of fragile beauty as these books of yours' (12 April 1895).

Yeats, a hero perhaps as eccentric as Verlaine or Villiers, made no move himself, but upon his return from Sligo in July 1895, Mrs Shakespear did. In a railway car *en route* to Kent, she gave the thirty-year-old poet 'the long passionate kiss of love'. It was his first. 'I was startled & a little shocked.'[16] He remained an uncertain partner in the slowly developing love affair, but he decided that summer, '[I]f I could not get the woman I loved it would [be] a comfort even for a little while to devote myself to another.'[17]

4

Iseult Gonne was born on 6 August 1894. The name makes sense: both Gonne and Millevoye were admirers of Wagner, and in particular of *Tristan and Isolde*, the story of a magical romance between a French knight and a Celtic princess.

In place of 'Mama' Gonne taught the child to call her 'Moura', an anagram of *amour*, love. Never, not even in old age, did Gonne refer to Iseult as her daughter; she was her 'ward' or her 'niece'. These were the rules for unmarried mothers. She again rented a house in Samois, a place with a walled garden in the Rue de Barbeau. A widow, Madame de Bourbonne, was put in charge of the child's upbringing.[18]

5

When Lucien Millevoye was offered the editorship of a newspaper, *La Patrie*, Maud Gonne encouraged him to accept. It would put him back on his feet; he could again become a force in the politics of France. She took a new apartment at 7 Avenue d'Eylau, not far from the Trocadero with its splendid panorama of the Eiffel Tower. Following Iseult's birth, Gonne established a salon in support of Millevoye and his causes, as well as her own.

One of Millevoye's first articles for *La Patrie* concerned the recent arrest of Captain Alfred Dreyfus on a charge of being a spy for Germany. Originally secret, the indictment was leaked by military headquarters to Edouard Drumont, editor of *La Libre Parole*, on 31 October 1894. There was not much evidence against Dreyfus, apart from his being a Jew and having access to the military details that had been passed to the German Embassy in Paris. Yet Millevoye's article, published on 8 November, did not concern itself with the question of guilt or innocence. The crime was taken as proven. What Millevoye insisted upon was that the only punishment acceptable to France was the death penalty.[19]

Drumont's *La Libre Parole* and Millevoye's *La Patrie* became allies in the anti-semitic movement of 'France for the French'. In 1895 Drumont's paper sponsored an essay contest on the topic 'The best practical means for the annihilation of Jewish power in France.' The members of the jury were Clovis Hugues, Maurice Barrès and Lucien Millevoye. They awarded the prize to a priest for his work on the Jewish masonic conquest of the Third Republic.[20]

In the autumn of 1895 Millevoye repaired the breach that had opened between himself and Paul Déroulède. After the debacle of the Norton Affair, Déroulède had retreated to his estate in the Charente countryside of south-western France. He started writing historical dramas to reveal his political vision. *Messire Du Guesclin* was staged in late October 1895. It dramatizes the case of a leader of a France torn apart by anarchy. Du Guesclin sees the need for a strong government, and, with disinterested patriotism, takes whatever action he believes is necessary to save his country. On 25 October Millevoye asked Déroulède if he had made plans to re-enter political life.[21] Déroulède replied that he was just waiting for an opportune moment. He would be back, and he would bring Millevoye with him.

6

In the period after the birth of her daughter, Maud Gonne did not immediately plunge herself into her role as an outside agitator in Britain and Ireland. She put her energies into being a *salonnière* and woman of letters at her apartment at 7 Avenue d'Eylau. Her circle included the leading female activist writers in Paris: Madame Caroline Rémy de Guebhard, whose pen name was 'Séverine'; Sibylle Aimée Marie-Antoinette Gabrielle de Riquetti de Mirabeau, Comtesse de Martel de Janville, whose pen name was 'Gyp'; Maguerite Durand, Madame Laguerre, Boulangiste, feminist, and journalist, whose pen name was 'Néva'; and Ghénia de Sainte-Croix, Madame Avril, who wrote under the name 'Savoiz'.

Postcard of Avenue d'Eylau, Paris, with Eiffel Tower in the distance.

Séverine ran away from the husband she married at seventeen to work with the socialist editor Jules Valles. She was chic, modern, inconsistent and impulsive – both an incendiary and a lady of charity. Léon Daudet reported the rumour that whenever Séverine had children, she abandoned them.[22] As a writer, her speciality, like Gonne's, was an inexhaustible maternal sympathy for the miserable and downtrodden (apart from Jews). She was in succession a socialist, a Boulangiste, an anti-Semite, and (in a *volte-face*) a Dreyfusard. A male journalist discriminatorily observed that, like a cat, Séverine could scratch, but being scratched was a pleasure 'since we can expect as compensation that one day her little hand will deign to heal the wound'.[23]

In 1897 Séverine began to write for the all-woman newspaper founded by Marguerite Durand, *La Fronde*. Gyp, another former Boulangiste and current anti-Semite, wrote for *La Fronde* as well. Goncourt observed Gyp closely when she visited the home of Alphonse Daudet:[24]

> A large nose, a slightly faded blondeness, but a bent elegance of the body in a white dress of a thoroughly distinguished taste, and voluptuous, exciting. She speaks lovingly about animals, about her horse, who tramples her feet and to whom she cannot resist bringing lumps of sugar daily, about cats she adores, about dogs, for whom her house is a refuge; and as the conversation revolves around food, she says she likes only chops, and boiled eggs, and that sometimes she eats only for lunch and dinner.

'Gyp', *Sibylle Aimée Marie-Antoinette*
Gabrielle de Riquetti de Mirabeau,
Comtesse de Martel de Janville.

Author of over a hundred novels, Gyp was endowed with both talent and malice.[25] (One of her real-life heroes was the Marquis de Morès: he moved through Paris accompanied by a bodyguard of a dozen butchers hired from the slaughterhouse district, whom he armed with leaded canes. He would begin his hunting expeditions in the streets of Paris with the cry 'Tally-ho for the Jews.')[26] In December 1897 Gyp was forced to withdraw from *La Fronde* because she refused to stop submitting anti-Semitic copy. She explained her political position very neatly to an interviewer:[27]

> I like neither the Republic nor any other parliamentary regimes, and I'm instinctively on the side of those who are against those people. I'm an imperialist – a Caesarist, to be more precise. My dream is of a leader whose neck could be severed if he betrayed the country … a man … personally and directly responsible … As I am at the same time authoritarian and democratic, I find myself very close to Déroulède, who is a plebiscitary republican, and there you have it.

Of these four women, Ghénia de Sainte-Croix was the closest to Maud Gonne. One of the great early organizers in French feminism (vice-president of the International Conference of Women in 1920), her personal cause was to outlaw prostitution.[28] She became a sort of second mother to Iseult, travelled to Ireland with Maud Gonne in 1898, and stood by her through the break-up with Millevoye and the divorce from Major MacBride. Gyp, Séverine and Madame Durand may at times have been role models, rivals or allies for Maud Gonne; Ghénia de Sainte-Croix was always her trusted advisor and friend.

On 19 January 1895 Maud Gonne was among the select audience for the first in a series of nine lectures on the history of feminism, 'adapted to the milieu of the *mondaine* in a *joli* salon'. The following Saturday the second lecture was given by the scholar of the occult, Julies Bois, on the 'unquiet heart of the modern woman': 'the ingénue, the cosmopolitan, and the free young woman.'[29] At the opening of the salon in May, Maud Gonne borrowed a fashion masterstroke from Gyp by dressing entirely in white (thought to be appropriate only for unmarried young girls). Her costume was reported in the *Freeman's Journal* on 23 May:

> In defiance of French prejudice, Miss Gonne appeared in white from head to foot – her hat was an arrangement of white wings, her gown was of white crépon, and a boa of white feather was about her throat. I am told that the effect was far too striking, especially as Miss Gonne's beauty is in itself sufficiently remarkable.

The mother of Iseult, now nine months old, was ready to take on the world afresh.

7

Maud Gonne returned to Ireland for a big rally in Limerick to celebrate the election of John Daly to Parliament. She had been campaigning for Daly's release from Portland Gaol and his election to office would increase pressure on the government to exercise mercy on his behalf. Barrels of burning tar and bonfires illuminated the streets. Bands led two parades – one of Parnellites, the other of anti-Parnellites – as they made their ways from different parts of Limerick to Bank Place, where the Mayor addressed the crowd. He (falsely) said that he did 'not speak empty words' when he declared he had never felt prouder or happier in his life than he did in 'presiding there under the circumstances under which they had met together'.[30] The quarrelsomeness and futility of Irish parliamentary politics were wearisome.

When Maud Gonne learned that a new departure in republican politics had been initiated at a Convention of the Irish National Alliance (Yeats declined an invitation to attend, so young John MacBride went in his place), she was interested. The INA criticized John O'Leary's Irish Republican Brotherhood for always postponing the fight. Jeremiah O'Donovan Rossa, a former dynamitard, gave a speech saying the time for revolution had arrived. Ireland should train soldiers to join an attack on Britain by France or Russia; surely one was imminent.[31] Maud Gonne became an early adopter of this physical force policy.

Her first duty as she understood it was to get the men of deeds out of prison and back into the movement. She lent material assistance to the family of Thomas Clarke, sending his mother Mary money in November 1895, the same month in which Gonne published a defiant defence of the dynamiters in a Belfast newspaper:[32]

> I hear some say, 'Do not darken the Irish cause by speaking of such as they – they are dynamiter criminals; what have we to do with them?' As I look at the men who speak thus in their smug respectability and cheap patriotism, I think of those others, like Dr Gallagher [Dr Thomas Gallagher, an Irish-American sentenced to life in 1883 under the Treason and Felony Act], who exchanged a happy home and wealth and all that makes life sweet for a convict's cell in Portland, and I echo their question, 'What indeed have we to do with men like these?'

Terrorism was justified. Those jailed under the Treason and Felony Act 'did not fail. They accomplished the end they had in view. They forced the attention of England to the necessities of Ireland'.

8

Yeats's relationship with Olivia Shakespear was winding its slow way toward the purchase of a double bed. The couple had agreed to negotiate their liaison through sponsors. In mid November 1895 Shakespear and her sponsor, Valentine Fox, were to come to the rooms Yeats shared with Arthur Symons in Fountain Court to plan the next step in the affair. Suddenly, Maud Gonne crashed back into Yeats's mental life with a number of mischievously flirtatious letters.

On 3 November she wrote to ask if he had been doing 'any occult work or visions in which I have been in any way mixed within the last week?'[33] The chances were that he had, because Yeats rarely stopped either thinking about Gonne or doing occult work. She had a particular reason for asking, but, teasingly, she informed him she would tell him about it another time. He would only have to wait a week. She was coming to London on 13 November, and would be happy to dine with him that evening. In a second letter, she describes a spine-tingling encounter with the astral body of the poet. Yeats had manifested himself in a hotel drawing room where only she was aware of him; others present knew nothing. So she mentally issued him with an invitation to come to her bedroom at midnight. They could then go together wherever he liked. That night, with his presence alongside her, she had a dream of floating in the air. She wisely told Yeats to burn this clearly improper letter. Naturally he put it away in a safe place.

When Yeats came to meet Gonne on 13 November at the Charing Cross Hotel, he was 'troubled and worried', Gonne's phrase for 'sick with love'. In the hotel, she retreated from the implicit promises of her letters, and reminded him of 'the honour of our country' and his 'first duty' to be 'one of the Great Poets of the century'. He should never allow himself, she advised, to get 'tied down by lesser duties'.[34] Why was she talking about duties? He just wanted to know what she wanted from him – not his love after all? Maybe he talked again of marriage; maybe she was thinking of how she herself was tied down by her duty to Iseult.

All these manoeuvres of daring advance and ambiguous retreat by Gonne made it difficult for Yeats to move ahead in his relationship with Olivia Shakespear, but the married woman helped him along, and he made it eventually.

9

In 1896 Gonne kept up her social profile with an appearance, along with Lucien Millevoye, at Varnishing Day of the Salon in Paris (noted by *Le Gaulois*, 25 April), and in a 'fearful and wonderful' garment at the Dublin Horse Show in late August. The *Irish Times* strained to analyse her costume:[35]

> Imagine dark blue, with light green silk slashings in the sleeves, the dark blue zouave opening in front over the most bewildering arrangement of fancy blue and white silk and cream lace, which hung, *en désordre*, as if it had been flung at her and had caught on by accident. Her hair was done in thousands of little curls all over her head, which made it appear a tremendous size, and some bright pink roses rested on her hair. There was a hat besides, but that baffles description. Everyone was turning to look at her.

The main preoccupation of Maud Gonne that year, however, was the Amnesty Association. It was in fact now a front for the Irish National Alliance. On its behalf, she was in London in April, Waterford in May, London in June, Belfast in August, London again in August and Dublin in September.[36] In September John Daly was granted release from Portland Gaol, and Gonne was present first at the pier in Kingstown (now Dun Laoghaire) to meet his ship, and she was on the platform at the giant rally organized for his formal welcome back to Ireland. Daly thanked Gonne for his release:[37]

> When I was in prison a little bit of news we chanced to hear was that an Irish lady identified herself in the cause of Ireland, and I said that the country that could produce such a woman was worthy of being a nation [*cheers*].

At the time of Daly's release from prison, a group of Irish-American republicans was arrested in Boulogne. Both the Amnesty Association and the INA had been infiltrated by spies and *agents provocateurs*. Documents and dynamite were found with those arrested, which indicated that a plan was afoot for explosions in Britain, in order to protest or even prevent the Queen's Jubilee visit to Ireland, scheduled for 1897.[38] One of the plotters was Patrick J. Tynan, a member of the 'Invincibles' who had carried out the Phoenix Park murders in 1882. Whether or not Gonne was party to INA plans for these bombings, she came to the defence of the arrested men, both by giving speeches ('These men could not bear the sight of Ireland lying prostrate at the feet of England, and so they went forward, madly if you will, but still heroically, to strike a blow for their country') and by hiring Dublin barrister J.F. Taylor to defend Edward Bell, one of the men arrested.[39]

According to *A Servant of the Queen*, Gonne called upon Millevoye to employ his influence to prevent Tynan from being extradited from France. Millevoye had been outraged by the first press reports of the dynamiters, which claimed that they had conspired with nihilists to target the Czar. Such an attack on French soil could upset the Franco-Russo alliance, Millevoye's cherished foreign policy. In front of Gonne's friend Arthur Lynch, Millevoye scolded her (the condescending tone is interesting):

> Your Irish revolutionaries are even worse fools than I took them to be … You will undo all the work you have done to create sympathy for Ireland in France if you do not repudiate them at once.

Maud Gonne has herself replying with spirit:

> How you go on, my friend. And you know nothing of what you are talking about, any more than the Irish Revolutionists know about a plot to assassinate the Czar! All I ask you to do is to prevent the extradition of Tynan; hold him in jail as long as you like until the truth is proved, but don't hand him over to the English. Holland is sure to follow France's example about the men. Don't set a bad example by handing over a political prisoner. My friends, the Irish revolutionists, may have been arranging a little dynamite plot in England – more power to them … I certainly will not repudiate them; but I have come to Paris to say that I know for certain that this talk of a plot against the Czar, as far as Irishmen are concerned, is an English lie.

Out of the hearing of Lynch, she then whispered to Millevoye, 'I ask that [favour] in the name of our alliance.'[40] This is Gonne's story, and the fact is that on 13 October France refused to extradite Tynan.

10

Yeats came to Paris on or about 2 December 1896 for a six-week stay at the Hôtel Corneille, paid for by an advance from A.H. Bullen on his novel-in-progress, *The Speckled Bird*.

The story was to be partly located in Paris. Its hero was 'to see all the modern visionary sects pass before his bewildered eyes', such as the Order of the Golden Dawn, the Swedenborgians, the Brother of the New Life, the Order of the Rosy Cross and the Oneida Community.[41]

A second purpose of Yeats's visit was to work on the rituals for a new Celtic Mystical Order; one purged of all elements not Celtic, just as Sar Péladan's Catholic Order of the Rosy Cross was cleansed of all elements that were not Roman Catholic. Maud Gonne, William Sharp and the Mathers were keen to help create rituals, ceremonial garments and amulets for this new sect.

A third purpose of Yeats's Paris visit was to establish new cultural fronts for the Irish National Alliance's subversive activities. Yeats and Maud Gonne set up a branch of the Young Ireland Society in Paris, L'Association Irlandaise, and the beginnings of a 1798 Celebration Committee. The London headquarters of these organizations was 55 Chancery Lane. This was already the address of the Amnesty Association, the Gaelic Athletic Association and the National League. Dr Mark Ryan, head of the Irish National Alliance in Britain and Ireland, was an officer of all these groups. This central office certainly had the effect of making it easy for British G-men to keep an eye on the many Irish subversive organizations; they had only one building to watch.

There was, of course, one more purpose of Yeats's prolonged Parisian visit: to court Maud Gonne. He had tried his best to love Olivia Shakespear, but he could not get Gonne out of his mind. He dramatizes the regretful return of his passion for Gonne in 'He tells of a Valley full of Lovers':[42]

> I dreamed that I stood in a valley, and amid sighs,
> For happy lovers passed two by two where I stood;
> And I dreamed my lost love came stealthily out of the wood
> With her cloud-pale eyelids falling on dream-dimmed eyes:
> I cried in my dream *O women, bid the young men lay*
> *Their heads on your knees, and drown their eyes with your hair,*
> *Or remembering hers they will find no other face fair*
> *Till all the valleys of the world have been withered away.*

John Harwood points out that this lyric ascribes to Gonne a surreal witch-like power to steal the hearts of men from other women; she is both entrancing and disabling.[43] What she gave Yeats looked to him so much like love, he could not believe it was not the real thing. As he wrote in *A Speckled Bird*:[44]

> It seemed to Michael that he had never been so intimate with anybody and never could be so intimate with anybody again, for the things she told him were his innermost thoughts and feelings and certainly nobody but one who had thought and felt just such things could understand him.

Yeats wondered at times if he were not 'really mad'. At night the hero of *A Speckled Bird* goes over the words and looks of his beloved to try to come to a reckoning with the real self that lay behind them, 'but in time he saw nothing except the image he had made'.

After Yeats's departure from Paris and Gonne's lecture at a Young Ireland Society meeting in Glasgow on 28 February 1897, Maud Gonne invited the poet to dine with her when she passed through London.[45] She had, he believed, 'no thought of the mischief she was doing', but just then he had an imminent assignation with Olivia Shakespear. After his dinner with Gonne, Mrs Shakespear arrived at Yeats's rooms at 18 Woburn Buildings for the rendezvous. It was his custom – just as some drink alcohol and others light candles – to read 'much love poetry … to bring the right mood round'. On this day, however, he wrote letters while Olivia sat waiting to be made love to. She suddenly burst into tears and said, 'There is someone else in your heart.'[46] This was the end of his affair with Olivia Shakespear. He turned the event into a poem expressive of a mixture of feelings – pathetic, resentful, and pleading – addressed to Maud Gonne:[47]

> Aedh Mourns for the Loss of Love
>
> Pale brows, still hands and dim hair,
> I had a beautiful friend
> And dreamed that the old despair
> Might fade in love in the end:
> She looked in my heart one day
> And saw your image was there;
> She has gone weeping away.
>
> [1898]

11

In early March Yeats attended a meeting of the Dublin 1798 Commemoration Committee. A quarrel broke out among various personalities and factions – the Irish Republican Brotherhood, the Irish National Alliance, and Parnellites and anti-Parnellites of the Irish Parliamentary Party. The poet was helpless to reconcile them.

He wrote to Maud Gonne about the brawls, and about another thing too: someone had been attacking her reputation. Would it have been Charles

MacCarthy Teeling? Gonne asked by return of mail, 'all such things never trouble me at all'.[48] Still, she continued, was it Teeling?

In a letter now lost, Yeats told of 'the awful accusations and slanders'. Gonne claimed to find them very amusing; 'They are certainly not worth contradicting'.[49] This became her settled position with respect to moral charges, and it was a wise one. They were all deemed to be instances of a man talking scandal against a woman, a crime in the code of chivalry.

Teeling clearly did not follow that code. An elderly man with a white moustache, he was an old enemy of John O'Leary, going back to an August 1885 encounter at the memorial service for novelist Charles Kickham. On behalf of the Young Ireland Society, O'Leary had acknowledged the leadership of Parnell: Teeling wanted nothing to do with a parliamentary quest for Irish freedom, and he did not, he declared, care how much blood was shed by a physical force movement.

'What nonsense!' O'Leary replied. 'You should care.' Teeling kept up his quarrel with O'Leary until 19 February 1886, when he was expelled by vote from the Young Ireland Society.[50]

Maud Gonne herself had invited Teeling to join the 1798 Commemoration Committee (conceived to be an umbrella organization for all types of nationalism). Since Teeling's great-uncle had been an *aide-de-camp* to General Humbert, head of the French invasion forces in 1798, his presence would have been desirable at commemorative events. Generals Hoche and Humbert were the focus of Gonne's attempt to revive a Franco-Irish military alliance by means of joint commemorations of 1798. She invited Teeling to the St Patrick's Day celebration in Paris, attended by descendants of Irish exiles.

Teeling believed that Gonne was a British spy, only a single instance of widespread (and justified) paranoia about informers within the 1798 Committee. Furthermore, he gathered that she was a 'vile abandoned woman who has had more than one illegitimate child and that she is suspected by the French of giving information to the English'.[51] Teeling took up Gonne's invitation to the St Patrick's Day banquet, but only in order to tell the dignitaries present that she was a spy and adventuress. As a spokesman for Ireland, she was nothing but a fraud. While Teeling was canvassing the diners with her crimes, Gonne was delivering the banquet address on General Hoche, 'whose immortal example has animated many a patriot heart to draw once more the sword for the dear old land'.[52]

Gonne affected indifference to Teeling's malice when he was in Dublin, but in Paris he made himself an intolerable nuisance. At her request, Yeats rounded up letters from the heads of Irish nationalist organizations disavowing Teeling. Yeats wrote one himself, and they were all posted to the Comte de Cremont, secretary of the Société de St Patrice. As a result, Teeling was expelled from the Société.

This became Yeats's standing role with respect to Maud Gonne and scandal: it was his job to take her side unquestioningly, to publish attacks on the character of the accuser, and to lobby key people in her support. He had a lot of this sort of work on his hands in the next decade.

12

Apart from the Teeling mess, St Patrick's Day 1897 included a public relations success for Maud Gonne. She threw a political banquet at her apartment at 7 Avenue d'Eylau, which was decorated with silk flags, a golden harp against green on one side, and the French tricolour on the other. Sprigs of shamrock tied with green bows were at each place setting. Maud Gonne, in a white gown of *crêpe de chine*, sat at the head of the table between the Mayor of Paris and the proprietor of *La Patrie*, Millevoye's newspaper. To accompany her toast, Maud Gonne pledged: 'What Germany is to France, England is to Ireland – your Alsace is our Ireland, and we wish for her deliverance no less ardently than we desire our own,' [53] a sentence that succinctly restates the terms of the Gonne/Millevoye 'Secret Alliance'.

Another manifestation of that alliance was the launch of a newspaper supplement to *La Patrie*, under Gonne's editorial guidance. The first issue of *L'Irlande Libre* appeared in May. Contributors included James Connolly, John Daly, Edouard Drumont, Clovis Hugues, Stephen MacKenna, Lucien Millevoye, Ghénia de Sainte-Croix, and of course Gonne herself, a balance of Irish and French nationalists, most of whom were in favour of propaganda and force over debate and legal process.

In her statement of 'Our Programme' in the first number of *L'Irlande Libre*, Gonne makes three points. First, both the French and the Irish are hampered by a parliamentary form of government, which has failed to achieve *revanche* on one hand, or independence on the other. Second, the deep friendship of Ireland with France is based on a military alliance, and France remains, Ireland trusts, generous, strong and able to defy one of Europe's great powers. Third, France and Ireland are united by their common repugnance towards

Britain.[54] Gonne sets forth clearly her main foreign policy goal through these three points. She wants the French military to support an Irish insurrection against Britain. The two-year programme of 1798 commemorative activities is a means to this end.

Lucien Millevoye provided *L'Irlande Libre* with a prize piece of Anglophobia to lead off the first issue:

> Greatness is not in the pompous equipage of magnificence and sovereignty. The well done alone is great. What can one say about a reign to which Providence gave more than half a century to leave some trace of kindness and charity, of mercy on earth, and yet enters eternity bearing only … a heavy burden of iniquities? The accents of *God Save the Queen* were hollow in the three years of famine that piled up fifteen hundred thousand corpses. Queen Victoria did not come once in that time to pray at this monstrous gigantic pit of the rotting bones of a people … a race exterminated. She believes that the killing of the innocent served the interests of Britain. Her reign is splashed by hideous carnage in the face of God.

Millevoye's personalized attack on Queen Victoria was carried by Maud Gonne into her 1798 propaganda. A meeting of the 1798 Committee was scheduled for 22 June, and Gonne laid plans to turn it into a protest against celebrations in Dublin at the time of the Queen's Jubilee.

Yeats was in Sligo, and reluctant to involve himself any further. Committee meetings of fractious republicans dismayed him. His disgust with both his love affair and public affairs comes out in 'He mourns for the Change that has come upon him and his Beloved, and longs for the End of the World.' The change that has come upon him is that he has become a 'hound with one red ear', while his beloved is a 'white deer with no horns' (an asymmetry in one, a lack in the other). He calls to her, but what she hears is not a love call, just the yapping of a strange dog that wants to bring its quarry down. The poem ends with a vision of an apocalyptic pig that 'lay, grunting in the dark, and turning to his rest.'[55]

Maud Gonne continued to insist by letter that Yeats come to Dublin for these important meetings,[56] and finally he could not say no. She also roped in James Connolly to support her incendiary plans. Connolly's Irish Socialist Republican Party was tasked with organizing a coffin, banner, wagonette and some black flags for a mock burial ceremony.[57] A band rehearsed a funeral march, which would accompany a parade to the Liffey, where a coffin labelled *British Empire* was to be dumped into the river.

Charles Oldham was persuaded to allow Gonne to use the upstairs window of the Contemporary Club on Dame Street. From there lantern slides of British atrocities in Ireland could be projected – photographs of evictions, statistics on deaths in the Famine and the numbers of men in British prisons. Announcements were posted that Maud Gonne would be giving an oration in Foster Place, in front of Trinity College and next to the former site of the Irish Parliament. On 20 June, decoration day for patriot graves, Gonne went to St Michan's Church to lay a wreath on Robert Emmet's tomb, only to find the gate chained. This fact served to inspire the rhetorical climax of the speech she was preparing.

On the evening of 21 June Maud Gonne told the crowd, spread across Dame Street, that the reign of Queen Victoria had deprived Ireland of half of her children. It would be fitter for those now assembled at the foot of their old House of Parliament, the use of which England had deprived Ireland, to celebrate the anniversary of the martydrom of the heroes of 1798 than to take part in the hideous and shameless celebrations of the Queen. She ended with the story of the locked church in which Emmet was buried, then added, after a long pause, in her best quavering Sarah Bernhardt voice, 'Must the graves of our dead go undecorated because Victoria has her Jubilee?'[58] The crowd erupted. Jubilee decorations were ripped from lamp posts, mostly by boys, according to the Unionist *Irish Times*, of the 'corner boy class'.[59] 'The Boys of Wexford' was sung by gangs. Followed by the crowd, with Maud Gonne beside him on the brake, Connolly drove up Dame Street past Dublin Castle, and then down to the river, where the coffin was dumped in the river. The crowd next turned up Sackville [now O'Connell] Street. Windows were smashed. At Rutland [now Parnell] Square, W.B. Yeats accompanied Maud Gonne up the stairs to the National Club. Soon a man ran into the room shouting that the police were executing a baton charge into the crowd in Rutland Square. It was awful. The people were being bludgeoned.

When Maud Gonne rose to go out into the street, Yeats demanded to know what she meant to do. 'How do I know until I get out?' Concerned for her safety, Yeats ordered the door to be locked.[60] Down in the street, one sergeant got a scalp wound, another a gash on the chin. Two constables were bleeding from their encounters with the crowd. But after the police charge, hundreds of citizens had to be treated in Jervis Street Hospital, and two elderly people were trampled, one of whom, a woman of seventy, died of her injuries.[61]

For his part in driving the brake, James Connolly was jailed in the Bridewell. He was Maud Gonne's hero. 'You were the only man with the courage

... to carry through in spite of discouragement, even from friends.'[62] Gonne paid Connolly's fine, then visited the family dwelling, arriving with her Great Dane, Dagda. Mrs Connolly was just then bathing her baby daughter Johanna Mary, watched by Ida Connolly, then five years old. Mother and daughters were astonished by this apparition of Parisian beauty with her preposterously large dog. 'Let me hold the dear little infant. I've never held one so small,' Gonne lied. She picked up Johanna, though she was covered in baby powder. Ina Connolly remembered Gonne's hands as being enormous.[63]

For Maud Gonne, the Queen's Jubilee was a triumph; for Yeats, it was a disaster. He could see that she had been magnificent. She had a genius for street theatre, for making other people do her bidding, and for creating live performances that moved the masses. Reaching for a comparison, he wrote that she was like the Pope entering St Peter's Square, so great was the charisma of her person. This praise, however, does not do justice to her *coup de théâtre*, such as the *mise en scène* with the coffin of the British Empire. Like James Connolly, Maud Gonne had a particular talent for (in Anna Magny's phrase) *actions symboliques au caractère sensationnel*.

In the eyes of Maud Gonne, however, Yeats had shown himself to be the next thing to a coward. In her table of values, nothing stood higher than courage, nothing lower than cowardice. A month later, she gave Yeats the bad news:[64]

> Our friendship must indeed be strong for me not to hate you, for you made me do the most cowardly thing I have ever done in my life ... You have a higher work to do – With me it is different. I was born to be in the midst of a crowd ... Everyone who stayed in the Club & did not go out to the rescue of the people who were batoned by the police ought to feel ashamed ...

That a woman died in the riot she organized, Gonne claimed, was not her fault, but Yeats's, because he had prevented her from going out into the street where she could have taken control of the situation:

> Do you know that to be a coward for those we love is only a degree less bad than to be a coward for oneself? The latter I know well you are not, the former you know well you are. It is therefore impossible for us ever to do any work together where there is likely to be excitement or physical danger & therefore now let us never allude to this stupid subject again.

Yeats, it seemed, was finished as a suitor. Maud Gonne had a sexual preference for a bold, even a foolhardy, man. Bringing the word 'coward' into relation with Yeats, and then shutting down all further conversation – 'let us never allude to this stupid subject again' – was deadly. These were 'the worst months of my life', Yeats later wrote, and surely getting this letter from Maud Gonne was his lowest moment in all those distressing months.[65]

He was left like Helmer at the end of *A Doll's House*, standing in the emptiness after the door has slammed.

VIII

MILLENARIAN EXALTATIONS

I n July 1897 Yeats returned from Dublin to Tillyra, the 'Big House' of Edward Martyn near Loughrea. Lady Augusta Gregory found him there. He was 'white, haggard, voiceless, fresh from the Jubilee riots, which he had been in the thick of, having been led into them as escort to Miss Gonne – However he had by main force & lock & key kept her from reaching the mob when they came into collision with the police.'[1]

Lady Gregory invited the poet back to Coole for later in July, then cared for him through the summer. Yeats drafted a weepy Petrarchan lyric.[2]

Subject For Lyric

O my beloved you only are
   not moved by my songs
Which you only understand
You only know that it is
   of you I sing when I tell
   of the swan on the water
   or the eagle in the heavens
   or the faun in the wood.
Others weep but your eyes
   are dry

II

O my beloved. How happy
I was that day when you
came here from the
railway, and set your hair
aright in my looking glass
and then sat with me at
my table, and lay resting
in my big chair. I am
like the children o my
beloved and I play
with images of the life
you will not give to me o
my cruel one.

Fortunately, he did not soon send her a poem arising from these pitiful, nostalgic jottings; instead, he sent her a lyric, which lightly satirized her celebrity while calling upon her nobler instincts not to forsake an old friend:[3]

Old Friends

Though you are in your shining days,
Voices among the crowd
And your new friends busy with your praise,
Be not unkind or proud,
But think about old friends the most:
Time's bitter flood will rise,
Your beauty perish and be lost
For all eyes but these eyes.

On 6 September 1897 Gonne replied a little severely that she was 'not in the least inclined to forget old friends'. Moreover, she 'had a horror of all the little things & materialities of life'. She was not, in other words, a self-infatuated celebrity.

In her subsequent letters, she grew 'kind and friendly', Yeats reported to Lady Gregory, 'but whether more than that I cannot tell'.[4] In an October letter Maud Gonne put him out of all doubt: she told him plainly that she did not like him to 'give me so much place in your life'.[5] She would be his friend and co-worker, but that was all. For the immediate future, she was sailing for America on 17 October 1897, on a fundraising tour organized by the Irish National Alliance.

2

For three months Maud Gonne crossed the United States, from New York to Chicago, through St Louis, Missouri and Omaha, Nebraska, all the way to Cripple Creek, Colorado. During these months, the Dreyfus *case* was turning into the Dreyfus *affair* in France. The initiating events had occurred in 1894: in July 1894 Major Esterhazy began to sell French military secrets to the German military attaché; in September 1894 the French Intelligence Service recovered a memorandum, or *bordereau*, from the wastebasket of the German attaché. This document was evidence that there was a French traitor at work, an artillery officer and member of the General Staff. In October 1894 Captain Alfred Dreyfus, an Alsatian Jew with a slightly German accent, was mistakenly identified as the spy. By the end of that month, his name was leaked to the anti-Semitic press, in particular to Edouard Drumont, editor of the *Libre Parole*, and Lucien Millevoye, who debated between them not Dreyfus's innocence or guilt, but only the best form of capital punishment for the Jewish rat. In December 1894 Dreyfus was court-martialled.

The evidence against Captain Alfred Dreyfus was circumstantial. There was a supposed similarity of handwriting; Dreyfus also had the means and opportunity. Jewishness stood in for the motive. Because the case against him was obviously a weak one, it was bolstered by a 'secret dossier' given to the military judges and not to Dreyfus's defence attorney. Dreyfus was duly found guilty, and exiled to Devil's Island off the coast of French Guiana. Case closed.

The conduct of those who prosecuted Dreyfus became more heinous in 1896, when to the original false accusation and prejudiced court proceedings, a cover-up was added. In March of that year the German attaché once again carelessly left a torn-up letter in his wastepaper basket, which was again passed on to French intelligence, now headed by Colonel George Picquart. He had not been party to the original proceedings against Dreyfus. This time the document – an express letter called a *petit bleu* – was signed, and in exactly the same handwriting as the *bordereau*. Since Dreyfus, confined on Devil's Island, could not have written both, he could not have written either. Picquart learned that the author of the letter was Major Esterhazy, a French officer who had had the same means and opportunity that Dreyfus had had, and more motive – he was badly in debt.

In August and September of 1896 Colonel Picquart tried to explain to the General Staff that a mistake had been made about who was spying for Germany. Dreyfus was innocent, and the guilty man – Major Esterhazy – was not only at large, but still betraying his country. The General Staff, however, showed no desire at all to admit that mistakes had been made. The generals of the French army assumed it was a thing so obvious as to be unquestionable that the Jew should be left to die on Devil's Island, and Esterhazy quietly deprived of the means to continue to harm the nation. The thing to avoid at all cost, Picquart was told, was the bringing of the army into disrepute.

At that instant Picquart – in an instinctive moral action, one of the most consequential in modern European history – perceived that this decision by the generals was infamous. Before walking out of the meeting, he declared that he would not keep one particular secret: Alfred Dreyfus was innocent.

Adding more blocks to a tower of injustice, the General Staff removed Picquart from the intelligence services and sent him off to the first of many provincial postings. He wound up in farthest reaches of Algeria, ordered to undertake a military mission so ill-advised and dangerous that it was obviously designed to get him killed in action.

The next escalation of the tower of blocks involved the addition of a piece of false evidence. Having realized that, should Picquart blow the whistle, the original case against Dreyfus would not bear scrutiny, the generals tipped off newspapers in September 1896 that the case was stronger than it appeared to be: there had been a secret dossier that included a letter mentioning *this scoundrel Dreyfus*. No such letter mentioning Dreyfus by name in fact existed, but there *was* a secret dossier. So the Dreyfus family began to demand, with good reason, that if a secret dossier existed, it be made public, and a new trial be held on the basis of the full disclosure of evidence. In anticipation of a public trial, Captain Henry in the intelligence department forged a document to strengthen the case against a man the General Staff now knew for a fact to be innocent. The forged document would become known, like the *petit bleu* and the *bordereau*, by its own pet name: the *faux Henry*. The whole tower of blocks rested on these three little pieces of paper, none of which ever actually came from the hand of Dreyfus.

The argument for a retrial of Dreyfus was carried forward by Alfred's wife and his brother Mathieu Dreyfus. They were prepared to sink the whole of the sizeable family fortune into his exoneration, but apart from the admission that a dossier had been withheld from the defence, they had little fresh evidence.

Then, in the summer of 1897, while Maud Gonne was organizing a Dublin riot against the Queen's Jubilee, Colonel Picquart obtained leave to come to Paris. He was by then afraid for his life. He went to his school friend and lawyer, Louis Leblois, and told him what he knew, but swore Leblois to silence, unless the colonel happened suddenly to come to a bad end. Leblois gave his promise.

Two weeks later, he broke the promise. He told the vice-president of the Senate, Auguste Scheurer-Kestner, a man well known for his probity, that an innocent man had been sentenced to Devil's Island, and the real traitor was still at large.

Scheurer-Kestner, once he had convinced himself of the truth of Picquart's claim, began to hold conversations with Dreyfus's family, with the General Staff of the army and even with the President of France, Felix Faure. On the left, Scheurer-Kestner's revelations were welcomed; on the right, they met a wall of resistance. Meanwhile, the General Staff secretly began to arrange for the protection of the real traitor, Major Esterhazy, warning him that he might publicly be named as a suspect in the original case of espionage, but that people in high places would protect him; he should just lie low.

Enraged and terrified, Esterhazy went in search of help. The first place he went was to the offices of *La Patrie*, Lucien Millevoye's right-wing paper.[6] He needed someone to be his spokesman.

3

On 8 and 10 November Louis Leblois, Picquart's lawyer, called on Émile Zola. Leblois laid the truth before the great novelist and asked him to speak out in the name of justice.[7] Jewish writers and intellectuals like Léon Blum, Daniel Halévy and Marcel Proust went around with a petition on behalf of Dreyfus.

Léon Blum, much later to be Prime Minister of France, called upon Maurice Barrès,[8] a particular intellectual hero of Blum's generation. Barrès was smart, lycée-educated, ironic and egotistical. 'He only talked of himself,' one young writer recalled, 'but himself was ourselves.'[9] That is, for the young, he was 'one of us'. Yet Barrès told Blum, a Jew, that he would have to keep faith with his old friends, men like Rochefort and Millevoye, anti-Semites. In other words, for Barrès, a Jew could never be 'one of us'. The slogan of Barrès as a parliamentary deputy was 'France for the French'. After this meeting with Blum, Barrès brought Léon Daudet, the anti-semite son of novelist Alphonse Daudet, to visit the editor of *Le Figaro*. They asked this editor, in the name of 'neutrality', to refuse to publish anything by anyone who questioned Dreyfus's guilt and by Zola in particular.[10]

The thinking of Maurice Barrès about the Dreyfus case was for much of this period the dominant thinking of both the press and the parliament. Barrès agreed with the formula worked out by Paul Déroulède: 'It is highly improbable that Dreyfus is innocent, and it is absolutely certain that France herself is innocent.' In the affair, Dreyfus figured, Barrès explained, not so much as a man as a symbolic instrument. One side was using him as a tool to defend the Jews, to attack the army, and to ruin the Roman Catholic Church. The Dreyfusards did not, in Barrès's view, really care about this little Jew on Devil's Island. They simply wanted to 'remake France in the image of their own prejudices'. The other side, which Barrès represented, wanted instead to 'preserve France', and for that, an army undisturbed by criticism was required. Besides, it was very wrong to complain about anti-Semitism 'when the enormous power of the Jewish race had become obvious, a power which threatened France with a total change in her nature.'

Actually, Barrès argued, as far as true guilt or innocence was concerned, Kant was wrong. (It was typical of Barrès to bring Kant or another philosopher into the midst of a political speech.) It was silly to say, he explained, that [11]

> 'I must *always* act in such a way that my action could be a *universal rule*.' Not so, gentlemen! Leave aside those pretentious words *always* and *universal* and then you are true Frenchmen. Make it your business to act according to the interests of France at this time.

In other words, there was no morality. There was only nationalism.

4

Once Zola brought his weighty mind to bear on the Dreyfus case, he took a very different line from Barrès. For him, there was something called truth, and it was an absolute. It marched. At the end of the day, it triumphed. It found the criminals in their shadowy corners. It went about naked, and stripped others of their coverings. 'Truth is on the march' became the anthem of his campaign for Dreyfus's exoneration. It would be almost literally the marching song of Zola's followers.

As early as 5 December 1897, less than a month after his conversations with Louis Leblois, Zola was writing not just that Dreyfus was innocent, but that[12]

> ... this whole lamentable Dreyfus affair is the work of anti-Semitism. It and it alone made the miscarriage of justice possible; it and it alone is driving the public to hysteria; it and it alone is preventing the miscarriage from being quietly, nobly acknowledged, in the interests of this country's health and good name.

The health and good name of the country were being run down, Zola declared, by men with newspapers, people like Edouard Drumont in *Libre Parole* and Lucien Millevoye in *La Patrie*, [13]

> ... a whole foul swathe of the press that I cannot read without my heart bursting with indignation. [It] has been convincing the public that a syndicate of Jews, paying fantastic bribes to corrupt decent men, was bent on carrying out a most loathsome plot. Their first aim was to save the traitor and replace him with an innocent man; then it was the Army itself that would be dishonoured and France that would be sold to the enemy, as it was in 1870. I will spare you the details, the flights of fancy, concerning this sordid machination.

In one way, Barrès was correct. Zola and the Dreyfusards were making the Dreyfus affair into a symbol of the conflict between one side and the other in French society, a conflict that had organically developed ever since the French Revolution. From late November 1897 to January 1898, as Zola turned out one treatise after another, he addressed himself not just to the authorities involved in the original case against Alfred Dreyfus, but to France as a whole. He scolded the people like a father scolds a child. 'Do you know, France, where you are headed?' he wrote on 5 January 1898. To the past, to the Church, to military dictatorship. That is where anti-Semitism leads. Then, finally, on 13 January 1898 came the issue of Clémenceau's newspaper *L'Aurora* with the headline 'J'ACCUSE!' – perhaps the greatest piece of polemical journalism ever written, and with the greatest instant sales.

This was the apotheosis of the writer in politics. Zola was not the only writer involved, and all those involved were not on the side of Dreyfus. Anatole France, Marcel Proust and Octave Mirbeau stuck their necks out as Dreyfusards. But Maurice Barrès, Léon Daudet, Edouard Dujardin and Paul Bourget were all vehement anti-Dreyfusards. Of the fifty-five daily newspapers in France, in January 1898 forty-eight of them were anti-Dreyfusard.[14] The response of the General Staff to 'J'ACCUSE!' was to charge Zola with libel.

5

In the first week of January 1898 Maud Gonne disembarked from New York not in France but at Queenstown, County Cork, although she had been away from Millevoye and her daughter Iseult for three months. She gave speeches at French Hill in Cork and at Castlebar in County Mayo on the theme of the 1798 Rebellion.[15] On 23 January she was in London working with Yeats on the rituals for the Celtic Mystical Order, while still trying to make him accept a situation in which she would give him 'a perfect friendship and nothing else'.[16] Not until February did she make it back to Paris, where the trial of Zola was the talk of the town.

Lucien Millevoye may have been too busy to miss her during her absence in America. He wrote to a friend on 18 January that he was 'at the moment completely absorbed in the Dreyfus affair'.[17] The trial of Zola ran from 7 to 23 February. At a meeting of socialist workers in Suresnes in Paris on 15 February, Millevoye announced that he had acquired sensational new proof of Dreyfus's guilt. He would not be handing over the document at the meeting, but he had seen it. To prevent a war in Europe, it had to be kept quiet. He himself had been brought to the secret room where the dossier was held. Millevoye said that on fine bonded paper was handwritten the following note: 'Make sure that this *canaille* Dreyfus sends the pieces he promised earlier. Signed ... William.'

In other words, William II, Emperor of Prussia, was the one running the spy network in Paris. The army had physical evidence of his involvement. When Millevoye looked up to gauge the effect of his bombshell on his audience, he saw a roomful of working men shaking with laughter. For five long minutes, he was drowned in ridicule.[18]

During the trial, Lucien Millevoye and his fellow leader of the Ligue anti-sémitique, Jules Guérin, hired bands of booted toughs, most of them butchers, to come to the courthouse. 'Their eyes full of threats and their fists clenched,'[19] they menaced Zola, his legal team, and his supporters. They chanted 'Long Live France' and 'Down with the Jews'. The mood of the scene outside the courtroom after Zola was declared guilty on 23 February 1898 is captured by a reporter for *La Libre Parole*: [20]

> I saw men who in ordinary life were incapable of cowardice shout 'Coward!' to this feeble little man, who was protected only by a handful of friends; they were ready to spit in Zola's face, so great was their hatred for Dreyfus.
>
> I was not better than them; I was one of them, yelling from the bottom of our lungs like dogs, baying at the moon, or screaming for death itself: 'Down with Zola! Down with the Jews!' If the path from the stairway to the carriage had been just a little longer, it is by no means certain that Emile Zola would have returned home alive on that night ...
>
> Not for a moment did the thought cross my mind that this man who had endured all these affronts had suffered so long for a cause that he thought was just. Believe me, that thought never occurred to me. In *Libre Parole* I described the scene just because I thought it was both comforting and beautiful.

6

While Maud Gonne was an anti-Dreyfusard, she did not become caught up in the coils of the trial of Zola. In February 1898 she was organizing a plan of action in response to news that famine conditions were reoccurring in the Erris peninsula, Co. Mayo. As if playing a scene out of *The Countess Cathleen*, Gonne sold her jewels with a view to giving money to starving tenants.[21] She worked with James Connolly on drafting a defence of communal property, printed as a pamphlet entitled *The Right to Life and the Rights of Property*. It explained with unconditional brevity that theft of the landlord's sheep and cattle in times of famine was not a sin, citing popes and saints in support of this view.

When Yeats told Lady Gregory about this enterprise, Gregory, a landlord herself, was shocked. She tried to persuade Yeats to stop Gonne:[22]

> We who are above the people in means & education, ought, if it were a real famine, to be ready to share all we have with them, but that even supposing starvation was before them it wd be for us to teach them to die with courage [rather] than to live by robbery – Miss Gonne would, if she suffered by imprisonment also gain by it the notoriety she wants – but the poor people sent to prison would have no such consolation – In all the crimes that have been condoned in Ireland, sheep stealing has been held in horror by the people, & it wd be a terrible responsibility to blunt their moral sensitiveness by leading them to it.

This *noblesse oblige* argument stunned Yeats, so far removed was its point of view from that of Maud Gonne, yet so sensible and so grand.

The 5 March 1898 issue of the *Freeman's Journal* reported Maud Gonne's speech to a large crowd in Belmullet. She attacked Britain for its barbarous system of relief: workhouses, the construction of famine roads going nowhere, relief works far removed from those in need, and the hopelessly slow system of distribution of food to the provinces.[23] British aid was no help at all. Spotting a land grabber and a grazier in the audience, she condemned him from the stage as an enemy of the people.[24] With a number of priests in support, Gonne preached her doctrine that in circumstances of dire need, the rights of property were suspended; the people should help themselves to the landlords' flocks.

The *Irish Daily Independent* published Maud Gonne's 'Famine in the West' on 10 March, a good example of her fully committed style of eyewitness reporting.[25] She began with a distinction between different types of tears:

> I believe it to be our duty to drown the sobs of hopeless suffering and pain in the wild, fierce ones of hope, anger, and defiance.

When I saw tears come into the eyes of the men as they heard their children cry for food; when I saw the half-naked little ones and heard their mothers answer the priest's questions why they were not at school, 'they have no clothes,' when I saw them turning, in vain, the wet, boggy mould off their empty potato ridges down on the seashore, and above on the opposite side of the road saw the fat cattle grazing peacefully on the good pasture lands, from which human beings had been driven; when I saw the mute despair on the faces of men and women, I said, 'I will be the voice of these helpless victims of England's policy, I will speak for them before the world, even if it be but to call down the execration of mankind upon England's civilization and England's Government, which is responsible for all this ruin and misery.'

On 13 March 12,000 people came to hear Gonne speak in Ballina. Men removed the horse from the wagon on which she sat, and pulled it themselves through streets lit up by burning tar barrels. Famine conditions could be good conditions for rebellion.

Gonne did not just make speeches and write articles in Mayo. She worked with village women to set up an organization to distribute boiled oatmeal and condensed milk to the hungry. To the local men she proposed the construction of a factory to dry fish as a protection against future crop failures. Working with local committees, she drew up a list of reasonable demands to present to government:

1. Sixpence a day for famine work to be increased to 1 shilling

2. No woman to work if a man could be gotten

3. 1s. 6d. a week extra lodging money to anyone who had to walk more than one mile to relief works

4. Free seed potatoes immediately

5. Preparation of the ground and sowing seed to be paid like relief work a rate of a shilling/day.

Maud Gonne was hugely popular in the west of Ireland and not just because she was tall, beautiful and eloquent. She also had a gift for good works.

7

In the midst of her work all through March 1898 as an outside agitator in Mayo and Sligo, Maud Gonne wrote Yeats another provocative letter. It falls into the genre of a report on a paranormal experience, but the obvious subtext is an erotic fantasy:[26]

> Mar 16, Tubercurry
> My dear Friend,
>
> At 7 driving across Gap by Glen Ersk lake into your beautiful county of Sligo. I thought I would get you to come & show it to me, so I *went* to you & putting my hands on your shoulder asked you to come with me. We stood by that beautiful lake amid the twilight shadows, then you were on the car beside me driving among the mountains. Here we were interrupted by my travelling companion. James Daly had been talking to me of matters which required my attention. Some half hour or so later it had grown almost dark, I looked for you but you were gone so I went again to *fetch you* but this time you were eating your dinner with friends so I did not even try to attract your attention.
>
> All this sounds slightly mad, but you will not think it so, & it is not at all – now please tell me exactly and truthfully were you conscious of any of this or not? Also what you were doing at 7 o'clock this evening, or at 7.30 or 8 o'clock. Write to me at Ballina.

Her invitation to reply in kind opens the way to join in a game of mutual intimacies. Upon her return from the west to Dublin, Gonne and Yeats combined their powers in 'seeing visions' together. The initiates would engage in 'deliberate reverie',[27] reporting their mental journeys afterwards. The participants lit upon similarities in their oneiric experiences as proof of the reality of the places and characters they had mentally visited.

It is surprising that this 'occult work' should have proceeded side by side with Gonne's Mayo relief work, the 1798 Centenary committee work of Yeats and Gonne and the involvement of both in the subversive activities of the Irish National Alliance. Yeats, however, as Terence Brown observes, saw these labours as ultimately one. To him, Gonne seemed to have made herself into 'an image possessed of magical powers that could sway the multitude and embody its unified mind',[28] and Gonne may have thought so too. The magic they made together was both erotic and political. They were to act symbolically as the male and female leadership principles in a resurgent Celtic nation.

In April Maud Gonne returned to Paris to recuperate from bronchitis, and Yeats followed her. He stayed with the Mathers in their two-storey house in Auteuil in the 16th arrondissement. The main room was done up in an Egyptian manner, with an altar to the god Thoth,[29] but MacGregor Mathers's task when Yeats was there was to compose rituals for the new Celtic Order. He excelled in the fresh invention of ancient rituals. Yeats himself was adept at telling fortunes with a pack of Tarot cards. On 7 May 1898 Maud Gonne asked him to come to her apartment at 7 Avenue d'Eylau and read the future for her sister, Kathleen Gonne Pilcher.

This period of mutual occult phantasy may have been when Maud Gonne entered into a 'spiritual marriage' with Yeats, though that event is often dated by scholars to the end of 1898. What did such a marriage contract its parties to do, and not to do? This marriage did not imply communal property or a vow on the part of the woman to obey the man. They acknowledged love for one another; they saw their futures as one future; they committed themselves to a friendship beyond the ordinary.

Yeats's understanding was that the spiritual marriage meant that wedlock with another was impossible. In so far as the marriage was 'spiritual', it would not be a marriage in the flesh – this was Gonne's idea. The spiritual marriage was monogamous yet celibate. As time went on, it became clear that, in the spiritual marriage, Maud Gonne permitted and indeed encouraged a frank indulgence in mutual sexual phantasy.

Meeting in Dublin in June for 1798 commemorative events, Gonne and Yeats made plans to go together to Newgrange in County Meath, a centre of Neolithic culture in Ireland, in order to collect talismans for use in the rituals of the Celtic Mystical Order. Before the two could get away together, however, when Maud Gonne was on her way to the unveiling of a plaque to a 1798 rebel, the horse drawing her carriage fell, and she was thrown to the road, hitting her head and breaking her arm. Yeats gave his beloved every kindness as she lay in her room on Nassau Street. He appears to have undertaken the quest for talismans on his own, for after leaving Gonne in the care of Sarah Purser, he waited in London to give her some magical amulets he had acquired.

En route from Dublin to London, Maud Gonne read two poems by Yeats in the May issue of *The Dome*. The title of the first, 'He thinks of those who have Spoken Evil of his Beloved', alludes to MacCarthy Teeling's attacks on her in Paris, as well as those by F. Hugh O'Donnell in Dublin and London, and various members of Clan na nGaedheal in America:

> Half close your eyelids, loosen your hair,
> And dream about the great and their pride;

> They have spoken against you everywhere,
> But weigh this song with the great and their pride;
> I made it out of a mouthful of air,
> Their children's children shall say they have lied.

If the first line sounds like a masterful lover issuing commands to his pliant mistress, the second reveals that the speaker is not going to make love to the woman after all; he is a hypnotist at work. Moving along, the speaker takes a third role, the confident press agent to eternity. Poems like this one, he promises, will clear her name of passing scandal and make her famous for ever. The last line may distantly hint at the metaphysical children that will be born of the union of the poet and his muse, all of them adoring their mother.

Norman Jeffares may be right in reading the second Yeats poem in the May issue of *The Dome*, 'He hears the Cry of the Sedge', as a lyric solemnization of the spiritual marriage:[30]

> I wander by the edge
> Of this desolate lake
> Where wind cries in the sedge:
> Until the axle break
> That keeps the stars in their round,
> And hands hurl in the deep
> The banners of East and West,
> And the girdle of light is unbound,
> Your breast will not lie by the breast
> Of your beloved in sleep.

Admittedly, this poem does not at first look like a lyric marriage vow. It is a poem of loss and emptiness ('wander', 'desolate'); the speaker does not plight his troth, just the reverse: he is cursed by a wind among the reeds with the absolute hopelessness of his sexual desire ever achieving fulfilment. Yet that surrender of hope for his desire to be satisfied may have appealed to Maud Gonne as a beautiful offering to her; it is just what she has been asking for. On her journey from Dublin to London, Maud Gonne 'read over & over again your poem until I didn't need the book to read it, it is so beautiful.'[31] Which of the two poems from *The Dome* she found so beautiful, she does not say – the one in which he says he will fight her enemies and make her famous, or the one in which he says he finally accepts that he will never have sex with her as long as this world shall last.

Gonne writes that in order to thank him for all his kindness in Dublin, and for the poems, she 'went' to Yeats the previous night, but he may not have understood, she supposes, the purpose of her apparition in his sleep. The sexual possession he could never have in life, she implies, he could enjoy in his dreams with her permission and psychic participation.

After Maud Gonne left London for Aix-les-Bains, Yeats asked by letter if she had consciously paid him an astral visit on Monday morning, 4 July. In his 'Visions Notebook', Yeats noted that, while he was in a 'curious trance like state, before fully waking in the morning ... she stood by me & seemed to dissolve as I woke. She seemed anxious to give me some good message.'[32] Gonne replied that she 'did not consciously go to see you on Monday but I probably did so *unconsciously* as I was thinking of you, & I find one's *thoughts* often *really* carry one to places & people'. At that 'hour – 7 to 8 AM – having got up at six' in her hotel, Gonne had a letter from Yeats before her and was thinking of writing him, but 'felt too tired'. It was in that drowsiness she must have come to him while he lay not yet fully awake in his own bed in Woburn Buildings, London.

In September (she had joined him in person during August for the culmination of the 1798 commemorations) Maud Gonne sent Yeats a 'care package' with instructions for the use of the contents:

> 1st a little box of earth from NEW GRANGE from the very centre of that wonderful Irish pyramid
>
> 2nd a white bottle (it ought to be white & gold) containing water from the golden Boyne I got it in the morning sunlight & the river shone like gold.
>
> 3rd the bottle you [saw?] containing water from a wonderful holy well at Ballina where I *saw* the FISH. By it was buried the wife of King Dathai, they have just destroyed her grave to put her in the graveyard it was so wicked & the man who did it got an attack after & has lost all his strength.
>
> That grey water seems to me to symbolize the *West*, & the cloudy hosts of the Sidhe, while the Boyne water will tell you I think of more material things of Ireland. Try some experiments with them. I am doing so & I will write & tell you more when I have time. Touch your lips & ears & breast before sleeping & I think they will give you dreams.

Along with the instructions regarding the female talismans (the two bottles and the little box), the accompanying letter thanks Yeats for the 'most beautiful' poem he had sent, 'Mongan thinks of his past Greatness':[33]

I have drunk ale from the Country of the Young
And weep because I know all things now.
I have been a hazel tree & they hung
The Pilot Star and the Crooked Plough
Among my leaves in times out of mind.
I became a rush that horses tread:
I became a man, a hater of the wind,
Knowing one, out of all things, alone, that his head
Would not lie on the breast or his lips on the hair
Of the woman that he loves, until he dies;
Although the rushes and the fowl of the air
Cry of his love with their pitiful cries.

Apart from giving voice to an ancient Celtic wizard who lived many lives, this poem restates the key term of the 'spiritual marriage': as long as they both shall live, he and the woman he loves shall never be of one flesh. The assertion is fervently made, but also treated as a pitiful fact: the young drinking their ale, the birds in the sky, even the leaves on the trees, enjoy sexual generation; he alone cannot feel what they all can feel, and this fact makes the whole living world sad. Yet the choice to be celibate separates the man from all other things in nature, and may be the source of his powers as a wizard. He is possessed of what he does not possess. To quote the French religious phenomenologist Jean-Luc Marion:

> Nothing belongs to me more than that which I desire, for *that* is what I lack; that which I lack defines me more intimately than all the things that I possess which remain exterior to me while what I lack inhabits me; such that I can exchange what I possess, but not the lack that possesses my heart.[34]

The combination of Yeats's poem and Maud Gonne's relief package is striking. In *Memoirs*, Yeats candidly reflected on the bodily anguish he experienced after he had broken off his affair with Olivia Shakespear for the sake of Maud Gonne, and his helpless sense of shame over his return to the habit of masturbation:[35]

> It was a time of great personal strain and sorrow. Since my mistress had left me, no other woman had come into my life, and for nearly seven years, none did. I was tortured by sexual desire and disappointed love. Often as I walked in the woods at Coole it would have been a relief to have screamed aloud. [CANCELLED: It was the most miserable time of my life.] When desire became an unendurable

torture, I would masturbate, and that, no matter how moderate I was, would make me ill. It never occurred to me to seek another love.

By giving Yeats instructions about how he should touch himself at night with her talismans, Maud Gonne participates knowingly, albeit discreetly, in these onanistic practices.

The combination of the occult with varieties of sexual experimentation was common near the end of the millennium. MacGregor and Moina Mathers had a white marriage – 'we have nothing whatever to do with any sexual connection – we have both kept perfectly clean.' Yet in 1895 both defended Dr Edward Berridge when he introduced 'Karezza' into the practices of the Order of the Golden Dawn. This was a trance state achieved by breath control during Tantric sexual intercourse; the participants, sitting face to face, the man inside the woman, remained strictly still, never permitting even the slightest movement that would lead to emission. Berridge and MacGregor Mathers were both interested in the possibility of sexual intercourse by elite adepts with 'Elementals', otherworldly beings, for the purpose of procreation; Mathers had written a paper on the subject. Successful intercourse with immortals might sometimes require a female facilitator of a mortal kind, as a symbolic stand-in. Annie Horniman was outraged by this carry-on in the Isis Urania Temple, London, but Moina Mathers told her she had not achieved a high enough grade in the hierarchy of the Golden Dawn to understand fully 'the composition of the human being', and therefore had no right to discuss these arcane questions.[36] Horniman was such a bad sport about Dr Berridge, she had to be expelled from the Order of the Golden Dawn.

Intercourse with angels and devils, succubi and incubi, is a subject of learned discourses in Huysmans' *Là-Bas* (1891):[37]

> 'I want to ask you,' said Des Hermies, 'does a woman receive the visit of the incubus while she is asleep or while she is awake?'
> 'A distinction must be made. If the woman is not the victim of a spell, if she voluntarily consorts with the impure spirit, she is always awake when the carnal act takes place. If, on the other hand, the woman is the victim of sorcery, the sin is committed either while she is asleep or while she is awake, but in the latter case she is in a cataleptic state which prevents her from defending herself. The most powerful of present-day exorcists, the man who has gone most thoroughly into this matter, one Johannès, Doctor of Theology, told me that he had saved nuns who had been ridden without respite for two, three, even four days by incubi!'
> 'I know that priest,' remarked Des Hermies. 'And the act is consummated in the same manner as the normal human act?'

'Yes and no. Here the dirtiness of the details makes me hesitate,' said Gévingey, becoming slightly red. 'What I can tell you is more than strange. Know, then, that the organ of the incubus is bifurcated and at the same time penetrates both vases. Formerly it extended, and while one branch of the fork acted in the licit channels, the other at the same time reached up to the lower part of the face. You may imagine, gentlemen, how life must be shortened by operations which are multiplied through all the senses.'

In the summer of 1898 the mad, young, polymorphous perverse Aleister Crowley (an admirer at the time of Yeats's poetry) published his first collection of verse, aptly entitled *White Stains*. Many of the other peers of Yeats and Gonne in Paris and London were also venturing into new sexual territories. The nineties entertained varieties of conjugality, unnatural, natural and supernatural; monogamous and polygamous; with oneself, another, or immaterial beings; for the sake of procreation, pleasure or enlightenment. The perverse was by some seen as both glamorous and spiritual. Symboliste paintings and drawings by Jan Toorop, Fernand Khnopff, Félicien Rops, Gustave Moreau (a Gonne favourite), and Yeats's friend Althea Gyles illustrated the many possibilities. These artists mingled occult iconography, nude figures of dreamily attractive men and women and configurations suggestive of obsession or trance to produce something apparently pornographic but ostensibly profound.

Maud Gonne may not have been giving Yeats what, as a man, he hoped to get from a woman (total acceptance, mutual surrender), but she was leading him far from well-travelled paths, while torturing his sensibility in ways that were productive of the exhausted and disturbed lyricism of *The Wind Among the Reeds*.

8

After arriving in Aix-les-Bains in early July 1898 and before going to Dublin in August for the laying of the foundation stone for the Wolfe Tone Memorial, Maud Gonne prepared an issue of *L'Irlande Libre* on the 1798 centenary. It included articles from Marguerite Durand's feminist *La Fronde*, Drumont's anti-semitic *La Libre Parole*, and Millevoye's right-revolutionary *La Patrie*. The issue also included a piece on socialism in Ireland by James Connolly. Pierre Ranger argues that Maud Gonne integrated the socialism of Connolly with the Caesarism of her Paris friends by means of her 'unfailing anti-Semitism'.[38]

Certainly, she took on the colour of French anti-Semitism, and never learned to see it as a stain. Yet what brought these otherwise discordant contributors within the same covers of *L'Irlande Libre* in August 1898 was probably the simple fact that Maud Gonne believed the friends could be of use to her.

Three French delegates and several friends were brought along by Maud Gonne for support in the various 1798 centenary events. Ghénia de Sainte-Croix, the revolutionary Amilcare Cipriani and two French journalists (not including Millevoye) were with her both in Dublin and Mayo. When their ship arrived in Kingstown on 14 August 1898, Yeats, Maud Gonne and her Paris retinue were greeted by a large crowd. 'The horses were taken from the carriage and we all addressed the mob, even Cipriani, who spoke in French,' Yeats wrote to Lady Gregory.[39] Wolfe Tone Day was 15 August, and the crowds along Sackville (now O'Connell) Street in Dublin were huge, as the brakes carrying the dignitaries from Rutland Square by way of places of interest in Wolfe Tone's life made their way to St Stephen's Green, where Yeats and John O'Leary gave orations from a platform. It was all very fine, but after so many months' work, Maud Gonne herself was disappointed. Only a spontaneous revolution would have been equal to her hopes.

A week later she was in Ballina to lay the foundation stone for General Humbert's monument. Cipriani spoke in French, Willie Rooney in Irish and Maud Gonne gave a speech in English of 'hatred and contempt for England'.[40] A police report concluded that the event was far less troublesome than the authorities had feared, but the police failed to realize the significance of the fact that Dr Mark Ryan and Solomon Gillingham were among Gonne's party.[41] Ryan was the head of the Irish National Alliance, while Gillingham, a Irish colonial with a profitable bakery in Pretoria, was canvassing for support of the Boer War in South Africa.[42] The Boer War would soon become the focus of Gonne's next campaign against Britain, and one of her most effective. It would prove troublesome indeed for the police.

On 11 August Lucien Millevoye was in Pouilly-le-Châtel, north of Lyon. On 18 August he was reported among the arrivals at Royat, the spa where his alliance with Maud Gonne had begun over ten years earlier. The account of his arrival does not mention the French deputy as having a travelling companion, and Gonne was in Ireland, but one's knowledge of his character compels one to look for evidence of a consort at the spa.

Taking his rest in Royat, Millevoye had no idea that by the end of the month, Captain Hubert-Joseph Henry, forger of the documents that incriminated Alfred Dreyfus, would be arrested. The following day Captain Henry was found dead in his cell, his throat cut twice, a razor in his hand. The undeniable evidence – though anti-Dreyfusards still denied it – that the case against Dreyfus, so long indignantly defended by Millevoye, was unjust would lead to a new period of crushing disappointment and public humiliation for the French deputy.

9

For a point of view different from that of Maud Gonne on the explosive divisions in France, consider George Moore's visit to Fontainebleau in August 1898. While rewriting *Evelyn Innes* at the Hôtel de Londres, Moore asked his friend Jacques-Émile Blanche to arrange a dinner so that Moore could meet Maurice Barrès. The encounter, however, went badly. The conversation turned almost immediately to the Dreyfus affair. Perhaps Barrès gave the rationale that he was accustomed to publicizing at the time: 'That Dreyfus is guilty, I deduce not from the facts themselves, but from his race.' Moore got up from his seat, grabbed Barrès by the collar, threw a napkin in his face, then stormed out of the dining room. Monsieur and Madame Barrès left immediately, declaring they would never again accept an invitation to dine with George Moore.[43]

When the coast was clear, Moore emerged from his bedroom. He complained about Barrès's lack of education. The charge is unusual: Barrès was well known for his deployment in fiction of the philosophical vocabulary of Kant, Fichte and Hegel.[44] His whole claim to superiority in style was erudition. Moore's point is that Barrès had no mother-wit, that he was a maniac with a vocabulary. Then followed a conversation that Blanche found so interesting and funny that he transcribed it:

> Rose Blanche: My dear George, suppose it is Jacques and I, who are so often present in London, would we contradict your views of British politics? No, we would struggle to understand the political situation by combing through your newspapers.
>
> GM: My dear Rose, in a matter of military treason, the conviction without evidence of an officer is infamous. It could not take place in a country of honour, justice and morality.
>
> Rose: So what would happen in England?

> GM: The accused would be taken to the Tower of London, and held incommuni-
> cado. He would have been found innocent, or he would have been shot. It would
> not have mattered. No one would know. 'State Secrets' 'National Interest.'

In *La Pêche aux Souvenirs*, Blanche says he finally saw the light in the Dreyfus
affair when Moore spoke. His opinion thereafter was irremovable: it was all a
matter of state secrets, as important in France as in Britain.

Yet this is not where Moore's thinking was going. It is often said in excuse
of the prejudices of people of an earlier time that everyone had such blind spots
in that benighted era, but many French, Irish and English people at the turn of
the century were not anti-Semitic. Moore himself was not prejudiced against
Jews. True, Moore told Eliza Aria how much he liked Jews while explaining
that he was particularly fond of Eliza on account of the fact that she possessed
none of the features with which they were traditionally associated.[45] To hate a
person because he or she happened to be a Jew was as ridiculous as to hate a
man because he was English or Irish. Moore was interested in individuality, in
personality, not in group identities.

Barrès was preaching France for the French (that is, not for Jews, or for
cosmopolitans like Moore), and also a certain kind of nationalism: a conservative state – Catholic, royalist, and family-centred, the kind of state Action
Française later wanted to put into place. All forms of nationalism were absurd
to Moore, but this particular proto-Fascist one was a horrifying example of
what he meant by 'uneducated'.

Maud Gonne and Lucien Millevoye were both propagandists for the
type of republicanism that Barrès defined.[46] The nationalisms of France and
Ireland at the turn of the century were near cousins. Like the French right-wing
elements who rejected democracy and bourgeois society, Maud Gonne united
her contradictory ideas by means of anti-Semitism. It was an insistent, recur-
rent part of her attitude to life, and one that she expressed in letters to Yeats
(he ignored it) and often imposed on the *United Irishman* once she obtained a
controlling interest in that weekly.

The following sample of citations is taken from letters to Yeats and her
articles in the *United Irishman*:

> Letter to Yeats, 24 June 1899: Waldeck Rousseau *opportuniste* the lawyer of the
> jews and financiers has chosen Millerand socialist collectiviste as minister of
> commerce ...[47]

> Article in *United Irishman*, 23 September 1899: [England's] able diplomatists and,
> above all, her Jewish allies, who foment quarrels and internal strife among the

different countries whom her policy of grab have exasperated, may be able to stave off the day of reckoning for a time, but sooner or later it will come.[48]

Article in *United Irishman*, 21 October 1899: The liberation of the traitor Dreyfus immediately after his re-condemnation has been the last stroke to convince Russia that no French institution is now safe from the domination of the agents of the synagogue.[49]

Letter to Yeats [September 1900]: [Kathleen Gonne Pilcher] like myself was rather repelled by the Semitic tendency of the teaching [in the Order of the Golden Dawn].[50]

United Irishman, 3 November 1900: The Celts, differing widely in this from the Semitic race, have always reverenced the feminine equally with the masculine principle.[51]

Letter to Yeats, 27 July 1909: [In Aix les Bains] the atmosphere created by the people one meets that the proximity of jew bankers & enterprising fair ladies & fat vulgar creatures of all sorts gets so on my nerves that after the first day or two I have not been in the gaming rooms at all.[52]

Such anti-Semitism was incongruous in articles in the *United Irishman*, there being so few Jews in Ireland. A Jew for Maud Gonne was a kind of Englishman, and an Englishman a sort of Jew. She associated both with greed, treachery, cunning and filth. Like Millevoye, she was in favour of a violent, military and non-parliamentary movement for Irish independence. Like Millevoye, she had a liking for secret conspiracies, and also like him, she used as her means for political change newspaper propaganda (that is, slanted reporting), heavy applications of financial capital, clubs and leagues, marches, leaflets, posters, open-air oratory, commemorative events and other forms of mobilization of the masses.

When Moore returned to Ireland in 1900, he wanted Ireland to become an independent nation in modern Europe. He found that things had changed in the country of his birth since he had left decades earlier. A military style of patriotism – uniforms, marches, expressions of a desire to die – had been idealized. The patriarchal family was the only social unit to be tolerated. Worst of all, a newly arrogant Church was being awarded knee-knocking subservience, while all things English – good or bad – were belligerently abominated. To Moore, it seemed as if the whole country wanted to turn away from modern individual life.

Moore offered to Irish people instead the example of modern France. Imitate, he said, their kind of experimental literature, their kind of personal painting, their very lax Catholicism or outright scepticism. Like Zola, Moore looked forward to the day when religious illusions would lose their hold over people, when the varieties of the human sexual instinct and their pleasant fruits would be acknowledged, and when art would declare the naked truth. But he was really recommending one France in place of another France – Zola's France, in place of the France of Barrès and Millevoye.

10

After the death of Captain Henry, Millevoye believed himself to have been insulted by Zola's friend, novelist Octave Mirbeau, and sent him a challenge.[53] This was just one of five duels Millevoye tried to start in that summer and autumn, and even if they came to nothing, the prospect of a duel is frightening, and he was alone, without Maud Gonne beside him, lending him her courage. The anti-Dreyfusards as a whole pursued a strategy of killing their opponents one by one; as a block they were bloody-minded. Mirbeau, however, declined the offer.[54] From his place of exile outside London, Zola passed a secret letter through his mistress to Mirbeau, telling him never to risk his life in a duel with Millevoye; the man was just 'an idiot' and not worth the bother.[55]

In this stormy and stressful period Millevoye sought comfort in the arms of another woman. In *A Servant of the Queen*, Maud Gonne tells the story of the end of her affair with Lucien Millevoye in the following way.[56] Before leaving Paris for a Swiss holiday with her sister, Maud Gonne went with Ghénia de Sainte-Croix and Millevoye to hear one of her favourite singers, Eva Bréval, in a Wagner opera.[57] During the intermission, Millevoye said that he knew a woman who, though just a café-concert singer, had a better voice than Bréval. He offered to present this singer at Maud Gonne's salon. On the way home, Ghénia de Sainte-Croix confided to Gonne: 'You are away from Paris too much, Maud *chérie*.' Soon, Maud Gonne confronted Millevoye about an article in his newspaper that stated that Germany was the single enemy of France, saying nothing at all of Britain. This was a violation of their 'alliance'. Millevoye testily said the article was by a woman who loved Alsace-Lorraine just as Maud Gonne herself loved Ireland. Gonne's Irish revolutionaries were absurd, he went on; she should give up on them and support the Home Rule party – a low blow, given his knowledge of Gonne's anti-parliamentary politics. Gonne asked if the author of that article were not the same woman whom

Millevoye claimed sang as well as Bréval. It was as she feared. This was all the work of a Clémenceau conspiracy, she declared; Millevoye had been caught in a honey trap. 'He has triumphed at last through her and has broken our alliance. Goodbye, old friend, I go on my way alone and carry on the fight.'[58]

In November Gonne wrote to Yeats from Paris. She was so glad, she said, to have him in her life; he was always the same. For weeks, she had been 'incapable of any sort of work', her mind 'blank and stupid'. 'I thought it must be some of the forces that work for Britain were paralysing my will.' Although unable as yet to explain it to Yeats, or perhaps even to herself, Maud Gonne was shattered by the news that Millevoye had jilted her for another woman. Say what you wish about him – that he was a cad, a fiend, and a fool – still, Lucien Millevoye was her first love and the father of her two children. He had schooled her in political journalism. She had brought him back more than once from the brink of self-destruction. He had opened doors for her in Paris. She had thought she could count on him always to be the same. He was a cad in the beginning and a cad in the end.

11

On 29 November 1898 Maud Gonne arrived at Kingstown.[59] Yeats met her in Dublin, and they were quickly 'deep in occult science' together.[60] For 'occult science', as usual read 'flirtatious play-acting'. On 6 December Yeats recorded in his diary that he had dreamt during the night that she had kissed him on the lips. As had become their custom, he checked with Maud Gonne to see if she had dreamt a complementary dream. In his 'Visions Notebook' Yeats left a memorandum of what happened next: [61]

> She said 'I was with you last night but do not remember much' but in the evening she said some such words as these 'I will tell you what happen[ed] last night. I went out of my body I saw my body from outside it & I was brought away by Lug [an ancient Irish god] & my hand was put in yours & I was told we were married. Then I kissed you & all became dark. I think we went away together to do some work.'

Then, according to *Memoirs*, 'for the first time with the bodily mouth, she kissed me.'[62] Yeats's phrase – 'bodily mouth' – is peculiar, especially for those who have no experience of consorting with immaterial spirits. The strangeness is increased by Yeats's use of the definite article 'the' in place of 'her', as if the 'bodily mouth' is an objectified instrument normally employed for other purposes, such as eating, speaking, biting or breathing through, while previously another mouth, the disembodied one, had sometimes been used by Gonne for the purpose of kissing him.

The peculiar usage brings out the extreme strangeness of the very human and ordinary thing she did, kissing him. In *The Erotic Phenomenon*, Jean-Luc Marion gives a painstaking, thoughtful microanalysis of what occurs in a kiss.[63] To allow oneself to be loved, to be transformed from a 'body' into 'flesh', to use Marion's terms, one must allow oneself to be penetrated by the other. Maud Gonne, desperate after the loss of Lucien Millevoye, was, through her own sudden condition of lack, opening herself to give to Yeats what he lacked, the lack that had come to define him as a poet and a person. Her kiss offered him the chance to make the journey from touching himself to touching her and being touched by her:

> By touching one another mouth to mouth, our two mouths set off a wave that traverses our two bodies, so as to transcribe them wholly into two fleshes, without remainder; the mouth begins the process, because, already open, without distinction between exterior and interior, it offers itself from the outset as flesh; it incarnates first the lack of distinction between touching and touching oneself, feeling and feeling (oneself) feeling. But, if nothing resists it (and precisely, the flesh that it begins to give to the other is defined by its non-resistance), that is, since nothing resists it, the kiss of my mouth upon her mouth … inaugurates the infinite taking of flesh … The eroticization of everything is involved.

This opening by Maud Gonne was momentous for Yeats. He was stunned by it. At that moment, he neither gave himself nor took possession of her. He went back alone to his own hotel.

The next day Yeats returned to Maud Gonne's rooms on Nassau Street. He found her sitting gloomily by the fire. She should never have spoken to him as she did the day before, she said, for in truth she could never become his wife. Yeats then asked her directly, possibly for the first time, if she loved someone else. No, she replied, but there had once been someone. Then she let the whole web of lies unravel, thread by thread: the meeting with Millevoye in Royat, a baby born, the baby dying, another baby born, that child now a girl of four. She had for some time been finished with Millevoye sexually, she said. She added a tale of Satanism. In her adolescence, she said, she had made a Faustian pact with the Devil: control in this life exchanged for damnation in the next world.

The whole operation derived from a book of arcana in her father's library.[64] Even now, she continued to feel morally responsible for Millevoye; she was necessary to him; without her, he would be lost. She would never completely give him up.

Although Yeats already knew much of this 'as through a glass darkly', it was another thing altogether to remove the illusion under which the two of them had formed a long-lasting relationship, not just his long, devoted, always frustrated, but in some ways free and irresponsible, courtship of her, but also the 'spiritual marriage' that locked that courtship into place seemingly for ever. That was gone too. She had broken the spell with a kiss of the bodily mouth, by becoming flesh to his flesh.

But what was she asking of him? It was hard for him to work out. He confided his misery and bewilderment in a letter to Lady Gregory:[65]

> Today & yesterday I have gone through a crisis that has left me worn out. MG is here & I understand everything now. I cannot say more than that if I am sorry for my self I am far more sorry for her & that I have come to understand her & admire her as I could not have done before. My life is a harder problem to me than it was yesterday.

W.B. Yeats by Alvin Langdon Coburn.
(Namur Archive, London; Scala)

Understanding and admiring the fallen woman is not the same as permitting her to give herself to him. But what could he do with a wife and stepchild in Paris? Would he have to live there too? Would they live on her money? Was he being asked to allow a situation to continue in which she was still a necessity to Lucien Millevoye? Was her past to be kept a secret between the two of them that no one must ever know? Or did most of her acquaintances already know? As his letter to Lady Gregory indicates, it was his crisis more than Maud Gonne's, although she was the more to be pitied.

What Yeats did next was to do nothing. He let Maud Gonne wait around in Dublin for something to happen until she finally returned alone to Paris. He gave her many signs of his pity. More than once she kissed him 'very tenderly', while he was 'careful to touch [her only] as one might a sister'. In as much as a mutual kiss requires a continuous communication of non-resistance and positive reciprocity, and thus a wordless utterance of 'Yes' over and over, conversely by his 'brotherly' responses, Yeats was saying 'No' again and again. In his *Memoirs* he gives a noble reason for what seems either cold calculation or unconscious hostility: 'If she was to come to me, it must be from no temporary passionate impulse, but with the approval of her conscience.' This line of thought gave his own conscience troubles. He admits that he often lay awake afterwards reflecting that maybe he did not in fact act 'from a high scruple' but 'from a dread of moral responsibility', meaning presumably the double responsibility for Maud Gonne and her daughter Iseult that a fully mutual kiss would signify.[66] Still, it does Yeats great credit that he realized what was going on in his unconscious rationalizations, and that he recorded everything in detail for posterity to contemplate.

As Deirdre Toomey was the first to realize, Yeats placed this moment in which he stood in judgment upon himself for his refusal of Maud Gonne at the centre of one of his major poetic sequences, 'The Tower' (1927):[67]

> Does the imagination dwell the most
> Upon a woman won or woman lost?
> If on the lost, admit you turned aside
> From a great labyrinth out of pride,
> Cowardice, some silly over-subtle thought
> Or anything called conscience once;

Toomey surmises that what put Yeats off at the last moment was phobia about women's bodies, and in particular fear of female genitalia.[68] They are the 'great labyrinth'. In that labyrinth dwells a monster born of the lust of Pasiphae, and ephebes who enter there are entering their own graves, unless they are great artists, like Dedalus, and fly free from the trap.

While Maud Gonne was still in Dublin, she said to Yeats out of the blue, 'I hear a voice saying, "You are about to receive the initiation of the spear."' They then had a double vision. She thought herself 'a great stone statue through which passed flame'. He experienced himself as becoming a 'flame and mounting up through and looking out of the eyes of a great stone Minerva'. When he honourably spoke of marriage just before her return to Paris, she said, 'No, it seems impossible,' because she had 'a horror and terror of physical love'.[69]

It is impossible now to know what was in Maud Gonne's mind when she said that she thought she was about to receive the 'Initiation of the Spear'. Did she expect to get it from the next world, or from Yeats himself, in fantasy or in the flesh? The double vision that Yeats reports in such detail is transparently a fantasy of coition, but coition entirely on the astral plane, returning the relationship once again to the terms of the 'spiritual marriage'.

Although Maud Gonne's statement, 'I have a horror and terror of physical love' is often quoted to establish a permanent fact of her nature, it should not be taken at face value. Maud Gonne may have had a justifiable horror and terror of the consequences of physical love, given that she had had two illegitimate children, and, according to her husband John MacBride, two miscarriages, one of which seems to have put her life in danger;[70] but her presentation of herself to Yeats in early December 1898 seems that of a woman of normal appetites. Some poems by Yeats describe her as fully sexed ('her blood ran wild'); one of these, 'The Grey Rock', appears to allude specifically to December 1898:[71]

> I knew a woman none could please,
> Because she dreamed when but a child
> Of men and women made like these;
> And after, when her blood ran wild,
> Had ravelled her own story out,
> And said, 'In two or in three years
> I needs must marry some poor lout,'
> And having said it, burst in tears.

Maud Gonne's statement that she had no appetite at all for physical love was a way of letting Yeats off the hook, and a way of doing so that involved the least embarrassment to herself. She had discovered with that first kiss, and confirmed it with many tender but unreciprocated kisses in the following days, that it was Yeats himself who had a horror and terror of physical love.

In December 1898 Maud Gonne herself seems like the heroine of Colette's *Vagabond*, afraid of growing old, of being deceived again, of suffering, but who cannot rid herself of 'that woman', her own flesh, 'dumb and hell-bent on animal pleasure', and also, a hundred times more dangerous and harder to conquer than her external enemies, the 'greedy child who trembles within, weak, nervous, ever ready to hold out her arms and beg, "Don't leave me alone!"'

IX

SEXUAL LOVE,
SPIRITUAL HATRED[1]

Previous page: *Maud Gonne MacBride (Bain Collection, Library of Congress)*

On 19 December 1898 W.B. Yeats read Maud Gonne's future by means of a 'horary', a form of astrology. Yeats scribbled his findings in his 'Visions Notebook', saying that Gonne would[2] 'find her plans & arrangmt upset changing fealings & dreams & by occult intuitions & will find herself in a revolt against <the established order> settled conditions ... will suffer from depression'. Yet, Maud Gonne, after receiving his forecast, wrote to Yeats that she was not in fact depressed. Her own visions were of fair omens. On her return to Paris, she saw in her mind's eye 'a very big shield held over me & I also saw the spear, it seemed protecting & encouraging'.[3] She sent along with this letter a prurient description of the 'Initiation of the Spear':

> I saw Lug [*sic*] in his chariot. He touched me on the chest with the spear & I fell down on the ground & the fountain of fire played over me. Then held out the spear over me & I grasped it & was raised to my feet through the fire fountain. I then got into the chariot & knelt there under Lug's [*sic*] great shield. The chariot rose to a great height & stopped at last on what seemed to be a sort of dazzling white platform on which stood a white altar & on it was inscribed a golden sun & a red rose lay on it, I was told that rose incense should be used for Lug [*sic*]'s ceremonies. I found myself dressed in a long white shining garment.

A week later, Gonne confided to Yeats that since her chariot ride with Lugh, she had been 'partially' initiated not just with the spear but with the sword too.

'This too we must try together.'[4] The spiritual marriage appeared to continue in force. Or was Maud Gonne still putting out feelers regarding a marriage of the ordinary kind?

Lady Gregory, believing in the sincerity of the poet's stated wish to marry Maud Gonne,[5] urged him to pursue her to Paris. Yeats found he first had many other things to do in Dublin and London, but he did manage to arrive in Paris by the end of January 1899. When he came to Maud Gonne's apartment, however, he found nothing of the warmth expressed in her recent spicy letters. She allowed him to visit as often as he wished, but she was 'almost cold' to him in person.[6] She unguardedly answered his questions about her past life. Yeats responded evangelically, by trying to make her see that she had been leading a 'life of hatred', and thus had put herself in 'her deepest hell'. If only she would 'labour for divine love', she would find her 'highest heaven'. 'Hers was a war of phantasy and of a blinded idealism against eternal law.'[7] This interpretation of Gonne's character is the reverse of that given in *The Countess Cathleen*, the play Yeats was preparing for its May 1899 Dublin premiere. The countess acts from motives of self-sacrifice and love for others; in the play's conclusion, the Divine of Divines blesses those motives, even after she has sold her soul to the devil. Listening to Yeats's new, severe interpretation of her character cannot have been pleasant for Maud Gonne, nor were his invitations to a vague and lonely heaven likely to prove compelling.

2

The French deputies, Gonne found, were now even 'more *bitterly* divided' than the leaders of Irish opinion.[8] Millevoye's associates had formed a new league of anti-Dreyfusard intellectuals on the revolutionary right, the Ligue de la patrie française. It was designed to be the mirror opposite of Clémenceau's Ligue des droits de l'homme ('League of the Rights of Man'). To borrow a description from Anatole France, it was 'violent in tone, full of a malevolent love of France and a destructive patriotism. It was continually organizing rather savage demonstrations in theatres or churches.'[9] Members included Degas, François Coppée, Jules Lemaître and Paul Bourget, along with a rump of old Boulangistes like Jules Guérin, Barrès, Déroulède and Millevoye. Fifteen hundred members appeared at the Salle des Agriculteurs de France in Paris, in order, Lemaître declared, 'to reassure good people that not all the intellectuals were on the other side'.[10]

An unexpected event then changed the face of the Dreyfus affair. On the night of 16 February 1899 the president of France, Felix Faure, suddenly called for his chief of staff. Coming to the door, the chief of staff saw in the shadows the president, his flesh ashen and his face contorted; behind him stood the slender figure of his mistress, Marguerite Steinheil, nude. 'Help me to sit in the chair,' the president whispered. 'I do not know what happened; I felt a sudden blow, there,' he said, gesturing to the back of his neck. 'I think I am about to die.' Marguerite Steinheil left the Elysée Palace quickly, dressed in a man's coat and wearing a man's hat. According to the reports of those who came to attend to the president, locks of her hair had to be cut from the fingers of the dying man.[11]

That the death of Faure was an assassination was an article of faith among the far right. Barrès wrote: 'In whatever way the poison was administered, in a cigar, or a glass of water, Marguerite was charged to close the book. She rendered an immense service to the Dreyfusard party.'[12] Faure had been strongly Catholic and friendly to monarchism. With his death, the Dreyfusard republicans were in a position to elect a president more to their liking. Clémenceau wasted no time in nominating Émile Loubet, who received two-thirds of the votes.

In this crisis for the right, believed by them to be the result of a clandestine murder, Paul Déroulède planned to turn the funeral of Faure into a coup.[13] His old Boulangiste confederates – Millevoye, Barrès and Marcel Habert – were part of the conspiracy. After lunch on 23 February Déroulède got into a closed fiacre, with Barrès by his side, and headed for the Place de la Nation. Other conspirators arrived in small groups, so as not to attract the attention of the police. Déroulède carried a 100,000 francs, one part in gold pieces, to convince waverers and to open doors. At the Place de la Nation, Déroulède and Barrès hid in a porter's lodge, waiting for the honour guard of troops to return from Père Lachaise cemetery. Déroulède had convened the Ligue des Patriotes, and Jules Guérin the Ligue antisémitique at Place de la Bastille, supposedly to assemble for a procession to Faure's grave, once the military parade had come to an end. Déroulède arranged matters beforehand with General de Pellieux, whom he expected to be leading the troops. However, when the troops arrived, General Roget was at their head.

Déroulède went forward nonetheless, grabbed the bridle of Roget's horse, pointed in the direction of the Elysée, and cried out, 'Follow me, General! To the Elysée! Friends are waiting for us. It will be a *Quatre Septembre* military coup without bloodshed.' General Roget stayed in his saddle, and continued to ride down the boulevard, followed by Déroulède and 2000 of his friends, who, imagining things were going well, were singing the 'Marseillaise'. At the Rue de Reuilly, the General pointed his sword in the direction of the barracks. The troops turned out of the boulevard. Déroulède marched alongside them past the gate right into the yard of the barracks, shouting to General Roget, 'Save us from anarchy and Dreyfus! General, save the country. You will have deserved well of France.' The gate was then closed, and Déroulède put under arrest.

All the leaders of this attempted coup could have been sentenced to prison for sedition, if not to a worse punishment. Yet, among the ranks of the right revolutionaries were the clergy, the magistracy, the army, the landed gentry, industry, commerce, part of the Chamber and most of the press. Neither Millevoye nor Barrès was ever arrested. Déroulède was put on trial for treason in May and found not guilty.

Maud Gonne was horrified that, after the fall of Faure, socialists and liberal republicans had received ministerial appointments in the new government. In June she explained the situation in France to Yeats. Things were so bad that she dreamed of a Napoleonic sword arising from a witch's kettle:[14]

> Here the political atmosphere is thick & heavy. It seems like a boiling cauldron & one does not know what will emerge from all the seething bubbles and vapour – I hope it will be the pure bright light of a shining sword which will guide France once more to glory but at the present all is dark & troubled & England may well look on with satisfaction.
>
> [T]he president of the *Entente Cordiale* is Minister of the Navy! Waldeck Rousseau *opportuniste* the lawyer of the jews and financiers has chosen Millerand socialist collectiviste as minister of commerce & General Gallifet the murderer of 30,000 French men, women, and children – defenceless prisoners after the Commune – is Minister of War! & half of the revolutionists today ... applaud.

Gonne had returned to talking the language of her anti-Semitic, Anglophobic alliance with Millevoye: 'I feel our cause is bound up with the cause of France – we have the same deadly enemy to fight – the horrible plutocracy of which the English Empire is the symbol.' A *rapprochement* with the father of Iseult had in some fashion come to pass.

3

On 4 March 1899 the *United Irishman* published its first issue. The idea for the publication (named after an earlier one by John Mitchel) belonged to Willie Rooney. He had invited Arthur Griffith, a close friend of John MacBride, to return from South Africa to serve as editor. In its seven years of publication, this weekly would have a profound impact on raising the consciousness of Irish nationalists. Its articles were sometimes laboriously sarcastic, and sometimes cloyingly sentimental, but its self-help propaganda shaped both the intelligentsia and the foot soldiers for the 1916 Rising. It favoured the Irish language, Irish manufactures, Irish everything except the Anglo-Irish. Griffith could be sharp in his dealings with departures from the party line, although not so nasty as his rival D.P. Moran in *The Leader*.

It is uncertain if Maud Gonne took any part in the initial planning of the weekly. In March, after agitating for popular justice against land grabbers in Ballina, Co. Mayo, Gonne went to Belfast for the Gaelic *feis* (festival). There she met her friends from the Wolfe Tone Commemoration Committee, Anna Johnston and Alice Milligan, both Protestant republicans. Since 1896, they had published a radical weekly entitled the *Shan Van Vocht* ('poor old woman', a traditional name for Ireland), in whose pages they sometimes celebrated Maud Gonne's activities, and particularly her 'womanly tact', her 'faculty for arranging and managing everybody and everything, and in making people act as they ought to, even when they are quite unwilling'.[15] The *Shan Van Vocht* was closing its operations; there was little support in the north for a nationalist newspaper. Perhaps owing to Gonne's faculty for managing everybody, the two women gave their subscriber list to Arthur Griffith, an instantaneous lift for the new publication.

Maud Gonne provided direct assistance to the *United Irishman* by putting Griffith on a salary of 25 shillings a week. This covered his room and board. When, after some months of publication, the paper's expenses exceeded its income, Gonne undertook a fundraising tour of the United States on its behalf.[16] Yeats spoke casually of the *United Irishman* as Maud Gonne's paper, but if she did not actually own it, by her investment, fundraising, reputation and strength of personality, she obtained a controlling interest in it. In return, Griffith published her articles (approximately one every other month in the first year) and provided favourable, extensive coverage of her political activities with evicted tenants, the Amnesty Association, the Irish Transvaal Committee, Inghinidhe na hÉireann (Daughters of Ireland) and the Patriotic Children's

Treat.[17] The *United Irishman* was far more effective in carrying out Gonne's propaganda purposes than *L'Irlande Libre*. It had a historical impact.

Whether or not Gonne influenced Arthur Griffith's treatment of the Dreyfus affair and Jews more generally is a matter of debate.[18] Griffith published paragraphs sympathetic to the sufferings of Dreyfus in March and June 1899, when the Court of Appeals overturned the 1894 verdict and ordered that the prisoner on Devil's Island be returned to France for a new trial, but Griffith changed tack by August 1899, when the second Dreyfus trial began in Rennes. One reason that has been given for Griffith's swift switch in direction is that Dreyfus was supported in his second trial by English newspapers, and he was constitutionally inclined to oppose whatever Britain supported. Yet the British press had by and large been pro-Dreyfus for over a year, since Zola's *J'Accuse* (13 January 1898).

Gonne's own anti-Semitism was a lurid thread running through the *United Irishman*. In the 23 September 1899 issue, following the pardon of Dreyfus and the arrests of French nationalists, Griffith printed her article (writing as 'The Foreign Secretary') setting forth the theory that there were three evil influences in the nineteenth century: the Pirate (Britain), the Freemason and the Jew. In a subsequent article over her own signature, Maud Gonne threatened Jews, English people and Dreyfusards with an Armageddon:

> [Britain's] able diplomatists and, above all, her Jewish allies, who foment quarrels and internal strife among the different countries whom her policy of grab has exasperated, may be able to stave off the day of reckoning for a time, but sooner or later it will come.[19]

Not all the anti-Semitic remarks in the weekly are by Gonne or Griffith; a number are by F. Hugh O'Donnell (also writing as 'The Foreign Secretary'). As editor, Griffith did not excise such comments, and in their letters to the editor, readers of the *United Irishman* complained about many things, but never about its anti-Semitism. One may conclude that they either shared it, or, like Yeats, overlooked it.

4

During the second Dreyfus trial at Rennes, parts of France verged on civil war. Nationalists organized bellicose demonstrations in many cities, particularly in Rennes itself. In the course of the trial, Dreyfus's lawyer, Fernand Labori, was badly wounded in the street; the assailant fled on foot and was never apprehended. On 12 August Paris police, getting wind of plans for a fresh attempt at a coup, finally began to arrest leaders of the nationalist street demonstrations, including Déroulède. This caused the February conspiracy for a coup at last to be investigated. To prevent arrest for his own part in that February conspiracy, Jules Guérin, editor of *L'Antijuif*, barricaded himself in the fortified headquarters of the Ligue des Patriotes in the Rue de Chabrol.

Guérin had begun his career as a police informant, but his gift for organization and his unscrupulousness led him to a high position among the right revolutionaries. With his band of henchmen recruited from the slaughter-houses, he paradoxically became a cult hero of decadent intellectuals. Hannah Arendt saw in Guérin's admirers the origins of totalitarianism:[20]

> These men, who despised the people and who had themselves but recently emerged from a ruinous and decadent cult of aestheticism, saw in the mob a living expression of virile and primitive 'strength'. It was they and their theories which first identified the mob with the people and converted its leaders into national heroes. It was their philosophy of pessimism and their delight in doom that was the first sign of the imminent collapse of the European intelligentsia.

Troops laid siege to Guérin's 'Fort Chabrol' and blocked its drains. On the twenty-sixth day of the siege, 9 September, the military court in Rennes, in defiance of the evidence presented, found Dreyfus guilty once again and sentenced him to ten years for treason. On the thirty-sixth day of the siege of Fort Chabrol, news arrived that Captain Dreyfus had accepted a pardon from President Loubet, and was now free. On 20 September, the thirty-seventh day of the siege, a smart carriage drove up the Rue de Chabrol, and a famous beauty (unnamed in press accounts) stepped out, then presented the sergeant on duty with a bouquet of flowers for Guérin.

Lucien Millevoye was the next to arrive on the scene on 20 September 1899. It was understood that if Guérin did not leave peacefully with his old friend, the troops would attack.[21] Millevoye returned from his parley alone. Reporters asked what had happened inside.

He explained:

We kissed, Guérin and I, with emotion. Guérin showed me the preparations he had made for resistance. Then he examined the conditions that were offered to him. But nothing was decided by this interview. I went out promising to bring him the government's response to his own offer that evening.'[22]

The chief of police was unwilling to wait any longer. He knocked on the door and said that if there was no surrender within five minutes, the attack would begin. Guérin reflected, then surrendered. In the trial of nationalists that followed that November, he was sentenced to ten years in prison, and Déroulède to ten years in exile. Millevoye and Barrès, who had reason to fear, got off scot-free.

5

It is unlikely that Maud Gonne was the unnamed famous beauty who brought Jules Guérin flowers at Fort Chabrol. In September Gonne was in Ireland preaching popular justice against 'land grabbers' and the suspension of laws of property. On the last day of the siege of Fort Chabrol, a feeble-minded old man was on trial in the winter assizes in Connaught for listening to her advice. He had forcibly evicted a new tenant ('grabber') from the cottage from which he himself had been evicted. When the local sergeant knocked on the door:

> A voice said, 'Yes I am here.' Door then opened. Saw prisoner inside. No one else. I asked him what brought him there, and he said he did not come there without his authority. I asked if Ginley [the sitting tenant] had given him authority, and he said, No; but that Miss Maud Gonne had told him on the previous day in Ballina to go and take possession of the house, and if there were a dozen locks on the door, to break them. Durcan had a lock in his hand and also a bar of iron.

The sergeant requested leniency for the defendant:

> This old man – who appeared a weak-minded man – heard some of these fine theories [of Maud Gonne], and he got it into his head that he could take possession of this place, and he went up there and drew the staple out of the door, and evicted the pigs [*laughter*]. He thought he was all right.

The judge suspended sentence.

Another prosecution arose from Maud Gonne's speech at Knockmore, Co. Mayo, on 17 September 1899, when some 900 people gathered to hear her rail against land grabbers, and against one man in particular, William Hughes, who had taken over a property formerly inhabited by a widow. From the platform, Maud Gonne pointed Hughes out in the crowd:[23]

> He is here in your midst, and the grabber is a traitor to your class, a traitor to himself, and a traitor to his country; he is a robber, a miserable wretch like Hughes. I tell you today to take up the case of Mrs Feeney and her orphan daughter until such time as she is re-instated in her holding. Let no man of you speak to Hughes. Be ready and be watchful to strike a blow against England.

Frightened for his life, William Hughes sent a note up to those on the platform. It indicated that he was willing to return the cottage to the widow and her children, provided he was reimbursed the nine pounds of back rent he had paid to obtain the lease. He was told he must give the house back freely, with no conditions, and if he did so, all would be well for him. They all then marched off to restore the widow to her cottage, but Hughes later claimed in court that he had never got what he was owed. He was awarded £5 in damages and £1 in costs.

In 'A Question of Policy' (*United Irishman*, 11 November 1899), Gonne explained that she agreed with the United Irish League's goal of 'land for the people', but not with its tactics. They were too peaceful, too law-abiding. Irish peasants had their fair share of courage, but they had, she believed, too much respect for the law, even a 'childish, unreasoning terror of the law'. Nationalist organizers should teach the people to bravely defy the law. She had wanted to bring a mob to surround the courthouse for the trial of the land grabber William Hughes, and she was well able to assemble one and to incite it to deeds, but the United Irish League would not permit her to do so, because it was illegal. This, she believed, was a mistake: 'We disapprove of English law in this country, we know that English justice is a farce, and we are prepared to fight against it, and the first thing is to teach people to look on it with contempt and defiance.'[24]

6

The situation in the Boer republics gave Maud Gonne an opportunity to preach courage and military defiance. Over the summer of 1899 Britain was asserting its claim to the whole of South Africa, but the presidents of the Orange Free State and the Transvaal Republic refused to accept British conditions upon freedoms they already enjoyed, and they prepared for war. Over a month before the 11 October declaration of war, Irish residents of Johannesburg, led by Arthur Griffith's friend John MacBride, 'decided it was our duty to Ireland to seize the opportunity of paying back a little of the score we owed England.'[25] They formed an Irish brigade to fight alongside the Boers.

Back in Dublin, Griffith and Maud Gonne rallied behind this golden opportunity for a vicarious war with Britain fought on foreign soil. On 7 October Griffith, Gonne, Yeats, and John O'Leary met in the rooms of the Celtic Literary Society at 32 Lower Abbey Street and established the Irish Transvaal Committee. They claimed to be raising money and recruiting men for an ambulance corps for those who would be wounded in the coming war, but they also planned a full-scale programme of resistance to the recruitment of Irishmen to fight on the British side against the Boers. The police heard talk of a secret fund that was being used to pay currently enlisted Irishmen to desert. Those Irishmen already in the colonial army were urged to shoot their officers. The meetings of the Irish Transvaal Committee, chaired by either Gonne or O'Leary, were fiery, seditious, extremist and popular. New committees were started in other Irish cities. When Griffith and Gonne arrived on 14 November to make Boer War speeches in Cork, the crowd unhitched the horses from their carriage, and pulled it themselves from the railway station to the Victoria Hotel.[26]

The police forces were more worried about Maud Gonne's anti-recruitment drive than they had been about her earlier efforts to make trouble for the British in Ireland. The Irish Transvaal Committee was, police report noted, 'a great source of danger because of the finances of Maud Gonne and her friends'.[27] Some of the money appeared to be coming from Belgium, where the Boer financier Dr W.J. Leyds was stationed. In November, Gonne's Irish-Australian friend in Paris, Arthur Lynch, had contacted Leyds about his desire to contribute to the Boer War effort. Lynch, supplied with money by the Boer consul in Paris, left to set up a second Irish brigade in South Africa.[28]

The anti-recruitment drive was a potentially effective tactic in the first months of the Boer War because the Dutch colonists initially had a numerical advantage of troops on the ground, which, combined with their superior knowledge of the terrain and support from the local white population, enabled them to win a string of decisive victories over the British army. However, more British troops were being recruited for the South African war. When the Queen's forces in the field were resupplied, the Boers could be overwhelmed.

In December 1899 Gonne joined forces once again with James Connolly to organize an anti-British rally at Beresford Place. It was scheduled for

17 December as a protest against the visit of Joseph Chamberlain, British Secretary for the Colonies, to receive an honourary degree from Trinity College. Connolly and Gonne hoped to turn a rowdy meeting into a spontaneous rebellion and the seizure of key public buildings in Dublin, which, Connolly argued, the British would never bomb; as capitalists, they were bound to respect private property. That notion, and the whole plan, seemed foolish to Arthur Griffith. The Irish protestors were unarmed, and would be killed.[29] Other constitutional nationalists withdrew when the Beresford Place protest was prohibited by the authorities. John Redmond and Michael Davitt begged Maud Gonne not to go ahead with the meeting because many citizens were likely to be injured. She defied the advice of the head of the Irish Parliamentary Party and the leader of the Land League: 'I said I should go to Beresford Place whatever happened as when a meeting was announced it must be held or attempted at any cost so as not to set an example of cowardice to the crowd.'[30]

In spite of the fact that the 17 December assembly had been outlawed, people gathered in front of Trinity College at one o'clock, the hour announced for the speeches. Mounted on a borrowed hearse, Connolly and Gonne arrived at Beresford Place near the Custom House, and pulled to a stop. When they attempted to address the crowd, police surrounded the wagon and arrested Connolly. The crowd pressed in upon them, and the police mounted a baton charge, but were repulsed by shovels and broomsticks. Connolly broke loose from his captors, and with Gonne by his side, took the reins of a two-horse brake. Flaunting Boer and Irish flags and followed by a mob cheering Kruger and the Boers, they set off up Talbot Street. A contingent of panting policemen came after them. As the wagon passed by him, the future playwright Seán O'Casey saw Maud Gonne 'smiling happily, like a child out on her first excursion'.[31] Connolly drove to North Earl Street, where a speech was hastily given. The wagon eventually pulled up opposite the Irish Transvaal Committee rooms. When Maud Gonne began her speech, the police closed in once again. Leaflets mocking the British army for its losses to the Boers were released from the upper windows of 32 Lower Abbey Street, landing on the constabulary.[32] For two artists of street demonstrations like Maud Gonne and James Connolly, the anti-Chamberlain protest was a total success, although Connolly got a jail sentence for his part in it. The *New York Times* noted that Maud Gonne 'bravely faced the music, but was of course protected by her sex'.[33]

7

Exalted by thrilling months of law-breaking, Gonne made contact with Dr Leyds about a means to contribute more directly to the Boer War effort. Before Christmas 1899, the Boer diplomat received the Irish Joan of Arc. She explained that she was asking for £500. Her plan was to place bombs disguised as lumps of coal in a British troopship. Dr Leyds was horrified: 'But this is not a recognized means of warfare.' What does it matter, Gonne asked, whether you kill British soldiers on land or at sea? The object was to kill them. Such an explosion would discourage enlistment. Dr Leyds said that an atrocity of this sort would cause the Boers to lose their Liberal support in the British Parliament, as well as elsewhere in Europe.

Maud Gonne returned to Paris. According to her account, a secretary to Dr Leyds arrived the next day with a message that the Boer diplomat had changed his mind. She would soon receive £2000, considerably more than she requested. Before the money was sent, however, another Irish revolutionary collected the sum from the office of Dr Leyds.

Gonne immediately suspected that the thief was F. Hugh O'Donnell. She turned to Dr Mark Ryan, head of the Irish National Alliance, and demanded that O'Donnell be dealt with severely.[34]

In fact, F. Hugh O'Donnell, already established as a Boer agent in Europe, had written to Dr Leyds warning him to keep clear of Maud Gonne:[35]

> I have always warned you against letting yourself be in any way connected with this notorious woman. Any good she may do is outweighed by the evil of her conduct and the grossness of her language … You can easily understand the effect upon the military circles in Germany and Russia of this 'friend' of the Boers advising soldiers to shoot their own officers. This shameless woman is a disgrace and a danger to every cause to which she attaches herself.

O'Donnell's low opinion of Gonne's discretion was, unknown to her, shared by Dr Mark Ryan, who wrote to Dr Leyds:

> WARNING: An Irish woman is coming to ferret around tomorrow or the day after. Too much has already been said to her. Her chatter and her conceit could jeopardize the freedom and lives of many people. We have placed our confidence in your discretion. Do not say a word to inform this woman or everything could possibly go wrong. THE CHIEF.

There is a receipt in Leyds's archives from F. Hugh O'Donnell for £2000, the first of a number of payments, because O'Donnell rather than Gonne became the conduit for Boer support of anti-British activities in Ireland. The main beneficiary was the Irish Parliamentary Party.

Dr Leyds's mission in Europe was to use the wealth of South African gold mines to bribe politicians and newspapers to make the case for the Boers, or (in less pejorative language) to subsidize the work of the Boer Republic's European friends. His operations required a degree of discretion; editors and statesmen did not want to be seen to be receiving money. Discretion was never any part of Maud Gonne's valour. With her travelling menagerie, her great height and her famous face, Maud Gonne was possibly the most easily identifiable subversive in Europe. She delighted in making speeches to crowds in which she said things openly that others uttered to one another only in clandestine whispers. She was an awkward sort of collaborator for someone in Dr Leyds's position.

Maud Gonne was incensed when the door had been metaphorically shut in her face by Dr Leyds and her military mission scuppered by F. Hugh O'Donnell. She asked Yeats to put things right with the secret revolutionary organization in London, but Dr Ryan, Dr Leyds, and F. Hugh O'Donnell maintained a united front against her. In his surviving letters to the South African diplomat, O'Donnell showed himself to be mainly outraged by the fact that Maud Gonne was an unmarried mother:[36]

> Millevoye's young lady came to our chief's house, quite furious at not having received what she demanded. She was accompanied by one named Yeats who it is said is the latest successor to Millevoye, and before this young man she said all she had heard at your house, and further … She declared that you had claimed to be in communication with Irish revolutionaries 'through a person who did not belong to their organization'!!! Without a doubt, within 24 hours all Dublin will know …
>
> If she is not a spy, she is almost one and her bragging is more dangerous than treachery itself.
>
> Except among the common people, she has the most detestable reputation. Stories are being circulated of 'three children put out to nurse in Paris,' but she shows herself everywhere at our meetings, and we are obliged to put up with her. But one could not be too prudent when she is near.

Gonne continued to press her services upon Boer officials. The Chancellery of the Republics of South Africa sent an official note on 20 January to Arthur Griffith about the matter:[37]

> While thanking Mademoiselle Gonne for her warm sympathy with the Republics of South Africa, I am instructed to request you as quickly as possible to point out that both in Brussels and in Paris our diplomatic representatives inhabit neutral territory and we cannot allow ourselves to be accused to neutral governments of abusing their hospitality by entering into relations with indiscreet advocates of resurrection in Ireland or elsewhere. We have already declined the services of M. Cipriani and similar gentlemen for related reasons ... we should accordingly wish Miss Gonne to cease sending telegrams and paying visits to our chancelleries and consulates. We shall continue all the same to be grateful to her and all other Irish ladies for expressions of their good wishes.

In June 1900 the *United Irishman* closed its columns to F. Hugh O'Donnell, formerly a frequent contributor. That was the only revenge that it lay within Maud Gonne's power to exact for O'Donnell's smearing of her name and his foiling of her plans for a splendid, terrifying outrage – the sinking of a British troopship and the drowning of all on board.

8

On 12 January 1900 Maud Gonne boarded *La Normandie* for New York, to undertake a lecture tour of the United States. The theme of her lectures was 'England's difficulty is Ireland's opportunity'. If the immediate causes for which she requested donations were Boer hospitals and the *United Irishman*, the real cause was revolution in Ireland.

A 'Maud Gonne Reception Committee' organized her welcome in New York: steamers flying Orange Free State and American flags sailed out to meet her ship, and a crowd gathered on the pier to applaud.[38] At her first address on 5 February, Gonne told the audience at the Academy of Music that whenever the British captured an Irishman fighting for the Boers, he was shot on the spot. It was the sole duty of every Irishman to 'oppose, thwart, and hinder' England at every step.[39] Receipts at the gate for this one event added up to $2000. On 9 March Maud Gonne embarked on a return ship for Le Havre.

She came back to Paris to find her daughter Iseult, now six, seriously ill with influenza and an infected lung. Gonne caught the illness, so both mother and daughter were confined to bed. Her amazingly active life of trains, boats, carriages and horses, from one hotel to another across Britain, France, Ireland and the USA, came to rest for a few weeks. Yet by the end of the month she was well enough to take pleasure in Yeats's plan to nominate Major MacBride of the Irish Brigade as a Home Rule candidate for a seat to be vacated by Timothy Harrington. (The idea was not that MacBride would actually represent the electorate at Westminster; the election would be a symbolic act to show Irish contempt for British institutions and foreign policy.)

By early April, fully recovered, Gonne wrote her most famous and ferocious article, an attack on Queen Victoria entitled 'The Famine Queen'. The venom for the queen as a bad mother runs so deep it makes one ask if it arises from a well of self-hatred.

9

The 7 April issue of the *United Irishman* printing 'The Famine Queen' was suppressed by Dublin Castle. By the time the chief inspector arrived at the newspaper's offices, the issue had been in the shops for more than a week. Detectives ran around to the newsagents, but word of the suppression had caused a run on sales.[40]

Ramsay Colles, the unionist editor of the *Irish Figaro*, came to the defence of Queen Victoria in his 7 April editorial. Maud Gonne, he wrote, was a discredit to her sex:

> This lady – if a liar can be considered a lady – lately communicated falsehoods to the French gutter press to the effect that the Irish soldiers now serving in South Africa were put on board the transports with 'manacled wrists' and she added that the majority laid down their arms and refused to fight the Boers.[41]

Arthur Griffith was outraged by this smear on Maud Gonne (whom in preference to Victoria he called 'Queen'), and what he took to be the libel that she was not Irish. He went to the *Figaro* office on Grafton Street, where Colles was hoping to get a view of the Empress passing, and attacked him with his *sjambok*, a South African whip made from hippopotamus hide. Neither man was seriously injured, but Griffith was arraigned for assault.

On Easter Sunday, 15 April, after the twelve o' clock mass, Gonne gathered together with fifteen young women, almost all of them sisters of members of the Celtic Literary Society, at 32 Lower Abbey Street. They decided to honour the chivalry of Arthur Griffith, then doing twenty-eight days in gaol, by giving him a blackthorn with a silver ring to replace his broken *sjambok*.

Maud Gonne proposed that the women form themselves into an organization; maybe it could be called Daughters of Ireland. Willie Rooney, acting editor of the *United Irishman* while Griffith was in confinement, was in the outer room. He offered a Gaelic translation of the name, Inghinidhe na hÉireann.[42] The society took its objects from those of the Celtic Literary Society, the fostering of Irish language, literature, music, history and industries, only adding 'among the young'. A patriotic children's picnic, Rooney said, should be organized for those little ones who refused to attend Queen Victoria's treat, which, Gonne believed, was really only a Boer War recruiting drive. 'Then the girls all looked at each other and said, "Let's do it."'[43] Maud Gonne was elected president, Ethna Carbery and Máire Ní Cillin vice-presidents, and Máire Quinn secretary.[44]

The women adored Maud Gonne. They were inspired by her indomitable, playful and spectacular political style. The Ladies Committee for the Patriotic Children's Treat urged Irish children to 'love and honour Miss Gonne, more perhaps than any other human being outside of your fathers, mothers, brothers and sisters. She has sacrificed station and friends for your sake and for the sake of Ireland.'[45] This women's organization was to have a lasting effect on the Irish nationalist movement right through to 1916, sixteen Easters later.

Maud Gonne sued Ramsay Colles for libel for stating on a placard that she was in receipt of a British pension. The 21 April issue of the *Irish Figaro* claimed that the assistant commissioner of police had verified that she was on £300 per annum in recognition of Colonel Gonne's military service. Gonne asserted, strangely, that the placard implied that she was a British spy.[46]

Maud Gonne would have to testify in court, and everything she said would be taken down by shorthand reporters and published in newspapers. She would have to be careful to keep clear of perjury. On the day of the arraignment, the Queen's counsel made Maud Gonne's time on the stand uncomfortable:

> Are you ashamed of your father's past? No.
>
> And it was no discredit to him that he was for years in the pay of the British Government? Not when holding the views that he had.
>
> He attained to the post of … ? Colonel.
>
> While holding those views he was in receipt of substantial income? He was.
>
> And drew it steadily? Of course.
>
> Are you ashamed that your sister married a British officer? I have nothing to do with that. [*applause*]

Would you agree that it is not a very courageous or manly thing to defame a woman? I think opinion is pretty general on that subject.

I suppose, then, that any person that would defame the greatest woman in our country – I am not referring to you [*laughter*] – would merit your censure? I think if anyone defames a woman as a woman, yes, but as a public character, it is not defaming to say the truth of her.

Your idea is that you might defame a woman for her public character? No.

Would you think that a cowardly and unmanly act? I would.

And would you consider it a cowardly thing to defame men who are fighting for their country in the service of their Queen? I would think it a cowardly act to defame men who are fighting for their own country.

Would you think it a shocking thing to describe Irishmen who are fighting as soldiers on behalf of her Majesty the Queen as 'creatures with minds so degenerate and ignorant that they are fittingly compared with beasts of the field'? I would approve of that. [*applause in the gallery*]

Mr Swifte directed a constable to stand at the gallery steps and remove anyone who disturbed the court.

Witness further said in cross examination that for the last four months she had been publicly proclaiming that the Irish soldiers of the Queen were traitors to their country. She was present at a meeting in Beresford Place.

A meeting at which one speaker recommended that Irish soldiers should shoot their officers! I cannot answer for what the other speakers said, but only for myself.

Would you approve of that statement? I would.

Therefore, if the statement was made in your presence, so far from contradicting it, you would approve of it. I would. But how is this relevant? The clearer you make my opposition to the British Government the graver Mr Colles's defence becomes.

The British Government will survive your opposition. This is the way you describe the Queen – 'A woman of vile, selfish, and pitiless soul'? I don't think that is the way I describe her. I did not write what you say.

'After all she is a woman; however vile, selfish, and pitiless her soul may be, she must sometimes tremble as death approaches.' That is a translation of what appeared in my paper in Paris.

Do you wish to repudiate it? Not in the slightest. The translation may change it; but I take the fullest responsibility for that article.

'She has always been ready to cover with her Royal mantle the crimes and turpitude of her Empire'? I believe that to be right. That is my belief.

'Taking the shamrock in her withered hand?' Does that show good taste? I consider it to be true.

Listen to this. 'Victoria in the decrepitude of her eighty-one years?' I think it describes her exactly.

Are you an Irishwoman? I am an Irishwoman.

Was your father an Irishman? He was, and proud of it, and told me to be proud of it.

And proud of the fact that he was for so many years in the pay of Her Majesty's Government? As I said already, my father held different ideas to what I do.

Of what part of Ireland are you a native? I was brought up in Dublin.

That is not my question. I was born while my father's regiment was quartered in Aldershot.

That is the reason you stated a while ago that you were Irish by birth? I am an Irishwoman. My father was Irish.

What part of Ireland did your father come from? I don't know where he was born.

Mr Swifte, who was on the bench, concluded that while Miss Gonne's views were shocking, she was entitled to put the criminal law into operation. The natural effect of Ramsay Colles's placard was to hold her up to hatred and contempt. He would make no comment about her claim that the placard implied that she was a spy; the injury to her reputation rested on other grounds. Nothing could be more mean than to oppose the government as she did and at the same time to take a pension from that government. A *prima facie* case had been made, and Swifte judged that he must send Ramsay Colles for trial. That decision forced Colles to apologize, and the case was closed.[47]

The cross-examination proved 'a terrible nervous strain' for Maud Gonne, but her friends said she appeared to be 'wonderfully cool and collected'.[48] Certainly, the unflustered clarity of her verbal performance is astonishing; her responses to questions are prompt, succinct and to the point. Owing to this performance, her reputation as an Irish republican remained intact. John O'Leary, still chief of the IRB in Ireland, gave her his blessing.

However, no sooner was she free from the libels of Ramsay Colles than F. Hugh O'Donnell privately circulated a truly scandalous pamphlet about Maud Gonne. Yeats once again was summoned to her defence, but he had no luck in arraigning O'Donnell before a secret IRB court of inquiry.

10

Saturday 30 June 1900 was the Patriotic Children's Fête. According to the *Freeman's Journal*, 30,000 children paraded from Beresford Place to Clontarf Park, where they were addressed by Maud Gonne. Three tons of sweets and 50,000 buns were consumed. According to a surprisingly witty police report, 'the young people were treated to moderate refreshments and unlimited treason in the shape of disloyal emblems and speeches'. Some of those who would be 'out' in 1916 reported in old age that their political lives began on this day.[49]

In mid July Gonne hosted in Paris a group of friends from Inghinidhe na hÉireann, the IRB and the staff of the *United Irishman*. This was not just a junket to the 1900 Paris Exhibition; it was the 'Irish delegation' (if a self-appointed one) to the World's Fair, in which many nations were represented. Maud Gonne organized an event to celebrate Irish volunteers who had fought for France in the past, and French soldiers who fought for Ireland – in effect, propaganda for French military support of an imminent Irish rebellion, so that it could be 'a nation once again'.[50] A police report noted that Maud Gonne and the IRB were seeking official authorization from France for an Irish brigade trained and stationed on French soil, ready to sail for Ireland whenever opportunity for rebellion arose.[51]

Maud Gonne spent the month of August in Aix-les-Bains. Her sister Kathleen had taken Iseult for a holiday elsewhere, so she had no child to mind. While attempting to rest, Gonne stewed over the infamies in F. Hugh O'Donnell's *ad feminam* pamphlet, and worked away at an article of retaliation for the *United Irishman*, which Yeats and Æ ultimately persuaded her not to publish.[52]

Lucien Millevoye may have been in Aix-les-Bains too. A number of Gonne scholars – Norman Jeffares, Karen Steele, Anna Magny and Deirdre Toomey – date her final break with Millevoye to this summer.[53] After studying O'Donnell's pamphlet, Gonne, one may speculate, was moved to make Millevoye understand how much she had been forced to suffer as a result of her affair with him. In September Gonne wrote to Yeats that her month in Aix-les-Bains had been a 'time of stupid little worries which got on my nerves & made my temper bad'. This forced understatement could easily apply not just to a final break with Millevoye, but to her attempt to protect herself from F. Hugh O'Donnell's slanders, or any number of other irritations. There are no clear signs that Gonne and Millevoye were intimate in the months immediately before August 1900, or those after it. The frequent republication of opinion pieces and news items from *La Patrie* in the pages of *L'Irlande Libre* and the *United Irishman*, and vice versa, continued. Millevoye now and again saw Iseult. His daughter remembered him giving her a coin while she was with Ghénia de Sainte-Croix. Not that he was a cosy paternal figure: Iseult and her cousin Thora Pilcher nicknamed him *Le Loup*, The Wolf.[54]

After the summer of 1900, however, Maud Gonne clearly did turn in search of a new male companion – one who was neither Millevoye nor Yeats. In September and October Gonne ordered the printing of 40,000 leaf-lets admonishing Irishmen not to enlist in the British army; she organized Inghinidhe na hÉireann; and she gave public addresses in which she said that Irishwomen should not walk out with British soldiers and that Irishmen who joined the army were traitors. The Boer War, however, was a lost cause in the autumn of 1900, though skirmishes continued and the last of the Boers would not surrender until May 1902.[55] President Kruger had gone into exile, and was making his way towards France.

On behalf of the Irish Transvaal Committee, Gonne had an elaborately lettered 'Address' to Paul Kruger prepared for presentation, and Inghinidhe na hÉireann designed its own ceremonial parchment for Kruger, in Gaelic, 'on behalf of the women of Ireland'.[56] By this time the Irish Brigade had disbanded and Major John MacBride was also on his way to Paris. He arrived on 6 November and Kruger on 22 November. Maud Gonne, with John MacBride, six Irish delegates – and Millevoye, joined the crowd of 10,000 that had gathered to welcome the president at the railway station.[57] In the *United Irishman*'s report, the Irish were by no means lost in the crowd (though Millevoye was overlooked):[58]

> The old lion of the veldt has come to Paris ... Miss Gonne, of course, is there at the head of the band, John O'Leary, a venerable, and if he will permit it, picturesque reminder of old battle days of the land; Major MacBride, who is himself fresh from the fight, reeking with cannon smoke, a tried veteran now, consecrated in I know not how many fights – standard-bearer of the Irish cause; Count Dalton O'Shea, descendant of an ancient exiled Irish family, still true to the old land's cause, and W. O'Leary Curtis, representative of the Irish Transvaal Committee – a consistent enemy to English rule.

The next day, Gonne joined a long queue of dignitaries waiting at President Kruger's hotel to pay their respects. John MacBride lodged at the Hôtel de l'Europe with his mother Honoria, his brother Anthony, his old friend Arthur Griffith and IRB chief Dr Mark Ryan. Gonne invited MacBride and Griffith to dine at 7 Avenue d'Eylau. Deep into the night, she lay back in her armchair smoking one cigarette after another, studying the short, wiry, red-haired soldier with a sunburnt face, while he told of galloping without fear into the face of British fire, and sending Tommies running across the veldt in terror. Days later, when MacBride's mother and brother left Hôtel de l'Europe to return home, Gonne insisted that he take up residence at her flat, a fact he let slip to an interviewer for *The Times.*[59] This hospitality was quite outside of MacBride's notions of what to expect from a lady of quality. On 26 November MacBride and Gonne went with O'Leary Curtis to Hôtel Scribe for the presentation of the two Irish testimonials to President Kruger. After the ceremony, an Irish journalist asked MacBride how he felt. He was, he said, never so moved in all his life; the last time he had seen Kruger was in South Africa:[60]

> I sail on Saturday for New York ... I am not much of a speechmaker. I believe more in the efficacy of one well-directed bullet than in a hundred appeals to the foreign parliament that has its seat at Westminster. But I may give some lectures in America.

The journalist then asked Maud Gonne how she, 'a daughter of Erin', felt about having met Kruger:

> Well, to tell the truth, I felt as if I could have burst into tears! It seemed to me so dreadful that we, who represent Ireland, the land of born soldiers and of heroes, could offer nothing more to that aged enemy of our country's foe than addresses, howsoever beautiful and kindly meant.

During his last days in Paris, Maud Gonne helped MacBride to write a speech he could deliver in the United States. He pleaded with her to accompany him on 1 December when he set off for his lecture tour. While he was not frightened of war, the prospect of giving lectures left him terrified. She, however, was scheduled for appearances in Belfast and Limerick in the first week of December, and in Liverpool during the second week. Still, she was clearly taken with the brave major. In her Limerick lecture, she announced to the crowd her high estimate of him: 'I consider that John MacBride has done more for Ireland than any living man.'[61]

Once MacBride arrived in New York, he wired Gonne that, while he had received a hero's welcome in America, his lecture tour might be cancelled unless she joined him as a speaker. On 15 December Tom Clarke, then in New York, sent his fiancée Kathleen Daly a bit of gossip: Maud Gonne was coming to join John MacBride in America.[62]

11

Gonne gave Yeats warnings that their spiritual marriage did not, in her view, tie down its partners. In July she had declined his 'kind, sweet' proposal that they enter into a white marriage.[63] Yeats's proposal took it as given that she would never be more to him than a sister, but, by means of a formal union, he could offer her the protection of his name, which would be a defence against scandalous attacks, like F. Hugh O'Donnell's pamphlet. Her answer was that she would 'not accept protection from anyone'. Yeats had 'his own natural life to live', and should not feel any duty towards her. Lady Gregory gave him the peace and ease his writing required; that was good. As for herself, she needed the whirlwind. This letter spelled out plainly that the spiritual marriage, in her view, was not exclusive. She set him free to find a lover or a wife, or just to remain as he was with Lady Gregory.

On 14 December 1900 after deciding to join MacBride in America, Maud Gonne wrote to Yeats about a 'most beautiful girl about 18' she had come across.[64] The young Irishwoman was on her way to join the cast of a lewd musical comedy in London. It would be much better, Gonne reasoned, for her to get a part in a decent Irish play. She had given this, Gonne repeated, 'very beautiful girl' Yeats's address in London. It seems possible that Gonne's letter of recommendation is not just a characteristically charitable act, but a signal to Yeats that she is anything but jealous where he is concerned.

12

Maud Gonne and her little dog Patsy arrived in New York on 10 February 1901. In a letter to her future husband Tom Clarke, Kathleen Daly asked about the nature of the relationship between Gonne and MacBride.[65] The two were staying in the same hotels in Chicago, Kansas City, St Louis and elsewhere, taking meals and travelling on trains together. Gonne gave fiery, eloquent speeches about British perfidy and Irish courage; MacBride, with his hands in his pockets, stood on stage and described battles in the Boer War from the vantage point of one who had been in the midst of them.[66] When they were alone, MacBride pressed his suit. From what he knew of women, little enough though that was, it seemed that she must be in love with him. She had come so far at his request, and she made so much in public of his heroism. The way she rambled across the continent, never complaining about the 'knocking about', 'for a woman,' he wrote to his mother, 'it is wonderful'.[67] It may be that during this tour, or before, she accepted him as her lover. A woman who did that, by MacBride's code of conduct (which differed little from that of F. Hugh O'Donnell), desperately wanted to get married; otherwise, she must be a trollop. On St Patrick's Day in St Louis, he asked Maud Gonne to be his wife. She did not quite say no. Her answer was that there was no room in her life for marriage while the war continued. If she meant the Boer War, that was pretty much over. If she meant the Irish war with Britain, its end was two decades away.

The pair continued to be together in America until the third week of May. Gonne sent remittances to the *United Irishman* – two of ten pounds and one of fifteen pounds were reported by Dublin Metropolitan Police spies.[68] When they returned to New York City, MacBride was able to persuade John Devoy of Clann na nGael to funnel money to the Gonne's paper.[69] In New York they spent time with Tom Clarke, one of the dynamitards for whose amnesty Gonne had long laboured. He liked MacBride: 'His manner is not very taking but the more one knows him, the better you like him. He is a first-class fellow I find in every respect'.[70] MacBride agreed to act as best man at Clarke's wedding. Maud Gonne, an old friend of the Daly family, hoped to be present for the event too, but Kathleen's arrival in New York was delayed past Gonne's 13 May sailing for Europe on the *Lorraine*.

After the 16 July wedding in the Bronx, MacBride was ready to return to France. He wrote to Gonne that in Paris he could make a living as a journalist. There he would be close to the action in case an opportunity for war arose in Ireland (in MacBride and Gonne's correspondence, war had a euphemistic or metaphorical character, comparable to the occult in the Yeats/Gonne letters). In Paris, MacBride was awarded a post – more for his nationalism than his journalism – as secretary to Victor Collins, correspondent for the American *Sun*.[71]

On 10 September Maud Gonne visited Westport, MacBride's home town, after unveiling a 1798 monument in Castlebar. Honoria MacBride, John's mother, had a general store (with a counter for alcoholic drinks) along the quays. Maud Gonne stayed with his brother Joseph for three days in his cottage at Rossbeg.[72] She was getting to know the family.

The progress of the Gonne-MacBride relationship did not escape the notice of scandalmonger F. Hugh O'Donnell. An announcement had been published that Major MacBride was to be honoured in Paris in November, with a presentation of appropriately martial tokens of esteem: a sword of honour from John O'Leary, and an engraved revolver from Maud Gonne on behalf of the 'Major MacBride Club'.[73] Someone took out an advertisement in *Reynolds' News* (a British Sunday newspaper): 'Sword of honour to be presented to an Irish literary warrior in Paris, to avoid him any alarms in the presentation to be performed by a complaisant English woman'.[74] It was signed 'Mary Jane Griffith & Anarchino' but Gonne reasonably suspected F. Hugh O'Donnell of being the author, given the allusions to herself as being both 'complaisant' and 'English'. She had also identified his hand in a *Pall Mall Gazette* article accusing MacBride of cowardice and Gonne herself of being English. It added that the ceremony of presentation to MacBride would be attended by 'French national-ists of the Rochefort Millevoye type'. On top of O'Donnell's sneaky insinua-tions, Gonne had been accused by IRB members of 'felon-setting' for making speeches urging open revolution. Could Yeats not do something? Gonne may have assumed that Yeats would suppose that something was going on between herself and MacBride, or perhaps she believed his often-tested love of her was blind love.

13

If Maud Gonne was enamoured with Major MacBride, love did not temper her politics. In the first week of July 1901 she came to Dublin for the funeral of her doctor, George Sigerson. Greeted by an English acquaintance in the street, she accepted his handshake. Afterwards, she wrote an article about how ashamed of herself she was for doing so. Because of the use of concentra-tion camps by British forces in South Africa, all English people were outside the 'pale of civilization'. To show them any courtesy at all was to tolerate evil.[75]

In a September speech to the Dublin Workmen's Club, she described Ireland as a dying mother, unable to support her children.[76] This was the doing of the longstanding British policy of racial extermination. The Irish Parliamentary Party was really to blame, because its members tolerated Britain's sham political institutions. It was time to prepare for a physical force solution to Ireland's problems.

In an interview with *Le Figaro* (10 October) she explained that her new policy of intolerance was that Irishmen elected to Parliament should not take their seats. British goods should be boycotted in Irish stores. Irishmen should prepare for open insurrection.[77] In November she proposed that when nationalists were not selected for jury duty on account of their beliefs, they should obstruct the court until they were arrested, and in this manner make impossible the false justice of British law.[78]

These are all radical measures. They are also steps taken much later by Sinn Féin in the War of Independence. One should be careful not to underestimate the effect of Maud Gonne on Irish politics, although it is difficult to measure that effect precisely. The publicity, funding, organization, public speaking and mass mobilization, for the Anti-Eviction movement, the Amnesty Association, the Wolfe Tone Memorial Committee and Irish Transvaal Committee were all her work. Often she was the only woman in these organizations. Maud Gonne was essential to them all. Her aim was always the violent overthrow of the British government of Ireland. Her vast financial resources, uniquely charismatic power on the speaker's platform and ruthless clarity of purpose were essential to the increase in militant activism during the Irish Revival.

14

Maud Gonne, in Dublin for the Christmas holidays of 1901, became involved, as president, in the activities of Inghinidhe na hÉireann. In addition to its classes in Irish language, history and literature, the members of the organization had started putting on pageants and plays with the help of Frank and W.G. Fay's 'Comedy Combination'.[79] Over the holidays, several of the women were in a performance of Æ's *Deirdre* at George Coffey's home. Gonne thought Ella Young 'quite exceptionally good' in her part. She judged that Mary Walker (Máire Nic Shiubhlaigh) had the makings of a fine actress too. She wrote to Yeats to ask if he had decided what to do with his new play *Cathleen ni Houlihan*. Gonne urged him to give it to the Fays and the women of Inghinidhe na hÉireann for performance.[80] She had not yet put herself forward for the leading role, but within a week she did just that, to overcome Lady Gregory's resistance to allowing the Fays to undertake the production.[81] Her sudden desire to take the stage had little to do with wanting to please the author of the play. In this script, she perceived an opportunity for an Inghinidhe na hÉireann political spectacle to match the Patriotic Children's Treat.

In mid February, after reaching agreement to perform *Cathleen ni Houlihan* during Easter Week 1902, Gonne wrote to Yeats. She said she was glad to hear that Lady Gregory had been taking good care of him while he was ill. Then she talked about the great meeting she had put on with MacBride in Paris; 4000 were in the audience. What the letter implies is that if he had someone, she did too. Then she explained:[82]

> I keep getting a vision of a beautiful grey shrouded figure holding a wonderful jewelled chalice, which I think at times contains fire, for I see flames sometimes rising [from] it. Through the grey veils one can see the glimmer of precious stones & jewels. I don't think she has anything to do with the grey woman I used to see. She is very calm & seems to be great & holy. Do you know what it means?

It would require neither one deeply versed in occult arts, nor a Freudian analyst, to interpret this 'vision'. The chalice is the vagina. The vagina is happy. The grey woman is no longer grey. This is semaphore, not a real dream.

15

In later years, when Yeats was defending the idea that the Irish National Theatre Society was dedicated to art and not to propaganda, those of another view always brought up *Cathleen ni Houlihan*.[83] Yeats argued in a patent application for the Abbey Theatre that this play could not be propaganda in essence even if it were so in effect, because it was based on a dream he had had in the summer of 1901. There are many problems with Yeats's ascription of authorship to his dream. Lady Gregory, for instance, wrote most of the play's dialogue. Some key aspects of the action and *mise en scène* arose in rehearsal. But it is possible that Yeats had a dream, maybe even a nightmarish dream, in the summer of 1901, about a woman who had put on years, too many years for Lucien Millevoye, a woman who had had lovers, who was in league with the French, who was always trying to whip up war, who spoke in nationalist clichés, who had a mystic power over Irish crowds, and who then suddenly became a beautiful young woman again, with the gliding walk of a queen. It was as if she had had a bath in that famous ancient pool that renews the virginity of Greek goddesses. Whatever *Cathleen ni Houlihan*, as written by Lady Gregory, and acted by Maud Gonne, may have come to mean to others, it may have originally been something entirely different to Yeats: 'Heart mysteries there, and yet when all is said/ It was the dream itself enchanted me' ('The Circus Animals' Desertion').[84]

As for Maud Gonne, it is an understatement to say the part of Cathleen ni Houlihan was made for her. It was her own ultimate wish-fulfilment dream.

She had a problematic, actually a false, claim on Irishness, but Yeats's play made her into its embodiment. This was better than the implied flattery of *The Countess Cathleen*. There she was a pity-crazed, bleeding-heart aristocrat ready to sell all that she had, even her soul, for the peasantry. In *Cathleen ni Houlihan* she inhabited a different order of reality, a symbolic space, both near to and infinitely far from ordinary Irish cottiers, but still she was the impersonation of the Spirit of the Nation.

There was one aspect of the play that Gonne did not like: its ending. In mid March when the play was being rehearsed, 'it went splendidly', she told Yeats, except for the scene when the curtain closed. In the play, the year is 1798, and the place somewhere near the landing spot of the French invasion force under General Humbert. An old woman on the road appears at a cottage seeking comfort. Inside, the family is preparing for young Michael's wedding, but as the old woman sits by the fire she recalls – as if reciting old rebel ballads – all the young men who, out of love of her, had given up their lives. Still, she continued to need someone to help her to drive the strangers out of her house and to recover her four green fields. Michael falls under her spell, and, when she goes out the door, makes as if to follow her. In the original draft by Yeats and Gregory, Michael stands at the door hesitating when the play ends. Gonne objects to this vacillation:[85]

> We are all of opinion that Michael ought to go *right* out of the door instead of standing HESITATING. It doesn't seem clear if he doesn't go out. If he goes out Delia can throw herself on Briget's shoulder in tears which makes a much better end. Please write at once and say if we may do that. Russell & Miss Young & the Fays & all the actors want it & think it is much better and indeed *necessary.*

Yeats conceded the change, and it was not an insignificant one. It alters the play from one that dramatizes vacillation about the value of blood sacrifice to a play that wholly recommends such sacrifice above all other values – prosperity, parents, promises and romantic love.

In the performances on 2, 3 and 4 April, Maud Gonne vanished into the character, and the character became Maud Gonne. The stage of St Teresa's Hall of Total Abstinence was tiny; there was a full but entirely sober house. Gonne made her way through the crowd to the stage, wearing a stagey mop of long white horse hair, and hunched under a black cloak, but everyone knew who this six-foot-two female must be. As the play unfolded, Yeats was disconcerted by the peasant comedy side of the play (why were people laughing?), but then found himself swept away by the 'weird power' of Maud Gonne; 'creepy' was Joseph Holloway's word for her acting.[86] Gonne arose at the ending as if mounting a speaker's platform, focused her eyes in a 1000-yard-stare, and gave an oration in a quavering voice: 'They shall be reee-mem-be-rrred ... *for everrr!*' The combination of a simplistic rendering of peasant life and an other-worldly revelation aimed at the audience was startlingly effective. Here is the contemporary report from the *New Ireland Review*:

> The well-known Nationalist orator did not address the other actors as is usual in drama, but spoke directly to the audience, as if she was addressing them in Beresford Place ... She can scarcely be said to act the part, she lived it. When she entered the little firelit room there came with her a sense of tragedy and the passion of deathless endeavour.[87]

In that performance, Yeats's own private dream, and the dream-work behind it, vanished from sight: one could only see Maud Gonne, icon of insurrection, and hear Lady Gregory's dialogue.

The play was instantly successful. It led directly to the formation of a permanent theatre company by the Fay brothers for producing plays in Ireland by Irish authors with Irish actors (eventually housed in the Abbey Theatre). But its thrilling dramatization of a boy's moment of political commitment, and the report from off stage that the old woman had therefore turned into a young girl with the walk of a queen, made the little one-act into a machine for the manufacture of militant patriots. It was staged over and over as a curtain-raiser at the Abbey in the years before 1916, and by amateur theatre clubs all over Ireland. The play was simplicity itself for actors to perform and audiences to understand. On Tuesday fourteen Easters later, Joseph Holloway, the Dublin diarist, made a note on the 1916 rebels being blasted by British firepower, 'Poor brave fellows. It is sad to think that those who serve Cathleen ni Houlihan must give her themselves, must give her all.'[88]

16

According to R.F. Foster in *W.B. Yeats: A Life*, the incident on which the poem 'Adam's Curse' is based occurred in May 1902 in the Kensington drawing room of May Gonne, Maud's cousin. *A Servant of the Queen* gives a detailed recollection of the scene, in which she identifies 'that beautiful mild woman, your close friend' from the poem as her sister Kathleen:

While we were still at dinner Willie Yeats arrived to see me and we all went into the drawing room for coffee. Kathleen [her sister, Mrs Pilcher] and I sat together on a big sofa amid piles of soft cushions … I saw Willie Yeats looking critically at me and he told Kathleen he liked her dress and that she was looking younger than ever. It was on that occasion Kathleen remarked that it was hard work being beautiful which Willie turned into his poem 'Adam's Curse'.

Next day when he called to take me out to pay my customary visit to the Lia Fail [Coronation Stone from the hill of Tara, held in Westminster Abbey], he said: 'You don't take care of yourself as Kathleen does, so she looks younger than you; your face is worn and thin; but you will always be beautiful, more beautiful than anyone I have known. You can't help that. Oh, Maud, why don't you marry me and give up this tragic struggle and live a peaceful life? I could make such a beautiful life for you among artists and writers who would understand you.'

'Willie, are you not tired of asking that question? How often have I told you to thank the gods that I will not marry you. You would not be happy with me.'

'I am not happy without you.'

'Oh yes you are, because you make beautiful poetry out of what you call your unhappiness and you are happy in that. Marriage would be such a dull affair. Poets should never marry. The world should thank me for not marrying you. I will tell you one thing, our friendship has meant a great deal to me; it has helped me often when I needed help, needed it perhaps more than you or anybody know, for I never talk or even think of these things.'[89]

The emptiness of the spiritual marriage between Gonne and Yeats, the torpidity of his dutiful adherence to chivalric codes, and the patent pleasure of crafting beautiful verses are all embodied in the poem's conclusion:

> We sat grown quiet at the name of love;
> We saw the last embers of daylight die,
> And in the trembling blue-green of the sky
> A moon, worn as if it had been a shell
> Washed by time's waters as they rose and fell
> About the stars and broke in days and years.
>
> I had a thought for no one's but your ears:
> That you were beautiful, and that I strove
> To love you in the old high way of love;
> That it had all seemed happy, and yet we'd grown
> As weary-hearted as that hollow moon.

From its first lines to its last, 'Adam's Curse' conveys the sense of an ending: the day, the summer, the beauty of a woman, the moon, even his love – they all are coming to a close, and try though a person might, and perhaps must, nothing can stop the death of everything.

A short time after the event that inspired 'Adam's Curse', from her newly acquired house next door to Æ's home on Coulson Avenue in Rathgar, Dublin, Maud Gonne wrote to her sister Kathleen that '1st I am to become Catholic; 2nd I am to marry Major MacBride':

> Neither you nor anyone on earth quite knows the hard life I have led, for I never told of my troubles and I have preferred to be envied rather than pitied. Now I see the chance, without injuring my own work, of having a little happiness and peace in my personal life, and I am taking it. We are made that way, that we need companionship, and with Iseult growing up, I cannot get this companionship outside of marriage. Marriage I always consider abominable, but for the sake of Iseult, I make this sacrifice to convention. Now my dearest, MacBride and I are interested in the same work and the Irish movement is a people's movement.

Kathleen had her doubts about this decision. MacBride had neither money nor position. Maud had never actually said she loved him. If she wanted to get married, why not marry W.B. Yeats? Maud replied:[90]

> Of course as regards social position in the worldly sense you are right in what you say but dear one you must consider my life is different from yours – I only like those who are doing something.
>
> I am getting old and oh so tired and I have found a man who has a stronger will than myself and who at the same time is thoroughly honourable and whom I trust.
>
> As for Willie Yeats I love him dearly as a friend but I could not for one minute imagine marrying him.

Maud told Kathleen the part about marrying MacBride was secret. That was in June 1902. The following month Gonne told Yeats that she had stayed a week in the Carmelite Convent in Laval in western France, where Iseult was baptized a Catholic. She prevaricated about her own intentions: 'I felt a little inclined to be [baptized] also but felt it would mean limitations of thought so didn't.'[91] Still, the lie is a hint about the real truth. Some anxiety about Yeats's reaction to the impending change in her life, or some consideration for his feelings, may also have led her to embroider a letter box for the poet's papers during her July holiday at Aix-les-Bains.[92]

Certainly, it was of practical importance to keep Yeats on side. They were both officers of Cumann na nGaedheal and the new Irish National Theatre Society. He was a man she could trust to help her whenever she called. In October, when Inghinidhe na hÉireann was planning a programme of plays for the Samhain festival, late in the rehearsal period W.G. Fay withdrew Yeats's *The Hour-Glass* because he wished to keep it for the opening of the theatre society's new performance space on Camden Street. Máire Quinn of Inghinidhe na hÉireann was outraged. She accused the Fays of being afraid of political plays (though *The Hour-Glass* is not obviously a propaganda play). In a confidential letter to Yeats, Gonne took up Máire Quinn's battle for her. Yeats was not to mention Quinn's name when he told the Fays to reverse their decision about *The Hour-Glass*. She presumed that her own influence over Yeats would remain irresistible.

In January 1903 she again urged Yeats to intervene and tell the Fays what to do. Máire Quinn wanted the part of Cathleen ni Houlihan now that Gonne was giving up the stage. Yeats was to inform the Fays that Quinn was to have this signature role, a casting decision normally belonging to a director.[93] Fay had a temper, and this interference set him off:[94]

> Miss Quinn is a member of my company whom my brother & self have taught what ever she knows of acting and it seems rather humourous [*sic*] to me that she should begin to think that she is the best judge of how parts should be given out in my company. I bitterly dislike underhand dealing of any sort and as far as I can prevent it, it won't find room in my company. As long as I stage manage my crowd I will give parts to the persons who seem to me most fitted for them.

Nonetheless, Máire Quinn got the part she wanted.

In the last week of January 1903 Maud Gonne waded into theatrical affairs once again. She was outraged by the cheek of W.G. Fay because he had altered the ending of a Cumann na Gaedheal prize-winning play, Padraic Colum's *The Saxon Shillin'*. This was an agitprop skit rather like *Cathleen ni Houlihan*. Two sisters are resisting eviction from their cabin; their Fenian father is in prison, and their brother, sick of politics, is in the British army. He comes home, and, inspired by the plight of his sisters, takes up a rifle: 'I'll defend the place till the last,' he cries, 'For land an' home, Irishmen join me!'[95] The final tableau has him shot dead in the doorway by order of his own commanding officer. W.G. Fay thought the ending melodramatic, more suitable for Queens' Theatre populism than the new form of Irish theatre to which he aspired. He had Colum rewrite the ending. At a read-through of the new version, Maud Gonne berated Fay in front of his actors with fierce majesty, saying he had ruined the play, and done it out of cowardice, or out of a wish to get in with Unionist backers of the new theatre. Gonne often told men that they were cowards and Unionists; it was a powerful rhetorical tactic. She was a lot bigger than Fay, and a lot richer, but he stood up to her. He didn't care about her 'damned' nationalist societies; he was in charge of the play as a play. Did he say 'damned'? To me? Gonne laughed to cover up her embarrassment. Later she issued a threat to resign over the insult.[96]

In a letter to Yeats, the president of the Society (she was a vice-president), Gonne unreeled a line of complaints against W.G. Fay, ending up with 'He blustered & was rude to me & to Cumman na Gaedheal.' W.G. Fay also appealed to Yeats. He did not care a damn about offending the *United Irishman*, and he obviously did not care a damn about saying 'damn'. He had just one fixed opinion: 'that a Theatre is no more a Political Party than it is a Temperance platform … For pity sake, let Art at least be free.'[97] Intellectually, Yeats was on W.G. Fay's side of this argument, but he had always come to Maud Gonne's side when she appealed for his help. That was about to change.

17

In January 1903 J.M. Synge crossed over to London with three new plays in his suitcase, unseen as of yet by anyone in the theatre. Over the next two months, first in Lady Gregory's rooms at Queen Anne's Mansions, and later, in the Woburn Buildings at Yeats's regular Monday 'At Home', he read out his writings of the summer before, in January and February *Riders to the Sea*, and on 3 March *In the Shadow of the Glen*. The audiences were mainly London men of letters, such as John Masefield, G.K. Chesterton and Arthur Symons. They all loved it. It was the debut of Synge as a man of letters. He was looking for a publisher for his Aran prose book and his plays, and opportunities for literary journalism. Mostly, however, he was hoping to get his plays put on stage by what was still called the Fays' company, but was rapidly being taken over by W.B. Yeats and Lady Gregory.

On 2 February Maud Gonne herself came to a reading of *Riders to the Sea* in Yeats's rooms.[98] She had known Synge in Paris six years earlier, when he came regularly to her Paris branch of the Young Ireland Society for the first four months of 1897. Then by means of a rather officious letter, Synge informed

Gonne that he would come to no more of her meetings: he couldn't 'get mixed up with a revolutionary and semi-military movement'.[99] That *mixed up with* suggests a distaste for potentially shameful doings, doings she herself had a taste for. Now they met again, in a London literary drawing room.

Gonne was still indignant at the time that W.G. Fay had made 'rude remarks' in front of the company, and she was a vice-president and he was only the stage manager; she could not, she said, 'remain a Vice-President of an Association where only the stage-manger's opinion counts'.[100] Surely Yeats would put things right.

Yeats changed the subject to Synge. What did it matter how *The Saxon Shillin'* ended, or what rules and regulations Æ had concocted to resolve disputes, now that they had plays like *Riders to the Sea* in their hands? Yet Maud Gonne was unlikely to admire this play or its playwright. She can hardly have found its profound fatalism – so many young men dying, in a struggle against the sea – a rousing alternative to Colum's *Saxon Shillin'*. His last line – 'Irishmen, join me!' – from her point of view was a great ending for a play; Maurya's 'No man at all can be living for ever, and we must be satisfied' was less inspiring.[101] Did she perhaps realize the ending of *Riders to the Sea* contradicted the line about the dead young men, which, just the previous April, she spoke as Cathleen ni Houlihan –'They shall be alive for ever'? If men were made to reflect that their time in life was short, and you only live once, and the universe will always be what it is, then it would not be easy to get Irish boys to die for Ireland.

On 18 March 1903, when Synge left London for Paris, he had the support of Yeats, Gregory and London's literary elite, but he did not have any guarantee of backing from Maud Gonne, or from the new Reading Committee of the Irish National Theatre Society. In fact Gonne was already determined to found a new theatre group, directly under the aegis of Cumann na nGaedheal, which would produce plays in Irish by Douglas Hyde and propaganda plays such as *The Saxon Shillin'*, and, if she could get it, a 'very direct, short' anti-King Edward VII play. Direct, short, and propagandistic was what she wanted, and she was not much interested in anything else.

18

There was little likelihood of W.B. Yeats and Maud Gonne working out their differences once he received on 7 February, just before giving a lecture on 'The Future of Irish Drama', a telegram announcing the engagement of Maud Gonne to John MacBride. Regardless of any adumbrations from Maud Gonne, he was thunderstruck. She was to be received into the Roman Catholic Church on 17 February 1903, and married four days later. Yeats dashed off three letters to her, one right after the other, attempting to persuade her neither to become Catholic nor to marry MacBride. Those letters are lost, but her reply of 10 February is extant; it tries to assure him that she will be the same as ever: 'Marriage won't change me I think at all.'[102] A draft of Yeats's fascinating, bizarre fourth letter exists.[103] In language that mingled Protestant bias, Nietzschean superman theory and Rosicrucian pretension, Yeats wrote that if Maud Gonne turned Catholic and married a common Irishman, she would 'fall into a lower order & do great injury to the religion of [pure] free souls that is growing up in Ireland'. This was at bottom an appeal to Anglo-Irish values, but those were not Maud Gonne's values.

The objections of other friends were more sensible. All who knew either the bride or the groom thought the marriage ill-conceived. MacBride's brother warned him: 'She is accustomed to money. You have none. She is used to going her own way and listening to no one ... these are not good qualities for a wife.'[104] Arthur Griffith knew each of the parties well:

> Queen, forgive me. John MacBride, after Willie Rooney, is the best friend I ever had; you are the only woman friend I have. I only think of both your happiness. For your own sakes and for the sake of Ireland to whom you both belong, don't get married. I know you both, you so unconventional – a law to yourself; John so full of conventions, you will not be happy for long.[105]

Iseult Gonne, when told of the upcoming marriage, said that she hated John MacBride. Honoria MacBride was direct in a letter to her son: 'She will not make you happy. You will neither be happy. She is not the wife for you.' In spite of all this sound advice, marriage seemed to Maud Gonne at the time the right thing to do, and she was true to her habit: 'I never analyse or reason out personal things very deeply or at least not consciously.'[106]

There were signs of serious trouble even before the nuptials. Maud Gonne had told both her sister and Yeats that she disliked the institution of marriage. She intended to go on after marriage just as she had before, not even changing her name (in France, her name remained the same; in Ireland and Britain, she would be called Mrs MacBride). However, according to a notebook MacBride prepared when the marriage broke apart, Gonne told him another story altogether. His testimony was that at a time when he had decided to leave France for the USA, she begged him not to go, wept, and confessed that she had for years been leading an 'immoral life'. She had had, she explained, a child by her lover, a French deputy named Lucien Millevoye. Then she asked him to make her his wife. [107]

> She would place her whole life in my hands, to direct as I wished, if I would make her my wife: that she had suffered greatly and wanted to try and be a good woman. I was moved by her and felt sad for her, and thinking I was doing a good thing for my country, I married Maud Gonne.

This is like a scene from a play by Arthur Wing Pinero, such as *The Second Mrs. Tanqueray*, so popular in the 1890s. But if the scene did in fact occur, and if Maud Gonne *was* playing a part, MacBride may seriously have come to believe he would be doing her a favour by giving her a life as a decent Irish Catholic wife and woman of the house. Yet their wishes were diametrically opposed.

The night before the wedding Maud Gonne insisted on writing a letter of explanation to Lucien Millevoye. MacBride objected. There was a violent scene. MacBride warned her to reflect on what it meant to marry him. After the ceremony, no communication with her former lovers would be permitted. He knew well that Millevoye was one of them. He believed Yeats to be another. He suspected there had been more.[108] Still they went forward.

The warlike and truly republican ceremony was held at two venues, the English Consulate and the parish church in Avenue d'Eylau. Its assertively political form was, from Maud Gonne's point of view, a public revision of the 'Secret Treaty' or Alliance with Lucien Millevoye in 1887. The couple feared that the groom would be arrested at the consulate, so MacBride kept one hand on his revolver throughout the vows.[109] Victor Collins, the America *Sun* journalist and MacBride's employer, gave away the bride at the church. Reginald Collins (brother of Victor) was drafted in as best man; he carried the battle-tested Irish Brigade flag made by Inghinidhe na hÉireann. A Belgian priest, Father Van Hecke, former chaplain of the Irish Brigade, officiated. Maud Gonne's wedding toast was 'To the complete independence of Ireland!' Seamus Ó Cathasaigh (James Casey), a close friend of MacBride and later an important figure in Sinn Féin, was one of the small party. At the wedding breakfast at the Hôtel de Florence, he presented the couple with a decorated

Irish harp by McFall of Belfast, a Kapp and Peterson pipe, a silver *mether* (Irish drinking cup) from Inghinidhe na hÉireann, a case of Belleek pottery from amnestied prisoner John Daly of Limerick, and Father Nolan's *Irish Prayer Book*. Ó Cathasaigh recited a poem in Irish, and (this would have been necessary) its translation – about a fair maiden who married a 'warrior generous and open-hearted',[110] yet she was not a maiden and he was not open-hearted. In the afternoon, Mr and Mrs MacBride went off on their terrible honeymoon, to begin a disastrous marriage.

X

THE CRACK-UP

Previous page: *John MacBride, best man at the 1901 wedding of Tom and Kathleen Clarke. On the reverse of the studio card is impressed "Purdy / 146 Tremont St. / Boston / LaCorona". (Image used courtesy of the National Library of Ireland)*

It is unclear how many days passed before the newlyweds began to understand that they had made a terrible mistake. In the first week of May, only five weeks after the marriage, Maud Gonne confided to Yeats in London that she had 'married in a sudden impulse of anger' against Lucien Millevoye.[1] In later years she said the couple married only because their 'work' (agitation for an insurrection) had come to a standstill, and they were both depressed.[2] Yet she had been entertaining MacBride's proposal for two years before the wedding, and had told her sister nine months earlier that she intended to accept it. Why did things go so quickly wrong? Or rather, why did she ever believe things could have gone well?

In the years before the wedding, Maud Gonne's campaign to create the conditions of war between Ireland and Britain had grown ever more frenzied. One of the primary attractions of Major MacBride from the start was his readiness to kill and be killed in a fight against Britain.

It is a puzzle why Gonne's long-standing Anglophobia had turned into a frantic, insatiable desire for immediate violent action. One hypothesis would be that it was an outcome of the painful break with Millevoye and her disillusionment with Yeats. Yet Millevoye's life was, since the Dreyfus affair, equally violent, wild and irrational. She was, one might conclude, still acting in harmony with the radical right nationalist, rather than in reaction against him.

At the time of Gonne's wedding, Millevoye was running a daily series of hysterical diatribes in *La Patrie* against the emerging *entente cordiale* between Britain and France. Newly crowned King Edward VII, an old friend to France, was strongly in favour of improved diplomatic relations and the settling of disputes over rival colonial claims in Africa. President Loubet issued a cordial invitation for Edward VII to be his official guest in May 1903. The current period of Anglo-French hostility (which Maud Gonne had believed would inevitably lead to international war, then an Irish rebellion backed by France) was coming to an end. Even Paul Déroulède, exiled in Spain, thought the *entente* ultimately good for *revanche*. He wrote a letter to Millevoye objecting to his advice that readers should hiss at the British king in the streets of Paris.[3]

While it seems incredible and utterly mad, on the last page of *A Servant of the Queen* Maud Gonne may be telling no more than the truth when she says that when the couple married they believed they were both about to die in an attempt to assassinate Edward VII in Gibraltar. Their honeymoon holiday was, in other words, a suicide mission to foil the *entente cordiale* by means of a terrorist act. Right after the marriage, Mr and Mrs MacBride informed the public that they would be taking their honeymoon in Algeciras, Spain, just opposite Gibraltar. Edward VII arrived in Gibraltar on 8 April 1903. Gonne expected to be shadowed by the police. She was to serve as a decoy, while MacBride reconnoitered with Clann na nGael operatives arriving from the USA.

When the king's yacht berthed, it was surrounded by a guard of honour. All along His Majesty's route, the road was lined with soldiers. The King was the guest of Sir George White at The Convent, the governor's official residence. The only outsiders to come near him there were a choir of children singing 'God Save the King'.

When on the day of the monarch's arrival, Major MacBride returned late to the hotel in Algeciras, Maud saw that he had been drinking. MacBride refused to explain to her how the plan had gone wrong. He later wrote to his brother Anthony:

> Needless to say I did not put foot on Gibraltar and consequently do not know how the C.B.s [Companions of the Bath, a British order of merit] are doing there. We were at Algeciras (opposite Gib) the day the king arrived and as he forgot to send me an invitation I did not go.[4]

It was disappointing. Since Maud Gonne and John MacBride had not died, they were going to have to live together. By the end of the month, she was pregnant.

The major did not by means of his marriage come into equal ownership, much less sole control, of his wife's property. She gave him £3000 as a present, which generated £100 a year in income. That was what she spent on 'dresses and journeys', and ought, she judged, to suffice for his needs.[5] She did not wish to humiliate him, or herself, by a situation in which he kept asking for small sums. Still, it may have been awkward for the major to have such determinations made independently by his new wife.

After a month of marriage Madame MacBride had to get away. Her cousin May was to be married in England, and in June Edward VII was making an official visit to Ireland. It would be up to her this time to disrupt a royal visit. The major could not come with her, not this time, nor on her future journeys. On British soil he was liable to be arrested for having fought for the enemy in the Boer War. Ahead of her departure from France, Gonne wrote to Yeats an effusive and grateful note asking if she could come to 18 Woburn Buildings for tea on her arrival in London, 4 May 1903. She was no sooner in the door than she told Yeats she wished she had never been married.

Madame MacBride had expected to carry on the life of Maud Gonne, without any change, but the major was shocked at the idea that being a wife should make so little difference to her. He had plenty of time while she was away to talk the matter over with his friend and boss, Victor Collins, at the American Bar in Paris.[6]

2

It took Maud Gonne MacBride, as she now signed herself, no time at all, after arriving in Dublin on 7 May, to whip up a lot of trouble. *The Saxon Shillin'*, rejected by the Irish National Theatre Society, was performed on 15 May by Inghinidhe na hÉireann.

On Sunday 17 May she sent telegrams to Edward Martyn, George Moore, Alderman Tom Kelly, Arthur Griffith, Henry Dixon (an IRB man) and Seamus MacManus, inviting them to tea at her house on Coulson Avenue. Her plan was to form a 'People's Protection Committee' to disrupt the meeting two days later at the Rotunda of the United Irish League for the purpose of setting up a parliamentary election fund. They were going to make a motion demanding that Tim Harrington, Lord Mayor and head of the United Irish League, formally refuse to welcome King Edward VII on his visit to Dublin. Moore, after hearing their plans, said he was a writer not a politician, and bowed out (thus, according to Gonne's stated opinion, proving himself a coward).[7] Moore's friend Edward Martyn, an often out-of-sorts ascendancy landlord, both Catholic and homosexual, was in the habit of accepting the presidency of any organization likely to annoy his fellow landlords. He became the nominal head of the People's Protection Committee. Several of those present at the Coulson Avenue Sunday tea remembered the gathering as the real beginning of the Sinn Féin party. Those involved soon renamed themselves the National Council of Cumann na Gaedheal, an organization dedicated to a united movement of opposition to both the parliamentary Home Rule movement and the British authority in Ireland.[8]

The 19 May 1903 'Battle of the Rotunda' was, in Maud Gonne's own view, one of her finest hours. Before the United Irish League could take up the first item on its agenda, the members of the People's Protection Committee pushed their way up on stage, in spite of barracking by League members. Martyn was unable to make himself heard in such circumstances; he passed the list of demands to Maud Gonne. She held it in her right hand, tapped it with her left, and made an answer inaudible to reporters to John Redmond's question of what she was doing there. Redmond expostulated, but she 'stood her ground defiantly.'[9] Tim Harrington asked her to wait her turn until the end of the meeting; the floor would then be open to 'all other business'. Yet the lady would not be delayed. Redmond called for silence so that she could be heard.

> Mrs MacBride: I will not detain you a moment.
>
> A voice: 'Thank you.' [*ironical laughter, cheers and boos*]
>
> Mrs MacBride: I am here with this deputation from the People's Protection Committee …
>
> A voice: We don't want your deputations. [*cheers and boos*]
>
> Mrs MacBride: Whether in the event of a visit to Ireland from the King of England, the Lord Mayor will, as head of this Municipality, carry out the wishes of his citizens by attending the meeting of the Dublin Corporation at which an address to the King may be moved [*cries of 'Bosh'*], and oppose it by his voice, vote, and influence. [*cries of 'rot' and renewed disorder*]

Tim Harrington, the Lord Mayor, rose and made a loquacious speech. His record as a nationalist was, he said, spotless, unlike that of some, gesturing to Martyn, who had until lately opposed even Home Rule. Maud Gonne shouted, 'Answer the question.' Harrington complained about a libellous paragraph that was appearing week after week in a newspaper that represented Mrs MacBride's views, the *United Irishman*. Martyn said this was no answer to the question. 'Voice:

They have come just to disturb the meeting. The Lord Mayor: [*fiercely to Martyn*]: I am no flunkey, sir – that is the only answer you will get [*loud applause*].'

Harrington started pushing Martyn off the platform, and he retreated, but Mrs MacBride stood her ground and courageously faced the meeting, which was in the majority opposed to her, asserting, 'I want a plain answer.' She and Harrington became engaged in a heated altercation, in the course of which he was heard to say, 'You know perfectly well that I would not.' Redmond begged Harrington to go ahead and give a definite answer; he himself declared to the crowd he would oppose any address to the king. But Harrington kept refusing to be bullied, until he finally shouted 'Very well then, No!' Some members of the United Irish League (Harrington's organization) shouted 'Throw her off!' Other men – Seán T. O'Kelly thought they were from the IRB – rushed the stage to force Harrington to answer the question then and there.[10] A chair was pitched up onto the platform. Harrington lifted up his own chair and hurled it at a man, injuring him. Then everyone started throwing chairs, onto the platform and down from it. The People's Protection Committee made a rapid retreat, with Mrs MacBride acting as an effective rearguard. The Lord Mayor 'jumped clean off the platform, and, plunging into the middle of the affray, seized several of the protagonists and separated them'.

After reading reports of the 'Battle of the Rotunda', Maud Gonne was concerned that some might think she had fled the scene before the fighting had come to a stop. *Judy: The London Serio-Comic Journal* openly teased her:[11]

> There is a moral to be drawn from the free fight organized by Miss Maud Gonne at Dublin last week. Although several persons, including an MP, sustained injuries, the lady's name is conspicuously absent from the list of the slain. We hesitate to impute cowardice to the wife of Major MacBride, but the inference is forced upon us. That she was present at the earlier stages of the meeting is indisputable; but, alas! when the trouble began it was gonne she was, entirely – into the garden, perhaps.

To put matters right, Maud Gonne had Seamus MacManus write a letter to the press in which he assumed complete responsibility for her early exit and swore that she herself wanted to remain until the end.[12]

3

Maud Gonne MacBride, knowing herself to be pregnant, spent most of the month of June in France. She returned to Dublin in July in order to lead the 'National Council' (formerly known as the People's Protection Committee) in a planned disruption of a 3 July 1903 meeting at City Hall. A vote was scheduled on a motion to offer a formal welcome to Edward VII during his visit to Ireland (21 July–1 August). The motion was defeated, with the assistance of Lord Mayor Tim Harrington; the king was, by vote of the city government, not welcome. Mrs MacBride remained in the city to organize a hostile reception for the king. In order to whip up sectarian feeling, with help from the women of Inghinidhe na hÉireann, she put up 10,000 copies of the anti-Catholic Coronation Oath on lamp posts and hoardings:

> Archbishop of the Church of England: Will you to the utmost of your power maintain the laws of God, the true profession of the gospel and the Protestant reformed religion established by law, and will you preserve unto the bishops and clergy of this Realm, and to the churches committed to their charge, all such rights and privileges as by law do or shall appertain unto them, or any of them?
>
> King Edward VII: All this I promise to do.

Preparations were made for burnings of the Union Jack at street corners along the king's parade route.

On Coulson Avenue in Rathgar, Maud Gonne MacBride noticed with annoyance that her neighbours had hung out red, white and blue bunting and Union Jacks. This was, she thought, disgraceful in a Catholic country, because Pope Leo XIII had only just died on 20 July. She was already infuriated by the welcome given to the king at Maynooth College by Irish bishops:[13]

> As I sat in my kitchen, waiting for the kettle to boil, my eye rested on a broom in the corner – it would make a good flag pole; so I went upstairs and found an old black petticoat I decided might be sacrificed, tore it in half, nailed one half to the broomstick and hung it out of the sitting room window as a contemptuous though childish answer to the Union Jacks.

The next morning Gonne's charwoman told her the police had removed the black French petticoat and taken away the broomstick. Mrs MacBride told the maid to borrow another broomstick from Violet Russell, Æ's wife, and use the remaining half of her black petticoat for another flag. When the police approached to remove this one, she carried it to an upstairs window and had her garden gate locked. When two G-men knocked on the door (they were the pair who customarily followed her), she refused to oblige them. One detective laughed and tried to push her aside, but she stood firm. Neighbours had come out of their houses to watch. Her charwoman cried out, 'You dirty scoundrel! Daring to lay hands on a lady; you murderer, you double murderer, daring to touch a lady in her condition!' The second G-man then called, 'Come on, the police will have to get a warrant.' The two disappeared up Rathgar Road. By the time the police returned with a warrant and reinforcements, Máire Quinn and Violet Russell had joined forces with Maud Gonne MacBride, and word had been sent to the Celtic Literary Society offices for men to come to her aid.

The policemen were in doubt about the meaning of the black petticoat. A black flag could be a sign of mourning, or it might be a sign of affiliation with an anarchist group (assassinations by anarchists of titled or elected European leaders were common during this period). A policeman asked Mrs MacBride if the black undergarment on display was a gesture of respect for the pope, or disrespect for the king. If the second, it had to come down. Whatever her intention was, she refused to say, but declared that she would defend her property. She showed the policeman a handgun (it looked real but Gonne told her friends it fired only puffs of perfume). Meanwhile, a policeman had, without her permission, climbed up on her roof to catch hold of the black flag/French petticoat. Máire Quinn hit him with a bottle of ginger beer; he fell off the roof and broke his arm; the women only laughed at his misfortune. By then, reinforcements arrived from the Cumann na Gaedheal Club, a thousand of them in a street now lined with police.

Both Yeats and MacBride congratulated Maud on the 'Battle of Coulson Avenue'. A zany mixture of radical propaganda, mob excitement, injured participants and inspired feminine mayhem, it was the kind of thing she did like no one else.

After the Jubilee Riots in June 1897 Maud Gonne explained to Yeats why the two of them could never work together again in political activism. She politely put it to him that he had a higher work to do, while she was 'born to be in the midst of a crowd'.[14] At a comparable juncture in February 1903, after Yeats had learned of her imminent marriage, she explained to him their differences once again in terms of their opposed attitudes to the 'mob': 'You say I leave the few to mix myself with the crowd, while Willie I have always told you I am the voice, the soul of the *crowd*.'[15] Yeats wanted to move the people by his poems and plays, even to shape the nation, but he feared the 'mob', that is, the masses as a collective, instinct with its own motion, but, in his view, when acting as one, blind, driven by appetite, without reason, like a colossus on a rampage. By saying she was 'the soul of the crowd', Maud Gonne did not mean she thought of herself as just one of their number, but that she took power from the many, and gave them a single purpose; she was made real through actuating their frustrated energies. The relationship between Maud Gonne and the mob is not perfectly analogous to that between a star of the stage and her supporting cast and audience, but the analogy does suggest the forms of inter-dependency involved and the dramatic, improvisational and sometimes festal character of the combination. The members of the mob brought out the best in her, even as she sometimes brought out the worst in them.

4

The month of August was spent on the coast of Normandy. A year earlier Maud Gonne had taken a lease on Les Mouettes, a tall house by the sea in Colleville, not far from Caen. She had learned about the place from Madame de Grandfort and Ghénia de Sainte-Croix, who ran a rest home for 'ladies of ill-repute' beside it. Major MacBride, who was already in residence before Gonne went to Dublin for the 'Battle of Coulson Avenue', did not approve of the Grandfort/Sainte-Croix operation. He took all his walks on the beach in the opposite direction.[16] Victor Collins, Mrs Collins and their two children were his houseguests. The party also included Iseult Gonne (then nine years old), Eileen Wilson (Maud's eighteen-year-old half-sister), Ghénia de Sainte-Croix and her husband, M. Avril. There was also a cook, Marie Bosse, a gover-ness, Madame Dangien, and sometimes a dressmaker, Madame B. It was a big household, mostly female.

After her arrival Maud suggested to her husband that it would be a nice gesture to invite Lucien Millevoye to visit. MacBride found the proposal outra-geous. His anger was more aggravated than appeased by the efforts of Gonne's friend, Canon Dissard of Laval (an old Boulangiste), to get him to change his mind.[17] 'This lack of delicacy led to friction,' MacBride recalled with evident understatement. She was sending Yeats letters, and she received books and letters in return. Her husband did not approve of that either.

She was, however, not flirting with Yeats. On the contrary, she was making trouble for him. What she took to be the rude behaviour of W.G. Fay in January, and Yeats's failure at the time to play Sir Galahad, still rankled with her. She was more than ever determined to settle scores with Fay and the Irish

National Theatre Society. Synge's play that Yeats liked so much – *In the Shadow of the Glen* – was, she said, 'horrid'. Yeats kept forgetting, she complained, that it was she who had started the Irish National Theatre Company, by getting the Inghinidhe na hÉireann to put on plays and by taking the lead in *Cathleen ni Houlihan*. Now Yeats and the Fays were claiming credit for her work and turning the Irish National Theatre Society into a club for the entertainment of unionists; the whole thing was a 'terrible disappointment'. She would now have to start a rival Cumann na nGaedheal society for the production of truly political plays. Her letter of resignation read:[18]

> When I joined the Society I understood it was formed to carry on National & propagandist work by combating the work of the English stage. I find it has considerably changed its character & ideals & while I shall always be interested and glad of its success I can no longer take an active part in the direction & work.

Given how thrilled Yeats was with the early promise of the theatre movement, and particularly with the literary value of Synge's work, Gonne's energetic hostility and practical opposition was a sorry turn of affairs. Once they had been allies; now they were at loggerheads.

Gonne came with Dudley Digges and Máire Quinn for the opening of Yeats's *The King's Threshold* and Synge's *In the Shadow of the Glen* on 8 October 1903, only so that the three of them could create a spectacle by walking out of the performance in a huff. To the press, she stated that Synge was unable to give a true picture of Irish life because 'he spends most of his time away from Ireland, and under the operation of foreign influences'.[19] If so, surely she suffered from the same disqualification. Fair-mindedness was not, however, her aim. For more than a month, a great part of the *United Irishman* was turned over to an attack on Synge's play, in a concerted, vindictive effort to crush the new theatre.

5

Mr and Mrs MacBride had taken up new quarters at 13 Rue de Passy, Paris. She was in the late stages of pregnancy and miserable, so much so that she asked a French doctor if he could not give her something to bring on an early labour, horrifying the medic and her husband. She may have been suffering from a pregnancy-related illness such as pre-eclampsia, but MacBride was uncomfortable with talk about female matters. That was unfortunate because he lived in a house of women: Maud, her half-sister Eileen and her constant companion Mary Barry Delaney, the governess Madame Dangien, Iseult, and the servants.[20] He was especially disgusted, listening at a partition between his bedroom and the sitting room, by Gonne's conversation with the midwife about how to prevent pregnancy while continuing to engage in sexual intercourse.[21]

A month or two before the birth of the child, Madame MacBride went to visit Ghénia de Sainte-Croix. Upon her return she told her husband that Millevoye had been there just when she arrived, but that she had not actually seen him. Had MacBride been with her, she would have been able to talk with her old friend, and she would have liked that. MacBride replied that he would not allow her to talk with Millevoye, not ever, under any circumstances, and if she did so, he 'would have to take the child away after it was born'.[22] That was a dangerous way to talk to Maud Gonne, a person not easily frightened.

At Christmas MacBride went out to celebrate the holiday with a friend, Vance Thompson. The two men drank some eggnog at one place, then met up with other friends for more drinks in a café in Rue de Mozart. Thompson returned with MacBride to Rue de Passy for dinner. They had red wine with dinner, then some champagne. According to his wife's later account, MacBride, drunk, got into a quarrel with Thompson, and pulled a gun on him. Eight months' pregnant, she had to calm down her husband and get him up to bed. She claimed that in the course of her ministrations, he kicked out at her. He vomited, then fell asleep on the bed, fully clothed. The next morning MacBride knew an apology was in order. His wife appeared to him to accept his explanation, closing the conversation with the words, 'Say no more about it'.[23] However common it was for Irishmen who had the money to get drunk at Christmas time, and to fight when they were drunk, this was not the kind of behaviour that Maud Gonne had seen before. What kind of man had she married? A stereotypical Irishman, but she did not know that.

Maud was delighted with baby Seaghan, born on 26 January 1904. She 'imagined all sorts of wonderful things for his future'.[24] MacBride himself told the New York *Sun* he hoped the boy would be the first president of an Irish republic, which put the day of liberation pretty far into the future.[25]

Maud wrote to May Gonne, now Mrs Bertie Clay, that the child looked just like Georges, her child by Millevoye. This made her happy; the boy who had died lived once more. She did not tell her husband, who knew nothing about the transmigration of souls. He was so conservative, John, 'too pious'. 'On Fridays he upsets the whole house as he will not eat meat and makes us all feel very wicked.'[26] Generally, Catholics did not eat meat on Fridays, unless they had a particular reason for exemption. But Maud Gonne MacBride was not very Catholic at this point.

Even after the birth of their son, the couple were not happy together. That is plain to see in the joyless expressions of the parents in a family photograph. They are seated with their child in Paris, beside the Irish Brigade flag, and behind a table on which an ammunition belt and two revolvers are displayed, in surely one of the strangest snapshots of a newborn ever taken.

MacBride was particularly dissatisfied with his prospects in France. Around the end of March he decided to seek his fortune in the United States. He accepted an offer from Clann na nGael to be a fundraiser and speaker. Once settled in New York, he wrote to his wife that he wanted her to leave France, sever connections with all her past immoral associations, and join him in America; maybe then they could be happy.[27] She did not agree, but she wrote that she loved him and pleaded with him to come back to her.

John's brother Joseph MacBride had, after meeting Eileen Wilson, Maud's half-sister, corresponded with her. Between themselves, the two had made a match, and they were married in London on 3 August 1904. They then returned to Joseph's cottage near Westport. Neither John MacBride nor Maud Gonne MacBride were present for the wedding, which was the beginning of a long and evidently successful marriage. (One of their grandchildren is the poet Paul Durcan.)

In August John MacBride returned by ship to Le Havre. His wife collected him, and they went to Colleville for a holiday. MacBride was still very troubled by Maud's sexual history; he would have preferred that she had none at all. He was not sure which of the men to whom he had been introduced in Paris had formerly been her lovers. Was Arthur Lynch?

Lynch was a friend of hers for years in Paris, a member of the Paris Young Ireland Society, a radical candidate in a Galway election for Parliament, Paris correspondent of the *Daily Mail* and a leader of his own Irish Brigade in South Africa. He had the credentials.

Or Amilcaire Cipriani?[28] Maybe he was one of them. He had been close to her for ten years. He had fought with Mazzini and Garibaldi, and, a diehard anarchist, he was always looking for a new revolution to join. He had accompanied Gonne to Ireland for the 1798 centenary.[29] Maybe that was just a romantic getaway. Æ was another suspect. She had his photograph on her writing table. There was also gossip in Paris that it had been Gonne who was fellating Felix Faure at the time of his stroke. MacBride came to accept this rumour as true as well.[30]

By the end of August 1904, to stem the tide of suspicion, Maud made a confession to her husband. She had been the mistress of only three men.

By one, Millevoye, she had two children, and two or three miscarriages. By the others, she had had no children.[31] This confession did not help matters. MacBride was horrified: it was to a harlot he was married.

Towards the end of September Maud brought baby Seaghan, nine months old, along with her to 26 Coulson Avenue, Dublin, the base of operations for starting up her new theatre company and mobilizing opposition to the Irish National Theatre Company. Jennie Wyse Power, an Irish activist, was often in the house, and Mrs MacBride gave her to believe 'that the utmost affection and confidence' existed between herself and her husband, but that Maud very much hoped, however unhappy he might be in France, John would not risk his freedom by coming to Ireland.[32]

Before her departure John MacBride had asked his wife to leave Seaghan with Honoria MacBride in Westport. He was determined to enter Ireland secretly and take up residence there. Maud, however, did no such thing; she returned to Paris with Seaghan in November 1904.[33]

While his wife had been away, MacBride had been drinking heavily. He had taken to the bottle in October, according to his statement to the divorce court, after receiving a portion of a letter written by his wife to her cousin, May Gonne Clay, the previous February. In the letter, Maud described a conversation that had taken place with her doctor. It was very unfair, she had joked, that women should have all the pain of childbearing without men having their turn at it. The doctor replied, with equal humour, that God was male and he made the laws of nature to suit his own sex. She continued the letter saying, 'It is too horrible to have any more children, but John thinks that no precautions should be taken and that all should be left to God; I call that cheap on his part.'[34] The letter was dated in February 1904, three weeks after the child was born, and a few weeks before MacBride's departure for the USA. Evidently, he had sought to resume conjugal relations not long after the birth, and she had refused him. The letter also said that the baby seemed to its mother a reincarnation of her son by Millevoye.

These communications determined MacBride to leave the marriage once and for all. If Maud's letter was indeed, as appears likely, forwarded to MacBride by May Gonne Clay, his exit may have been the end she had in view; however, reading the letter also had the effect of hardening MacBride's resolution to remove Seaghan from his mother.

According to Maud Gonne's account, summarized by Anna MacBride White, and usually followed by biographers:[35]

> She returned to find the household at 13 Rue de Passy in a distressful condi-
> tion. The women of her household and Madame Avril de Saint-Croix, to whom

Iseult had gone, had a sad story to relate. Whatever dreadful state John MacBride had been reduced to by stress, anxiety and disappointment, he was now accused of indecent behaviour while drunk towards various members of the household including the cook and Miss Delaney, of 'tempting' Eileen Wilson, and, most seriously of all, of frightening the ten-year-old Iseult in the same fashion. Iseult was vulnerable not only because of her childish beauty but also because she was the unacknowledged illegitimate child of a prominent French politician … Such behaviour toward a child was a criminal offence carrying a sentence of over twenty years in France.

Maud Gonne recalled that she had been summoned back to Paris from Dublin by Ghénia de Sainte-Croix because her home at 13 Rue de Passy was being ill-used. On 25 November 1904 MacBride had left for Ireland with Victor Collins. On her arrival in Paris on 26 November, she heard about Iseult's terrifying sight in MacBride's bedroom. In her husband's absence, Maud went to England during December to ask lawyers how to obtain a separation that would assure her custody of Seaghan. Four years later, she told Yeats she had been waiting for such an opportunity in order to strike.[36]

Early in 1905 she applied to Yeats for his support: 'Of a hero I had made, nothing remains & the disillusion has been cruel.'[37] She still admired MacBride for his 'fidelity to the National cause', but his drunkenness was a disgrace. There were other reasons why she was seeking an amicable separation, and she had given May Gonne Clay permission to quietly let Yeats know them. 'For the children's sake as well as from an Irish point of view, I wish this thing to be kept out of court.' Mrs Clay then told Yeats:

> MacBride has been a half insane brute from the very first. On one occasion he kicked his wife in a drunken fury. He has carried on with the servants & now at last there has been a very serious offence and the children cannot be trusted with him & Mrs MacBride came to London three weeks ago to start divorce proceedings.

When he was informed of the charges, MacBride denied them *in toto*. The first intermediary between the quarrelling husband and wife was Irish nationalist MP Barry O'Brien. He tended to believe MacBride's version, but he was mainly concerned that their split should not harm 'the cause'. MacBride was informed that his wife would not make public her charges of indecency to her child, and to her half-sister, if he quietly accepted separation and surrendered the custody of Seaghan. Otherwise, she would not spare him; it would be warfare.

On 9 January 1905 she wrote to John O'Leary, president of the IRB:[38]

To avoid going into the law court, where I should have to publicise and dishonour a man who fought against England, I have offered terms of separation, which my family who know the whole circumstances, considers far too generous. I hope for John's sake that he will accept these terms, for if not, I shall have to apply in the usual way for a judicial separation, and the scandal will be horrible.

She also informed Victor Collins of her charges. Collins did not believe them. He told Maud that all the charges originated with children and servants, people likely to make up tales whenever a husband and wife fall out. They were all her dependants. Was their testimony reliable? Collins then wrote MacBride that, in his judgment, Maud was trying to frighten him into surrendering his son.

Maud gave MacBride until 14 January 1905 to accept her terms of settlement. After that, she would take her case to the courts. MacBride made counter-charges of immorality on the part of his wife. He told Barry O'Brien that she had been the lover of Millevoye, Cipriani, W.B. Yeats and an unnamed man (Yeats thought he meant W.T. Stead; Maud Gonne believed Arthur Griffith was the one). Whatever about the others, O'Brien could not believe it of the poet: 'That kind of thing never seemed to interest Yeats.'[39]

MacBride refused to settle, so Maud Gonne pursued a separation in the French courts. She was alarmed to find out that incidents of drunkenness were not grounds for divorce in France. She was going to have to charge her husband with gross indecency if she wished to gain both a divorce and custody of the child: 'The case has to be made more heavy against him than I wished & the Eileen affair will have to be gone into.' Otherwise, MacBride could still claim custody of the child following a divorce. On 24 February the Civil Tribunal of the Seine heard her plea for a preliminary divorce decree. If MacBride declined to contest it, there would be no investigation of the charges; if he did, she would bring up, from her accusations of sexual assault upon four different women in her household, whatever was required to do the job in court.

At the first encounter in court, MacBride wept the whole time. He was charged with infidelity, cruelty and habitual drunkenness. MacBride's lawyer said that his client would not contest the divorce, or even temporary custody of the child, provided the boy spent nine months of the year in a 'national and Catholic atmosphere'. Maud Gonne MacBride did not accept this limitation. The judge granted Maud control of the child pending the final hearing and judgment, and ordered that the father be allowed to see his son for one hour a week. Gonne insisted that visits be supervised, to prevent kidnapping. These events were reported in the *Irish Independent* under the headline: 'Mrs Gonne MacBride Applies for Divorce, A Paris Sensation.'[40]

Through Yeats, Gonne commissioned a number of people to gather damaging information about the reputation of the MacBride family in Westport. She had heard they operated a 'low shebeen house'; Patrick, the brother in charge, looked 'like a man who drinks'.[41] The family had a pub-cum-general store on the quays. Æ asked a friend in the area to find out about the business. He replied that MacBride's brother Patrick, who ran the concern, was 'a hardworking decent man'. His mother Honoria had a 'refined gentle manner'. They were both devout Catholics. Their public house was 'clean, well-conducted, and orderly'.[42]

That information was of no use to Maud Gonne. Annie Horniman, English owner of the Abbey Theatre, then undertook to spy on the MacBrides in Westport. Wearing rings set with gigantic gems and gowns of ostentatiously lavish materials, Horniman cannot have managed to make herself inconspicuous in an Irish western seaboard town. She sent voluminously descriptive reports of her interviews with people in town, but all she learned was that Patrick MacBride was never seen drunk, John MacBride was often seen in church, and the mother looked very much like Queen Victoria.[43]

The women of Inghinidhe na hÉireann were also charged with finding evidence of MacBride being drunk in public, but, while they did their best, proof was hard to come by. In New York, Máire Quinn's efforts met with 'opposition and silence'.[44]

6

Yeats came to see Maud Gonne's struggle with her husband in terms of the contemporary struggle of women for equal rights. By turning Catholic and marrying an Irishman, she had, in his view, surrendered the freedom she had enjoyed. She had been a remarkable example of the New Woman, but 'I feal [*sic*] at every turn that by turning catholic she put herself in their hands – she accepted their code & that is for woman a code of ignoble submission'. Quite rightly, in his view, Maud Gonne had bridled at MacBride's demands for obedience. Yeats himself had sympathy with independent women, but MacBride and his type did not: 'The trouble with these men,' Yeats wrote, 'is that in their eyes a woman has no rights.'[45] He urged Gonne to realize that, by taking a stand, she was serving the cause of all women, and particularly of Irish women: 'The woman's question is in a worse state in Dublin than in any place I know, and [Maud Gonne] seems naturally chosen out by events to stir up a rebellion in what will be for her a new way.'[46] No woman could have had a better friend than Maud Gonne had in Yeats throughout this time of trials: he was thoughtful, unwavering, unselfish and reliable.

In early August 1905 Maud Gonne (she had gone back to her old name) disburdened herself by giving a feminist critique of marriage to the New York *Evening World*. Asked if marriage was a mistake for an independent woman, she replied:[47]

> If a woman has really something worthwhile to do in the world, I say unhesitat-ingly that marriage is a deplorable step ... If she is an ordinary commonplace woman, then she might as well marry as not. No matter how loving he is when he first marries, a man is sure to become jealous or sarcastic about his wife's career. In the end, he is likely to make his wife's life a hell ... In these days the woman is likely to be better educated than her husband. It is a fatal error for such a woman to take on such a man. Then he makes another kind of hell by misunderstanding her and ridiculing her from the standpoint of his hopeless inferiority.

Maud Gonne's court case was certainly a woman's struggle. There were many postponements, and not until 24 July 1905 did she even receive a copy of MacBride's legal submission. He was represented by Fernard Labori, lawyer for both Zola and Dreyfus, who no doubt cherished the chance to oppose the former mistress of Millevoye. On behalf of his client, he denied every one of the charges. MacBride was not a drunkard, just a *rude buveur*, a heavy drinker, yet one whose 'brain is always clear – nay, brilliant'.[48] MacBride's definition of drunkenness differed from that of his wife. He judged a man to be drunk only when he could no longer keep his drink down; i.e., when he vomited. He swore this had happened on only two occasions in the course of his marriage, once at Christmas 1903 when he unwisely mixed his drinks, and once in October 1904 after a third party sent him a disturbing letter written by his wife.

Testimonials were provided to his bravery, hard work and high standing among Irish nationalists. MacBride himself requested a divorce from his wife on account of her false charges against him, her credulousness in listening to the gossip of children and servants, and her insane belief in reincarnation (that Seaghan MacBride was Georges Gonne-Millevoye reborn). She was not in full possession of her mental faculties. Furthermore, his wife was not, as she so often pretended, Irish. Were it not out of concern for the reputation of the mother of his son, MacBride could have brought, he said, specific charges of various gross immoralities against her.

Charges and replies were heard in court, and reported by the *Irish Independent* on 27 July. Jean Cruppi, Gonne's lawyer, put on the record that MacBride had made an indecent approach to the cook, improper speeches to the school-teacher, and enjoyed adulterous relations with a young girl (Eileen Wilson MacBride, eighteen at the time) who was under Maud Gonne's protection.[49]

The lawyers began to present their cases four months later, on 21 November 1905. Over the course of five hours Maître Cruppi called witnesses and presented his charges against MacBride. On Monday 27 November it was Labori's turn. Eileen Wilson MacBride took the stand and protested that she was innocent of any sexual relations with John MacBride. Her husband Joseph then declared his belief in her, and said that those 'who slandered his wife were vile women in the pay of the vilest creature upon earth', words that stuck in the memory of Maud Gonne.[50]

After witnesses had been heard, French legal procedure required an *enquête*, or fact-finding inquiry. The final stage of the trial was scheduled for 28 February 1906, more than a year after Maud Gonne had begun her action. That court date was then postponed until August. The slow process was wearing for Gonne, but her rage still burned, as if it were the only thing still alive in her. She was furious with MacBride and his friends for refusing her initial offer of a settlement out of court, thus, as she perceived the matter, compelling her to bring charges of adultery against her half-sister in order to win custody of her son Seaghan.[51]

Maud Gonne understood that the divorce proceedings would bring about a big change in her political position in Ireland. All the forces of prejudice opposed to a strong woman would be unleashed against her if she were to return to public life. She still felt within herself the power to 'move the crowds if I could show them a fiercer & wilder way to freedom', but she was weary, and if others had taken up the baton where she had been forced to drop it, she was now content to let them carry it forward without her.

In August 1906, during his summation, Labori openly spoke of Iseult as Gonne's daughter 'by a former marriage … I mean "union"'. He said that Gonne had brought an accusation against MacBride to his own family that she had left out of her formal charges in court, because she knew it to be untrue: that he made an indecent assault on this child of this former union. Gonne was terrified she might then be forced to make Iseult testify in order to retain custody of Seaghan.

On 8 August Gonne reported the verdict to Yeats. The charge of drunkenness was judged to have been proven, but not the charges of immorality. For the next four years the mother was to retain primary custody of the child, but the father was granted visiting rights every Monday until the child was six years old, at which point the father was to have him one full month each year. This judgment was a terrible disappointment to Maud Gonne. It meant she had not been believed.

Do we believe her charges? It is possible that, sick of a marriage of mutual hatred and fearing that she was going to lose her son, Maud Gonne brought those charges against her husband, which were most likely to guarantee her sole custody of Seaghan under French law. It is also possible that John MacBride, after drinking heavily, trapped in France and raging with disappointment, had done all the things she accused him of doing.

In his written submission to the divorce court, MacBride gave a circumstantial account of why he could not have had immoral relations with Eileen Wilson at Colleville during his wife's absence in Ireland during the summer of 1903.[52] He admitted as relevant the fact that her bedroom communicated with his, but Eileen, he pointed out, slept with Iseult, and Ghénia de Sainte-Croix slept across the hall. The walls were thin, and it was easy to hear movements in the house.

As for the charges that he had exposed himself to Iseult in October 1904, about which Iseult told Ghénia de Sainte-Croix after Sunday Mass, if she believed what Iseult said, MacBride asked, why did Madame de Sainte-Croix return the child to 13 Rue de Passy where he was staying? He recalled that Iseult had once entered his room unannounced just as he was emptying a chamber pot (in other words, when he was exposed). That incident, he speculated, was probably the origin of her story.[53]

Certainly, in a house full of women, with MacBride living in their midst, being particularly unaccustomed to feminine civilities, angry and drinking to drown his sorrow, he could have become a fright to them all. His jealous hatred of Millevoye might have been projected upon Millevoye's daughter, or have simply been intuited by her, giving her a profound sense that he was a threat. Iseult hated MacBride before the marriage, and she was terrified of him during it; she saw in him the 'eyes of an assassin'. For a 10-year-old in such circumstances to speak of her stepfather to a trusted friend as a horrible indecent monster who uncovered himself before her eyes is entirely plausible, even if he did not make an intentional overture to her.

In MacBride's later life, all the way up to his execution in 1916, there is nothing to show that he was either a serial child molester or an alcoholic. Even though her charges remained unproven in court, MacBride should have known better than to start a fight with Maud Gonne.

XI

FALLEN MAJESTY AND THE RISING

After the conclusion of her trial for divorce, Maud Gonne risked a return to the public eye in Dublin. She dared not bring Seaghan with her, for fear that her custody would not be recognized on Irish soil. On 20 October 1906 W.B. Yeats accompanied her to a performance at the Abbey Theatre. Nineteen-year-old Mary Maguire (later Mrs Padraic Colum) was in the audience. The crowd awaited the arrival of the playwright so that the performance might begin:[1]

> At last we saw Yeats hastily enter, accompanied, not by the short Queen Victoria-like figure of Lady Gregory, but a tall woman dressed in black, one of the tallest women I have ever seen. Instantly a small group in the pit began to hiss loudly and to shout, 'Up John MacBride!'
>
> The woman stood and faced the hissers, her whole figure showing a lively emotion, and I saw the most beautiful, the most heroic-looking human being I have ever seen before or since ... she was smiling and unperturbed. Soon a counter-hissing set up, the first hissers being drowned by another group, and then I realized who she was ... She was a legend to us young persons in our teens.

This attempt at the public shaming of a woman, according to Roy Foster, 'crystallized' Yeats's hatred of the 'narrow-minded nationalism' of republican clubs, while also establishing him 'in the public position of Gonne's escort and protector'.[2]

Yeats invited Maud Gonne back to Dublin for the debut of Synge's new play, *The Playboy of the Western World*, on 25 January 1907. This, however, was one fight she was willing to miss. She decided to stay out of Ireland until her divorce appeal had been heard. Nonetheless, she kept abreast of the news, and followed the story of the riots sparked by the performance of Synge's master-piece. Years before, she would have been among the rioters, inciting them to damage property. Now, however, her concern was for the feelings of Yeats. She advised him that while no doubt he thought he was in the right in defending the play, those opposing him were 'equally sure they are right and suffering for a good cause'.[3] The impulse to step back from a fight, and the willingness to look at both sides of a situation, signal a deep change in her.

She showed generosity in comprehending the hostility to her of MacBride's republican friends in Dublin. Yeats was convulsed with antipathy for those who took sides with a pervert and a drunk, while pretending to be scandalized by a 'woman with a past'. She thought he was being unjust to 'the people':[4]

> [The people] have taken up MacBride because they have been told he was a hero & because they *know* he *actually* fought England & because they *believe* (here they are wrong) that he will fight England again.
>
> They considered that a woman's life should not count, if by not sacrificing it they could keep their hero, *their one fighting man* intact.
>
> It is not an ignoble idea, the only misfortune is that their hero is not a hero.

This letter gave him a poem, 'The People' (although it was not composed until 27 January 1915). The beginning of the poem manifests Yeats's indignation at what he had to put up with from the rabble in Ireland, which is contrasted with the life of a scholar-author in the court of an Italian Renaissance prince. The poem then introduces the voice of Gonne:

> Thereon my phoenix answered in reproof,
> 'The drunkards, pilferers of public funds,
> All the dishonest crowd I had driven away,
> When my luck changed and they dared meet my face,
> Crawled from obscurity, and set upon me
> Those I had served and some that I had fed;
> Yet never have I, now nor any time,
> Complained of the people.'[5]

2

Maud Gonne was now, she wrote in May 1907, 'living my own life more than I have ever done before'. She had taken up painting at the beginning of her lawsuit; now she was ready to send a picture to the Salon. Her occult interests had moved back toward the centre of her life. Yeats had told her about a hallu-cinogenic powder; she was eager to try it. She was drawing upon her occult visions for the illustrations she was providing for Ella Young's *Celtic Wonder Tales*. One of her designs shows a naked bard holding a harp in one hand, his other hand pulling the head of a half-dressed maiden into a kiss. She sent it to Yeats and asked for this thoughts.

While summering in Colleville in 1907, Gonne, so often impenetrable to herself, began to have insights into her past life. In the years leading up to her marriage, she felt, her obsession with bringing about an insurrection had caused her 'to lose all sense of proportion & all sense of life'. Perhaps she would never have been freed from her enslavement to the cause without 'the horrid crash in my affairs'.[6] For years 'I had worn blinkers, so as to … only see the one end'. 'Now I have taken them off & find so much to look at'.[7]

Yeats had remade himself too. From the time of the nightmarish choice he faced in December 1898, when he failed to return her kiss, Yeats used himself as material for an experiment in his evolving theory of the mask.[8] He had come to perceive that the image of himself in his poems was the image of a man detestably weak, feminine and passive. He had been stung by Gonne's accusation of cowardice at the time of the Jubilee Riots. Nietzsche's celebration of the superman provided him with a new model of masculinity: 'Creative life is a rebirth as something not oneself'.[9] To write a different kind of poetry than that of *The Wind Among the Reeds* he had to become a different kind of person, more masculine and dominating. He may have once turned aside from the labyrinth of his beloved in December 1898, but he subsequently had gone into the abyss of himself. He made literature out of what was still blind and dumb within himself.[10] Self-understanding was slow, dangerous and laborious for him; he held back from quick generalization; followed no set code of conduct. Who he was and what he felt were mysteries even to himself. Feelings became apprehensible only as they took shape in the verbal forms he crafted, and he became the self that the greatness of the poetry required of him.

In the period of mutual bitterness following Maud Gonne's marriage in February 1903, Yeats openly fought for the freedom of literature from politics, and its superiority to politics. He chose the plays of Synge as his field of battle.

He and Arthur Griffith, like knights before their queen, engaged in a tournament of champions that lasted from the production of *In the Shadow of the Glen* in October 1903 well past the *Playboy* riots of January 1907. In this protracted struggle, Yeats proved his mettle to everyone. Mary Colum watched with wonder his display of magnificent belligerence in the *Playboy* controversy:[11]

> He was a wonderful fighter, eager, sardonic, tireless, and undoubtedly he had the racial quality of liking to trail his coat ... The battle he waged for *The Playboy of the Western World* was a display of fighting strategy, of immovable courage, of indifference to public hostility such as I have never seen anywhere in anybody else ... I never witnessed a human being fight as Yeats fought that night [of the *Playboy* debate], nor never knew another with so many weapons in his armoury.

The insecure and ineffective committee man, rubbing along with Catholic IRB members of the Wolfe Tone Commemoration Society, was replaced by an Anglo-Irish gentleman whom it would be inadequate to say had become a snob only because of prolonged association with Lady Gregory. Mary Colum again:[12]

> I do not think he needed any external influence to make him snobbish; at this period he was afflicted with a variety of snobbishnesses that were a sight to behold and an experience to encounter ... First of all, his genius, the nature of his intellectual interests, placed him to some extent apart from the bulk of humanity; then, in addition to the common Irish notion of his descent, he had, like Villiers d'Isle-Adam [*sic*], the idea of a noble and chivalrous ancestry, an ancestry devoted to high causes. If he had had his choice he would have liked to be at the court of a Renaissance prince or duchess, or even with Goethe's Duke in Weimar. Added to this romantic snobbery, he had a curious bourgeois snobbery mocked at by George Moore.

On top of the snobbishness, Yeats had also acquired a degree of sexual confidence. Lady Gregory and Annie Horniman had doted on him and quarrelled over him since 1897. The witty, tolerant and pretty Florence Farr went to bed with him in 1903.[13] Star actress Mrs Patrick Campbell flirted with him and staged his romantic verse-plays, and from March 1908 he enjoyed a relaxed sexual relationship with 33-year-old 'medical gymnast and masseuse' Mabel Dickinson. If Maud Gonne was a different woman after her divorce, Yeats had in the meantime become a new and bigger man.

3

In ways that suggest feelings of something more than friendship, Maud Gonne began once again to report to Yeats her dreams and visions. In one, amidst 'titanic forms of light and immense energy', Yeats was faced with a choice of great importance; he trembled with anxiety. She had a message to impart to him: he must 'choose the higher'.[14] In another dream, he was scaling a mountain but encountered an impassable obstacle. She wanted so much to come to his aid, but in the dream, she was unable to move her limbs. If Yeats drew no conclusions merely from the fact that Maud Gonne was often dreaming about him, he could not miss the sexual longing expressed by her 26 July 1908 letter, in reply to his own admission that he had 'evoked union' with her. After everyone in her Rue de Passy household had gone to bed, she prepared to visit him 'astrally'. Together they flew up into the starlight and over the sea. It seemed then that he took the shape of a great serpent, but she was not sure of this because she looked only into his eyes:[15]

> [Y]our lips touched mine. We melted into one another till we formed only *one being, a being greater than ourselves* who felt all & knew all with double intensity – the clock striking 11 broke the spell & as we separated it felt as if life was being drawn away from me through my chest with almost physical pain.

After this interrupted union, she came to him two more times, but each time a noise in the house broke the spell before total ecstasy was achieved. When she finally fell asleep, she dreamt that they were in Italy together.

Yeats met Gonne in October 1908 in London, and found her 'sad & gentle'. She spoke of 'her old politics of hate with horror'.[16] That is just how he thought of them too. When Gonne went to Dublin with Ella Young for several weeks, Yeats followed. When she returned to Paris, he went as well. In December he took a room for a month at Hôtel de Passy, near her residence at 13 Rue de Passy. What he had long wanted, or claimed to want, was about to be his.

4

It is generally agreed by scholars that it was in December 1908 in Paris that 'the first of all the tribe' lay at long last in Yeats's arms, and – this seems strange – 'cried into this ear/ Strike me if I shriek'. An incident reported by Ella Young suggests that by this time the poet had overcome his former phobia about the intricate complications of female genitalia. Yeats, Gonne, and Ella Young visited the studio of Auguste Rodin, arriving to find the sculptor[17]

> ... chiselling at a block of marble without a model of any kind ... He received us graciously, and explained that the marble he was working at would be a rapture of Sainte Therese. We gazed at it solemnly ... The room was full of Rodin's sculptures. He led us from one to the other talking of them, and gesticulating as he talked. He invited us for a week-end at Meudon, and said finally: 'But you must see my pictures in the other room, my sketches. They are my great works.' The other room opened off the first ... The sketches hung in a line from wall to wall. When I had contemplated two or three of them, I looked into the garden. Yeats went reverently from sketch to sketch. Maud Gonne joined me at the window.

According to Yeats scholar John Kelly, what the poet was 'reverently' gazing at, and what provoked the sudden interest of the two women in horticulture, were Rodin's erotic sketches, an almost obsessive series of depictions of vaginas.[18] Ella Young concluded that Rodin had a sick mind. Not at all. Rodin's drawings could once have served as art therapy for someone like the young Yeats; now the reverence of the poet's gaze showed that he no longer required healing.

The great event when it finally transpired was a disappointment. To judge from poems published (somewhat cruelly) not very much later, Yeats discovered that the most beautiful woman he had ever seen was no longer quite so beautiful. According to 'Peace', published in 1910, time had touched her form.[19] The 'lineaments' remained, but he could only 'record what's gone' ('Fallen Majesty'). Nothing could compare with the oft-imagined flesh of the muse; the uncovered body of a 42-year-old mother of three disenchanted him. All through December in Paris, he was not happy and satisfied, but short-tempered. Soon after sexual relations began, Gonne put a stop to them. She let him off easy and took the blame on herself, treating it as a problem not of too little desire on his part, but of too much on hers:[20]

> I have prayed so hard to have all earthly desire taken from my love for you & dearest, loving you as I do, I have prayed & I am praying still that the bodily desire for me may be taken from you too. I know how hard & rare a thing it is for a man to hold spiritual love when the bodily desire is gone & I have not made these prayers without a terrible struggle, a struggle that shook my life though I do not speak much of it & generally manage to laugh. The struggle is over & I have found peace.

Paradoxically, love, once granted, rather than redressing Yeats's long-suppressed rage, released it. Feeling his motiveless malignity, Gonne presented him with a notebook. Its purpose was that she 'for whom and for myself I write may know me for good and evil, and that I may watch [my temper] and amend'. He accepted that he was irritable. He promised that this acceptance would force him 'to make my writings sweet-tempered and, I think, gracious'.[21] In the pages of this notebook he examined his fits of temper: with Ella Young, over something stupid she said; with Arthur Sinclair the actor. It was, he reasoned, degrading to fight with such people. He must become like a hero out of Plutarch, someone whose pose was like a second self. He had to surrender his intellect – that faculty that goes around saying 'Thou fool' all day long to every stupid person – and cultivate his religious genius, which sees all things as equal, that even the merest Catholic Paddy had a 'sweet crystalline cry'.[22]

In spite of this programme of anger-management and self-improvement, Yeats could not keep a lid on rage that arose from decades of past humiliations. Even though Maud Gonne had been alone since 1904, and since then had been stuck in France out of all Irish affairs, Yeats kept going back to how she had hurt him between 1897 and 1903, with her attempts to 'hurl the little streets upon the great' ('No Second Troy').

True forgiveness was not to be. In September 1908, he drafted 'Recon-ciliation':[23]

> Some may have blamed you that you took away
> The verses that could move them on the day
> When, ears being deafened, the sight of eyes blind
> With lightning, you went from me, I could find
> Nothing to make a song about but kings,
> Helmets, and swords, and half-forgotten things
> That were like memories of you – but now
> We'll out, for the world lives as long ago;
> And while we're in our laughing, weeping fit,
> Hurl helmets, crowns, and swords into the pit.
> But, dear, cling close to me; since you were gone,
> My barren thoughts have chilled me to the bone.

Those phallic Rosicrucian swords and vaginal helmets had been the very para-phernalia of their Golden Dawn play-acting and his Arthurian code of honour, as well as the substitute satisfactions of heroic age verse-dramas such as *On Baile's Strand*. Now they were pitched into the aboriginal 'pit'. His passion did not preclude wit. The rhyme-word in the final couplet 'since you were gone' includes a pun on her name as forceful as, yet less forced than, Shakespeare's 'will' sonnet to the Dark Lady (Sonnet 135) or Sidney's 'rich' sonnet on his mistress Penelope Rich (Sonnet 24).

'Reconciliation', like 'No Second Troy', works the figure of speech *praeteritio* (bringing something up by saying it need not be brought up) with harsh irony: 'Why should I blame her that she fill my days / With misery ...'[24] In the positive column of the balance sheet, it was only her uncomprehending incomprehensibility that evoked the poetry in the first place ('Words'). His losses in the other column were simply 'The hourly kindness, the day's common speech, / The habitual content of each with each'– in short, a happy marriage. He was 'a King and No King': love, while finally returned, could never now be fully requited; his past desires remained unfulfilled, and the woman who could have fulfilled them no longer existed; an older one had taken her place. This was love talking the language of rage, or rage mimicking the language of love – it is hard to tell which.

In all the autobiographical love poems of *Responsibilities* (1914) there is unfairness, but also to be found there are the very lineaments of great poetry: electric, immediate feeling, some honesty in the court proceedings of self-judgment, and a highly perfected craft. What he felt to be shameful, and hard to forgive, was not that Gonne had passed him over in favour of MacBride in 1903, or that she had not told him about Millevoye before December 1898. If he were to be honest with himself, he had to admit that he had known a good deal about what was going on between her and both men well before he showed that he knew anything at all. When Gonne made him a present of herself in December 1898, he had not grasped what he quickly perceived to be a nettle. What was ineradicably shameful was that in the poems of *The Wind Among the Reeds* he painted himself publicly as her pathetically disappointed, always devoted lover. Judging by those poems, the world must believe him to have been fooled about Millevoye and outmanned by MacBride. He holds her responsible for the ridiculous, un-Nietzschean figure he cuts in the early poetry. What he really hated was the image he had made of himself.

5

In the years after her break-up with MacBride, Maud Gonne had come to feel conscious pride in having inspired a love like that of W.B. Yeats, and she was able to tell him so, while being certain that a sexual relationship would never work between them. The day after he left Paris at the end of December 1909, she wrote:[25]

> You asked me yesterday if I am not a little sad that things are as they are between us – I am sorry & I am glad. It is hard being away from each other so much there are moments when I am dreadfully lonely & long to be with you – one of these moments is on me now – but beloved I am glad & proud beyond measure of your love, & that is strong enough & high enough to accept the spiritual love & union I offer ...

She was still willing and eager to pay him regular astral visits, but she could not expose herself again to the humiliation of love in the flesh.

Yeats, however, was not satisfied with a return to the status quo on the astral plane. He told her of a message received by way of a dream: sexual intercourse was essential to a man's health and to a great artist's creative life. Gonne was willing to argue the toss with the dream messenger. She instanced the cases of Raphael, ruined by sexual indulgence, and Michelangelo, celibate for a whole year while painting the ceiling of the Sistine Chapel.[26] Yeats returned to the subject immediately in two letters now lost, and was still at it in November 1909, but Gonne's replies made it clear that she was not going to be persuaded to have sex with him again, even for the sake of his poetry.[27]

The Royal Irish Constabulary logged Maud Gonne's arrival from Holyhead on 6 May 1909, and alerted the Dublin Metropolitan Police so that she could be followed upon her arrival in that city; her return to London on 21 May was also noted. But she was no longer a threat to national security. On her arrival in London she paid a call on Yeats. From her subsequent apology, it appears that he again asked her to be his lover, and, angered, she laid the blame on him for having refused her love in December 1898. That was what had forced her to marry MacBride, she said. After her outburst, she suffered remorse. It had been her own fault entirely, she wrote, that she had married the major. She had been 'carried away on the wave of hate which I had thought righteous'. If only she had stuck to their spiritual marriage, she would have been safe from 'all the crushing sorrow that came on me'.[28]

The question of who really was to blame for the failed consummation of their love haunts two opposed Yeats poems of this period. In January 1911 he wrote 'Friends' (what he was reduced to being with Maud Gonne) about Olivia Shakespear, Augusta Gregory and Maud Gonne:[29]

> Now must I these three praise –
> Three women that have wrought
> What joy is in my days:

One because no thought,
Nor those unpassing cares,
No, not in these fifteen
Many-times-troubled years,
Could ever come between
Mind and delighted mind;
And one because her hand
Had strength that could unbind
What none can understand
What none can have and thrive,
Youth's dreamy load, till she
So changed me that I live
Labouring in ecstasy.
And what of her that took
All till my youth was gone
With scarce a pitying look?
How could I praise that one?
When day begins to break
I count my good and bad,
Being wakeful for her sake,
Remembering what she had,
What eagle look still shows,
While up from my heart's root,
So great a sweetness flows
I shake from head to foot.

Most of the critical discussion of 'Friends' concerns the order of the first two women praised: John Harwood thinks Olivia Shakespear is the second woman described, because it was she who unbound, by means of her sexual know-how, 'Youth's dreamy load'. Roy Foster thinks that section must concern Lady Gregory, since it was she who enabled the poet to 'live / Labouring in ecstasy' at Coole.[30] My concern is with the third woman, about whose identity there can be no doubt; Yeats even puns on her name again ('my youth was gone'). What is also unquestionable is that the poem puts into print the idea that she treated him unforgivably. Pitiless, for years she left him starving for love, until her beauty – when it was at last his to enjoy – was only something to remember. Yet it is still her image he pictures when he masturbates. This is a reductive reading of the joy expressed in the final three lines, but that act is what is basically indicated.

The second poem, 'The Cold Heaven', does not, on the other hand, blame Maud Gonne for the failure of their love; the poet blames himself. Deirdre Toomey observes that this poem follows 'Friends' in the first Cuala Press printing of the poems; the poems are alternative readings of a single life experience. Each displays a powerful somatic response – 'shak[ing] from head to foot' in the first, and 'trembl[ing] and rock[ing] to and fro' in the second:[31]

> Suddenly I saw the cold and rook-delighting heaven
> That seemed as though ice burned and was but the more ice,
> And thereupon imagination and heart were driven
> So wild that every casual thought of that and this
> Vanished, and left but memories, that should be out of season
> With the hot blood of youth, of love crossed long ago;
> And I took all the blame out of all sense and reason,
> Until I cried and trembled and rocked to and fro,
> Riddled with light. Ah! when the ghost begins to quicken,
> Confusion of the death-bed over, is it sent
> Out naked on the roads, as the books say, and stricken
> By the injustice of the skies for punishment?

In this vision of the Last Judgement, Yeats goes back over memories of his star-crossed love affair with Maud Gonne, and breaks down, taking all the blame, 'out of all sense and reason'. It is easiest to take that phrase as meaning it was not sensible/reasonable for him to feel guilty for the failure of their love to achieve natural fulfilment, but it could also mean that, so great was his grief upon realizing his own responsibility for this failure, that he lost his good sense and his rational faculties and was reduced to a bout of weeping. Toomey hypothesizes that the poem relies on an occult belief that the poet had fallen in love with an avatar of a woman he had wronged in a previous life – a far-fetched concept, but Yeats entertained a lot of notions others find far-fetched. In this case, however, the likely meaning is that when the poet is punished for his sins in the next life, he is going to suffer for his conduct in his early relationship with Maud Gonne. She offered herself to him at one of the lowest points in her life, and he treated her cold-bloodedly, like a sister and not like his beloved. Another of Yeats's beliefs relevant to an understanding of the poem (again noted by Deirdre Toomey) is his conception of purgatory as the reliving of past transgressions by ghosts until at last the consequence of those transgressions is at an end. The last line of 'The Cold Heaven' seems to put the blame for the speaker's fate once again on the stars, 'the injustice of the skies', as if all one's conduct in life is the result of the position of planets and stars at the moment of one's birth. That would make it pointless for anyone to accept any blame at all. If this ending contradicts the early recognition of responsibility, the contradiction is not a flaw: 'The Cold Heaven' does not aim to make a coherent judgment, but to dramatize the speaker's night thoughts.

6

After her retirement from the lecture circuit and her subversive work, Maud Gonne gave herself to being a mother, to judge by the recollections of her niece, Thora Gonne Pilcher. Two years older than Iseult, Thora went to school in Lausanne and loved to spend her holidays in the Gonne households, both in Paris and Colleville. At 13 Rue de Passy:[32]

> There was an arched doorway cut out of a wooden fence in the street, through which one entered into a courtyard. By the doorway, a large bob-tailed sheepdog was chained, his name was 'Brutus'. He was on guard in case John MacBride came to take away his son … Downstairs was a big drawing room with sea green walls on the left; a dining room & kitchen on right. Lots of twittering birds were in the kitchen, kept in a row of cages all on one side.

The main rooms had Persian rugs on polished wooden floors; a green parrot had the freedom of the house. Compared to Aunt Maud, her own mother was 'cold and distant'. Greeting Thora at the door of 13 Rue de Passy, 'Aunt Maud's outstretched arms with all the warmth and love in them embrac[ed] me, [and] I felt so full of joy. Every minute in that house was vibrant with intense life.'

In a letter to Lady Gregory at the time of a fortnight's visit to France after Easter 1910, Yeats pictured the house at Colleville:

> I can see the sea from the window & I can hear the waves breaking on the sand. There is no one to speak to, even if one did know French or to call on except villagers & one old Countess in a deserted looking old chateau. There are some villas along the sands but they are still empty. Iseult is away, but the little boy & a number of brown & black dogs, a parrot & about a hundred caged birds & a cat excite each other at intervals. There is also a haunted picture.

The 'haunted' painting was a full-length portrait of Maud Gonne standing in a white dress. During August 1909, Iseult saw the figure in the painting open and shut its eyes and move its lips. It then lifted its arms, and folded them under its chin. The next day at tea, visitors saw in the mirror the eyes of the portrait move. That evening, Maud Gonne, her cousin May, and Ella Young performed an evocation in the room, and all three women agreed that the figure in the portrait moved. Maud suspected her 'grey woman' had returned, but this time it was as the source of a funny frisson rather than as a morbid fantasy or memory trace.[33] The haunted portrait counted as a special feature of the Colleville house. Another feature was the day trip west along the coast to Mont Saint-Michel. Yeats was awestruck by the monastery: 'Those great pillars, the whole incredible vastness of all those empty buildings has impressed me more I think than any building I have ever seen.'[34]

Nearly every letter Gonne wrote to Yeats between 1910 and 1916 illustrates her concern for her children's health. She lives in fear that Seaghan will come down with meningitis, as Georges had done; or appendicitis, or tuberculosis. When either child falls ill, she cancels all her travel plans. If the illness continues, she takes the child off to a health spa for a month. Being a mother is the centre of all her cares. Once Iseult passes puberty, Maud takes her duty as chaperone very seriously; she does not want what happened to her to happen to her daughter. At one time she feels that Iseult is working too hard at school (a threat to her health), and at another that she is being lazy, and will not amount to anything. When Iseult begins to smoke cigarettes, her mother counts the number she smokes, and crabs at Iseult for ruining her health. Maud Gonne became a mother like any mother.

Never accustomed to do things by halves, having become Catholic, Maud Gonne proceeded to become devout in every way. She painted pictures of the Sacred Heart, went on pilgrimages to Lourdes and received communion from the Pope. When she read that villagers had seen visions of Joan of Arc, she travelled to the village in the hope of seeing the saint herself.

7

In 1911 her own children seemed well enough, and sufficiently attended by the household staff, to enable Maud Gonne to re-engage with public life in Ireland for the first time since the break-up with MacBride. She joined forces with James Connolly's trade union and women from both Inghinidhe na hÉireann and the Women's Franchise League to provide daily meals for 250 Dublin schoolchildren. The Roman Catholic hierarchy was hostile to anything that had to do with trade unions or socialism, even feeding the hungry. Gonne made herself useful in overcoming this clerical opposition. In a friendly parley with the church authorities, she indicated that they surely did not want her to 'rouse the socialists & hold indignation meetings outside priests' doors'.[35] Gonne also arranged for the New York patron John Quinn to channel his charity for once to those who were not artists. According to the balance sheet she later sent Quinn, he was the one who chiefly paid for the 250 dinners a day.[36]

Regularly in danger of malnutrition, Dublin's tenement children were placed in acute peril in 1913. Following a 26 August strike by tramway men belonging to Jim Larkin's Irish Transport & General Workers' Union, the Dublin Employers' Federation began a lock-out of all union members. Æ followed Yeats's 'September 1913' in the *Irish Times* with an open letter 'To the Masters of Dublin' a month later. Much of the Dublin citizenry, even those with jobs, lived close to starvation. Because of the lock-out, workers' families, and especially their often numerous children, were seriously at risk of starvation. A Jewish and English socialist, Dora Montefiore, organized a scheme for the feeding of Irish children in England by families sympathetic to the union. In response Archbishop Walsh issued a letter on 21 October reminding 'Catholic mothers' of their 'plain duty' not to send 'their little children to be cared for in a strange land, without security of any kind that those to whom they are handed over are Catholics'.[37] By means of the Archbishop's letter, a capitalist/socialist conflict morphed into English/Irish, Judaeo-Protestant/Catholic, and matriarchal/patriarchal axes of conflict.

The controversy brought out tensions within Gonne's own set of values too. On the one hand, she belonged with the feminist activists and socialists; on the other hand, she was Anglophobic and newly pious in her Catholicism. As a member of the Ladies School Dinners Committee, she pursued a cautiously respectful line with respect to the Church's position.[38] The Archbishop ultimately provided his own truly Irish and truly Catholic 'Children's Distress Fund'. Maud Gonne was not the leader of the 'Save the Dublin Kiddies' campaign; several activist women from Inghinidhe na hÉireann played a role more important than hers, regardless of Dora Montefiore's leadership; but Maud Gonne's solidarity with the women she was the first to organize indicated that her political life had not entirely come to an end.

One of Gonne's woman friends from Inghinidhe na hÉireann, Helena Molony (also an Abbey Theatre actress), was by her side in a village near Argelès, a seaside town in the Pyrenees, when war was declared between

France and Germany on 14 August 1914. Trains were then commandeered for the war, so the women, along with Seaghan and Iseult, had to stay put. Maud and Iseult helped nurse the wounded in a casino that had been converted into a hospital. A year later, Gonne moved to a vast military hospital complex on the north coast of France near Étaples. Both Iseult and Maud helped patch up 'poor mangled, wounded creatures in order that they may be sent back again to the slaughter'.[39] After Maud and Iseult returned to Paris, they continued to volunteer as nurses. For many years, Maud Gonne had praised a few men for courage, shamed many others for cowardice, and longed for war, but month after month of facing the fruits of war tempered her old bloodthirstiness. Of all the injured and dying she nursed, only a single one showed any inclination to return to the front; the heroic joy of battle she expected was otherwise non-existent. She became, for a while, a pacifist.

Lucien Millevoye had longed for war as well, and particularly for a war with Germany. There was nothing he had wanted more, though he never expected that France would be relying on Britain for help. His son Henri, a 33-year-old advocate in the Court of Paris when the war began, served as a lieutenant with the 74ᵉ Régiment d'Infanterie. Maud Gonne had tea with Lucien and Henri in mid September 1915 (Iseult worked in Millevoye's military aviation business).[40] Only days after this tea, on 25 September, Henri Millevoye's regiment took part in the 3rd Battle of Artois near the Belgian border. After French units became mixed up in the trenches, the battalion straightened itself out and managed to capture two trenches. It advanced close to the German front line. Lieutenant Henri Millevoye was among the many killed there.

Iseult, accompanied by Thora Gonne Pilcher, went to give her condolences to her father. Upon seeing him, Thora thought that Millevoye did not look like a Frenchman; more like a Russian prince, 'ragged looking, good looking'.[41] He was in tears when they arrived. When Iseult learned that the cause of his present sorrow was not that his son had been killed, but that his most recent mistress had left him, she was properly angry. What a father, what a man! He once offered career advice to Iseult, a somewhat melancholy, wistful girl. If she wished, she need not seek a trade at all either as nurse or employee of his aviation business, because she had the wherewithal to become the Aspasia of an industrialist or politician. She could then follow in what Millevoye conceived to be her mother's footsteps.[42]

8

In the years between 1910 and 1916, Maud Gonne came to a new appreciation of her own importance as Yeats's muse and as a character in the story his poems told. She was already accustomed to being a literary character. George Birmingham made her the villainess of *Hyacinth* in 1906, where, as Miss Groold, she imagines herself to be an object of dread to Dublin Castle, buys a newspaper much like the *United Irishman*, starts a donnybrook at a Rotunda parliamentary meeting and preaches that every deed against England, no matter what, is glorious, not shameful, including persuading Irish soldiers to murder their English officers; Miss Groold's way of meeting criticism is to fondle her pet monkey. The hero's fateful choice at the crisis of the novel is whether or not to accept Miss Groold's money in taking a job as editor of her newspaper; it is framed as a choice between good and evil. Maud Gonne did not complain about this representation of herself, only of the novel's insinuation that the Irish lads she recruited for the Boer War were from the Dublin criminal underclass.[43]

Before her appearance in *Hyacinth*, Gonne had also been a character in Colonel Emile Driant's *La Guerre Fatale* (1903), this time as the heroine in a boy's adventure tale. Driant was General Boulanger's son-in-law, and a thoroughgoing right republican.[44] He wrote novels of imaginary wars occurring in the near future, stocked with portraits of recognizable individuals in semi-plausible thrillers. In *The Fatal War* Henri d'Argonne, a French officer and a Breton, meets a woman much like Maud Gonne ('Maud Carthy'), except that the fictional Maud is 'descended from one of the noblest and oldest families in Ireland'. The feelings of Maud Carthy and Henri d'Argonne for one another are 'common, passionate, irresistible'.[45] They both detest England 'because [they] followed the cult of the beautiful and the good'. Together they manage to bring about the complete destruction of Britain.

Maud Gonne had also been honoured with praise poems by Clovis Hugues, Armand Silvestre and Achille Maffre de Baugé,[46] but her role in the work of W.B. Yeats was of another order altogether. French graduate students and scholars like Maurice Bourgeois sought her out. To them, she was important because of what W.B. Yeats had written, and mainly for that alone. They asked to borrow copies of his books. As a result, she began to take a proprietorial view of the poetry. The time Yeats spent on the theatre, she often told him, was wasted; she nagged him to give up the Abbey. His poetry was his greatest contribution to Ireland, and it sprang in part from her inspiration. What he had written for her 'would live because our love has been high and pure'.[47] She had actually been 'the Father' of his poems, 'sowing the unrest and storm which made them possible & you the mother that brought them forth in suffering & in the highest beauty'.[48] 'Our children were your poems.' She allowed that he had had a child by Lady Gregory too – the theatre – but that child was not so important. Maud Gonne commented that Synge's *Deirdre of the Sorrows* could not be as great as Yeats's *Deirdre* because Synge was only in love with 'rather an ordinary little girl'. That must, she wrote to Yeats, take 'somewhat away from the prestige' of his play.[49] In short, Yeats's work borrowed glamour from Maud Gonne's beauty, social status and fame. She was a stakeholder in the concern, and she could congratulate herself when the stock went up. When Yeats began to write his memoirs, Madame MacBride made no attempt to hide her curiosity (in what light would he present her?), and considered writing an account of her own early life for his use. By no means did she wish to be left out of his story; she now accepted that his had been no idle boast when he promised that she would live for ever in his rhymes.

Yet if her virtual place was beside him, Maud Gonne was not often actually in the company of Yeats between 1910 and 1916 – an Easter in Colleville in 1910, an August month on the beach in 1912, a rare intersection in London or Dublin. Often when she happened to pass through one of these cities, he was elsewhere or did not take the trouble to meet her. During that summer visit to Colleville in 1912, it seemed to Yeats for a moment, while sitting with her on the beach in the evening, with nothing new left to say to one another, that what they had had together – perhaps 'the best of love' – was possibly dead. But then, in a reversal of 'Adam's Curse', the Venusian miracle occurs once more, and he is in love again.

> A Memory of Youth
>
> The moments passed as at a play;
> I had the wisdom love brings forth;
> I had my share of mother-wit,
> And yet for all that I could say,
> And though I had her praise for it,
> A cloud blown from the cut-throat north
> Suddenly hid Love's moon away.
> Believing every word I said,
> I praised her body and her mind
> Till pride had made her eyes grow bright,
> And pleasure made her cheeks grow red,

And vanity her footfall light,
Yet we, for all that praise, could find
Nothing but darkness overhead.
We sat as silent as a stone,
We knew, though she'd not said a word,
That even the best of love must die,
And had been savagely undone
Were it not that Love upon the cry
Of a most ridiculous little bird
Tore from the clouds his marvellous moon.

But he did not respond positively to her invitations to spend Christmas in Paris, to join her at a spa in the summer or to come with her to Italy. Yeats was settling into London and the Home Counties. He had a mistress, the theatre, his poetry and his psychical investigations; Maud Gonne had her family and the Church. After World War I began, crossing the English Channel became dangerous. The relationship became epistolary.

9

In Easter 1916, however, things changed for both of them, changed utterly. Because of the censors in France and those in Dublin, Maud Gonne was slow to obtain the news of the 24 April Rebellion in Dublin. She was then 'overwhelmed by the tragedy & greatness of the sacrifice our country men and women have made. They have raised the Irish cause again to a position of tragic dignity'.[50] Again and again, she praises the courage of the rebels.

On 4 May a report was published that Patrick Pearse, Thomas MacDonagh and Thomas Clarke had been executed by firing squad. She knew all three. Pearse she thought the greatest Irish orator since J.F. Taylor; she had tried to get Yeats to help him find an agent to set up an American lecture tour. When French schools fell into disorder because of the war, she considered sending her son to St Enda's, Pearse's school. Her bond to Thomas Clarke was even closer. He had been one of the dynamitards for whose release from prison she toiled for throughout the 1890s. She was a close friend of his wife's family.

Three days later, the papers carried the news that her husband John MacBride had been executed. Maud went to Iseult

… paper in hand & looking pale and said 'MacBride has been shot' & then went to her little boy who was making a boat & said 'your father has died for his country – he did not behave well to us – but now we can think of him with honour' and then said to Iseult 'Now we can return to Ireland.'[51]

The fateful rapidity of these mental calculations is eerie. She had been hiding from her husband in France for twelve years, afraid that he would kidnap her son. Now he was a hero. Now she could live in Ireland.

The look of things changed suddenly from Yeats's point of view as well. He was at first bewildered that these men, with whom he too was acquainted – 'Connolly is an able man & Thomas MacDonagh both able and cultivated,' even if Pearse was 'a man made dangerous by the Vertigo of self sacrifice' – had started an insurrection.[52] It was 'tragic, heroic lunacy'.[53]

It dawned on Yeats when MacBride was executed that Maud Gonne was no longer prevented by marriage from being his wife. Iseult had spent much of May in the poet's company in London, and she brought him with her back to Colleville on 22 June 1916. He proposed once more to Maud Gonne, perhaps for old time's sake. He kept no secrets from Lady Gregory in his 3 July report:

> I asked Maude to marry me, a few days ago. She said that it would be bad for her work & mine, & that she was too old for me. 'I have been always ten years older than you. I was when we were both twenty & I still am.' Next day she said 'were you not very much relieved that I refused you'? & then 'I dare say it would be better for the children if we married but I do not think it would work'. Perhaps she was hesitating, perhaps not. I have not returned to the subject and she has not. I think she would find it hard to give up politics & I have given her a written statement of my political creed. Probably she has finally decided. She says 'I have always thou[gh]t a woman of my years should not marry.' I am very much taken up with Iseult, not in the way of love or desire, but her joyous childhood absorbs my thought, & I hardly know what I feel. It makes Madam Gonne seem older than she is. Should my feeling change towards Iseult I shall leave at once, as I think 30 years to[o] great a difference for her happiness, but I have little fear. I am more & more convinced of her genius.

It appears that he asked the question but did not try to persuade Maud to give yes for an answer. She had to probe to test the sincerity of his wish in the following days. It was possible that he was again just acting according to an antique code of conduct. He admits that she seemed at the time even older to him than she actually was; he had lost his desire for her. What he does not say in this letter to Lady Gregory is that he wanted children and had inwardly turned away from this 'barren passion' for whose sake, though he was past fifty, he had no offspring, 'nothing but a book'.[54] He was in search of a wife to live in the tower he had bought in Ballylee, Co. Galway and to bear his children. None of that was said or probably even formulated as a thought. This final proposal, after so many previous ones, attained an air of ceremony: he pretended to want to marry her, and she pretended the reluctance was all on her side.

The rapidity with which Yeats passes in this letter from his proposal to the mother to his interest in the daughter is startling. Usually so sensitive, Yeats seems obtuse. Can he have been unaware of how shocking and painful it would be for Maud Gonne when he asked her permission to court her daughter? Yeats was only repeating in a courteous manner the offence of which MacBride had been accused: wanting to have sex with her child. What mother could see without humiliation, rage, and repulsion her 51-year-old beau set his sights on her twenty-year-old daughter? Marvellously, Maud Gonne affected not to mind, and allowed him to make his case to Iseult, while telling Yeats he was not likely to succeed.

Something deep, laborious and slow was coming to pass within the poet, a reordering of fundamental poles in his existence. In his reports to Lady Gregory about his wooing of the child, he is witty, detailed and civilized, but he seems to be a moral sleepwalker looking for directions from Lady Gregory.

During the same summer that the rebels were executed, and Yeats proposed first to Maud then to Iseult Gonne, he was also working on 'Easter 1916' and the section of his autobiographies spanning the years 1897 to 1899. The whirling vortex of his mental activities is difficult to explore.

Yeats knew that it was incumbent upon him to write a poem about the Easter Rebellion.[55] Yet to write a funeral elegy in the twentieth century, as Helen Vendler has pointed out, presented unusual poetic difficulties. People no longer believed in the translation of men into demigods, or in the immortal rewards of the next life. The conventions of the form were outdated. Twentieth-century individuals were understood through their individuality, not by conformity to an archetype. So Yeats's 'Easter 1916' registers again and again both the resistance of his materials to the requirements of an elegy, and the inadequacy of the poetic form as a consolation for this historical tragedy. The heroes-to-be are only men who work at counters and desks. The female hero had been a genteel lady and an equestrian, but she had lost caste through her politics. One of the men had been a schoolteacher, another a potential poet, and a third, John MacBride, Yeats had before judged to be 'a drunken, vainglorious lout'; he 'had done most bitter wrong / To some who are near my heart', an allusion to both Iseult and Maud Gonne, and a sly confession that not just one but both women were at the moment near his heart.

Iseult Gonne

When ordinary humans, people with jobs and personality defects, avocations and aspirations, die in service to their country, the contemporary poet is unable to say, as poets had done in centuries earlier, that their deaths were only a sleep and a forgetting. Nor can he offer the solace of the traditional metaphor (now a cliché) that they had gone back to the bosom of Mother Ireland. Twentieth-century death was real death, the extinction of a self. Yet Yeats wanted to say, and as the author of an elegy had to say, that not all was lost; something had been born that now and in time to be would continue to exist.[56] The poem rehearses these nagging difficulties in preparation for a long-delayed triumphal assertion of contemporary heroism.

Terence Brown is right that Maud Gonne, while not explicitly prominent in the poem (Constance Markievicz is a 'stand-in' for her), is central to Yeats's thinking about the subject. He had often feared that she would sacrifice the sweetness of her voice and her beauty to politics, like 'a hysterical woman who will make unmeasured accusations and believe impossible things, because of some logical deduction from a solitary thought, which has turned a portion of her mind to stone'.[57] Fanaticism could petrify a heart and a mind, yet without fanaticism, this suicidal insurrection that at once destroyed the centre of Dublin and renewed hopes of national independence would never have come to pass.

While composing 'Easter 1916' Yeats was also finding it 'very exciting to work at' his memoirs. He wrote 'a great many pages', covering events from 1897 to 1899. This period in his life spans the 1798 centenary commemorations, his involvement along with Gonne in the subversive activities of the Irish National Alliance, the spiritual marriage, Gonne's explanation to him about Millevoye, his offer of sympathy when what she wanted was love, and her subsequent return to fanatical militancy. Reflection on this crucial passage in his life and her life could have reawakened Yeats's anger at the ways his love had gone wrong, but the period also could be seen as sowing the seeds of 1916. The commemoration of 1798 was, in fact, designed to spark a new insurrection; it just took a long time for that revolution to begin. Gonne's hectoring orations about courage and her street demonstrations were premature attempts to start an urban war. Her sacrifices for the cause set an example of patriotic irrationality. The play that she inspired and performed, *Cathleen ni Houlihan*, not only seemed a dress rehearsal for the event, but actually recruited soldiers for the Rebellion, and held out to them the illusory reward: 'They shall be remembered for ever.'

In his 1923 Nobel Prize lecture, 'The Irish Dramatic Movement', Yeats uses the metaphor of a people being unconsciously pregnant with a future event: after the death of Parnell, 'an event was conceived and the race began … to be troubled by that event's long gestation'. This figure of speech – the 'long gestation' – governs the refrain of 'Easter 1916': 'A terrible beauty is born.' The men and women who are the heroes of the Rising are just ordinary Dubliners; in the poem they are passive, unconscious, almost zombies; they have hearts of stone, not hearts of flesh. They do not so much do something, as something is done to them. They are changed, changed utterly. The event that came to pass was conceived much earlier, by other people, people like Maud Gonne and Yeats.

Not that 'Easter 1916' is a boastful poem; on the contrary, its tone is more like chagrin. The poet appears reluctant to tip his hat to the condemned rebels, and bend his knee; finally, he just surrenders to the force of unreasoned admiration. That chagrin arises, I think, from the poet's sense over many years that Maud Gonne had made a poor use of her life. She might have lived in the country; she might have, like the moorhen, heard the moorcock call; she might have been sweet and gracious. Yet the Easter Rebellion showed him he was wrong in his belief that her life had been wasted in fanaticism. It had come, unexpectedly, to this. She had played a part in keeping the revolutionary tradition alive. It would be silly for him to say she was the mother of the Rising, or its father (as she had claimed to be the father of his poems). Neither Yeats nor Gonne, one for years in England, the other even longer in France, could rightly claim credit for the 1916 Rebellion, but each was certainly a part of many things that brought it to pass.

While 'Easter 1916' is in a way a troubled meditation on the personal character and political life of Maud Gonne, she did not like the poem, nor did she misunderstand it:

No, I don't like your poem, it isn't worthy of you & above all it isn't worthy of its subject – Though it reflects your present state of mind perhaps, & isn't quite sincere enough for you who have studied philosophy & know something of history know quite well that sacrifice has never yet turned a heart to stone though it has immortalized many & through it alone mankind can rise to God …

[Y]ou could never say that MacDonagh & Pearse & Conally [*sic*] were sterile fixed minds, each served Ireland, which was their share of the world, the part they were in contact with, varied faculties & vivid energy! Those three were men of genius, with large comprehensive & speculative & active brains the others of whom we know less were probably less remarkable men, but still I think they must have been men with a stronger grasp on Reality a stronger spiritual life than most of those we meet. As for my husband he has entered Eternity by the great door of sacrifice which Christ opened & has therefore atoned for all so that praying for him I can also ask for his prayers & 'A terrible beauty is born'.

Maud Gonne had her own personal relationships to the executed men. She had been closer to James Connolly and his family, to Tom Clarke and his family, to John MacBride and his relations, and even to Pearse, than Yeats had ever been. She was right to be offended by the radical diminishment Yeats performs on those men before he elevates them to the skies of national history. In the first two stanzas of the poem, there is more than a touch of class condescension by Yeats to the named leaders of the Rebellion. Gonne had long urged men to give up their lives for their country, and these men in full knowledge had done just that. She was mourning friends for whose deaths she had to take some responsibility; she had to live on into the future with their widows. What she wanted from the poet was a proper memorial to those individual people, not another covert love-hate poem that took her to task for her politics.

Her own reaction to the deaths of the leaders in this letter is a Catholic one, a political Christology of the kind Pearse had preached. Death for one's country offered one a complete redemption of sin. MacBride, whom she had once made out to be a sex criminal, is now for her a martyred saint. She prays not only for him but to him.

10

Maud Gonne herself, if not utterly changed, was seriously altered by the Easter Rebellion. Politically, she reverted to how she had been before her divorce. Once she heard about the execution of MacBride, in a bolt she decided to give up her life in France. That meant an end to the daily domesticity, the fleet of household retainers, the dozens of singing birds, the dogs large and small, and the parrot.[58] Her whole luxurious lifestyle was traded for what could fit into a few suitcases. By November 1916 she had surrendered the lease on her Paris apartment.

She made the mistake of doing so before she had obtained permission to travel to Ireland. In fact, this permission was refused. She was allowed to travel to England but no farther, and she did not wish to be there at all. Infuriated, she was trapped in Paris with two well-grown children on her hands, and no home. While she appealed to authorities for permission to go to Ireland, and pulled strings with officials and friends in high places, including Yeats, she absolutely refused to comply with a formal request to give a verbal undertaking not to make political trouble in Ireland. Giving such an assurance would mean, she declared, 'acquiescing in a monstrous tyranny'.[59] Her ancient hatred of England was again in full flower, but in a time of war the authorities were not as patient with the eccentricities of an heiress as they had been in Victoria's time. The decision that she could not proceed from England to Ireland remained in force. Escorted by Yeats, Gonne finally travelled on her passport to England in September 1917. Three months later, wearing a disguise, she sneaked over to Ireland. In May 1918, having bought a house on St Stephen's Green, she was arrested under the Defence of the Realm Act and sent for detention to Holloway Prison, London. The British state, with which she had battled since she was twenty-one, finally in this manner recognized the 52-year-old Maud Gonne as an actionable threat to national security. She might have taken such recognition as an honour, but in fact she regarded it as an outrage to justice.

What happened to Maud Gonne after that – her permanent uniform of widow's weeds, her implacable stand as one of the republican widows, all of them enraged by the new government of the Irish Free State (established on 6 December 1922), her campaigns on behalf of women and of republican prisoners, her support for Hitler during the war, the survival of her gaunt beauty to her death in 1953 – is not part of the story of *The Adulterous Muse*. Nor is the later life of her children, not Iseult's elopement in 1920 with Francis Stuart, an eighteen-year-old Irish writer who idolized Yeats, but who turned out to be a sadist, a gambler, a supporter of the Nazis (he wrote radio scripts for 'Lord Haw Haw') and occasionally a bizarrely interesting novelist – *Black List Section H* remains fascinating if chilling reading. He was honoured in his old age by Aosdána ('people of the arts') in the Republic of Ireland.

After Francis Stuart left for Germany in 1939, Iseult made her home in Laragh Castle, Co. Wicklow, into a safe house for Herman Goetz. He was a German spy parachuted into Ireland in May 1940 to work as a liaison officer with the Nazi-friendly IRA. As a result, Iseult was arrested and sentenced to three months' detention for a violation of Irish neutrality. Given Millevoye's long enmity against Germany, it may at first appear surprising that the Gonne/MacBride/Stuarts actively supported the Nazis in World War II,[60] but it makes sense in view of their anti-Semitism, hatred of Britain and attachment to national socialism. Maréchal Pétain's France held no terror for the Gonnes, or for Millevoye's surviving confederates. The Vichy government was the true inheritor of Boulangism.

The political career of Seán MacBride also falls outside the scope of this book, although it has its own interest. He did not, as his father had hoped, become the first president of the Irish republic, but he did join the IRA at just fifteen years of age, rise to be its chief of staff, and earn a degree in law, which qualified him to defend IRA criminals in the Irish courts, before founding a new left-wing political party, Clann na Poblachta, purist in its Catholicism and republicanism. After his mother's death, Seán MacBride became a founding member of Amnesty International; for his defence of human rights he won the Nobel Peace Prize in 1974 and the Lenin Peace Prize in 1975.

The Adulterous Muse has two end points. In the first, Yeats, having accompanied Maud and Iseult from Paris to London on 17 September 1917, nine days later proposed to George Hyde-Lees, and married her on 20 October. While Yeats had difficulty getting the two Gonne women out of his sexual imagination – and his new wife into it – George by means of her automatic writing cast a spell over his thoughts sufficiently powerful to allow for two children to be born and a compendious, idiosyncratic occult system to be constructed (*A Vision*, 1925). The poet had found a new muse, and a new muse had found her poet.

The second point of closure is simply a death. On 25 March 1918 at age sixty-eight, after a few days' illness, Lucien Millevoye passed away just as the second Battle of the Somme was beginning. He never got to see the end of the war, or the victory of France on 11 November 1918.

Maud Gonne heard the news of Millevoye's death while in Ireland. The extent of his influence, through her, on the Irish struggle and on the shape of the new Catholic, nationalist, right-wing and Anglophobic Irish state is a matter of speculation, not as to its existence, but in terms of its quantity. By the time of his death she was twice widowed and thrice alone, without Millevoye, Yeats or MacBride, yet she had no further need of any of them. She had her glory.

She appears among the Olympians in one of Yeats's great late poems, 'Beautiful Lofty Things'. Appropriately, she is in Howth, the place of her childhood idyll: 'Maud Gonne at Howth station waiting a train,/Pallas Athena in that straight back and arrogant head.' The comparison to Athena, Greek goddess of wisdom, is striking. One does not usually associate Maud Gonne with that particular quality. She was sometimes unwise, or at least imprudent, in how she conducted her own life, yet in Yeats's experience, she did on occasion offer 'good counsel'.[61] When considering the justice of the allusion, one must allow for the fact that Athena was the sister of Ares, the god of war. She was in particular the war goddess of Athens, and also the deity of the *demos*, the mob that sometimes ruled that first democracy. Finally, recall that Athena was difficult to bring to bed, a virgin goddess. Vast and unbowed in her temple on the Acropolis, she was both courted and impugned but never subdued. Yeats's lifetime of observation boils down to 'that straight back and arrogant head'. Women who chance to be born immensely tall often stoop in life, so as not to stick out, or just to bring themselves down to the level of men, but she never did. She stood up into her full height. That she was arrogant was no fault, not in the eyes of Yeats (for whom pride was a virtue), nor given her iceberg-breaker role in the glacial shift in the status of women, in the eyes of posterity.

NOTES

Introduction

1. Yeats, *Autobiographies*, p. 272. Joseph M. Hassett, *W.B. Yeats and the Muses* (Oxford 2010), Ch. 3.

2. Denis de Rougemont, *Love in the Western World*, (New York 1940), p. 284; quoted by Hassett, Ch. 3.

3. Quoted by Amber Vogel in Marjorie Stone and Judith Thompson, eds, *Literary Couplings: Writing Couples, Collaborators, and the Construction of Authorship* (Madison 2007), p. 236.

4. *Ibid*, p. 235.

5. George Moore, *Confessions of a Young Man* (New York 1901), pp. 179–80.

6. Maud Gonne, 'In the Event of War', *United Irishman*, 22 December 1900.

7. Maud Gonne, *A Servant of the Queen* (Woodbridge 1983), p. 329.

8. *The Gonne-Yeats Letters, 1893–1938*, eds Anna MacBride White and A. Norman Jeffares (Syracuse 1994), p. 302.

9. Gonne to Yeats, [2/9 October, 1899]; *Gonne-Yeats Letters*, pp. 111–12.

10. Octave Mirbeau, *Torture Me! A Dark Depraved Tale of Sin and Sex in the Garden of Evil Ecstasy*, Loc. 1010–16. Mirbeau's representation of Clara is misogynistic; she is more symbol than person. In the male drinking party that begins the novel, somewhat like Plato's *Symposium*, the subject of debate is whether at bottom all men are not murderers. At the end of the night, it is concluded that Woman, 'being the matrix of life, is by that very fact the matrix of death, since it is from death that life is perpetually reborn'. The womb really is the tomb; the reverse being also true.

11. *Ibid*, 1937–46.

12. *Le Gaulois*, 8 September 1898.

I. The Origins of Maud Gonne's Hatred of the English

1. Ann Saddlemyer, *Becoming George: The Life of Mrs W.B. Yeats* (Oxford 2002), pp. 421–23.

2. Richard Ellmann, *Yeats: The Man and the Masks* (New York 1979), xxi.

3. *Daily Mail* article quoted in *Freeman's Journal* (21 October 1899), 8.

4. Samuel Levenson, *Maud Gonne: A Biography of Yeats' Beloved* (London 1977),

p. 165; *The Collected Letters of W.B. Yeats*, gen. ed. John Kelly, InteLex Electronic Edition 2002, vol. 2, p. 511.

5. *Gonne-Yeats Letters*, pp. 123–4.

6. *Gonne-Yeats Letters*, pp. 213–4.

7. The marriage is recorded in General Register Office, London, as having taken place at East Peckham Parish Church, 19 December 1865; Levenson, p. 9.

8. Ann Matthews, *Renegades: Irish Republican Women 1900–1922* (Cork 2010), p. 40.

9. *The Times* (22 April 1869). William Cook was a director of the Legal and Commercial Life Assurance Society and the Imperial Plate-Glass Company amongst others.

10. For a biographical article on Monier de la Sizeranne, see *L'Univers illustré* (2 February 1878), 80. In *A Servant of the Queen*, Maud Gonne transfers 'Aunt Mary' from the Cook line, her mother's family, to being a sister of her father.

11. *Times* (30 August 1871), p. 4; (2 January 1873), p. 12; (18 May 1894), p. 4; (5 January 1895), p. 3.

12. *Times* (29 July 1873), p. 12.

13. *Times* (28 December 1886), 11. Francis Cook's obituary appears in the *Times* of 19 February 1901, p. 8.

14. Church of Ireland records.

15. *Gonne-Yeats Letters*, 24 October 1905, 4 December 1905.

16. *Times* (11 June 1824), p. 4.

17. *Times* (4 September 1846), p. 8.

18. Madam Maud Gonne McBride [*sic*], witness statement (5 September 1949), Bureau of Military History.

19. Sinéad McCoole, *Easter Widows* (Dublin 2014), Loc. 635–38.

20. Thomas Gonne, letter to editor, *Times*, 27 May 1866.

21. *IB* 55, 20 Dec 1913, 803; illus. in Guy St John Williams, *The Racing Lodges of the Curragh* (Kildare 1997) p. 55.

22. Conrad A. Balliet, 'For the Love of Maud' (unpublished mss p. 120).

23. Maud Gonne, witness statement, Bureau of Military History.

24. *Times*, 7 February 1874.

25. *Irish Times*, 24 February 1879.

26. *Freeman's Journal*, 25 July 1879.

27. 'Military Intelligence', *Freeman's Journal*, 1 May 1881; Matthews, *Renegades*, p. 43.

28. Sinéad McCoole, *Easter Widows*, p. 10.

29. *Freeman's Journal*, 24 October 1882; *Irish Times*, 1 November 1882.

30. Maud Gonne, witness statement, Bureau of Military Archives. It is possible that Colonel Gonne talked with his daughter in 1885 about his newfound sympathy for Home Rule, and a plan to resign his commission and take up a political career, but there is no contemporary evidence of his having done so.

31. *Freeman's Journal*, 27 February 1885.

32. Both Thomas Gonne and George Moore are reported as being present at 'St Patrick's Ball', *Irish Times*, 18 March 1886.

33. A Dublin correspondent reported to *The Court and Society Review* that 'the greatest interest was excited' by the first appearances of the serialized *A Drama in Muslin*; the serial continued to June 1886 (*The Court and Society Review*, 21 January 1886, 39).

34. George Moore, *A Drama in Muslin* (London 1892), p. 157.

35. *Ibid*, p. 158.

36. *Ibid*, p. 171.

37. *SQ*, p. 27.

38. *SQ*, p. 40.

39. *Irish Times*, 6 March 1886.

40. 'Fashions and Varieties', *Freeman's Journal*, 17 March 1886.

41. 'Amateur Theatricals at the Royal Hospital', *Freeman's Journal*, 1 April 1884.

42. Adolphe Brisson, *Portraits Intime* (Paris 1896), p. 242ff.

43. George Moore to Henry Barnett, editor, *Court and Society Review*, 24 December 1885, 511.

44. McCoole, *Easter Widows*, p. 70.

45. Victor du Bled, *La société française depuis cent ans. Quelques salons du Second Empire* (Paris, 1923–24).

46. *SQ*, p. 33.

47. *SQ*, p. 34.

48. *SQ*, p. 34.

49. According to the *Irish Times* of 13 August 1886, the Prince of Wales, his wife, and children, had just left London for Hamburg (Matthews, *Renegades*, p. 46). The Bayreuth Festival ran from 23 July to August 20 in 1886, so it is possible that Maud Gonne's story of being noticed by the Prince in Hamburg before her visit to Bayreuth actually occurred.

50. *SQ*, p. 35. In this telling of the story by Maud Gonne, Colonel Gonne says nothing about giving up the military to become an Irish nationalist MP.

51. 'The Army', *Irish Times*, 2 December 1886.

52. Matthews, *Renegades*, p. 48.

53. *SQ*, pp. 45–46.

54. *SQ*, p. 51.

55. McCoole, *Easter Widows*, p. 21.

56. *Ibid*, p. 21.

57. *SQ*, p. 61.

II. The Secret Alliance

1. W.B.Y. to George Yeats (27 October 1938). W.B. Yeats, *Collected Letters*, InteLex electronic edition. *Unpublished Letters* (1905–1939). General Editor John Kelly, with co-editor Ronald Schuchard (1994).

2. Graham Robb, *The Discovery of France* (New York 2007), p. 310.

3. Eugen Weber, *France: Fin de Siècle* (Harvard 1986), p. 179.

4. George Henry Brandt, *Royat les Bains* (London 1880).

5. Marie Quinton, *Le journal de la belle meunière: le general Boulanger et son amie* (Paris 1895), np.

6. *SQ*, p. 62.

7. *SQ*, p. 63.

8. Marcel Prévost, *Les Demi-Vierges* (1894), loc. 1228.

9. Lucien Millevoye had married Adrienne Jeanne Marie Damiron (b. 1860) on 16 November 1879 in Lyon.

10. These various roles of Joan of Arc are analysed by Marina Warner in *Joan of Arc: Image of Female Heroism* (London 1981).

11. Frederick Brown, *For the Soul of France* (New York 2011), Loc. 1694–1703.

12. Venita Datta, *Heroes and Legends of Fin-de-Siècle France: Gender, Politics, and Nation* (Cambridge 2011), p. 142.

13. Henry James, *The Portrait of a Lady* (Boston 1882), p. 159.

14. Anne Magny, 'Maud Gonne: Réalitié et Mythe, Analyse d'une présence historique et litteraire', University of Rennes dissertation, 30 March 1992, p. 146. My thanks to Pierre Joannan for a copy of this work.

15. In pre-Revolutionary France, *notables* were members of a council of prominent persons called together by the monarch in times of crisis.

16. Vivienne Ann Schmidt, *Democratizing France: The Political and Administrative History of Decentralization* (Cambridge 1990), p. 42.

17. Lucien Millevoye's name appears in *Le Gaulois* (6 July 1880) in a list of those who resigned. For background on the laws of laicization, see Jean-Marie Mayeur and Madeleine Reberioux, trans. J.R. Foster, *The Third Republic from its Origins to the Great War, 1871–1914* (Cambridge 1984), p. 77; and Piers Paul Read, *The Dreyfus Affair: The Story of the Most Infamous Miscarriage of Justice in French History* (London 2012).

18. *Cartes des chemins de fer francais et tarifs des voyages circulaires* (1 January 1881), 540.

19. *Conseil héraldique de France. Maison de Castellane. Branche de Salernes* (8 August 1885), 76.

20. *La Justice*, 10 May 1886.

21. *Le Temps*, 23 July 1886. Millevoye was acquitted by jury.

22. 'Un précurseur de la droite républicaine: Edgard Raoul-Duval (1832–1887)', *Revue d'histoire moderne et contemporaine* (October–December 1999), 710.

23. James Harding, *The Astonishing Adventure of General Boulanger* (London & New York 1971), p. 64.

24. William D. Irvine, *The Boulanger Affair Reconsidered: Royalism, Boulangism, and the Origins of the Radical Right in France* (Oxford 1989), p. 5.

25. Mayeur and Reberioux, *The Third Republic*, p. 131.

26. Madeleine Zillhardt, *Louise-Catherine Breslau et ses amis* (Paris 1932), p. 205.

27. Harding, *The Astonishing Adventure*, p. 65.

28. 'In the days of M. Gambetta, it was said that the principal entitlement of the generals in the Army was that they were friends of Gambetta. Today, it is the friendship of M. Clémenceau of General Boulanger that counts. The radical shakes the hand of the minister of war. It is perhaps a symptom of how grave the situation in France now is.' *Le Figaro*, 11 January 1886.

29. Albert Dresden Vandam, *My Paris note-book* (Philadelphia 1894), Loc. 1994–2010

30. *Times*, 28 September 1887.

31. David Robin Watson, *Georges Clémenceau: A Political Biography* (London 1974), pp. 106–7. Maurice Agulhon, trans. Antonia Nevill, *The French Republic 1879–1992* (Oxford 1990).

32. Harding, *The Astonishing Adventure*, p. 113.

33. Mayeur and Reberioux, *The Third Republic*, p. 129.

34. Harding, *The Astonishing Adventure*, pp. 128–30.

35. Paul Lafargue, 'The Boulanger Question', *Le Socialiste*, 23 July 1887, trans. Mitchell Abidor.

36. W.H. Gleadell, 'General Boulanger', *Fortnightly Review*, September 1887: 360.

37. *Les maîtresses du général Boulanger, La vérité sur sa fortune* (Paris 1887).

38. Marie Quinton, *Le journal de la belle meunière*, pp. 30–31.

39. *SQ*, p. 65.

40. *Ibid*, p. 65.

III. Foreign Affairs

1. *SQ*, p. 67.

2. Watson, *Georges Clémenceau*, pp. 107–8.

3. Irvine, *The Boulanger Affair Reconsidered*, p. 74.

4. Roger L. Williams, *Henri Rochefort: Prince of the Gutter Press* (New York 1966), np. William D. Irvine says the Baron de Mackau presented the plan for a coup to Boulanger, who accepted it; rather than the other way around (*The Boulanger Affair Reconsidered*, p. 74).

5. Fresnette Pisani-Ferry, *Le General Boulanger* (Paris 1969), p. 95.

6. Williams, *Henri Rochefort*, p. 211.

7. Boulanger's conspiratorial machinations did not long remain hidden; they were knowledgably aired in the British press as early as June 1888 by Gabriel Monod: 'When Boulanger had been sent to Clermont-Ferrand, Republicans foolishly believed his popularity would steadily sink. They did not realize that, instead of being taken up with his military duties, he was incessantly employed in correspondence, in journeys to Paris without leave, and in preparing for an illegal electoral campaign, though his duties as a general in full pay rendered him ineligible. Thus, when elections came on, on the

25th of March, they were amazed to find one Thiébaud, an old Bonapartist journalist, undertaking on his own account to propose General Boulanger as a candidate in four departments at once,' 'Contemporary Life and Thought in France,' *The Contemporary Review*, 53, June 1888, 902–20.

8. Fresnette Pisani-Ferry, *Le General Boulanger* (Paris 1969), p. 95.

9. Peter Rutkoff, *Revanche and Revision: The Ligue des Patriotes and the Origins of the Radical Right in France 1882–1900*, (Athens, Ohio, 1981), p. 47.

10. Robert Harborough Sherard, *Twenty years in Paris; being some recollections of a literary life* (London 1905), Loc. 3830–40. This conversation occurred years after the events.

11. 'Veritas', BASSESSE!, 47.

12. Pisani-Ferry, *Le General Boulanger*, p. 99.

13. Harding, *The Astonishing Adventure*, p. 154.

14. Watson, *Georges Clémenceau*, p. 109.

15. This paragraph paraphrases Maurice Barrès' summary of the political situation in 'Monsieur Boulanger et la nouvelle generation', *Revue Independante* (April 1888), 55–63.

16. *La Justice*, 30 April 1888: 1. Téodor de Wyzewa was not impressed with this new turn taken by a former Blanquist: Vaillant is just 'this big fat man with glasses, with neither the talent to speak nor habits to suit a Marxist; his role as head of the socialist movement seems from now on finished,' Wyzewa, *Le mouvement socialiste en Europe* (Paris 1892), pp. 62–3.

17. Yves Chiron, *La Vie de Barrès* (Paris, n.d.), pp. 90–94. The line quoted is from *Sous l'oeil des Barbares* [AF translation].

18. Chiron, *La Vie de Barrès*, p. 90.

19. Jacques-Emile Blanche, *La Pêche aux Souvenirs* (Paris 1949), p. 210 [AF translation].

20. 'La Question Boulanger …', *La Justice*, 30 April 1888, 1.

21. René Kerviler, *Les Bretons* (Mayenne 1978), p. 28.

22. Grace Eckley, *Maiden Tribute: A Life of W.T. Stead* (Philadelphia 1978), p. 121.

23. *SQ*, p. 77. Maud Gonne has this rendezvous in Paris occurring immediately upon her return from a month in Constantinople (late November/early December 1887). She says she then set out for St Petersburg. But the trip to Russia was in May 1888. As often, her chronology is inaccurate.

24. Winifred Stephens, *Madame Adam* (London 1917), p. 178.

25. Stephens, *Madame Adam*, p. 181.

26. Robert Gildea, *Children of the Revolution: The French, 1799–1914* (London and New York 2008), Loc. 7269–90; p. 29.

27. *SQ*, p. 77.

28. Princess Catherine Radziwill, *Germany under Three Emperors* (London 1917), np.

29. Bertrand Joly, *Déroulède: L'inventeur du nationalisme* (Paris 1998), p. 146.

30. Eckley, *Life of W.T. Stead*, p. 294.

31. It is a fact that a Franco-Russian military alliance was formalized in 1892 as a safeguard against an attack upon either country by Germany, but it is incorrect to suggest

that had Maud Gonne never been to St Petersburg in 1888, that treaty would not have been made. The papers she carried did not amount to a 'draft' of the document signed four years later.

IV. From Millevoye to Yeats to Millevoye

1. *Freeman's Journal*, 20 September 1888.

2. Levenson, p. 45.

3. 'Society for the Preservation of the Irish Language', *Nation*, 13 October 1888, 7.

4. Levenson, p. 47.

5. 'A Grand Concert of Irish Music', *Freeman's Journal*, 1 November 1888.

6. *Freeman's Journal*, 12 November 1888. For this concert, the patronage of Prince Edward of Saxe-Weimar (a Gonne acquaintance from the Castle Season of 1886) had been secured.

7. *Freeman's Journal*, 19 December 1888. Architect and theatre diarist Joseph Holloway also took the stage for a recitation of 'Christmas Eve' by Thomas de Quincey.

8. John O'Grady, *Life of Sarah Purser* (Dublin 1996), p. 67, p.155 n56.

9. Quoted by Levenson, p. 63.

10. Hughes to Sarah Purser, quoted in Deirdre Toomey, 'Who Fears to Speak of '98? Yeats and the Nineties', *Yeats Annual*, no. 14, ed. Warwick Gould (Basingstoke 2001), p. 254 n6.

11. Quoted by Levenson, np.

12. W.B. Yeats, *Memoirs, Autobiography – First Draft, Journal*, ed. Denis Donoghue (London 1972), pp. 40–41.

13. Alfred Tennyson, *Idylls of the King*, Loc. 4290–97.

14. Irvine, *The Boulanger Affair Reconsidered,*p. 97.

15. Sherard, *Twenty Years in Paris*, Loc. 4298.

16. *Le Gaulois*, 3 December 1888, p. 3.

17. *Affaire Boulanger, Dillon, Rochefort*, Annexes / Haute Cour de Justice (Paris 1889).

18. Alfred Naquet, *Varia*, 144 (BNF). The date 5 December 1888 is scribbled after this report of Millevoye's speech, but that date may be approximate, and the same speech may have been given multiple times during the campaign.

19. Williams, *Henri Rochefort*, p. 218; Frank Harris, *My Life and Loves* (New York 1963), p. 435.

20. Harris, *My Life and Loves*, p. 438.

21. Harding, *The Astounding Adventure*, p. 189.

22. Sherard, *Twenty Years in Paris*, Loc. 4253–66.

23. *Affaire Boulanger*, p. 215.

24. The constitutional republican party went by the name 'Opportunist'. This title derived from the policy of Gambetta in the 1870s: Republicans should pursue election to parliament, he argued, and then extend secular and democratic institutions in

France *as opportunity allowed*, in a measured progress towards social justice. It would have been better to employ the name 'Progressives', given that 'Opportunists', especially in English, carries the derogatory significance of men without principle.

25. Maurice Barrès, *L'appel au Soldat*, p. 226; quoted in Pisani-Ferry, *Le Général Boulanger*, p. 182.

26. Bruce Fulton, 'The Boulanger Affair Revisited', *French Historical Studies* (1 October 1991: 310–329. JSTOR), p. 317.

27. *Le Gaulois*, 27 February 1889, p. 2.

28. Denis Brogan, *The Development of Modern France 1870–1939*, Rev. ed., (London 1967), p. 210–11; Harding, *The Astonishing Adventure*, p. 204; Williams, *Henri Rochefort*, p. 221.

29. 'Mermeix' [Gabriel Terrail], *Les Coulisses du Boulangisme* (Paris 1890), pp. 202–3.

30. 'General Boulanger's Prosecution', *Daily News*, 5 April 1889.

31. *Le Democrate, de Seine-et-Oise, Organe Republicain, Radical, Revisionniste*, 21 April 1889.

32. *Trewman's Exeter Flying Post*, 24 April 1889.

33. LWBY1, 140–41.

34. Quoted by Levenson, p. 64.

35. *Ibid.*

36. LWBY1, 154.

37. *Gonne-Yeats Letters*, p. 18.

38. Announced in *Freeman's Journal* on 2 July 1889.

39. Margaret Ward, *Maud Gonne: Ireland's Joan of Arc* (London 1990), p. 26, n18.

V. A Single Mother in the Nineteenth Century

1. Joly, *Déroulède*, 168; *Saturday Review*, 25 January 1890, 101; *Times*, 21 January 1890.

2. Rachel Holmes, *Eleanor Marx: A Life* (London 2014), Loc. 2198.

3. Gregoire Kauffmann, *Edouard Drumont* (Paris 2008), p. 177.

4. On 28 January Millevoye spoke to a crowd of 800 nationalists in Amiens. His theme was that the current parliament was in revolt against the wishes of the people of France. He gave another speech the following day, the anniversary of Boulanger's big electoral victory in Paris, in which he hailed the general: 'our head, our friend – you have not broken ranks; the army you raised is still in the field.' *La Presse*, 28 January 1890.

5. Kauffmann, *Edouard Drumont*, p. 179.

6. 'Mermeix', *Les Coulisses du Boulangisme*.

7. *Le Gaulois*, 9 September 1890.

8. *Times*, 17 September 1890.

9. *Times*, 29 September 1890.

10. Jeffares says that Maud Gonne returned to campaigning against evictions in County Donegal, leaving Georges Silvère in Samois, and that Millevoye followed her,

and he became ill (*Gonne-Yeats Letters*, p. 18) but, going by the evidence in local Irish newspapers, Gonne was not in Donegal until November 1890.

11. *Freeman's Journal*, 18 August 1890.

12. Gregory Allen, 'Maud Gonne and Home Rule', *Irish Times*, 18 January 1978.

13. 'Public Meeting at Gweedore', *Freeman's Journal*, 10 November 1890. See also *Freeman's Journal* accounts of 12 and 13 November.

14. *SQ*, p. 98.

15. *SQ*, p. 140.

16. 'Lord Arran's Evicted Tenant', *Western People*, 24 January 1891; quoted in *Freeman's Journal*, 7 February 1891, 5.

17. Magny, *Maud Gonne*, pp. 59–60. See also Pierre Ranger, *La France Vue d'Irlande : L'histoire du mythe française de Parnell à l'Etat Libre* (Rennes 2011), p. 187.

18. Yeats, *Letters to a New Island*, np; Magny, p. 71.

19. Yeats, *Variorum Poems*, p. 123; the text is from the version of 'A Dream of Death' published in the *National Observer* on 12 December 1891. The first draft of the poem is dated 'November 22nd'; see George Bornstein, ed., *The Early Poetry*, vol. 2, *Manuscript Materials by W.B. Yeats* (Ithaca and London 1994), p. 317.

20. *Times*, 31 July 1891, p. 8.

21. Yeats, *Memoirs*, p. 46. R.F. Foster covers these events carefully in *The Apprentice Mage*, pp. 115–6.

22. *Memoirs*, p. 47.

23. Yeats, *Variorum Poems*, pp. 121–22; version is that of *The National Observer*, 7 May 1892.

VI. The Millevoye Affair and the Norton Affair

1. Alfred Tennyson, *Idylls of the King*, Loc. 4290–97.

2. Yeats, 'Adam's Curse', *The Collected Poems of W.B. Yeats*, ed. Richard J. Finneran (New York 1983, 1989), pp. 80–81.

3. Quoted in Ellmann, *Yeats: The Man and the Masks*, p. 158.

4. Yeats, *Memoirs*, p. 41.

5. *Memoirs*, pp. 47–48.

6. R.F. Foster quotes the poem in full, concluding that it 'reflects' Gonne's 'secret sadness' (*Apprentice Mage*, p. 116).

7. *Memoirs*, p. 48.

8. Yeats, *The Early Poetry*, p. 484.

9. LWBY1, 266.

10. *Memoirs*, pp. 48–49. *The Apprentice Mage* identifies the 'corrupt priest' with Millevoye, and the desert as Gonne's life with him, p. 117.

11. *SQ*, p. 254. Surely the readiest interpretation of that dream of a woman bending over Gonne's childhood cot is that it was a wish-fulfilment about her mother, not that it

was the spiritual trace of an Egyptian priestess who had millennia earlier been sexually involved with a simoniac priest.

12. LWBY1, 266.

13. *Memoirs*, p. 60.

14. *Journal des Voyages et des Aventures de Terre et de Mer*, January–June 1892, 353.

15. Robert Tombs, *From Nationhood and Nationalism in France: From Boulanger to the Great War* (New York 1991), p. 132 and *passim*.

16. *Gil Blas*, 1 February 1892, 3.

17. The exaggerations and departures from the facts (the police shooting into the crowd, the trial and sentence, and so on) in this Paris interview indicate that Maud Gonne felt safe in France to elaborate a myth of herself without fear of correction; the same interview given in Dublin would inevitably have been read by people who knew better.

18. *Journal des debats politiques et littéraires*, 21 February 1892, 3.

19. Magny, 'Maud Gonne: Realité et Mythe', pp. 61–2.

20. 'Carnet Mondaine', *La Nouvelle Revue*, 1 May 1892; *Gil Blas*, 26 April 1892; *La Presse*, 24 April 1892.

21. LWGY1, 295.

22. See Deirdre Toomey, 'The Cold Heaven', *Yeats Annual*, no. 18, Loc. 4550–81.

23. Yeats, letter to the editor of the *Daily Express*, 2 June 1892; LWBY1, 299.

24. 'A National Literary Society', *Freeman's Journal*, 10 June 1892.

25. 'National Literary Society', *Irish Times*, 10 June 1892, p. 6.

26. LWBY1, 301.

27. Conrad A. Balliet, 'For the Love of Maud', p. 121. My thanks to the author for a copy of this unpublished manuscript.

28. 'Inauguration of the Irish Literary Society', *Irish Times*, 24 July 1892, p. 6.

29. 'National Literary Society', *Freeman's Journal*, 17 August 1892.

30. *Le Matin*, 18 September 1892; *Le Gaulois*, 18 September 1892.

31. Henri Bremontier, 'L'Actualite: Maud Gonne', *La Presse*, 26 October 1892, p. 1.

32. 'Conferences de Miss Maud Gonne', *Bulletin*, Société de géographie commerciale de Bordeaux, Ser2, A15 (November 1892), 635–6 ; 'Russia and Germany', *The Standard*, 7 November 1892, p. 5.

33. Maud Gonne gave a lecture on 23 November in Bethnal Green, London, on behalf of the Amnesty Association. According to a publicity interview she gave upon her return to Paris in December, while out of France she assisted at a sale of Donegal tweeds in Dublin to benefit evicted tenants; *La Revue mondaine illustrée*, 25 December 1892, 1.

34. Henri Spont, 'Conversation with Miss Maud Gonne', *Gil Blas*, 31 December 1892, 3.

35. Jacques St Cera, *Le Figaro*, 27 December 1892, p. 2.

36. *Journal des debats politiques et litteraires*, 16 January 1893, 2 ; 'Banquet', *La Presse*, 16 January 1893.

37. *Gonne-Yeats Letters*, p. 50.

38. Clovis Hugues, *Les Libres Paroles: Poésies* (Paris 18[94]), p. 88.

39. Millevoye to Barrès, telegram (1 January 1893); BNF.

40. Books on the Panama Affair include Jean Saint-Martin, *Clovis Hugues et moi dans l'affaire de Panama* (Avignon 1897) ; Maron J. Simon, *The Panama Affair* (New York 1971); Barry Evetts, *The Panama Affair* (San José 2000); Pierre-Alexandre Bourson, *L'affaire Panama* (Paris 2000).

41. The French press in the 1880s was relatively 'free' but not often 'independent'; the divisions between commerce, politics and objectivity were not maintained as a matter of custom.

42. Maxime Lecomte, *Les ralliés: histoire d'un parti (1886–1898)*, (Paris 1898), pp. 222–24.

43. Out of 545 duels fought in France between 1869 and 1884, only eight proved fatal. See Benjamin Cummings Truman, *The Field of Honor: being a complete and comprehensive history of duelling in all countries* (New York 1884), Loc. 276.

44. Maurice Barrès, *Le roman de l'energie nationale*, 3, *Leurs figures* (Paris 1902) p. 134.

45. *Ibid.*

46. Amédée Chassagne, *Les 40 mortels du boulangisme: elections legislatives 1893* (Paris 1893), Appendix 15G3.

47. 'Chronicle of Foreign Affairs', *The Speaker*, 31 December 1892.

48. Joly, *Déroulède*, p. 192.

49. *La Presse*, 28 March 1893.

50. *Freeman's Journal*, 24 April 1893, 10.

51. 'London', *Le Figaro*, 3 June 1893, 2; 'London', *La Lanterne*, 2 June 1893.

52. The words are Norton's, from his testimony at a subsequent trial; *La Presse*, 6 August 1893.

53. 'Heavy Sentences', *Freeman's Journal*, 7 August 1893, 10; *La Lanterne*, 7 August 1893.

54. Barrès, *Leurs Figures*, p. 231.

55. 'Paris', *Freeman's Journal*, 20 June 1893.

56. *Leurs Figures*, 232ff. My account follows that of Maurice Barrès, which itself is largely substantiated by many press accounts of the day.

57. *La Lanterne*, 25 June 1893, 5.

58. *Echo de Paris*, 24 June 1893, 3.

59. *Echo de Paris*, 25 June 1893, 3.

60. *Review of Reviews* 5: 4. The date of composition of this article is uncertain. Richard Pigott was the Irish journalist whose forged letters, published by the *Times*, aimed to destroy the political reputation of Charles Stewart Parnell.

61. Her arrival from Brussels is announced in *Le Matin* on 27 July 1893; she left on 14 August 1893, according to *Le Gaulois*.

62. *Le Figaro*, 29 July 1893; *Le Gaulois*, 29 July 1893.

63. *La Lanterne*, 7 August 1893.

64. This draft is quoted in Foster, *The Apprentice Mage*, p. 128.

65. Yeats, *The Early Poetry*, p. 491.

66. Yeats, *Variorum Poems*, p. 744.

67. *Gonne-Yeats Letters*, p. 51.

68. As he sat next to Maud Gonne at the August 1898 meeting of the 1798 Centennial Association, Lionel Johnson noticed that her hand was trembling: 'I think she has to force herself to speak' (Levenson, 140). My thanks for crucial information about 'The Glove and the Cloak' to Deirdre Toomey, who, it must be added, does not share the belief that Yeats understood that Gonne was the mother of a child well before December 1898, when Gonne told him herself.

69. Quoted by Norman Jeffares in *W.B. Yeats: Man and Poet*, p. 63.

70. Yeats, *Autobiographies*, p. 64.

VII. An Ibsenite Heroine

1. *Memoirs*, pp. 72–73.

2. *The Apprentice Mage*, p. 127.

3. 'Miss Gonne and the Political Prisoners', *Freeman's Journal*, 7 November 1893; 'Miss Maud Gonne', *Freeman's Journal*, 10 November 1893.

4. In *A Servant of the Queen*, Gonne suggests that the spy in her employ was planted there by Camille Dreyfus, editor of *Le Matin*, who provided information to Clémenceau, presumably in April or May 1893, ahead of the Norton Affair (*SQ*, p. 212).

5. Christopher McIntosh, *Eliphas Levi and the French Occult Revival* (London 1972), pp. 170–74.

6. *Gonne-Yeats Letters*, p. 21; Levenson, p. 92.

7. McIntosh, *Eliphas Levi*, p. 170.

8. Joséphin Péladan, *L'art idéaliste et mystique, doctrine de l'Ordre et du salon annuel des Rose+Croix*, (Paris 1894), p. 33.

9. McIntosh, *Eliphas Levi*, p. 181.

10. Joanny Bricaud, *Huysmans, occultiste et magicien: avec une notice sur les hosties magiques qui servirent à Huysmans pour combattre les envoûtements* (Paris 1913), Loc. 189–203.

11. LWBY1, 380, 382.

12. Villiers de L'Isle-Adam, *Axel*, trans. Marilyn Gaddis Rose (Dublin 1970), pp. 155–57. Yeats wrote about the play in *The Bookman*: 'A Symbolical Drama in Prose', *Uncollected Prose*, vol. 1 (New York 1970), pp. 323–34.

13. John Harwood, *Olivia Shakespear and W.B. Yeats: After Long Silence* (New York 1989), pp. 73–80.

14. *Memoirs*, p. 63.

15. LWBY1, 396, 414, 463.

16. *Memoirs*, pp. 85–86.

17. *Memoirs*, p. 86.

18. A. Norman Jeffares, 'Iseult Gonne', *Yeats Annual*, no. 16, 'Poems and Contexts', (Basingstoke 2005), pp. 204–5.

19. Joseph Reinach, *Histoire de L'Affaire Dreyfus* (Paris 2006), p. 130.

20. Vicki Caron, 'Catholic Political Mobilization and Antisemitic Violence in Fin-de-Siècle France: The Case of the Union Nationale', *The Journal of Modern History*, vol. 81, No. 2, June 2009, 294–346.

21. Rutkoff, *Revanche and Revision* p. 64.

22. Léon Daudet, *Sauveteurs et incendiaires* (Paris 1941), pp. 200–02. In fact, she put her two sons out to nurse, then sent them away to school, a common enough upbringing for middle-class French children in the nineteenth century.

23. Paul Desachy, *Le Boulevard: Croquis parisiens* (1893), p. 242.

24. Edmond Goncourt, *Journal*, vol. 3 (Paris 1989), 930–31; translation from Silverman, 102. Gonne and Gyp both spoke at a conference on 'Women and Feminism' organized for the launch of *La Fronde*; see *Le Gaulois*, 29 November 1896.

25. Madame Alphonse Daudet, *Souvenirs* (Paris 1910), p. 10.

26. Willa Z. Silverman, *The Notorious Life of Gyp: Right-Wing Anarchist in Fin-de-Siècle France* (Oxford 1995), p. 124.

27. *Le Matin*, 6 August 1899; translation from Silverman, p. 140.

28. Karen Offen, 'Intrepid Crusader: Ghénia Avril de Sainte-Croix Takes on the Prostitution Issue', *Proceedings of the Western Society for French History*, vol. 33 (2005), 354.

29. *Gil Blas*, 21 January 1895, 1.

30. 'Meeting at the Town Hall', *Irish Examiner*, 15 July 1895.

31. Léon Ó Broin, *Revolutionary Underground: The Story of the Irish Republican Brotherhood* (Totowa 1976), pp. 65–67; Toomey, 'Who Fears to Speak of '98?' pp. 215–16.

32. McCoole, *Easter Widows*, Loc 240–46; *Maud Gonne's Irish Nationalist Writings 1895–1946*, ed. Karen Steele (Dublin 2004), p. 6.

33. *Gonne-Yeats Letters*, p. 52.

34. *Gonne-Yeats Letters*, p. 55.

35. *Irish Times*, 5 September 1896.

36. *Gonne-Yeats Letters*, pp. 59–60; Irish Government. Anti-Government Organisations, 1882–1921 (CO 904, Volumes/Boxes 7–23, 27–29 and 157). Public Records Office, London, England; *Nation*, 13 June 1896, 15; *Freeman's Journal*, 5 August 1896, 5; *Nation*, 22 August 1896, 11; *Freeman's Journal*, 14 September 1896, 10.

37. 'Arrival of John Daly', *Irish Times*, 14 September 1896, 6.

38. 'The Dynamite Plot', *Times*, 25 September 1896, p. 6.

39. The police report of Gonne's activities included a newspaper article on her speech in defence of the dynamiters on 27 September 1896; quoted by Conrad Balliet, 'For the Love of Maud', p. 128.

40. *SQ*, p. 183.

41. LWBY2, 63, n7.

42. *The Wind Among the Reeds: Manuscript Materials*, p. 131. First published in the *Saturday Review* on 9 January 1897.

43. Harwood, *Olivia Shakespear and W.B. Yeats*, p. 70.

44. W.B. Yeats, *The Speckled Bird,* ed. William H. O'Donnell, (Toronto, 1976), p. 27.

45. Warwick Gould, ed., 'Yeats and the Nineties', *Yeats Annual*, no. 14 (London 2001), p. 223.

46. *Memoirs*, p. 89.

47. *Variorum Poems*, p. 152; the wording is from the publication in *The Dome* in May 1898.

48. *Gonne-Yeats Letters*, p. 64.

49. *Gonne-Yeats Letters*, p. 65.

50. Matthew Kelly, 'Dublin Fenianism in the 1880s: The Irish culture of the future', www.academicroom.com.

51. Teeling circulated a letter in the west of Ireland characterizing Gonne in these terms in the summer of 1898; *Gonne-Yeats Letters*, np.

52. 'St Patrick's Day in Paris', *Nation*, 27 March 1897, 6.

53. *Nation*, 27 March 1897.

54. Ranger, *La France Vue d'Irlande*, p. 189.

55. *The Wind Among the Reeds: Manuscript Materials*, p. 73. The poem is dated 'Sligo, June 1897'.

56. *Gonne-Yeats Letters*, pp. 70, 71.

57. From the minutes of the Irish Socialist Republican Party, quoted by Donal Nevin, *James Connolly: A Full Life* (Dublin 2005), p. 65.

58. *Autobiographies*, p. 244.

59. 'The Dublin Disturbances', *Irish Times*, 24 June 1897, p. 5.

60. LWBY2, 117.

61. 'The Injured of Tuesday Night', *Freeman's Journal*, 24 June 1897, 11.

62. Levenson, p. 123.

63. Ina Connolly Heron, witness statement; Military Archives; McCoole, *Easter Widows*, Loc. 1310.

64. *Gonne-Yeats Letters*, p. 73.

65. *Autobiographies*, p. 365.

VIII. Millenarian Exaltations

1. James Pethica, ed., *Lady Gregory's Diaries 1892–1902* (Gerrards Cross 1996), p. 148.

2. Ellmann, *Yeats: The Man and the Masks*, p. 161.

3. *Wind Among the Reeds: Manuscript Materials*, 165. The poem was published on 24 July 1897 in the *Saturday Review*.

4. LWBY2, 134.

5. *Gonne-Yeats Letters*, pp. 78–9.

6. Piers Paul Read, *The Dreyfus Affair: The Story of the Most Infamous Miscarriage of Justice in French History* (London 2012), p. 197.

7. Emile Zola, *The Dreyfus Affair and other writings*, ed. Alain Pages, trans. Eleanor Levieux (New Haven and London 1996), xvi.

8. Eugen Weber, *My France: Politics, Culture, Myth* (Cambridge, Mass 1991), p. 235; Léon Blum, *Souvenirs sur l'Affaire* (Paris 1935), pp. 84–89.

9. Weber, p. 227.

10. William C. Carter, *Marcel Proust: A Life* (New Haven and London 2000), p. 248.

11. J.S. McClelland, *The French Right from De Maistre to Maurras* (London 1970), p. 168.

12. Zola, *The Dreyfus Affair*, p. 24.

13. Zola, *The Dreyfus Affair*, p. 17.

14. Gildea, *Children of the Revolution*, Loc. 5033–38.

15. *La Revue hebdomadaire* [1902/11], Paris 1898, 149.

16. LWBY2, 178.

17. Rutkoff, *Revanche and Revision*, p. 79.

18. Louis Leblois, *L'affaire Dreyfus: l'iniquité, la réparation, les principaux faits et les principaux documents* (Paris 1929), p. 913; Jean Jaures, *Les preuves: affaire Dreyfus* (Paris 1898).

19. Raphaël Viau, *Vingt ans d'antisémitisme, 1889–1909* (Paris 1910), pp. 168–9.

20. *Ibid.*

21. Pethica, p. 167.

22. Pethica, p. 167.

23. Maud Gonne, 'Relief Work in Erris', *Freeman's Journal*; reprinted by Steele in *Maud Gonne's Irish Nationalist Writings*, pp. 122–25.

24. 'Belmullet', *Freeman's Journal*, 5 March 1898), 10.

25. Steele, *Maud Gonne's Irish Nationalist Writings*, p. 119.

26. *Gonne-Yeats Letters*, p. 88.

27. Ellmann, *Yeats: The Man and the Masks*, p. 129.

28. Terence Brown, *The Life of W.B. Yeats: A Critical Biography* (Dublin 1999), p. 101.

29. Ella Young, *Flowering dusk; things remembered accurately and inaccurately* (New York and Toronto 1945), pp. 105–6.

30. *Variorum Poems*, p. 165, p. 166.

31. *Gonne-Yeats Letters*, p. 91.

32. LWBY2, 251, n1.

33. *The Wind Among the Reeds : Manuscript Materials*, p. 185.

34. Jean-Luc Marion, *The Erotic Phenomenon*, trans. Stephen E. Lewis (Chicago 2007), p. 108. [Some of the phrasing in this quotation has been retranslated by AF.]

35. *Memoirs*, p. 125.

36. Mary K. Greer, *Women of the Golden Dawn: Rebels and Priestesses* (Rochester, Vermont 1995), pp. 160–62.

37. Joris-Karl Huysmans, *Là-Bas*, trans. Keene Wallace (New York 1928); Loc. 1952–63.

38. Ranger, *La France Vue d'Irlande*, p. 201.

39. LWBY2, 261.

40. 'General Humbert's Monument in Ballina', *Freeman's Journal*, 22 August 1898.

41. The 1798 Centenary Association has, according to the police report, 'shot its bolt' and 'the two meetings, so long talked of and from which great things were expected, have been held this month and were failures. One was held at Ballina on 21st of August, Miss Maud Gonne being the moving spirit. She brought over six unknown French delegates, an Italian named Cipriani, a couple of Irish Americans, and a man named Gillingham from South Africa with a couple from Dublin and London … the whole thing lacked enthusiasm …' (CO 904 60).

42. Donal Fallon, *16 Lives: John MacBride* (Dublin 2015), p. 62.

43. Jacques-Émile Blanche, *La Pêche aux Souvenirs*, trans. Walter Clement (London 1937), p. 147. The one event is described in different ways in these memoirs.

44. Yves Chiron, *La Vie de Barrès* (Paris 2000), p. 53.

45. Eliza Aria, *My Sentimental Self*, Foreword by Stephen MacKenna (London 1922), p. 196.

46. Ranger, *La France Vue d'Irlande,* p. 201.

47. *Gonne-Yeats Letters* (24 June 1899), p. 108.

48. Magny, 126; from the *United Irishman*, 23 September 1899.

49. 'Foreign Correspondent', *United Irishman*, 21 October 1899.

50. *Gonne-Yeats Letters*, pp. 134–35.

51. 'The Goddess Brigid', *United Irishman*, 3 November 1900, 3.

52. *Gonne-Yeats Letters*, pp. 275–76.

53. *Le Matin*, 8 September 1898, p. 2.

54. *Le Gaulois*, 8 September 1898, 2.

55. Zola, *The Dreyfus Affair*, 11 September 1898.

56. *SQ*, pp. 279–80.

57. According to *L'Orchestra*, Bréval sang from the Wagner repertoire several times through the middle of October 1898.

58. Levenson, p. 144.

59. 'Arrivals', *Freeman's Journal*, 29 November 1898, 14.

60. LWBY2, 312.

61. LWGY2, 314–15; Warwick Gould, 'Yeats, mescal, and visions', *Times Literary Supplement*, 13 July 1990, 762.

62. *Memoirs*, p. 132.

63. Marion, *The Erotic Phenomenon*, p. 125.

64. Since her father's death made her an independent woman, Gonne may have felt that she was herself guilty of making a pact by which he died to make her free; see Deirdre Toomey, 'Labyrinths', *Yeats and Women* (London 1992), pp. 21–22.

65. LWBY2, 314.

66. *Memoirs*, p. 133.

67. *Variorum Poems*, p. 413.

68. Deirdre Toomey, *Yeats and Women*, p. 20.

69. *Memoirs*, p. 134.

70. In his statement to the divorce court, MacBride wrote: 'I was aware that she had led an evil life before our marriage, but was not aware that it was so horrible as I afterwards found it out to be. By her own confession to me towards the end of August 1904, she had been the mistress of three different men. By one she had two illegitimate children and two or three miscarriages', quoted by Anthony J. Jordan, *The Yeats-Gonne-MacBride Triangle* (Westport 2000), pp. 127–28. In a trance state, Maud Gonne had once described herself as 'a murderess of children', and once in Dublin she was confined for a period and treated by Dr Sigerson; the nurse in attendance circulated a rumour that she had had an abortion and that Yeats was the father (*Memoirs*, p. 62, p. 67). It is difficult to date this health crisis; R.F. Foster suggests February 1893 (*The Apprentice Mage*, p. 127).

71. *Variorum Poems*, pp. 272–73.

IX. Sexual Love, Spiritual Hatred

1. 'I remember that Greek antiquity has bid us look for the principal stars, that govern enemy and sweetheart alike, among those that are about to set, in the Seventh House as the astrologers say; and that it may be "sexual love," which is "founded upon spiritual hate," is an image of the warfare of man and Daemon; and I even wonder if there may not be some secret communion, some whispering in the dark between Daemon and sweetheart.' Yeats, *Per Amica Silentia Lunae* (New York 1918), p. 39. See also Allan Wade, *The Letters of W.B. Yeats* (New York 1955), pp. 758–59.

2. LWBY2, 333–34, n1. Wade, *Letters*, p. 758–59.

3. *Gonne-Yeats Letters*, pp. 98.

4. *Gonne-Yeats Letters*, pp. 101–02.

5. Augusta Gregory, however, was not impressed with Maud Gonne's celebrated looks: 'Instead of beauty I saw a death's head', *Lady Gregory's Diaries*, p. 197.

6. LWBY2, 355.

7. LWBY2, 357.

8. LWBY2, 102.

9. Anatole France, *Monsieur Bergeret in Paris* (London and New York 1921) (trans. Bérengère Drillien), p. 217.

10. Arthur Meyer, *Ce que je peux dire* (Paris 1912), p. 264.

11. This account closely follows that of Thierry Billiard, *Felix Faure* (Paris 1995), p. 914.

12. *La Vie de Barrès*, p. 194; from *Cahiers*.

13. This account of Déroulède's failed coup follows *Le Figaro*, 24 February 1899; Billiard, *Felix Faure*, p. 930; Harvey Goldberg, *The Life of Jean Jaures* (Madison 1962), p. 247; and particularly Yves Chiron, *La Vie de Barrès*, pp. 200–03.

14. *Gonne-Yeats Letters*, pp. 108–09.

15. *Shan Van Vocht*, September 1897, 161. See Virginia Crossman, 'The *Shan Van Vocht*: Women, Republicanism, and the Commemoration of the 1798 Rebellion', *Eighteenth-Century Life* 22.3 (1998), 128–39.

16. Richard Davis, *Arthur Griffith and Non-Violent Sinn Fein* (Dublin 1974), p. 15.

17. Steele, ed., *Maud Gonne's Irish Nationalist Writings*, p. 42. This collection includes Gonne's writings for the *United Irishman*.

18. R.F. Foster, *Vivid Faces: The Revolutionary Generation in Ireland, 1890–1923*, Loc. 2953–60; Brian Maye, *Arthur Griffith* (Dublin 1997), p. 366. Patrick Maume gives a detailed account of the issue in *The Long Gestation: Irish Nationalist Life 1891–1918* (Dublin 1999), p. 52.

19. Levenson, p. 152.

20. Hannah Arendt, *The Origins of Totalitarianism* (New York 1966), pp. 77–78.

21. 'The Fall of Fort Chabrol', *Saturday Review*, 23 September 1899, 383.

22. *Le Figaro*, 21 September 1899.

23. 'Prosecutions at Ballina', *Freeman's Journal*, 1 November, 2 November 1899.

24. Steele, *Maud Gonne's Irish Nationalist Writings*, pp. 126–28.

25. Anthony J. Jordan, *Boer War to Easter Rising: The Writings of John MacBride*, Loc. 6618–22.

26. Levenson, p. 153.

27. Nov 21 1899; National Archives of Ireland, CBS, 3/716, box 6; Ranger, *La France Vue d'Irlande*, p. 219.

28. Donal P. McCracken, *MacBride's Brigade: Irish Commandos in the Anglo-Boer War* (Dublin 1999), p. 78.

29. G.A. Lyons, *Some Recollections of Griffith and His Times* (Dublin 1923), p. 14.

30. *Gonne-Yeats Letters*, p. 115.

31. Seán O'Casey, *Pictures in the Hallway* (New York 1942), p. 311.

32. *Freeman's Journal*, 18 December 1899, 11.

33. *New York Times*, 19 December 1899.

34. Donal P. McCracken, *The Irish Pro-Boers 1877–1902* (Johannesburg and Cape Town 1989), p. 76.

35. McCracken, *MacBride's Brigade*, np; *The Irish Pro-Boers*, p. 78.

36. McCracken, *The Irish Pro-Boers*, p. 77.

37. McCracken, *MacBride's Brigade*, pp. 80–81.

38. *New York Times*, 29 January 1900.

39. 'Maud Gonne Cheered', *New York Times*, 5 February 1900.

40. *Southern Star*, 14 April 1900, p. 7.

41. Levenson, p. 164.

42. Seamus Ua Caomhanaigh, 302 Howth Road, Killester, Dublin, witness statement.

43. Margaret Ward, ed., *In Their Own Voice: Women and Irish Nationalism* (Cork 1995), p. 19.

44. Máire Ó'Brolchain, Rocklawn, St Mary's Park, Galway, witness statement.

45. 'Patriotic Children's Treat', *United Irishman*, 14 July 1900, 7.

46. 'Application for Criminal Libel', *Freeman's Journal*, 23 April 1900, 8; 'Miss Maud Gonne and the *Irish Figaro*', *Irish Times*, 27 April 1900, p. 2.

47. After his apology was accepted, Colles returned to harry Maud Gonne in the 19 May issue of the *Irish Figaro*. He said he failed to see on what grounds Gonne's claim to be Irish rested. Since she did not appear to know where her father had been born, he had looked it up: 19 Gloucester Place, London.

48. *Gonne-Yeats Letters*, pp. 125–6.

49. See the witness statements by Mrs Tom Barry, *née* Leslie Price, 64 Patrick Street, Cork, and Joseph O'Rourke, 54 Herberton Road, Dublin.

50. 'The Irish Cause in France', *Freeman's Journal*, 24 July 1900, 13.

51. September 1900 police report; National Archives of Ireland, CBS Precis, box 5; quoted by Ranger, *La France Vue d'Irlande*, p. 218.

52. *Gonne-Yeats Letters*, p. 133; LWBY2, 560.

53. Jeffares in *Gonne-Yeats Letters*, p. 28; Magny, p. 137; Steele, np; Toomey, p. 27.

54. Balliett, 'For the Love of Maud', p. 113.

55. 10 June 1905, 15 June 1905; Irish Government. Police Reports, February 1898–December 1913 (CO 904, Boxes 68–91). Public Records Office, London; 'Irishmen and the English Army. A lecture by Miss Gonne', *United Irishman*, 20 October 1900, Steele, pp. 71–4.

56. *Connaught Telegraph*, 10 November 1900, p. 4.

57. *Le Gaulois*, 25 November 1900.

58. Stephen MacKenna, 'Over the Frontier, President Kruger, his Arrival in Paris, Reception of the Irish Delegates', *United Irishman*, 1 December 1900, 4.

59. *Times*, 16 November 1900; Jordan, *The Yeats-Gonne-MacBride Triangle*, Loc. 3344.

60. 'Ireland and the Boers, Reception of the Irish Transvaal Delegates by President Kruger', *Southern Star*, reprinted from the *Independent and Nation*, 8 December 1900, p. 6.

61. Levenson, pp. 179–80.

62. Tom Clarke to Kathleen Daly, 15 December 1900; Tom and Kathleen Clarke Papers, NLI.

63. LWBY2, 129–30.

64. LWBY2, 136.

65. Kathleen Daly to Tom Clarke, March 1901; Tom and Kathleen Clarke papers, NLI.

66. Levenson, pp. 184–86.

67. Nancy Cardozo, *Lucky Eyes and a High Heart: The Life of Maud Gonne* (Indianapolis and New York 1978), p. 207.

68. Léon Ó Broin, *Revolutionary Underground*, p. 117.

69. Jordan, *Boer War to the Easter Rising*, Loc. 3390.

70. McCoole, *Easter Widows*, p. 22.

71. Jordan, *Boer War to the Easter Rising*, Loc 3383, 6A.

72. 'Miss Maud Gonne', *Connaught Telegraph*, 14 September 1901, p. 4.

73. Jordan, *The Yeats-Gonne-MacBride Triangle*, p. 23.

74. *Gonne-Yeats Letters*, p. 143.

75. 'Toleration', *United Irishman*, 6 July 1901; Steele, p. 88.

76. 'Ireland To-Day', Steele, p. 79.

77. 'Other Threats', *Le Figaro*, 10 October 1901, p. 2.

78. 'Jurypacking', *United Irishman*, 2 Novemberr 1901; Steele, pp. 96–98.

79. Advertisement for recitations at the Coffee Palace, *United Irishman*, 21 December 1901, p. 3.

80. *Gonne-Yeats Letters*, p. 147.

81. LWBY2, 148.

82. *Gonne-Yeats Letters*, p. 148.

83. See Adrian Frazier, *Behind the Scenes: Yeats, Horniman, and the Struggle for the Abbey Theatre* (Berkeley and Los Angeles 1990), pp. 77–78.

84. *Variorum Poems*, pp. 629–30. See also Adrian Frazier, 'Cathleen ni Houlihan, Yeats's Dream, and the Double Life of Maud Gonne', *Sewanee Review* (Spring 2013). The reference in 'The Circus Animals' Desertion' is actually to *The Countess Cathleen*, although it may also fit *Cathleen ni Houlihan*.

85. *Gonne-Yeats Letters*, pp. 151–52.

86. LWBY3, 166–8. Holloway Diaries: A Dublin Playgoer's Impressions, NLI Mss 1798–1808, 3 April 1902, p. 169. This paragraph is taken from my chapter in the *Oxford Handbook of Modern Irish Drama*, 'Irish Acting in the Early 20th Century' (Oxford 2015).

87. Levenson, p. 195.

88. Robert Hogan and Michael J. O'Neill, eds, *Joseph Holloway's Abbey Theatre* (Carbondale, Edwardsville, London and Amsterdam 1967), p. 181.

89. *SQ*, pp. 328–29

90. *Gonne-Yeats Letters*, p. 154; Jordan, *The Yeats-Gonne-MacBride Triangle*, p. 33.

91. *Gonne-Yeats Letters*, pp. 155–56.

92. *Gonne-Yeats Letters*, pp. 158–59.

93. *Gonne-Yeats Letters*, p. 161.

94. LWBY2, 305n1.

95. Quoted in Lionel Pilkington, *Theatre and the State in Twentieth-Century Ireland: Cultivating the People* (London, 2001), p. 37.

96. Maud Gonne to My dear Willie; 25 September 1903; Paris; *Gonne-Yeats Letters*, pp. 176–77.

97. W.G. Fay to W.B. Yeats [February? 1903]; Ms. 13068, NLI; Robert Hogan and James Kilroy, eds, *Laying the Foundations 1902–1904*, Modern Irish Drama: a documentary history II (Dublin 1976), pp. 50–51.

98. According to Synge's diary, 2 February 1903, 'with Yeats *Riders to the Sea* read out to Chesterton, M.G., etc.'; Ann Saddlemyer, ed., *Theatre Business* (Gerrards Cross, 1982), 39n1.

99. Ann Saddlemyer, ed., *The Collected Letters of J.M. Synge*, vol. 1, 1871–1907 (Oxford and New York 1983), p. 47.

100. *Gonne-Yeats Letters* pp. 162–64, pp. 176–77.

101. Synge, *Complete Plays*, p. 106.

102. *Gonne-Yeats Letters*, p. 166.

103. LWBY3, 315–16.

104. Jordan, *Boer War*, p. 4.

105. Cardozo, p. 229; *A Servant of the Queen*, p. 348.

106. *Gonne-Yeats Letters*, p. 170.

107. Jordan, *Boer War*, Loc. 4040–44. MacBride prepared a notebook at the suggestion of Barry O'Brien, for use in discussions of an out-of-court settlement; Jordan quotes from this notebook.

108. Jordan, *The Yeats-Gonne-MacBride Triangle*, p. 82.

109. Maud Gonne to Dear Lady Gregory, 28 February 1903; Berg Collection 64B9544; NYPL; *Gonne-Yeats Letters*, p. 167.

110. *Freeman's Journal*, 3 March 1903, 5.

X. The Crack-Up

1. Foster, *The Apprentice Mage*, p. 293.

2. *Gonne-Yeats Letters*, p. 168.

3. Frederick Lawton, *The Third French Republic* (Philadelphia 1909), pp. 209–10.

4. *Gonne-Yeats Letters*, p. 168. 'C.B.' stands for 'Commander of the Bath', a British military award.

5. Mss. 29817 NLI; Jordan, *Boer War to the Easter Rising*, Loc. 3740.

6. Maud Gonne MacBride, witness statement.

7. *Gonne-Yeats Letters*, p. 173.

8. Seamus MacManus, witness statement; Maud Gonne MacBride, witness statement.

9. This account blends two detailed reports: 'The Parliamentary Fund', *Donegal News*, 23 May 1903, p. 8, and 'Mrs MacBride's Version', *Southern Star*, 23 May 1903.

10. Seán T. O'Kelly, witness statement.

11. *Judy: The London Serio-Comic Journal*, 27 May 1903, 242.

12. 'Repudiation by the Gaelic League', *Southern Star*, p. 5.

13. Maud Gonne MacBride, witness statement.

14. *Gonne-Yeats Letters*, pp. 72–73.

15. *Gonne-Yeats Letters*, p. 166.

16. Magny, p. 491.

17. Jordan, *Yeats-Gonne-MacBride Triangle*, p. 82.

18. *Gonne-Yeats Letters*, p. 174; LWBY3, pp. 425–26; pp. 434–35.

19. Hogan and Kilroy, p. 83.

20. Mary Barry Delaney is a curious figure in Maud Gonne's ménage. She settled in Paris in 1883 and after meeting Gonne in the mid 1890s, devoted herself to her until

her own death in 1947. She aspired to be a writer. In a September 1896 letter to Yeats, Gonne described Delaney's writings as 'not artistic but the sensational weirdness of some of them might suit a certain class of not overly cultivated people'. Assuming the role of general factotum, Delaney helped Gonne with the editorial and organizational side of *L'Irlande Libre*, and sometimes sent publicity material on Gonne's lectures to various English and Irish newspapers. Her passion for Gonne sometimes got the better of her, exploding in resentful letters that she did not get much in return for all she gave (*Gonne-Yeats Letters*, p. 104). Yeats described her as 'a morbid minded and very plain but quite worthy person' (WBY to A.H. Bullen, 10 July 1908).

21. The detail about the partition is from NLI MS 28, 517, quoted by Donal Fallon in *16 Lives: John MacBride*, p. 172.

22. Jordan, *Yeats-Gonne-MacBride Triangle*; pp. 82–3.

23. Jordan, *Yeats-Gonne-MacBride Triangle*, p. 80.

24. *Gonne-Yeats Letters*, pp. 180–81.

25. *Nenagh Guardian*, 7 May 1904, p. 4.

26. Jordan, *Yeats-Gonne-MacBride Triangle*, p. 81.

27. McCoole, *Easter Widows*, Loc. 839048.

28. In *The Speckled Bird*, the hero's intimate friend 'Margaret' had a friend much like Cipriani with whom she had been just as close: 'She had indeed felt just as intimate with an Italian musician who had talked to her about Wagner and about the greatness of music, and with a young Italian revolutionist who had talked to her about freedom, and would feel as intimate with others to come, but she did not know this and abandoned herself, with a joy that was like the joy of inspiration, to a sympathy that was awakening a new personality, among the darkness of her memories, that seemed to be her own inmost personality' (p. 170).

29. Yeats seems to have suspected Cipriani too; see *The Speckled Bird*, p. 170.

30. Balliett, 'For the Love of Maud', p. 55. Joyce put this rumour into *Ulysses*: 'Maud Gonne. Beautiful woman, La Patrie, M. Millevoye, Felix Faure, know how he died? Licentious men.'

31. MacBride's statement to the French divorce court; quoted in Jordan, MacBride's statement to the French divorce court; quoted in Jordan, *Yeats-Gonne-MacBride Triangle*, pp. 127–28.

32. Court testimony of Jennie Wyse Power, quoted in *Yeats-Gonne-MacBride Triangle*, p. 86.

33. Levenson, p. 227. Maud Gonne MacBride's movements in November 1903 are difficult to trace. MacBride wrote to John Devoy on 15 November 1904 that his wife had been in Paris for a couple of weeks (Jordan, *Boer War*, p. 10). She wrote to the secretary of the Skibbereen 1798 Memorial Comittee from Dublin on 25 November 1904 saying she was returning to Paris on that day (*Southern Star*, 25 November 1904). It is possible she returned from Dublin to Paris in early November, then made another trip to Dublin in the middle of the month.

34. From MacBride's 26 August 1905 statement to the Paris court, *Yeats-Gonne-MacBride Triangle*, p. 81.

35. *Gonne-Yeats Letters*, p. 184.

36. *Gonne-Yeats Letters*, pp. 247–48.

37. *Ibid.*

38. Jordan, *Boer War*, Loc. 4727–51.

39. Yeats to Lady Gregory, (12 January 1905); LWBY InteLex; *Gonne-Yeats Letters*, pp. 136–37.

40. 'Mrs Gonne MacBride Applies for Divorce', *Irish Independent*, 27 February 1905, p. 7.

41. *Gonne-Yeats Letters*, pp. 196–98.

42. Paul Gregan to George Russell; Berg Collection; 65B2172.

43. Horniman to Augusta Gregory, 11 April 1905; Berg Collection; 64B9516.

44. *Gonne-Yeats Letters*, p. 202.

45. LWBY4, 47.

46. LWBY4, 127. These feminist-friendly views of Yeats are very different from what many readers conclude from their reading of 'A Prayer for My Daughter' to be the poet's opinions.

47. Levenson, pp. 230–31.

48. Levenson, p. 229.

49. 'MacBride Divorce Case', *Evening Mail*, 10 August 1905, p. 3.

50. *Gonne-Yeats Letters*, pp. 216–18.

51. *Gonne-Yeats Letters*, p. 224.

52. Jordan, *Yeats-Gonne-MacBride Triangle*, p. 83.

53. McCoole, *Easter Widows*, pp. 60–61.

XI. Fallen Majesty and the Rising

1. Quoted in *Gonne-Yeats Letters*, p. 233.

2. *The Apprentice Mage*, p. 354.

3. *Gonne-Yeats Letters*, p. 237.

4. *Gonne-Yeats Letters*, p. 239.

5. *CBWBY*, p 151.

6. *Gonne-Yeats Letters*, p. 244.

7. *Gonne-Yeats Letters*, pp. 246–47.

8. For a deeply informed article on this subject, see Warwick Gould, 'Yeats's Mask', *Yeats Annual*, no. 19.

9. *Memoirs*, p. 191.

10. *Collected Works*, vol. 4, p. 231.

11. Mary Colum, *Life and the Dream* (Dublin 1966), pp. 119–21.

12. Colum, *Life and the Dream*, p.114.

13. *The Apprentice Mage*, p. 291.

14. *Gonne-Yeats Letters*, p. 252.

15. *Gonne-Yeats Letters*, p. 257.

16. Yeats to Lady Gregory (13 October 1908); LWBY.

17. Young, *Flowering Dusk*, p. 207.

18. Personal communication from John Kelly, 1 February 2014. According to Kelly, the visit must have occurred after 19 December 1908, and before Yeats's departure from Paris at the end of the month.

19. *Variorum Poems*, pp. 258–59.

20. *Gonne-Yeats Letters*, p. 258.

21. *Memoirs*, p. 157.

22. *Variorum Poems*, p. 291.

23. *Variorum Poems*, p. 257.

24. *Variorum Poems*, p. 256.

25. *Gonne-Yeats Letters*, p. 258.

26. *Gonne-Yeats Letters*, pp. 261–62.

27. LWBY4, 283.

28. *Gonne-Yeats Letters*, p. 271.

29. *Variorum Poems*, pp. 315–16.

30. *The Apprentice Mage*, p. 436, pp. 609–10; Harwood, p. 136.

31. Deirdre Toomey, 'The Cold Heaven', *Yeats Annual*, no. 18; Loc. 4591–4609. The reference to 'the hot blood of youth' is obscure; what was missing from Yeats's early courtship was hot-bloodedness.

32. *Letters to W.B. Yeats and Ezra Pound from Iseult Gonne: A girl that knew all Dante once*, eds A. Norman Jeffares, Anna MacBride White and Christina Bridgwater (London 2004), p. 19, pp. 21–22.

33. *Gonne-Yeats Letters*, p. 280.

34. W.B. Yeats to John Butler Yeats (19 May 1910); LWBY.

35. Yeats to Lady Gregory (10 November [ny]); LWBY.

36. Maud Gonne to John Quinn (3 November); my thanks to James and Jan Londraville.

37. Lucy McDiarmid, *The Irish Art of Controversy* (Dublin and Ithaca, New York 2005), p. 126.

38. McDiarmid, p. 157.

39. McCoole, *Easter Widows*, p. 77.

40. *Letters to W.B. Yeats and Ezra Pound from Iseult Gonne*, p. 48.

41. Balliett, 'For the Love of Maud', p. 113; *Letters to W.B. Yeats and Ezra Pound from Iseult Gonne*, p. 47.

42. *Letters to W.B. Yeats and Ezra Pound from Iseult Gonne*, p. 48.

43. Yeats to Lady Gregory, 29 March 1906; LWBY.

44. Martyn Cornick, 'Representations of Britain and British Colonialism in French Adventure Fiction 1870–1914', *French Cultural Studies* vol. 17 (2006), 137.

45. Émile Augustin Cyprien Driant, *La Guerre Fatale, France-Angleterre* (Paris 1904) pp. 51–52.

46. Clovis Hugues, 'Toast to Ireland,' *Les Libres Paroles*, p. 88; Achille Maffre de Baugé, 'Erin,' *L'Aube Meridionale* (January/February 1898), 22; Armande Sylvestre, 'Une patriote,' *L'Irlande Libre* (March 1898), 106.

47. *Gonne-Yeats Letters*, p. 294.

48. *Gonne-Yeats Letters*, p. 302.

49. *Gonne-Yeats Letters*, p. 273.

50. *Gonne-Yeats Letters*, p. 372.

51. Yeats to Florence Farr Emery (19 August 1916); LWBY. Yeats's information about Maud's response to the news of MacBride's death presumably comes from Iseult.

52. Yeats to Elizabeth Corbet Yeats (30 April 1916); LWBY.

53. Yeats to Lady Gregory (9 May 1916).

54. 'Introductory Rhymes', *Responsibilities* (1914); *Variorum Poems*, p. 270.

55. Yeats to John Quinn (23 May 1916); LWBY.

56. This line of thinking is remembered from a talk given long ago by Helen Vendler; my thanks to her and apologies if memory has misconstrued the original thought.

57. Yeats, *Essays and Introductions*, p. 314; quoted in Brown, *The Life of W.B. Yeats*, p. 232. Elizabeth Cullingford observes that Markievicz is a 'stand-in' for Gonne; Elizabeth Cullingford, *Gender and History in Yeats's Love Poetry* (Cambridge 1993), p. 121.

58. It is uncertain what dogs were part of the Gonne household in 1916, but Maud Gonne always had at least one. Dagda, a Great Dane, went everywhere with her in the mid 1890s; in the late 1890s she travelled with a lapdog, Patsy, to America; her basset hounds, Snake and Oona, won prizes at the May 1897, June 1898, and June 1901 Paris dog shows; her big shepherd Brutus guarded the house against MacBride during the divorce proceedings.

59. *Gonne-Yeats Letters*, p. 388.

60. *Letters to W.B. Yeats and Ezra Pound from Iseult Gonne*, pp. 152–53. Maud helped Iseult buy clothes for Goetz at Switzer's store, Grafton Street.

61. Aoife in *On Baile's Strand* (1904) is described as 'sitting at the fire with those grave eyes / Full of good counsel as it were with wine', (New York 1967), p. 169.

BIBLIOGRAPHY

NEWSPAPERS

The Connaught Telegraph
The Daily Express
The Daily News (London)
l'Echo de Paris
The Evening Mail
Le Figaro
Freeman's Journal
Gil Blas
The Irish Examiner
Irish Independent
The Irish Times
Journal des débats politiques et littéraires
La Cocarde
La Fronde
La Justice
La Lanterne
La Patrie
La Presse
La Revue mondaine illustrée
Le Démocrate de Seine-et-Oise
Le Gaulois
Le Matin
Le Temps
L'Univers illustré
Nation
National Observer Times (London)
The Nenagh Guardian
Shan Van Vocht
The Southern Star
Trewman's Exeter Flying Post
Western People

PERIODICALS

Cartes des chemins de fer français et tarifs des voyages circulaires
Conseil héraldique de France. Maison de Castellane. Branche de Salèrnes
The Contemporary Review (Pisani-Ferry)
The Court and Society Review
The Fortnightly Review
Journal des voyages et des aventures de terre et de mer
Judy: The London Serio-Comic Journal
La Nouvelle Revue
La Revue hebdomadaire
La Revue Indépendante
Le Socialiste
L'Irlande Libre
Review of Reviews
Revue de la Société Littéraire, et archéologique de Yerle
Revue d'histoire moderne et contemporaine
The Saturday Review
The Speaker

ARTICLES AND BOOKS

Anonymous, *Les maîtresses du général Boulanger, La vérité sur sa fortune* (Paris 1887).
Agulhon, Maurice, *The French Republic 1879–1992* (Oxford 1990);
—*Bassesse! Ou la vérité sur l'Affaire Boulanger, Veritas* (Paris 1888).
Arendt, Hannah, *The Origins of Totalitarianism* (New York 1966).
Aria, Eliza, *My Sentimental Self* (London 1922).
Balliet, Conrad A., 'For the Love of Maud' (unpublished manuscript, n.d.).
Barrès, Maurice, *L'appel au Soldat* (Paris 1926);
—*Le roman de l'energie nationale, 3, Leurs figures* (Paris 1902).
Billiard, Thierry, *Felix Faure* (Paris 1995).
Blanche, Jacques-Émile, *La Pêche aux Souvenirs* (Paris 1949);
—*Portraits of a Lifetime* (trans. Walter Clement) (London 1937).
du Bled, Victor, *La société française depuis cent ans. Quelques salons du Second Empire* (Paris 1923–24).
Blum, Léon, *Souvenirs sur l'Affaire* (Paris 1935).
Bourson, Pierre-Alexandre, *L'affaire Panama* (Paris 2000).
Brandt, George Henry, *Royat les Bains* (London 1880).
Bricaud, Joanny, *Huysmans, occultiste et magicien: avec une notice sur les hosties magiques qui servirent à Huysmans pour combattre les envoûtements* (Paris 1913).
Brisson, Adolphe, *Portraits intimes* (Paris 1896); *Portraits intimes* (Paris 1894).
Brogan, Denis, *The Development of Modern France 1870–1939*, revised ed. (London 1967).

Broin, Léon Ó, *Revolutionary Underground: the Story of the Irish Republican Brotherhood 1858–1924* (Totowa 1976).

Brown, Frederick, *For the Soul of France* (New York 2011).

Brown, Terence, *The Life of W.B. Yeats: A Critical Biography* (Dublin 1999).

Cardozo, Nancy, *Lucky Eyes and a High Heart: The Life of Maud Gonne* (Indianapolis and New York 1978).

Caron, Vicki, 'Catholic Political Mobilization and Antisemitic Violence in Fin-de-Siècle France: The Case of the Union Nationale', *The Journal of Modern History*, vol. 81, No. 2, June 2009: 294–346.

Carter, William C., *Marcel Proust: A Life* (New Haven and London 2000).

Chassagne, Amédée, *Les 40 mortels du boulangisme: elections legislatives 1893* (Paris 1893).

Chiron, Yves, *La Vie de Barrès,* (Paris, n.d.).

Colum, Mary, *Life and the Dream* (Dublin 1966).

Cornick, Martyn, 'Representations of Britain and British Colonialism in French Adventure Fiction 1870–1914', *French Cultural Studies* 17 (2006).

Crossman, Virginia, 'The *Shan Van Vocht*: Women, Republicanism, and the Commemoration of the 1798 Rebellion', *Eighteenth-Century Life* 22.3 (1998).

Cullingford, Elizabeth, *Gender and History in Yeats's Love Poetry* (Cambridge 1993).

Datta, Venita, *Heroes and Legends of Fin-de-Siècle France: Gender, Politics, and Nation* (Cambridge 2011).

Daudet, Léon, *Sauveteurs et incendiaires* (Paris 1941).

Daudet, Madame Alphonse, *Souvenirs* (Paris 1910).

Davis, Richard, *Arthur Griffith and Non-Violent Sinn Féin* (Dublin 1974).

Desachy, Paul, *Le Boulevard: Croquis Parisiens* (Paris 1893).

Driant, Émile Augustin Cyprien, *La guerre fatale, France-Angleterre* (Paris 1904).

Eckley, Grace, *Maiden Tribute: A Life of W.T. Stead* (Philadelphia 1978).

Ellmann, Richard, *Yeats: The Man and The Masks*, revised ed. (New York 1979).

Evetts, Barry, *The Panama Affair* (San José 2000)

Fallon, Donal, *16 Lives: John MacBride* (Dublin 2015).

Foster, R.F. *Vivid Faces: The Revolutionary Generation in Ireland, 1890–1923* (London 2015);

—*W.B. Yeats, A Life. Volume 1: The Apprentice Mage 1865–1914* (Oxford 1997).

France, Anatole, *Monsieur Bergeret in Paris* (trans. Bérengère Drillien) (New York and London 1921).

Frazier, Adrian, *Behind the scenes: Yeats, Horniman, and the struggle for the Abbey Theatre* (Berkeley and Los Angeles 1990).

Fulton, Bruce, 'The Boulanger Affair Revisited', *French Historical Studies* (1 October 1991: 310–29. JSTOR).

Gildea, Robert, *Children of the Revolution: The French, 1799–1914* (London and New York 2008).

Gleadell, W.H., 'General Boulanger', *Fortnightly Review* (September 1887: 360).

Goldberg, Harvey, *The Life of Jean Jaures* (Madison 1962).

Goncourt, Edmond, *Journal*, vol. 3 (Paris 1989).

Gonne, Iseult, *Letters to W.B. Yeats and Ezra Pound from Iseult Gonne: A girl that knew all Dante once*, Anna MacBride White, Christina Bridgwater, A. Norman Jeffares (Eds), (London 2004).

Gonne, Maud, *A Servant of the Queen* (Woodbridge 1983);

— 'In the Event of War', *United Irishman* (22 December 1900).

— *Maud Gonne's Irish Nationalist Writings 1895–1946*, Karen Steele (Ed.), (Dublin 2004).

Gould, Warwick (Ed.), *Yeats and the Nineties, Yeats Annual*, no. 14. (London 2001);

— 'Yeats, mescal, and visions', *Times Literary Supplement* (13 July 1990), 762.

— 'Yeats's Mask', No. 19. *Yeats Annual*, n.d.

Greer, Mary K., *Women of the Golden Dawn: Rebels and Priestesses* (Rochester, Vermont 1995).

Gregory, Lady, *Lady Gregory's Diaries, 1892–1902*, James Pethica (Ed.), (Gerrards Cross 1996).

Harding, James, *The Astonishing Adventure of General Boulanger* (London and New York 1971).

Harris, Frank, *My Life and Loves* (New York 1963).

Harwood, John, *Olivia Shakespear and W.B. Yeats: After Long Silence* (New York 1989).

Hassett, Joseph M., *W.B. Yeats and the Muses* (Oxford 2010).

Hogan, Robert and O'Neill, Michael J., eds, *Joseph Holloway's Abbey Theatre* (Carbondale, Edwardsville, London and Amsterdam 1967), p. 181.

Holmes, Rachel, *Eleanor Marx: A Life* (London 2014).

Hugues, Clovis, *Les Libres Paroles: Poesies* (Paris 1894).

Huysmans, Joris-Karl, *Là-Bas* (trans. Keene Wallace), (New York 1928).

Irvine, William D., *The Boulanger Affair Reconsidered: Royalism, Boulangism, and the Origins of the Radical Right in France* (Oxford 1989).

James, Henry, *The Portrait of a Lady* (Boston 1882).

Jaures, Jean, *Les preuves: affaire Dreyfus* (Paris 1898).

Jeffares, A. Norman, 'Iseult Gonne' 'Poems and Contexts/' *Yeats Annual* (Ed. Warwick Gould) (no. 16, Basingstroke 2005);

— *W.B. Yeats: Man and Poet* (New Haven and London 1949).

Jeffares, A. Norman and Anna MacBride White (Eds), *The Gonne–Yeats Letters 1893–1938* (Syracuse 1994).

Joly, Bertrand, *Déroulède: L'inventeur du nationalisme* (Paris 1998).

Jordan, Anthony J., *Boer War to the Easter Rising: The Writings of John MacBride* (Kindle Edition, 2012);

— *The Yeats-Gonne-MacBride Triangle* (Westport, 2000).

Justice, Haute Cour de, *Affaire Boulanger, Dillon, Rochefort* (Paris 1889).

Kauffmann, Gregoire, *Edouard Drumont* (Paris 2008).

Kerviler, René, *Les Bretons* (Mayenne 1978).

Kilroy, James, and Robert Hogan (Eds.), *Laying the Foundations 1902–1904: Modern Irish Drama: a documentary history II*, vol. 2 (Dublin 1976).

Lafargue, Paul, 'The Boulanger Question' (*Le Socialiste*, 23 July 1887).

Lawton, Frederick, *The Third French Republic* (Philadelphia 1909).

Leblois, Louis, *L'affaire Dreyfus: l'iniquité, la réparation, les principaux faits et les principaux documents* (Paris 1929).

Lecomte, Maxime, *Les ralliés : histoire d'un parti (1886–1898)* (Paris 1898).

Levenson, Samuel, *Maud Gonne: A Biography of Yeats' Beloved* (London 1977).

de L'Isle-Adam, Villiers, *Axel* (trans. Marilyn Gaddis Rose) (Dublin 1970).

Lyons, G.A., *Some Recollections of Griffith and His Times* (Dublin 1923).

Magny, Anna, 'Maud Gonne: Réalité et Mythe, Analyse d'une présence historique et littéraire' (Rennes: University of Rennes, 30 March 1992).

Marion, Jean-Luc, *The Erotic Phenomenon* (trans. Stephen E. Lewis) (Chicago 2007).

Matthews, Ann, *Renegades: Irish Republican Women 1900–1922* (Cork 2010).

Maume, Patrick. *The Long Gestation: Irish Nationalist Life 1891–1918* (Dublin 1999).

Maye, Brian, *Arthur Griffith* (Dublin 1997).

McClelland, J.S. *The French Right from De Maistre to Maurras* (London 1970).

McCoole, Sinéad, *Easter Widows* (Dublin 2014).

McCracken, Donal P., *MacBride's Brigade: Irish Commandos in the Anglo-Boer War* (Dublin 1999);

—*The Irish Pro-Boers 1877–1902* (Johannesburg and Cape Town 1989).

McDiarmid, Lucy, *The Irish Art of Controversy* (Dublin and Ithaca, New York 2005).

McIntosh, Christopher, *Eliphas Levi and the French Occult Revival* (London 1972).

'Mermeix' [Gabriel Terrail], *Les Coulisses du Boulangisme* (Paris 1890).

Meyer, Arthur, *Ce que je peux dire* (Paris 1912).

Mirbeau, Octave, *Torture Me! A Dark Depraved Tale of Sin and Sex in the Garden of Evil Ecstasy* (Kindle edition 2011).

Moore, George, *A Drama in Muslin: A Realistic Novel* (London 1892);

—*Confessions of a Young Man* (New York 1901).

Naquet, Alfred, 'Varia', Bibliothèque nationale de France, n.d.

Nevin, Donal, *James Connolly: A Full Life* (Dublin 2005.)

O'Casey, Séan, *Pictures in the Hallway* (New York 1942).

O'Donnell, William H., (Ed.), W.B. Yeats, *The Speckled Bird,* (Toronto 1976).

Offen, Karen, 'Intrepid Crusader: Ghénia Avril de Sainte-Croix Takes on the Prostitution Issue', *Proceedings of the Western Society for French History*, vol. 33 (2005).

O'Grady, John, *Life of Sarah Purser* (Dublin 1996).

Péladan, Joséphin, *L'art idéaliste et mystique, doctrine de l'Ordre et du salon annuel des Rose+Croix* (Paris 1894).

Pilkington, Lionel, *Theatre and the State in Twentieth-Century Ireland: Cultivating the People* (London 2001).

Pisani-Ferry, Fresnette, *Le Général Boulanger* (Paris 1969).

Prévost, Marcel, *Les Demi-Vierges* (Paris 1894).

Quinton, Marie, *Le journal de la belle meunière: le general Boulanger et son amie* (Paris 1895).

Radziwill, Princess Catherine, *Germany under Three Emperors* (London 1917).

Ranger, Pierre, *La France Vue d'Irlande : L'histoire du mythe française de Parnell à l'Etat Libre* (Rennes 2011).

Read, Piers Paul, *The Dreyfus Affair: The Story of the Most Infamous Miscarriage of Justice in French History* (London 2012).

Reberioux, Madeleine and Mayeur, Jean-Marie, (trans. J.R. Foster), *The Third Republic from its Origins to the Great War, 1871–1914* (Cambridge 1984).

Reinach, Joseph, *Histoire de L'Affaire Dreyfus* (Paris 2006).

Robb, Graham, *The Discovery of France: A Historical Geography from the Revolution to the First World War* (New York 2007).

de Rougemont, Denis, *Love in the Western World* (New York 1956).

Rutkoff, Peter M., *Revanche and Revision: The Ligue des Patriotes and the Origins of the Radical Right in France, 1882–1900* (Athens, Ohio 1981).

Saddlemyer, Ann, *Becoming George: The Life of Mrs W.B. Yeats* (Oxford 2002);

—*The Collected Letters of J.M. Synge 1871–1907* Ann Saddlemyer (Ed.), vol. 1. (Oxford and New York 1983).

—*Theatre Business* Ann Saddlemyer (Ed.), (Gerrards Cross 1982).

Saint-Martin, Jean, *Clovis Hugues et moi dans l'affaire de Panama* (Avignon 1897).

Schmidt, Vivienne Ann, *Democratizing France: The Political and Administrative History of Decentralization* (Cambridge 1990).

Sherard, Robert Harborough, *Twenty years in Paris; being some recollections of a literary life* (London 1905).

Silverman, Willa Z., *The Notorious Life of Gyp: Right-Wing Anarchist in Fin-de-Siècle France* (Oxford 1995).

Simon, Maron J., *The Panama Affair* (New York 1971).

Stephens, Winifred, *Madame Adam* (London 1917).

Stone, Marjorie and Judith Thompson (Eds), *Literary Couplings: Writing Couples, Collaborators, and the Construction of Authorship* (Madison 2007).

Tennyson, Alfred Baron, *Idylls of the King* (London 1983).

Tombs, Robert, *From Nationhood and Nationalism in France: From Boulanger to the Great War* (New York 1991).

Toomey, Deirdre, "The Cold Heaven". The living stream: essays in memory of A. Normal Jeffares', *Yeats Annual,* no. 18, a special issue, Warwick Gould (Ed.), (2013);

—'Who Fears to Speak of '98', Gould, Warwick, *Yeats and the Nineties, Yeats Annual,* no. 14 (Basingstroke 2001);

—*Yeats and Women*, Deirdre Toomey (Ed.) (London 1992).

Truman, Benjamin Cummings, *The Field of Honor: being a complete and comprehensive history of duelling in all countries* (New York 1884).

Vandam, Albert Dresden, *My Paris note-book* (Philadelphia 1894).

Viau, Raphaël, *Vingt ans d'antisémitisme, 1889–1909* (Paris 1910).

Ward, Margaret (Ed.), *In Their Own Voice: Women and Irish Nationalism* (Cork 1995);

—*Maud Gonne: Ireland's Joan of Arc* (London 1990).

Warner, Marina, *Joan of Arc: Image of Female Heroism* (London 1981).

Watson, David Robin, *Georges Clémenceau: A Political Biography* (London 1974).

Weber, Eugen, *France: Fin de Siecle* (Cambridge, Mass 1986);

—My France: Politics, Culture, Myth (Cambridge, Mass 1991).

Williams, Guy St John, *The Racing Lodges of the Curragh* (Kildare 1997).

Williams, Roger L., *Henri Rochefort: Prince of the Gutter Press* (New York 1966).

Wyzewa, Téodor de, *Le mouvement socialiste en Europe* (Paris 1892).

Yeats, W.B., *Memoirs, Autobiography – First Draft, Journal* Denis Donoghue (Ed.),
    (London 1972);

—*Per Amica Silentia Lunae* (New York 1918);

—*The Autobiography of William Butler Yeats* (New York 1965);

—*The Collected Letters of W.B. Yeats*, John Kelly and Eric Domville (Eds), vol. 1
    (Oxford 1986);

—*The Collected Letters of W.B. Yeats*, John Kelly and Ronald Schuchard (Eds), vol. 4
    (Oxford 2003);

—*The Collected Letters of W.B. Yeats*, John Kelly and Ronald Schuchard (Eds),
    (Oxford 1994);

—*The Collected Letters of W.B. Yeats*, InteLex electronic edition; *Unpublished Letters
(1905–1939)*, John Kelly and Ronald Schuchard (Eds), (1994);

—*The Collected Letters of W.B. Yeats / 2 : 1896–1900*, Warwick Gould and Deirdre
    Toomey (Eds), (Oxford 1997);

—*The Collected Poems of W.B. Yeats*, Richard Finneran (Ed.), (New York 1983, 1989);

—*The Early Poetry: Manuscript Materials by W.B. Yeats*, George Bornstein (Ed.), vol. 2
    (Ithaca and London 1994);

—*The Speckled Bird*, William H. O'Donnell (Ed.), (Canada 1976);

—*The Letters of W.B. Yeats*, Allan Wade (Ed.), (New York 1955);

—*The Variorum Edition of the Poems of W.B. Yeats*, Peter Allt and Russell K. Alspach
    (Eds.), (New York 1957);

—*The Wind Among the Reeds: Manuscript Materials*, Carolyn Anne Holdsworth (Ed.),
    (Ithaca and London 1993);

—*Uncollected Prose*, John P. Frayne and Colton Johnson (Eds), vol. 1 (New York 1970).

Young, Ella, *Flowering dusk; things remembered accurately and inaccurately* (New York
    and Toronto 1945).

Zillhardt, Madeleine, *Louise-Catherine Breslau et ses amis* (Paris 1932).

Zola, Emile, *The Dreyfus Affair and other writings*, Alain Pages (Ed.) (trans. Eleanor
    Levieux), (New Haven and London 1996).

INDEX

Abbey Theatre, 206, 208

Aberdeen, Lady Ishbel Maria Hamilton-Gordon, 22, 66

Académie Julian, 67, 77

actions symboliques, 147

Adam, Edmond, 59

Adam, Juliette, 59–62

Adam, Paul, 128

Agulhon, Maurice, 269n

Airfield House, 65–66

Aldershot, 15, 18, 198

Alsace-Lorraine, 40–41, 57, 144, 172

American *Sun*, 203

Amnesty Association, 119, 139, 141, 185, 205, 274n

Amos, Sheldon, 87

Andrieux, Louis, 74

anti-Dreyfusards, 156–57, 159, 169,172, 182

anti-Semitism, 13, 156–57, 167–71, 186, 263

anti-semitism, France for the French, 133, 155, 170

Arran, Lord, 273n

Arthurianism, 6, 245, 271n13, 273n1
    oath of courtly love, 70
    Lancelot, 6–7
    Sir Galahad, 6, 96, 226

Avril, Madame, *see* Sainte-Croix, Ghénia

Axel, 129, 276n12

Balliett, Conrad, 283n54, 286n3

Barrès, Madame, 169

Barrès, Maurice, 57, 81, 100, 107, 110, 114, 128–29, 133, 155, 157, 183, 270n15
    and George Moore, 169–72

Beresford Place, 191, 197, 199, 208

Blanche, Jacques-Émile, 169–70, 280n43

Blavatsky, Madame, 98

Blum, Léon, 155

Boer War, 168, 190, 192, 196, 200, 202–03, 221, 254,

Bois, Julies, 136

Bonnemains, Madame, 49–50, 56, 71, 75, 91

Boulanger, Georges, 4, 40–41, 46–49, 54–60, 71–75, 83, 100, 108–10, 126, 154
    clandestine operations, 56, 73
    duel, 71
    shoots himself, 75
    'skipped off like a pimp', 74

Boulangisme, 3, 57, 84–85, 263

Boulangistes, 3, 49, 54, 57–59, 68, 71, 73, 75, 83, 91–92, 97, 101, 106–07, 115, 134–35
    'Banquet de Versailles', 74
    at Faure's funeral, 183–84, 187
    plans for a coup, 48, 55, 57, 73, 84, 113
    dismal, 91
    old, 182–83

Boullan, Abbé, 129

Bourbon, Louis-Philippe, 44

Breslau, Louise-Catherine, 67, 76

Bréval, Eva, 172–73, 280n57

Brisson, Adolphe, 23, 126–28

Cambon, Paul, 46,

Campbell, Mrs Patrick, 242

Carbery, Ethna, 196

Cathleen ni Houlihan, *see* Yeats, W.B., plays

Celtic Literary Society, Lower Abbey Street, 190, 195–96

Clarke, Thomas, 105, 137, 201, 203, 256, 260, 225

Clémenceau, Georges, 46–48, 54, 108–17, 182–83, 268n28, 276n4
  dislike of Millevoye, 116–17
  and 'La Justice', 46, 108, 270n3
  splits with Boulangistes, 32

Clermont-Ferrand (military camp), 38–40, 48, 55–56, 104, 268n7

Colles, Ramsay, 14, 195–98, 283 3n47

Colleville, Maud Gonne's holiday home, 226, 229, 236, 241, 250–51, 255, 257

Colum, Mary, 239, 242

Colum, Padraic, 211, 213

Constans, Jean Antoine Ernest, 73–74

Cook, Caroline Louisa, MG's aunt, 16

Cook, Edith, MG's mother, 15–18

Cook, Francis, MG's uncle, 16, 28

Cook, Mary Anne, MG's aunt (*see* Comtesse de Sizeranne)

Cook, William, MG's grandfather, 16, 266n9

Coppée, François, 182

coup, attempted, 48, 55, 57, 73, 84, 113

Court and Society Review, 22

cowardice, 158
  MG on, 146, 191, 212, 241, 253
  of MG, 204, 223
  of WBY, 176, 212, 241

Crowley, Aleister, 167

Cruppi, Jean (lawyer), 15, 234–35

Daly, John, 105, 112, 119, 137, 139, 144, 216, 277n37

Daly, Kathleen (later Mrs Thomas Clarke), 201

Dangien, Madame, MG's governess, 226, 228

Daudet, Alphonse, 135

Daudet, Léon, 58, 134, 155, 157

Daudet, Madame Alphonse, 143

Daughters of Ireland, *see* Inghinide na hÉireann

Davis, Thomas, 67

Davitt, Michael, 27, 66, 190

Degas, Edgar, 182

Delaney, Mary Barry, 228, 286n20

Déroulède, Paul, 47, 54–55, 59, 73–75, 82–83, 108–17, 133, 136, 155, 182–84, 187–88, 220

divorce (of MG and MacBride), 97, 136, 230–36, 240, 242, 281n70

A Doll's House 148

Dreyfus, Captain Alfred, 133, 153–159, 168, 171, 187, 234

Dreyfus Affair, 9, 13, 153, 169–71, 186
  'faux Henry', 154
  'petit bleu', 153–54

Dreyfusards, 134, 172, 183

Driant, Emile, 100, 254,

Drumont, Edouard, 83–84, 108, 129, 133, 144, 153, 157, 167

Dublin, Castle Season, 21–24, 32

Dublin Corporation, 222

Dublin Employers' Federation, 252

Dublin Horse Show, 139

Dublin Metropolitan Police, 203, 247

Ducret, Edouard, 112, 116–17

duel, 9, 71, 109, 275n43
  Millevoye's duels, 84, 86, 110, 172

Dujardin, Edouard, 157

Duncan, J.A, 85

Dupuy, Charles (President of France), 113

Durand, Marguerite, 54, 72, 113, 133–36, 167

Durcan, Paul, 239

duty
  first, 136, 138
  Frenchman's, 56
  jury, 205

plain, 159, 252

tied down by lesser, 138, 251

to Ireland, 190, 194

to Maud Gonne, 202

dynamitards, 104–05, 137, 139–40, 203, 256

Easter Rising, 104, 115, 134–35, 146–47, 152

Édouard Vaillant, 33, 270n16

Edward VII, 16, 115, 117

Eiffel, Gustave, 59

Ellmann, Richard, 11, 137, 141, 144, 151

Elysée Palace, 29, 41, 96

Emmet, Robert, 38, 78

Empress Eugenie, 17

Empress Josephine, 24

England

anti-Catholic Coronation Oath, 224

hatred and contempt for, 7, 13, 28, 30, 40, 89, 114, 168, 194, 254

honourable enemies of, 139–40, 190, 232, 240

civilization, 160, 169

gaols, 66, 102

hypocrisy, 89, 127

oppressor, 103, 144, 146, 160

'Perfidious Albion', 30, 111, 116, 170

entente cordiale, 184, 220

The Erotic Phenomenon, see Jean-Luc Marion

Esterhazy, Major, 153–55

evictions, and anti-eviction campaign, 79, 84–88, 93, 101–02, 104, 146, 205, 211, 272n10

famine, 69, 144, 146, 195

conditions, 86, 159

works, 159–60

Farr, Florence, 242

Faure, Felix, 154, 183–84, 229, 286n30

Fay, Frank, 205

Fay, W.G., 205, 207–12, 226–27

Feline, Madame, 40

Floquet, Charles, 54

duel with Boulanger, 71

Fort Chabrol, 187–88

Fortnightly Review, 72

Foster, R.F., 125, 208, 239, 248, 281n70

Foster Place, 146

Fountain Court, 138

Fox, Valentine, 138

France

Chamber of Deputies, 45, 54, 56, 70, 71, 113, 116–17

fin-de-siècle, 9, 81

Third Republic, 42, 44, 133

Zola's versus Millevoye's, 172

France, Anatole, 157, 182

Franco-Irish military alliance, 143

Franco-Prussian War, 42, 44

Franco-Russian military alliance, 42, 58–61, 270n31

Freeman's Journal, 92, 105, 136, 159, 199

Gambetta, Léon, 44, 59, 81, 268n28, 271n24

Ghil, René, 110

Gillain, Lucien, poet inspired by Gonne, 102

Gladstone, William, PM, 104–05, 111, 127

Golden Dawn, Order of the, 128–29, 166, 171, 245

Hebrew letters, 128–29

Gonne

family conference, 32–33

Charles (MG's grandfather), 15

Charles (MG's uncle), 13, 19

Edith (MG's mother), 13

Francis (MG's uncle), 13

Georges Silvère (MG's first son), 45–46, 65, 122, 141

Georges Silvère, his booties, 65

Henry, 12, 162
Iseult, 125–26, 136, 138, 157, 176, 199,
    200, 226, 228, 235
    conception, 125–26
    birth, 132–33
    hated John MacBride, 214
    infected lung, 194
    alleged offence by MacBride,
        231, 236
    MG gets married for sake of, 210
Kathleen (later Mrs Pilcher), 20–21,
    162, 171–72
Gonne, Maud
    actress, 42–43, 102
        in *Caste*, 23
        in *Cathleen ni Houlihan*,
            207–08
        in 'Grand Public Recital', 67
        in *Heartsease*, 32–33, 37
    'agitatrice Irlandaise', 102
    appearance, 57
    beauty, 20, 26, 32, 68, 69, 91, 102,
        136, 146, 187–88, 248, 255, 259, 262,
        281n5
    eyes, 41, 61, 110 ('changeable as the
        sea'), 141 ('dream dimmed')
    appetite for physical love, 177
    as 'Aunt Maud', 250
    as 'Bragella', 14
    'celebrated *harangueuse*', 128
    charisma, 4, 147, 205
    conversation, 5, 101, 228 (with
        midwife), 230 (with doctor)
    education, Rosemont School, 21
    'father' of WBY's poetry, 254
    as feminist hero, 234, 252
    gift for good works, 85
    governesses, 19, 41 (Irish nurse),
        226, 228
    'the High-born Ladye', 67
    holidays, 37, 172, 205, 210, 220, 229,

household staff, 130, 136
illegitimate children, 281n70
interviews, 101–02, 104–05, 126- 28,
    136, 204
Irish Joan of Arc, 7, 10, 65, 85, 100,
    192, 251
    the role Millevoye's idea, 42–43
justifies terrorism, 137
in Aix-les-Bains, 164, 167, 171, 199
in Algeciras, 220
in Ballina, 160–64, 168, 185, 188
in Erris, 159
in Falcarragh, 87
in Italy, 20, 243, 256
in Kensington, 208
in Kildare, 17, 28, 76, 85
in Limerick, 119, 120, 137, 201
in Laragh Castle, 263
in Laval, 210, 226
in Liverpool, 201
in Marseilles, 53
in New York, 152, 157, 194, 201–03
in Paris with Aunt Mary, 25–27, 33
in Saint-Raphaël, 89, 90
in St Louis, 153, 203
in St Petersburg, 20, 31, 59–62,
    270n23, 270n31
in Switzerland, 172
in Tongham Manor, 15
lantern slides, 102, 146
leaves behind old politics of hate, 243
liking for conspiracies, 160
literary style, 90
lovers suspected by MacBride, AE,
    Cipriani, Faure, Griffith, Arthur
    Lynch, Millevoye, and Yeats, 215, 229
'magnificent virginity', 82
marriage proposals, 88, 92, 98, 100,
    125, 202 ('white'), 203, 219, 258
as 'Maud Carthy' (in Driant novel),
    254

as 'Miss Groold' (in Birmingham
  novel), 254
and the mob, 151, 168, 189, 225,
  226, 264
as 'Moura', 132
'out Hecubas Hecuba', 126
pets, 289
  'Dagda', 147
  'Chaperone' (monkey), 53, 69,
    77, 254
  'Patsy', 202
  'Snake', 289
pregnancies, 77, 126, 130, 220, 224,
  228, miscarriages, 177
proto-feminist, 7, 43,
residences, 7
  Avenue de la Grande Armée, 92,
    107, 108, 118
  Avenue d'Eylau, 133, 134, 144, 162,
    200, 215
  Coulson Avenue, 210, 221–22,
    225 ('Battle of')
  Les Mouettes, 226
  Nassau Street, 82, 88, 91, 162, 174
  Rue de Passy, 118–20, 123, 126,
    130
  Samois, 77, 81–82, 85, 92, 125,
    272n10
'Secret Treaty' (or 'Alliance') with
  Millevoye, 5, 42, 82, 144, 215
sexual relations, 42, 60, 81, 97, 125–26,
  130, 147, 164, 174, 228–29, 244
  horrified by sex? 177
skill at propaganda, 90, 100, 160, 212
terrible honeymoon, 216–18
as unwed mother, 82
visions
  great serpent, 243
  great stone Minerva, 177
  haunted painting, 250
  'Initiation of the Spear', 177

Lugh in his chariot, 180
  mental journeys, 160
  'titanic forms of light', 243
wealth, 15, 33
writings, 276–27
  'Le Martyre de L'Irlande', 92
  'A Question of Policy', 189
  A Servant of the Queen, 20–33, 37,
    40–42, 48, 53, 59, 60–62, 88, 90,
    172, 208, 220
Gonne, May, 32, 86, 112, 203, 208, 228,
  230–31
Gonne, Thomas, 15–21, 28
  commander of British forces in
    Ireland, 21
  intelligence officer, 21
  in Portman Square, 17, 31
Gonne, Thora, *see* Thora Gonne Pilcher
Gonne, William, 17, 28–33, 65, 78
Gore Booth, Eva, 131
Gould, Warwick, 271n10, 278n45, 280n68,
  287n7
Gregory, Lady Augusta, 151–52, 159, 168,
  175–76, 182, 202, 205–08, 212, 239, 242,
  248, 250, 255–58
Grévy, Jules, 54
Griffith, Arthur, 14, 185–86, 190, 193–96,
  200, 204, 214, 221, 232, 242
  on salary from MG, 185
Guaita, Stanislaus, 128–29
Guérin, Jules, 158, 182–83, 187–88
Gyles, Althea, 150, 167
'Gyp', Sibylle Aimée Marie-Antoinette
  Gabrielle, 47, 134–136, 161

Habert, Marcel, 183
Halévy, Daniel, 155
Harding, James, 268–70 (*passim*)
Harrington, Timothy, 195, 221–23
Harris, Frank, 72–73
Harwood, John, 141, 248

Hassett, Joseph M., 5, 265n1, 265n2
heart
    lonely, 131
    patriot, 143
    troubled, 122
    unquiet, 136
    weary, 209
    young girl's, 24
    young orphan's, 18
heartlessness, 61, 122
hero, 136, 155, 254
    cult, 187
    courageous, 146, 201, 202, 253
    eccentric, 132
    female, 134
    ideas of, 140
    illusory (MacBride), 231, 241, 257
    magician, 130, 142
    national, 139, 146, 187, 259
    Plutarch's, 245
    real-life, 73
heroine, 14, 22, 43, 125, 132, 254
    Ibsenite, 123–48
    Colette's, 178
    young, 43, 104
Herz, Cornelius, 82, 107–113
Hitler, Adolf, 13, 262
Holloway, Joseph, 208, 271n7
Holloway Prison, 262
Holmes, Augusta, 106
Holmes, Rachel, 141
Home Rule, 20, 27–28, 104, 222
    candidate, 85, 119, 195
    party, 172
    promised, 57
Home Rule Bill, Second, 57, 127
Horniman, Annie, 166, 233, 242
Hotel, Victoria, Cork, 190
Hôtel Belle Meunière, Royat, 38
Hôtel Corneille, Paris, 140
Hôtel de Londres, Fontainebleau, 169

Hotel des Marronniers, Royat, 38
Hotels, in spas, 37–38
Hôtel Scribe, Paris, 201
The Hour-Glass, 210
Howth, 17–18, 30, 91–92, 264
Hughes, John (sculptor), 68
Hughes, William (land grabber), 189
Hugues, Clovis, 101–06, 133, 144, 254
    his despicable verses, 106
Hugues, Jeanne Royannez (sculptor, murderer), 101
Humbert, General Jean Joseph Amable, 143, 168
Huysmans, Joris-Karl, 128–29, 166
    Là-Bas, 129
Hyde, Douglas, 213
    'my head spinning with her beauty', 68
    'we did not do much Irish', 75
Hyde-Lees, George, 262

Ibsen, Henrik, 148
illegitimate children, 32, 85, 100, 121, 143, 176, 231, 281n70
Inghinide na hÉireann, 185, 197, 199–200, 205, 211, 215–16, 221, 224, 227
Inghinidhe, women of, 205, 233, 251
Irish, enlisted soldiers, 194–95
Irish Brigade, 190, 195, 199–200, 215, 229
Irish Daily Independent, 158
Irish Figaro, 14, 195ff, 283n46, 283n47
Irish Independent, 232–34
Irish language revival, 66, 184, 196, 204
Irish Literary Society, 103
Irish National Alliance (INA), 136–42, 152, 161, 168, 192
Irish National Theatre Society, 206, 212, 220, 226, 230
Irish Parliamentary Party, 65, 142, 192–93, 204
Irish Republican Brotherhood (IRB),

66–67, 134, 198–99, 204, 221,223, 231,
242, 244,
republican women, 266
Irish Socialist Republican Party, 145
Irish Times, 22–23, 139, 138, 141–44, 146,
150, 252
Irish Transvaal Committee, 184, 190–91,
200. 204
Irish women, 85–87, 198–202
Irlande Libre (MG's newspaper), 144–45,
167–68, 186, 199
Isis Urania Temple, 166
L'Isle-Adam, Villiers de, 113, 129, 132, 242

James, Henry, 433
Jameson, Ida, 66–67
Jeffares, A Norman, 163, 199, 272n10
Jewish
conspiracy, 128
masonic conquest, 133
plot, 108
power, 132
race, 156
rat, 152
writers, 155
Jews, 154–57, 170, 184–86
bankers, 156, 171
threatened, 98
Joannon, Pierre, vii
Joffrin, Jules, 82
Johnson, Lionel, 132, 276n68
Johnston, Anna, 185
Joly, Bertrand, 60, 110
Jordan, Anthony J., 280–82, (*passim*)
Jubilee, Queen's, 139, 144–46
justice
English, 188
false, 204
popular, 194, 188
social, 270
wild, 8

Kant, Immanuel, 156, 169
Kelly, John, viii, 244, 288n17
Kelly, Tom (Dublin alderman), 221
Khnopff, Fernand, 167
Kickham, Charles, 143
kiss, 106, 173–78
applied, 40
with bodily mouth, 175
the long passionate kiss of love, 132
mutual, 176
unreciprocated, 177
Kruger, President Paul, 191, 200–01

Là-Bas, 129, 166
Labori, Fernand, 15, 187, 234–35
Ladies Committee, Patriotic Treat, 196
Ladies School Dinners Committee, 252
Lafargue, Paul, 28
Laguerre, Georges, 47, 54, 72–74, 82
Laguerre, Madame, 134
La Lanterne, 106
La Libre Parole, 108, 133, 153, 157–58, 167
Land grabbers, MG campaign against,
185, 189,
Land League, 22–24, 190
landlords, 22, 86, 104, 126, 158, 222
landlord syndicate, 86
Land War, 20
La Patrie (Millevoye's newspaper), 43, 71,
133, 144, 155, 157, 166, 182, 199, 220
La Presse, 73, 104–06
Larkin, James, 252
Laur, Francis, 83
Leblois, Louis, 154–56
Lee, Austin, 113
Lemaître, Jules, 182
Lenin Peace Prize, 262
Lesseps, Ferdinand de, 107–08
letters
confidential, 211
flirtatious, 138

forged, 275n60
improper, 138
officious, 212
open, 252
provocative, 160
published, 64
resentful, 286n20
secret, 172
spicy, 182
Levenson, Samuel, 67
Leyds, Dr W.J., 190–93
Lia Fail, 209
Liberal Party, 20
Ligue anti-sémitique, 158, 183
Ligue de la patrie française, 182
Ligue des Patriotes, 47, 55, 73–74, 182–83
Lissagaray, Prosper-Olivier, 83
Lister, Thomas V, 113
London Daily Mail, 14
Loubet, Émile (President of France), 183,
    187, 220
love
    acknowledged, 162
    blind, 204
    companionate, 82
    courtly love tradition, 6–7
    culpable, 129
    disappointed, 165
    lost, 141
    malevolent, 182
    often-tested, 204
    physical, 177
    romantic, 207
    spiritual, 244, 247
    and wisdom, 254
love affair
    developing, 122
    star-crossed, 248
love of truth, 70, 94
love poets, 6, 118, 142
lover

devoted, 246
literary, 6
masterful, 163
love story, great, 37
love token, ominous, 53
Lugh, 181
Lynch, Arthur, 140, 190, 229

MacBride, Honoria, 200, 203, 214, 230
MacBride, John, 15, 37, 137, 184, 190,
    200–10, 214
    admired, 200, 201, 204, 231–36
    candidate for Parliament, 195
    code of conduct, 201, 203, 215, 226,
        229–30, 233
    death of, 133, 149
    disgusted by idea of contraceptives,
        119–20
    divorce, 12, 121, 148
    divorce court, 123
    drinking, 220, 230–31, 233, 236
    exposes himself to Iseult, 231, 236
    'half-insane brute', 231
    hated, 236
    likeable, 203
    'lout, vainglorious', 258
    as public speaker, 201, 206,
    scandalized by a 'woman with a
        past', 125
    sexual relations, with MG, 202, 230
    in Westport, 202
MacBride, Joseph, 229
MacBride, Madame Maud Gonne, 221,
    224, 228, *see* Maud Gonne
MacBride, Patrick, 233
MacBride, Seaghan (son of Maud Gonne
    MacBride), 228–36
MacBride, Seán (aka Seaghan), 263
MacDonagh, Thomas, 256–57
Mackau, Baron, 54–55, 269n4
MacKenna, Stephen, 144

MacManus, Seamus, 221, 223
MacNeill, Swift, 86
MacPherson, James, 14
Maffre, Achille, 254
magic, 129–31, 160, 276
    bifurcated member, 129
    'deliberate reverie', 161
    Karezza, 166
    See also occult
Magny, Anne, vii, 43, 89, 147, 199
Major MacBride Clubs, 204
Mann, Tom, 31
Marinoni, Hippolyte Auguste, 112
Marion, Jean-Luc, 164, 174
Markievicz, Constance, 259
marriage, spiritual (MG and WBY),
    162–64, 175, 182, 202, 209, 247, 259
Martyn, Edward, 151, 221–23
Marx, Eleanor, 82
Masefield, John, 212
mask, 122, 241
Masonic order, 129
mass mobilization, techniques of, 48, 205
Mathers, MacGregor, 99, 128–29, 141,
    161–62, 166
Mathers, Moina, 99
    white marriage, 166
Maud Gonne Reception Committee, 194
Mendès, Catulle, 128
Meredith, Mary Ann, 18–20, 32
'Mermeix' (aka Gabriel Terrail), 84–85
Millevoye, Adrienne (wife of Lucien), 42,
    73–74, 268n9
Millevoye, Henri (son of Lucien), 253
Millevoye, Lucien, 35–78, 93–122, 237–63
    Bonapartist, 49
    death, 263
    with Gonne in London, 58
    height, 42
    'journalist arriviste', 69, 97
    'a kind of French Maud Gonne', 116

oratory, 71–72
    florid, 72
    politically undisciplined, 113
    proto-Nazi, 9
    public humiliations, 126, 169,
    sexual relations
        honey-trap, 173
        with Maud Gonne, 41–42,
            125–26
        with the woman who sings like
            Breval, 172
Milligan, Alice, 185
Mirbeau, Octave, 8–10, 157, 172, 265n10
    The Torture Garden, 9, 265n10
Mitchel, John, 185
Molony, Helena, 252
Montefiore, Dora, 252
Mont Saint-Michel, 251
Moore, George, 4, 131, 169–72
    Confessions of a Young Man, 8,
        137, 152
    'Don Juan trilogy', 6
    A Drama in Muslin, 21–24
    Esther Waters, 121
    idea of France, 171–72
    Mike Fletcher, 6
Moore, Thomas, 67
Moreau, Gustave, 129, 167
Morès, Marquis de, 83, 136
Morley, John, 88, 105
Morrígan, 7
Morris, William, 6
Morrow's Bookshop, 88
Morton, E.J.C., 103–04
mouvement socialiste, 270n16
movements
    anti-British and anti-parliamentary,
        172
    anti-semitic, 122
    land reform, 76
    non-parliamentary, 170

parliamentary Home Rule, 222
    physical force, 137, 143, 204
    reform, 74
    semi-military, 213
Murphy, William, 86
muse, 4–10, 70, 120, 130, 162, 244, 264

Napoleon, Louis, 16
Napoleon, Prince Albert Victor, 22
Napoleon, Prince Jérome, 55
Napoleon Bonaparte, 26
Napoleon III, 25, 38, 40, 44
Bonapartists, 55, 58, 84, 89, n7
Naquet, Alfred, 46, 48, 54, 74, 83
National Club, 146
National Council, 222
nationalism and nationalists, 10, 58, 68,
   143, 156, 170, 185, 202, 231
    conservative French, 40, 47, 170
    cultural, 67, 103
    French versus Irish, 5, 144, 170, 263
    'narrow-minded', 239
    'spotless', 222
    constitutional, 100
    radical right (see also 'right
      republicans'), 219
National League, 141
National Literary Society, 103–04
Newgrange, 162
New Ireland Review, 208
New Irish Library, 106
New Woman, 7, 233
Ní Cillin, Máire, 196
Nic Shiubhlaigh, Máire, 205
Nietzsche, Friedrich, 214, 241, 246
Noailles, Anna de, 45
Normandie, La, 194
Norton Affair, 93, 96–120, 141–43
Nouvelle Revue, 59, 89,
Novikoff, Madame Olga, 61–62

O'Brien, Barry, 231
O'Brien, William, 91
O'Casey, Seán, 191
occult, 128–38, 160, 166, 172, 176, 240,
   246–47
    composing rituals, 141
    Hebrew letters in, 129
    magical amulets, 141, 162
    magical reincarnation, 126, 230
    mutual phantasy, 162
    paranormal experience, 161
    psychical investigations, 256
    psychic participation, 164
    sex magic, 125
    Tantric sex, 166
    Tarot cards, 162
    trances, 164, 166, 167, 281n70
O'Connor, John, 86
O'Donnell, Frank Hugh, 162, 186, 192–94,
   198, 202–04
    pamphlet, 198–99
    sneaky insinuations, 204
O'Donovan Rossa, Jeremiah, 137
O'Grady, John, 76
O'Grady, Standish, 102
Oldham, Charles, 66–68, 86
O'Leary, John, 66–69, 75, 102–03, 137, 143,
   168, 190, 198, 200, 204, 231
O'Leary Curtis, William, 201
Olphert Estate, 86–89
Oneida Community, 140
Opportunists, French parliamentary
   grouping, 48, 70, 270–71
Orange Free State, 189, 194
Orleans dynasty, 44–45, 54–55
Orléans, Louis-Philippe, 44
Ossian, 14

Pall Mall Gazette, 60, 204
Panama Affair, 106–112, 274
Paris Exposition, 76, 198

Paris Commune, 107
Parliamentary Election Fund, 220
Parnell, Charles Stewart, 65, 83, 143, 260
    death of, 97–98
Parnell Fund campaign, 65
Parnellites and anti-Parnellites, 137, 142
Parti Nationale, 55, 106, 110
Patriotic Children's Fête, 199
patriotism, 170
    cheap, 137
    convinced, 100
    destructive, 182
    disinterested, 133
    military-style, 171
patriots
    celebrated Irish, 104
    militant, 208
    young Irish, 66
Pearse, Patrick, 256–61
Péladan, Sar Joséphin, 129
Pellieux, General George Gabriel de, 183
People's Protection Committee, 220–22
Pétain, Maréchal Henri Philippe, 263
Petit Journal, 112
Petrarch, 6, 151
Phoenix Park, 27, 65, 139
Picquart, Colonel Marie Georges, 152–55
Piggot, Richard, 64, 116
Pilcher, Kathleen (see also, Gonne,
    Kathleen), 162, 171, 172, 209
Pilcher, Thora Gonne (daughter of
    Kathleen), 200, 250, 252
Playboy of the Western World, 240–42
Pollexfen, George, 118
Pope Leo XIII, 224
Portland Gaol, 66
    prisoners in, 105, 111
Portrait of a Lady (Henry James novel), 43
Pouilly-le-Châtel, 168
Power, Jennie Wyse, 230
Prévost, Marcel, 41

prisoners (See Amnesty Association)
Proust, Marcel, 81, 154, 157
Prussia, 40, 44, 160
Puech, Lucien, 101
Purser, Sarah, 67, 76–77, 89, 162

Quinn, John, 252
Quinn, Máire, 196, 211, 225, 227, 233
Quinton, Marie, 49

Radziwill, Princess Catherine, 61
Ranger, Pierre, vii, 167
Ratazzi, Madame, Marie Bonaparte-
    Wyse, 89
Ready, Police Inspector, 86
Redmond, John, 191
Reinach, Jacques, 107–08, 110
Rémy, Madame Caroline, *see* 'Séverine'
Republic
    French, 44–48, 54, 72, 136
    purer French, 70
republicanism
    French versus Irish, 170, 262
republicans
    fractious Irish, 145
    French, 48, 56, 72, 82, 184, 268–70
    See also right republicans (French)
Republics of South Africa, 191–93
Revue de la Société Litteraire, 45
Revue Illustrée, 88
Revue Indépendante, 57, 270n15
Reynolds' News, 204
Rich, Penelope, 6, 246
Riding, Laura, 5–7
right republicans (French), 4, 40, 44,
    110–11, 184–185, 254
Rochefort, Henri, 47, 54, 72, 74–75, 82,
    114, 204
Rodin, Auguste, 244
Roget, General Gaudérique, 182–84
Rolleston, T.W., 102

Ronsard, Pierre de, 6
Rooney, Willie, 168, 185, 196, 214
Rops, Félicien, 129
Rosicrucianism, 98, 129, 214, 245,
Rothschild, Baron Lionel, 16
Rotunda, 103, 221,
    battle of the, 221–23, 254
Royal Barracks, Dublin, 27, 30
Royal Hospital Kilmainham, 23
Royal Irish Constabulary, 247
Royalism, French, 40–44, 48, 56–58,
  84, 170
Royat, 37–41, 48–49, 104, 168, 174
Roydon Hall, 16
Ruskin, John, 6
Russell, George ('AE'), 98, 206
Russell, Violet, 225
Russia, 20–21, 31, 42, 44, 53, 58–62, 70, 137,
  171, 192
Ryan, Mark, 141, 168, 192, 200,

Sainte-Croix, Ghénia de, Madame Avril,
  134, 136, 144, 168, 172, 200, 226, 228,
  231, 236
salon, 10, 24, 40, 48–50, 58, 110, 126,
  138, 151
Salviati, Cassandre, 6
Saxon Shillin', The 211–15, 221
Scheurer-Kestner, Auguste, 155
Schnaebele, Guillaume, 47
Séverine, Madame, Caroline Rémy de
  Guebhard, 74, 106, 134–36
Shakespear, Hope, 131
Shakespear, Olivia, 131–32, 138, 141–2,
  165, 247
Sharp, William, 141
Sidney, Philip, 6
Sigerson, George, 67–68, 89, 204, 281n70
Silvestre, Armand, 254
Sinclair, Arthur, 245
Sinn Féin, 205, 215, 222

Sizeranne, Comte and Comtesse de
  (MG's Aunt Mary), 16, 25, 33, 40,
  266n10
socialist movement, 44–46, 56, 134,
  158, 184
South Africa, 8, 18, 168, 194–206, 228
spas, French, 37–39 , 168, 251, 256
Spenser, Edmund, 30
spy, 20, 46, 60, 132, 178, 142, ,198, 232, 276
  infiltrators, 46
  MG maladroit, 67
  network, 158
Stead, W.T., 61, 116
  sex-mad, 61
Steele, Karen, 199, 277–84 (*passim*)
Steinheil, Marguerite, 183
Stephens, James, 111, 118
Stephens, Winifred, 270
St Maur, Marquise, 23
St Patrick's Ball, 23
St Teresa's Hall, Dublin, 207
Stuart, Francis, 263
St Woolstan's, Cellbridge, 28
Swinburne, Algernon, 6, 70
symbol, 42, 54, 156, 184, 264
  female, 130
  male, 130
  spear, 176, 180
  swords, phallic Rosicrucian, 184, 244
symbolic act, 195
symbolic instrument, 156
symbolic touch, 41
Symboliste paintings, 167
Symbolistes, 57, 129
Symons, Arthur, 138, 212
Synge, John Millington, 212–13, 227,
  240, 255

Tarlton, Augusta (MG's aunt), 18, 28,
Tarlton, Reverend Thomas (MG's
  uncle), 19

Teeling, Charles McCarthy, 143–44, 162

Tennyson, Lord Alfred, 6

Terrail, Gabriel, *see* Mermeix

theatre, amateur theatricals, 16, 21, 138

theatre movement, 210–11, 226

Theosophical Society, Dublin, 75

Thiébaud, Georges, 269n7

Thompson, Vance, 228

Tillyra (also spelled 'Tulira'), 151

Todhunter, John, 67, 103

Tongham Manor, 15

Toomey, Deirdre, 176, 199, 249, 276n68, 280n64

Toorop, Jan, 167

Trafalgar Square, 31

Turkey, 20, 52–53

Tynan, Katharine, 76

Tynan, Patrick J., 139–40

United Irishman, 14, 170–71, 185–89, 194–203, 212, 222, 226, 254

d'Uzès, Duchesse, 56

Vaillant, Marie Édouard, 57

Vallès, Jules, 134

Van Hecke, Father, 215

Vendler, Helen, 258, 289n55

Verlaine, Paul, 132

Victoria, Queen, and Victorianism, 6, 146, 194, 198, 262

Voleur illustré, 102

Wagner, Richard, and Wagneriansim, 26, 130, 132, 172, 286n28

Waldeck-Rousseau, Pierre, 170, 184

Walker, Mary, *see* nic Shiubhlaigh, Maire

Walsh, Archbishop William, 252

Weber, Eugen, 38

White, Anna MacBride, 230

White, George, 220

White, Lila, 53

The White Goddess, 6

Wilde, Jane ('Speranza'), 100–01

William II, King of Prussia, 158

Wilson, Daniel, 54

Wilson, Eileen (Mrs Joseph MacBride), 226, 229, 231, 235

Wilson, Margaret (mother of MG's half-sister), 25, 31

Wilson, Thomas George, 25

Wolfe Tone Committee, 185, 242

World War I, 256

World War II, 262

Wyzewa, Teodor de, 270n16

Yeats, George (Mrs W.B.), 13

Yeats, John Butler, 68

Yeats, Lily, 68

Yeats, William Butler
   'Amica Silentia Lunae', 281n1
   anger management, 96, 245
   Anglo-Irish values, 214, 242
   Arthurian notions of love, 6, 70, 245
   awareness of 'invisible rival', 132
   awareness of Maud Gonne's double life, 94
   established as MG's protector, 239
   fear of female body, 176
      overcome, 244
   in Fountain Court, 138
   'hair tent', 130
   masturbation, 165–66, 248
   meets MG, 68
   Memoirs, 165, 172, 176, 255, 258
   novel, *The Speckled Bird*, 140–42, 286n29, 286n28
   offers Gonne hallucinogenic powder, 241
   in Paris, 140
   plays
      Cathleen ni Houlihan, 28, 205–08, 211, 213, 227, 260

The Countess Cathleen, 91, 102,
125, 159, 182, 207, 284n84
Death of Cuchulain, 7
Deirdre, 205, 255
The King's Threshold, 227
poems
'Adam's Curse', 208–10, 255
'Aedh Mourns', 142
'Beautiful Lofty Things', 264
'The Cold Heaven', 249–50,
288n30
'A Dream of Death', 90
early, 246
'Easter 1916', 258–61
'Fallen Majesty', 244
'Friends', 247–48
'The Glove and the Cloak', viii,
120–21, 276n68
'The Grey Rock', 177
'He hears the Cry of the
Sedge', 263
'He thinks of those who have
Spoken Evil of his Beloved',
162–63

'A King and No King', 246
'A Memory of Youth', 255–56
'Mongan thinks of his past
Greatness', 164–65
'No Second Troy', 245
'Old Friends', 152
'The People', 240
'Reconciliation', 244–45
Responsibilities, 246
'The Tower', 176
Words', 246
sexual relations
with Mabel Dickinson, 242
with MG, 244–45
with Olivia Shakespear, 132, 248
'Visions Notebook', 164
'worst months of my life', 148
Young, Ella, 205, 241, 243–45, 251
Young Ireland Society, 142–43, 212, 229
Dublin, 66
Paris, 141

Zola, Émile, 130, 155–59, 172, 186, 234, *see
also* Dreyfus Affair